Bithika Mukerji

My Days With Sri Ma Anandamayi

Foreword by
Richard Lannoy

INDICA

Cover illustration: *Sri Ma with Renu and Gini*

© Bithika Mukerji 2002, 2005

First edition 2002
Reprint 2005

Indica Books
D 40/18 Godowlia
Varanasi - 221 001 (U.P.)
India
E-mail: indicabooks@satyam.net.in

ISBN 81-86569-27-8

Printed in India by

First Impression, New Delhi
011-22481754, 09811224048

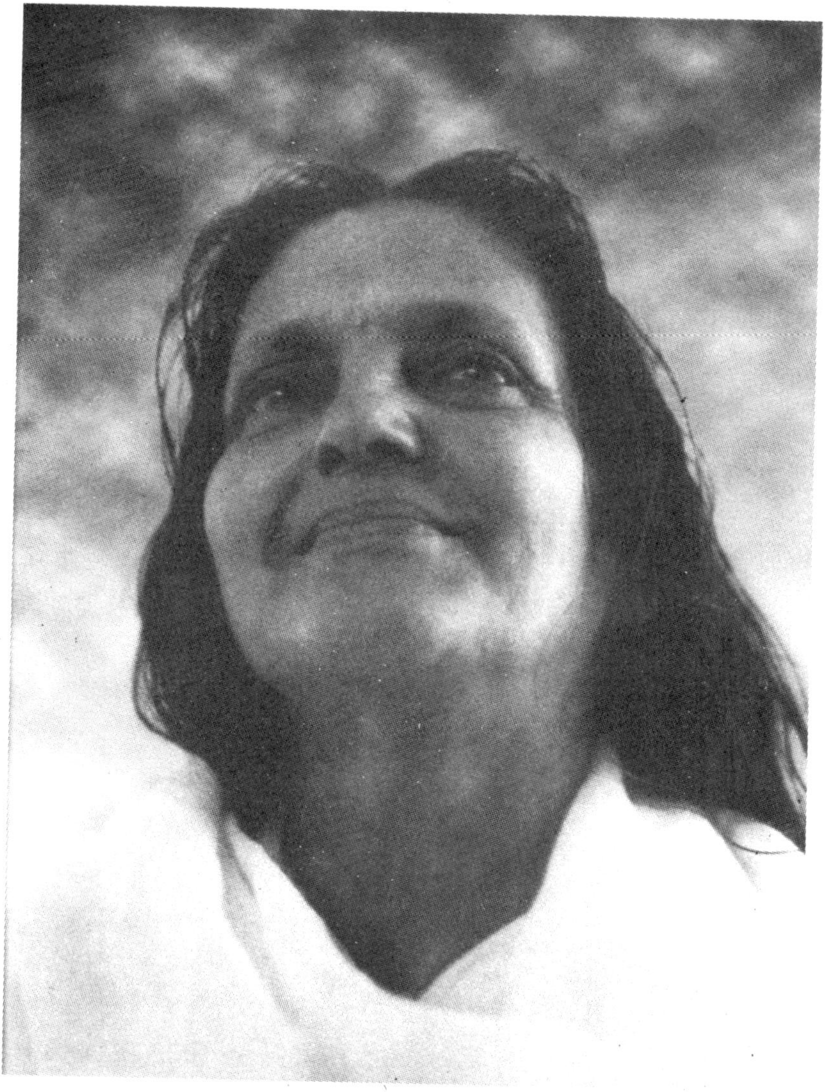

To "US"

fellow-pilgrims and friends;
and to all such like-minded people
in the world

Contents

	Foreword by Richard Lannoy	9
	Preface	15
1.	The Advent of Sri Ma in our Lives	21
2.	My Family	31
3.	My cousins Meet Sri Ma	46
4.	Changing Times	59
5.	A Marriage and a Death in the Family	76
6.	Our Entry into the World of *Sadhus*	91
7.	Renu's Marriage with N.P. Chatterji	103
8.	The Break in my University Career	117
9.	In Solon with Sri Ma (1946)	131
10.	Summer Vacation at Kishenpur Ashram (1947)	150
11.	Raipur and Solon Revisted	165
12.	One Year of my Life as an Ashramite	179
13.	The Best Years of the Ashram in Varanasi	195
14.	Sri Ma and the Kanyapeeth	211
15.	The Message of Sri Ma Anandamayi	227
16.	Bindu and I Take up Jobs	235
17.	Sri Ma's Birthday Celebration at our Home	256
18.	Random Memories	264
19.	An Invitation from Abroad	283
20.	At the Chateau de Bossey	299
21.	On the Way to Canada	313
22.	My Research Project	322
23.	The Ati-Rudra *Yajna* at Haradwar	335
24.	"I Am Ever With You"	347
	Glossary	363

Acknowledgements

My grateful thanks to Richard Lannoy for just being there! Without his unfailing help and encouragement this book would still be in its handwritten stage.

And then to Christopher and Zarine for their hospitality and for giving me the opportunity of *matr-satsang* in London. I remain impressed by their skill in computerising my book so speedily. It is in the fitness of things that I was able to give the finishing touches to the book in Horfield Rectory in Bristol. My affectionate thanks to Nicholas, Cathy and their children.

To my family for everything else.

To Sr. Alvaro Enterria, my publisher, for coping with the erratic method of work with patience and courtesy.

A word of apology to the reader if he feels that the text is encumbered by too many names. I shall be grateful if the reader bears with me and forgives any allusions to so many people I recall with much affection and regard.

Foreword

by Richard Lannoy

I have been a privileged witness to the gestation of this wonderful book. The personal memoir by a member of a distinguished family closely associated with Sri Anandamayi Ma for almost half a century, it is a uniquely intimate portrait.

The function of a foreword is to say briefly a few things about a book which the author cannot with modesty say herself. This is particularly true here, for Dr. Bithika Mukerji is so modest that the book very nearly failed to see the light of day. Fortunately, persistent encouragement, moral support and even a bit of good-natured badgering finally prevailed. Dr. Mukerji, already the author of a fine and authoritative biography of Sri Ma, *A Bird on the Wing*, was persuaded to return to her subject, but introducing a crucial new dimension to her several published accounts, namely her personal angle. For someone so preternaturally disposed toward self-effacement — a self-confessed inveterate "propper-up-of-walls" at the very back of the *satsang* hall — the prospect of advancing so far forward as to present a personal, semi-autobiographical angle upon a figure she regards as beyond the usual boundaries of human experience, seemed not only daunting but (I hope I am not revealing a secret!) presumptuous. Of course it wasn't in the least presumptuous; it was a guarantee of authenticity. Thank goodness she had the courage to complete her story, for it is in its openly-admitted subjectivity that its vividness and immediacy are rooted.

Something very special happens in the pages of this book. Allow me to share with you what I believe to be the "hidden treasure" in store for the reader, and certainly the source of a revelation to me personally. As a photographer who spent months photographing Sri Ma in the Fifties, I always sought, basically for aesthetic reasons, to pay very careful attention to the *total visual field*, the context, the atmosphere (*atman*-sphere, as that word originated long ago) of Sri Ma's environment. Personally, I had eyes only for Sri Ma; but photographically — I knew better than to isolate her from her setting, her people. What I didn't have the sense to appreciate until my visits came to an end and I had left India, never to see Sri Ma again, was the sum human total of the experience: Sri Ma and *everybody* around her. It is this totality which Bithika Mukerji's account encompasses. In a way which no one else can do — at least among English-language authors — she shows, with diligent descriptive accuracy down to the most minuscule and telling detail — the way Sri Ma was at all times totally fused into the lives of her people. While this story is essentially a double portrait of the author, and through the author's deep devotion, of Sri Ma, nevertheless without the actuality of all those people in Sri Ma's entourage being richly evoked as well, the life and person of Sri Ma could never attain such fullness and truth to life on the page. Not until I had read this book three times did it at last sink in that while at work as a photographer I certainly did have *darshan* of Sri Ma surrounded by her devotees, I actually had an even more remarkable kind of *darshan*: of *everybody* in the orbit of Sri Ma. The detailed characterisation in this book of all these good people has had an astonishing effect upon one reader for whom they had hitherto been, for the most part, just dear familiar faces without names, and with whom the language barrier hindered my ability to get to know them properly.

There is a lesson here which is very simple, but like all the best things, hard to put into words. However much one might be inclined to extol, eulogise, even rhapsodise Sri Ma as the veritable paragon of perfection, it is only through depiction of her manifest and multitudinous relation to "others" — she herself says this word is a contradiction in terms when considering her unitary being — that her full dimensionality, her all-inclusiveness may be fully revealed. In the visual arts we talk of *figure and field* as inseparable parts of one single pictorial unity. Bithika Mukerji's book gives us that in rounded dimensionality: figure *and* field.

The author — now my friend Bithika — combines the devotional and the scholarly. She has been closely involved in the Kanyapeeth at the Varanasi Ashram, and for many years taught philosophy at Banaras Hindu University, besides publishing, amongst other things, *Neo-Vedanta and Modernity*. She was four years at McMasters University in Canada, and one of the most interesting chapters in these memoirs is an account of how she carried her devotion to Sri Ma and the teaching she had imbibed from her since childhood into the Western world on both sides of the Atlantic. Her quiet faith is strong enough, for example, to have faced many years ago a major operation for cancer alone in a foreign country with perfect equanimity. Every member of her family also became associated with Sri Ma, including her saintly parents, while her sister Renu was constantly in attendance on Sri Ma for nearly forty years. The family home, 31 George Town in Allahabad, became, if I may be excused a barbarism, a "*grihastha*-ashram", in which devotees from all over India were welcome, especially during Sri Ma's many periods of residence in the garden cottage specially built for her. The Mukerji family typifies a quality of outstanding service and compassion which is among a number of distinctive features linked with the name of Sri Ma. And it is to their beloved *Bithu* that we owe such a detailed chronicle of this particular feature in the spiritual totality of Sri Ma's larger all-India family.

Bithika's memory for revelatory anecdotes — each one possessing a weight of significance — gives her book a marvelous liveliness. Her powers of characterisation colour her accounts of heroic *seva* and inner transformation, affording us insight into Sri Ma's inimitable *ways*. For this is a book which, above all, shows how Sri Ma ceaselessly channeled what elsewhere emerged as her *vani*, into ways of doing, by means of persuasion, exhortation, inspiration, humour, and a stream of instruction of the utmost practicality. The picture we have here is quite breathtaking; again and again we are launched upon a fresh tale without any preconceived notion how Sri Ma is going to handle the situation as it occurs, and each time we are left bemused by the inexhaustible resourcefulness which she brings to bear without a moment's hesitation. Sri Ma's effortless being is such that she seems, in some of Bithika's anecdotes, to break through the limits of her limitlessness and *act out of character*, with hilarious consequences, including inadvertent jokes at the expense of sadhus for whom she had boundless respect. Bithika shows how Sri Ma could express disarmingly simple, humble gratitude for words of praise, for her singing for instance, or her cooking skills, her acting skills during staged *lilas* or compliments on her domestic accomplishments from her sister-in-law in person later in life — praise she'd lap up like a village lass new to her in-laws' household! The agility of Sri Ma's compassion, the delicate precision of her comforting words to the victims of human grief, and most notably her especially sensitive and rapt response to deaths within the Ashram, strike one to the quick. More than any of her wise and lengthy discourses (and there are examples of these in published form elsewhere), Sri Ma's deep insight into the human heart, is communicated even more memorably in her actions. Bithika is also sensitive in her accounts of those moments when Sri Ma withdrew into herself on the deaths of those close to her. Bithika strikes a note here which is quite special: she has clearly adopted the style of Sri Ma's gentle compassion and her book is suffused with it on every page.

There are fresh insights to be found in these memoirs despite the wealth of material already written about Sri Ma. It is as an insider that Bithika can tell us what it is like to know with absolute certitude that it is specifically Sri Ma's *kheyala* to look after everything in the lives of particular individuals. For the author herself, along with other members of her family, enjoyed being in direct receipt of Sri Ma's grace and protection. Another vista opens when we observe Sri Ma's genius at granting individuals complete freedom of space in which to develop and expand. An especially delightful "sub-plot" here is the story of Bithika's brother Bindu, so named as a tiny little boy who

Foreword

slept under Sri Ma's *chowki*, who grew up to become a large-hearted, wondrously charismatic person, a musician, gifted with divine song who charmed multitudes. I think of the story of Bithu "stealing" a pebble from the Narmada riverbed, and its subsequent providential use, thanks to Sri Ma's flawless memory for detail. Then there's the tale, so tiny that its illuminating charm lifts it to magical intensity, of how Sri Ma remembered Bithika's squeamishness during a riotous dolloping of festival curds, just dropping a speck on the tip of her reluctant tongue! But it is the same Bithu who journeys half across North India to obtain Sri Ma's blessing for a six-month sojourn in Switzerland to attend a gathering of inter-faith students. At once she receives, alone, a sublime discourse on religious tolerance, Sri Ma lying on her *chowki* — as Bithu notes it all down in the half-light. We are subsequently given the gist of the speech which Dr. Mukerji distilled from this private talk, along with the response of her audience, drawn from twenty-six different nationalities. There are, in fact, several instances when Bithika is suddenly struck by the sheer vastness of Sri Ma's outreach to the many Indians and also peoples of other countries on her exhaustive travels through the Indian subcontinent.

Many of these anecdotes reveal the psychological subtlety, the boldness and lightning inspiration of Sri Ma's *kheyala*. And we get abundant insight into this most subtle and innovative of Sri Ma's *ways*, her *kheyala* functioning in unprecedented manner: authoritative, ineluctable, fathomless.

I am very proud to have played a minuscule part in getting this book into the public domain.

Preface

It may be of interest to the reader to know how this book was written. It has been my good fortune to have evoked the *kheyala* of Sri Ma in regard to being invited to conferences and seminars on philosophical themes for many years in various parts of the world. On none of these occasions, however, was I required to mention or talk about Sri Ma Anandamayi. It came as a great surprise, therefore, when I received an invitation from Spain to speak on Sri Ma in October 1992. A seminar was being organised by the International Institute of Mystical Studies in Avila, the town dedicated to the memory of its renowned nun, Saint Theresa. The seminar was on the contemporary mystic saints of India. The names chosen for this seminar were Sri Ramakrishna Paramahamsa, Sri Ramana Maharshi, Swami Ramdas, Sri Aurobindo and Sri Ma Anandamayi.

Searching for a clue to this invitation, I noticed the name of Professor Raimundo Panikkar as one of the co-directors of this Institute. He is a scholar of international fame; I am acquainted with him because he used to live in Varanasi off and on for many years and thus himself knew Sri Ma quite well.

Although feeling strangely nervous about this assignment, I lost no time in accepting it with delight and gratitude. It occurred to me that when I was a college student, Sri Ma had once said to me, "Why do you keep so quiet? You should speak more often — why don't you participate in philosophical discussions and occasionally write on these themes as well?" I remember, I did write a couple of essays on religious subjects in a school exercise book, since obedience to Sri Ma's expressed *kheyala* came naturally to us, but not knowing what I was supposed to do with them, they remained in my desk and are probably still lying around somewhere. Overcoming my natural diffidence, I also began to take part in school, college and university debates, learning to speak logically and to the point. It now occurred to me that perhaps she had asked me to prepare myself for such an occasion as this and not only for teaching at the University. To be asked to speak on Sri Ma, I would say, would be the fulfilment of a dream if I had ever dared to dream a dream of such magnitude! I determined to compose a paper, which would be just the very best that I was capable of writing. The ways of providence, however, are inscrutable. Nothing happened according to plan.

My sanyasini (renunciate) mother Swami Satyananda Giriji (her ascetic name) was not too well at this time (September 1992). She, however, insisted that I should not cancel my programme or the arrangements for going to Avila (near Madrid). She was very pleased that I would be talking about Sri Ma and gave me her blessing on the eve of my departure to Delhi en-route for Spain. Arriving in Delhi at my friend Dr. Premlata Srivastava's flat, I tried to revise my paper, which had turned out to be very inadequate; I had had no time or leisure to do any kind of justice to my subject before leaving Allahabad. Neither was I able to improve on it in Delhi before starting on my journey because the ultimate set-back came when my sister said on the telephone that though my mother was quiet and not suffering, the doctors held out no hope for her survival till my return from Spain. So instead of leaving for the airport, I returned to Allahabad by the overnight train but I was only in time to be with my family for the last rites. The manner of my mother's passing away and the subsequent concatenation of events, which arranged themselves for the last ceremonial rites, is a story of Sri Ma's grace and her *kheyala* for one of her most dedicated devotees.

Had it been an ordinary academic seminar, I would have sent in a last minute apology; but this was an assignment, which had seemed beyond my power to have arranged or now to cancel. Thus I returned to New Delhi the next day, again travelling overnight, and left for Madrid by the first flight available. I missed the opening session, the

Preface

welcoming address by the Mayor and other programmes for delegates, but was in time for the first meeting of the seminar. Before I had time to register the loss of my mother fully I was in Avila caught up in the milieu of the seminar.

I was very conscious of the poor quality of my paper and my not-quite-there feeling of unreality, but notwithstanding these inadequacies the reception to the talk was no less than astounding. I felt myself to be a mere cipher — Sri Ma seemed to reveal herself to those interested in her by her own inscrutable ways. It was as if she smiled at the audience and, like any such gathering in India, it became enamoured of her smile. Someone from the audience asked me to relate my own experiences. At first, I hesitated, because up to that time I had never written or spoken about Sri Ma from the personal point of view. I was completely unprepared for such a question. The audience, however, did manage to elicit something from me. The atmosphere was friendly and comfortable, as if we were talking together about Sri Ma — in fact a *satsang* (an assembly of devout people). To my surprise, Professor Panikkar who was presiding gave up his time for a final summing up. He is a man of fine sensibilities and perhaps he gauged the mood of the audience and their eagerness to listen to more on Sri Ma.

At the conclusion of the session, I was surrounded by men and women who wished to speak to me. But alas, the language barrier (without the simultaneous translation system of the hall) was insurmountable. We exchanged addresses, smiles, and a few halting words in both languages.

On my return to India, I was caught up in my usual routine. I was surprised and touched by numerous letters from Spain, particularly from friends who again and again requested an autobiography from me. They said it was not idle curiosity but a genuine desire to know about my relationship with Sri Ma. For the first time, the idea came to me that perhaps an openly personal approach to the *lila* of Sri Ma might prove to be of interest to readers, so this book began to take shape. (One of the letters from Spain is printed after the Preface).

My Days with Sri Ma Anandamayi

I have dedicated it to all the friends in Spain for whom it has been written. I hope it will also be of interest in India because many people will recognise the participants in this story and recall their own roles in many incidents. Looking back on the events, I realise that we lived through an era of tremendous changes in our personal lives and the life of the nation. Only now, in retrospect, do we see that Sri Ma stayed with us during these crucial times to guide and lend support and to teach us to hold fast to our tradition in the face of well nigh overwhelming tides of disruptive forces. In fact, I only began to appreciate this aspect of Sri Ma's message to us when I first went to Canada in 1973 and came in close contact with the eminent philosopher Dr. G.B. Grant. It was he who taught me to see the folly of the "we too" syndrome in the East. He would say, adapting words from Nietzsche, "Here in the West we are played out; 'the wasteland continues to grow'. Only the East is now in a position to contribute something toward the future of mankind. But will it realise the importance of its own heritage or dissipate it by aping the West?"

31, George Town
Allahabad - 211 002

A Letter from Spain

Dear Ms Mukerji

How are you? We hope you were well. It's a long time since we heard about you — sorry for that. We wouldn't like to lose contact with you. We hope you remember us, any case you have the picture we took in Avila last year which shows who we are.

Despite we were together a few minutes, couldn't talk too much and the little contact we have been later, we remember you a lot.

Something happen in our lives when we met each other. We don't know exactly why but we remind you many times. Perhaps because you represent a women who makes to know people that the Divine Being lives in everyone, no matter how was her/his way of life.

We'd like to know some thing more about you, something you could tell us about your spiritual experience. We know this is something personal and belong to our inner life but we hope you don't mind to do this. It is not curiosity but a sincere interest in learning from you.

Well, we hope, we can receive a letter from you soon, God's light and love were with you forever.

God bless you
Sincerely
    From "us"
(The group of nine friends I met in Avila in 1992)

Sra. Ana Mª Munos Pareja
Montilla, Córdoba
España

18 October 1993

CHAPTER ONE

The Advent of Sri Ma in Our Lives

In the summer of 1937, Sri Ma Anandamayi passed through the town of Bareilly more than once on her frequent journeys between the foothills of the Himalayas and the remote villages of Bengal.

Bareilly is a town which lies at the juncture of many routes to the hill stations of the northern region. At this time, Maharatanji, as she was known in the Sri Ananandamayi Ashram, was living in Bareilly. Her husband Sardar Balwant Singh Jaspal was posted in Bareilly. She was known to our family as Mrs. Jaspal. One day, she and my mother happened to be occupying adjacent chairs in the Ladies Club. Maharatanji asked my mother, if she would like to have *darshan* (audience, seeing) of a Bengali Mataji who was expected very soon and would be staying at the *dharamshala* (inn for pilgrims) near the railway station. Maharatanji probably thought my mother (Mrs. Mukerji to her) would be interested because she was also a Bengali. My mother hesitated because for gentlewomen to go to public places and pay court to religious personalities was not at all an acceptable norm of behaviour. She said she would ask my father. Mrs. Jaspal's fourth daughter Kamala was a classmate of my elder sister Renu, who had also heard something about Sri Ma in school. Kamala had a photograph of Sri Ma in one of her books. My sister Renu was shown this as a special privilege. It was one of the photographs of Sri Ma in an ecstatic state in Dhaka. Renu thought it was the photograph of a person who was not quite normal. Kamala was very annoyed and whisked the picture away. Much later, when we had all become great friends we appreciated these photographs of which they had a selec-

Sri Ma in a state of samadhi

tion at their home. At this time, they had known Sri Ma for more than one year.

My father made no objection to my mother's satisfying her curiosity but declined to accompany her. I think it was a Sunday when we joined my mother and visited this pilgrims' rest house to call on Sri Ma. The *dharamshala* was a busy place. One entered an enclosed courtyard with a small Siva Temple in the middle of a raised platform. A covered verandah led on to the rooms all around the courtyard. There was a big hall in the centre covered from wall to wall with a cotton carpet. At one corner of this hall, Sri Ma was sitting on the floor on a folded blanket. My mother hesitated for a moment, not knowing how to greet her. Brahmins are not supposed to bow or do *pranam* to any other caste. My mother wondered "Is she a brahmin?...shall I touch her feet...?" Somehow, these scruples evaporated as she gazed upon the radiant majestic form in front of her. She knelt down and did a *pranam*. We also followed her example.

Sri Ma addressed my mother in familiar terms, as if she had known her a long time. Maharatanji, Billoji her second daughter, my mother and Renu sat near Sri Ma and talked to her. Kamala, her younger sister Vimla, my brother Bindu and myself found ourselves among a bunch of young people who were grouped round Pitaji (Bholanathji)[1]. My early memories of these visits to the *dharamshala* centre round Pitaji and the *kirtana*s we learnt to sing with him. Sri Ma looked very beautiful but rather remote. She did join in our *kirtana* groups now and then but mostly she sat quietly in the hall talking to the ladies who came to visit her. We went with our mother every

---

[1] Sri Ma's husband, who, although an ascetic, usually travelled with her everywhere.

evening after school. It was a new world of joyous activity under the aegis of the two most fascinating personalities we had so far encountered in our young lives. Sri Ma was quite normal in her behaviour and talk, yet somehow aloof. We liked to sit near her and were happy when she smiled and spoke to us.

We were introduced to the game of *satcidananda*. This was played by throwing seven cowrie shells like dice on to the floor. There were two teams generally headed by Sri Ma and Pitaji. The team members would sit alternately in a circle. If a throw showed 3 face-up cowries then it would count as *sat*. If one of the same team could throw five face-ups then it would count as *cit*. All seven face-ups would mean *ananda* and so it would be a winning throw — but *sat-cit-ananda* needed to follow consecutively. If *cit* came before *sat*, or *ananda* before *cit* — they would stand cancelled. The winning team would sing *kirtana*, the losing team would do *japa* (repetition 108 times) of any name of God and then join in the *kirtana*. I realised later that in this way hundreds of children all over India were introduced to *japa* and *kirtana*, the two simple forms of *sadhana*. With some degree of wonderment, I also remember that we played 'Crocodile Crocodile' in the open courtyard. The courtyard was thought to be a river. We stood on the central platform or the verandah and descended into the 'river' from time to time. The 'crocodile' would try to catch the unwary. Whoever was caught became the 'crocodile'. I remember Sri Ma joining in with us once or twice for this game. The 'crocodile' never caught her because she was very swift and nimble in walking from the verandah to the platform or back. Joyous days!

My mother was as if bewitched. She has said that she would wait impatiently for my father to leave for the courts (he was a judge) so that she could go to the *dharamshala*. She would return home before him or before we children came back from school. One day, Sri Ma said to her, "The way your eyes return again and again to the clock, so should your mind be given over to thoughts of God. Even if distracted for a while, bring it back to God-remembrance continuously". My mother was a bit embarrassed that Sri Ma had noted her clock-watching, but pleased also with this *vani* (utterance); it may be said that she obeyed this *vani* scrupulously all her life even to her last moments because the very last words that my mother uttered a minute before her passing away were "Jai Guru, Jai Ma" (29th September, 1992).

My father did not go with us to the *dharamshala*. He apparently had said that he was not interested and in any case, he had a very low opinion of persons who followed the so-called mendicant's way of life. He had presided over too many legal disputes regarding property and management in ashrams and *akharas* (monasteries). To him ochre robes signified irresponsibility if not downright dishonesty of purpose. So, although he raised no objection to my mother's visits, he preferred to go to his club to play tennis as usual in the evenings, leaving her to proceed again to the *dharamshala* with us in eager attendance. By 'us' I mean my sister Renu (15) myself (12) and Bindu (8). My eldest brother Manu was with our grandparents in Allahabad and the youngest brother, Babu was only a small child at this time.

Babu, Bindu and myself

One evening Bindu developed a high fever. Even so, my mother was ready for her visit to the *dharamshala*. My father was annoyed that she should be so uncaring as not even to wait for the doctor who was coming to see Bindu. So my mother stayed back home. The doctor was concerned because there was a fear of typhus fever in the town at this time. While all this was going on somebody brought news that Sri Ma had come to the officers' enclave and was visiting the house of Mrs. Dixit, which was right next to ours. My mother ran to Mrs. Dixit's house. Sri Ma smiled at her and said, "Do you live nearby?" When my mother indicated our house, Sri Ma who was already on her way out of Mrs. Dixit's walked along with my mother, and came to our house with her whole entourage. My father and the doctor were standing outside and were surprised to see the sudden influx of visitors. My mother was beside herself with excitement — asking the servants to fetch chairs and carpets, the gardener to fetch flowers and us girls to sing a song of *agomoni* (welcome). Sri Ma sat down in one of the armchairs brought out for her. My father came forward and made a *namaskara* (joining palms together in a respectful greeting to welcome a visitor). Sri Ma said to him with a smile "See, I have come to your house, uninvited!" I do not know if he had imagined her in ochre robes and was surprised to see her in her graceful white dress. He made no reply. In any case he must have pondered over her words all his life!

In the meantime, Billoji, who had gone inside the house for something or other saw Bindu in his bed. She picked him up and brought him out to where Sri Ma was sitting and put him in another chair in front of her. He was flushed with fever but, obeying my mother, managed to gasp a few lines of the *agomoni* song. Sri Ma smiled at him and taking a garland from her own neck put it round his. Then it was time to go. Sri Ma went away to visit other houses in the vicinity.

When normalcy returned, the doctor made his examination and was surprised to find no sign of an ailment, not even a fever. Telling my parents to keep watch for a recurrence of the fever, he took his departure. Bindu, however, recovered and my mother could continue with her visits to Sri Ma. She was convinced that Bindu had recovered due to Sri Ma's grace. I do not know what my father thought about this, but henceforth he did accompany us to the *dharamshala*. He also took Mataji and Pitaji for drives to the public gardens and many temples in the town. Many group photographs were taken which are even now reminders of those happy days.

Bholanathji, or Pitaji as he was known to us, was tall and handsome with flowing hair and beard flecked with shining grey. He had a very outgoing personality, easily communicating with all the people who flocked to the *dharamshala*. The well-known *kirtana*-party of New Delhi came over to Bareilly and we and many others had the rare and unforgettable experience of participating in the special form of *kirtana* (*namayajna*), which was their forte. The entire Bengali

Community of Beharipur turned up for this festival. The cadre of officers remained exclusive no longer. They mingled happily with the joyous throng. It was an exhilarating experience. Pitaji was always at the centre of the *kirtana* and sometimes Sri Ma joined him for short spells. Pitaji discovered Bindu very early. As soon as he had a cluster of children near him, he would start a *kirtana*. He would hoist Bindu on his shoulders and ask him to lead the *kirtana*. We all knew that Bindu could sing beautifully, but it was Pitaji and Mataji who recognised in him a touch of the quality of a *parsada* (*lila* companion) who in later years came close to Sri Ma.

Bholanathji and Mataji

Sri Ma visited Bareilly thrice during this summer. On one of these visits after Bindu had sung for her she said to him, "Will you sing for me every day?" Bindu exclaimed, "But you are going away!" Sri Ma then said, "Give me a time. If you sing at that time every day, I shall hear your song from wherever I am. If you cannot sing a whole song, sing one line or just make a sound, any sound, I shall hear you."

The Advent of Sri Ma in Our Lives

After some consultations, the time of 8 o'clock in the evening was proposed to Sri Ma. For many years Bindu used to sing hymns at this time, but alas, as is the way of human frailty, he got out of this habit when he became busy in the world.

It is true that we did not realise or ascribe to these events their full significance. Sri Ma was moving through a society that was multicultural and multilingual. Religious orientations were also different. Sri Ma in Bareilly was as natural and at home as she was in Dhaka or Calcutta. When I read Didi Gurupriya's diary recording the same events I understood her surprise and appreciation of the degree of independence and freedom of movement enjoyed by the women of these northern towns. Housewives did their own shopping, and drove their own cars. Mrs. Dixit, for example, was the first lady who had the honour of seating Sri Ma in the passenger seat while she drove the car. As far as I know, Bindu was the only other person who invariably had this privilege in later years.

The commingling of different communities in Sri Ma's vicinity was a regular feature of her travels. It happened spontaneously. Another characteristic was the joyousness. I recall an incident that took place some years later in New Delhi. It was a public meeting and Sri Ma sat in our designated enclosure surrounded as usual by a group of young college girls. An American lady came up to Sri Ma, (probably from the embassy) and indicated a desire to talk with her, so I was detailed to translate the conversation. I do not quite recall her questions to Sri Ma but afterwards she talked to me for a while. She said, "In our country, a religious congregation is a serious affair, it can be quite grim and emotional at times. Certainly, nobody laughs. You seem to me to be very happy and relaxed." I had been feeling a bit embarrassed because of my young cousins Tara and Buba, who had the habit of giggling away at the slightest oddity occurring near them. Now I was reassured that this annoying habit was seen in a new light by an outsider. It had not occurred to me previously that we were a "religious congregation". I do not think that all of us young people had any religious aspirations while we were growing up. We simply wanted to be near Sri Ma.

In Bareilly, Maharatanji's daughters, Billoji, Shakuntala, Kamala and Vimala and the three of us were in constant attendance. My father met a cousin of his, Manoj Chatterjee, the father of Tara and Buba, who was one of the members of the *kirtana*-party from New Delhi. Other friendships were made at this time and subsequently, were forged into strong links. Later, when we went to Delhi, we already knew many of the devotees. This is how the family surrounding Sri Ma and Bholanathji grew by leaps and bounds. The people of one town would automatically play host to the visitors, making arrangements for their stay and meals.

I remember Sri Ma's principal devotee, Bhaiji, as a quiet retiring person who kept away from the centre of activities. I came to know him only because Sri Ma asked me one day to fetch him from where he was standing near the Siva temple in the courtyard of the *dharamshala*. I approached him and said, "Ma wants you" (*Ma apnake dakchen*). He came at once and knelt in front of Sri Ma, who was sitting on the floor. I do not know what they talked about but when Bhaiji was about to get up, Maharatanji pleaded with him to sing his own special song to Ma, that is to say, "*Jayah, hridayavasini*". Bhaiji — rather reluctantly, I thought — sang the first four lines and then excused himself and left the hall quickly. I noticed that he backed away from Sri Ma's presence as people do in temples. During Sri Ma's third visit to Bareilly, on her way to Almora, Bhaiji had talked at length with my parents. For many years we had thought that my parents had been initiated by him, but this was not so. When we were grown up and in a position to ask them, my mother said he had revealed to them something about his own understanding of Sri Ma and had opened up for them a new dimension of human aspiration.

He had said that in the nature of things we could only have vague ideas about the Supreme Deity who shapes our destinies. We are told that there is an ultimate power, which creates, sustains and annihilates; the *adya sakti* (primordial energy) without which nothing may stir. He believed that Sri Ma was the manifest form of this all-pervasive unmanifest presence, which we worship as the ultimate being. To be attuned to the cosmic rhythm of vibrant creation and its

The Advent of Sri Ma in Our Lives

equally tranquil process of withdrawal is to penetrate the mystery of life. Sri Ma is the key to the mystery of this ebb and flow of *ananda*, which lies at the heart of creation. She is Anandamayi, the personification of the Good and Blissful and who by her very presence awakens the aspiration for Supreme felicity, which lies dormant in every human heart. For my parents it was as if Bhaiji had opened a window in a closed room. The vista of *sadhana* as a way of life became a reality for people who had not previously been gripped by its allure. Life in the world seemed colourless without Sri Ma's presence to give it enrichment. We learnt some details about her life from new acquaintances. She was born in one of the remote villages of Bengal on April 30, 1896. From her infancy, she was an embodiment of radiant self-sufficiency. She never left home to become an ascetic. Her parents sometimes travelled with her. Her husband Bholonath was always with her. Although she had never been a wife to him, he chose to remain with her as a loyal companion. She never had been given any instructions regarding *sadhana*. She had no "guru", nor did she belong to any particular religious order. Then why was she well known as a personality of considerable spiritual eminence?

The answer to this question was not easy at that early date. The transformation of a quiet village maiden into a teacher of profound knowledge and understanding had been witnessed by the people of Dhaka about a dozen or so years ago. We had met Bhaiji who was one of them. He had been a high ranking Civil Servant in Dhaka. He had renounced his position in the world in order to devote his life to the service of his guru, Sri Ma Anandamayi. In our part of the country, he acquired many loyal followers of his own because he could communicate in English and interpret for them Sri Ma's utterances and many of her enigmatic ways of being in the world. I think his mediation was very fruitful and also very necessary till Sri Ma herself picked up Hindi and could converse fluently with her non-Bengali audience.

Sri Ma's personality was self-authenticating; even if she did not speak a word her majestic aura was awe-inspiring. On station platforms, in busy crowded places, her white clad figure drew attention. People stopped to look back and ask, "who is she?" When confronted by her, palms naturally came together in respect and heads were bowed in salutation. The details of her life and background were irrelevant. She was what she was, a person who obviously not only held the key to the mystery of life but who was ready to guide one's understanding of human destiny.

Did she have a mission for humanity? No, because she had no wishes or desires or will, her action or words were the outcome of a spontaneous *kheyala*. The word *kheyala* may mean a sudden whim, a thought, or an idea, which is unrelated to any of the ordinary springs of action. Sometimes this word is used to describe a non-rational process of thought such as a poetic fancy or an erratic whimsy. Sri Ma's *kheyala* was distinct from all such connotations. The best way to understand it was to see it as arising out of the needs and necessities of people surrounding her or situations which took shape around her, although it could not always be related to her immediate vicinity or to a specific time.

The journey toward an understanding of this *kheyala* however, had just started for us. A new chapter had begun. Life was never the same again.

Chapter Two

My Family

My forefathers were zamindars (landlords) in Uttarpara near Calcutta in West Bengal. By the early years of the nineteenth century Bengal had been profoundly affected by a broad-based educational system taught through the medium of English. My great-grandfather Jadunath Mukerji developed a love for English Literature and made himself proficient in it. He won the gold Metcalf Medal for English Literature for the year 1812, and became a scholar of note. He was appointed Principal of Ravenshaw College in Cuttack, a post of considerable prestige in those times. He was a good teacher, much beloved of his pupils. My grandfather inherited a love of learning from his father and continued the tradition of a wide interest in all branches of learning that were studied in his day.

My grandfather's uncle Pramoda Charan Banerjee was appointed the first Indian Judge of the Allahabad High Court in U.P. He wrote to his nephew to come to the United Provinces from Bengal, because my grandfather used to suffer from malarial fever in his village. There was a very close bond of friendship between nephew and uncle. My grandfather Bipin Bihari Mukerji immigrated to the United Provinces and joined the judicial service. As a Judge, my grandfather remained on a transferable circuit, visiting many towns of U.P. After his retirement, he chose to settle in Allahabad to be near his uncle. My mother recalls that this old gentleman used to arrive every evening at 31 George Town, our home, to spend some time with his nephew. His phaeton and pair were quite a notable sight in our locality.

My grandfather's one passion in life was the pursuit of knowledge. Although he had taken up a profession, he considered the imparting of knowledge his paramount duty as a scholarly brahmin. His flair as a teacher came to fruition after his retirement. He was proficient in Bengali, English, Sanskrit and Persian. The last two were necessary requirements for Judges of the time because the Hindu and Muslim codes were written in these languages. He taught himself Latin and French in his old age in order to supervise the studies of his grandchildren. He took as keen an interest in the cases argued by my advocate uncle as in the school subjects of students who came to him for his help and guidance. These ranged from university scholars to school-going children. Along with his own grandchildren, he also tutored the son of his clerk who lived in one of the outhouses in our compound. Neighbours and friends would invite him to perform the ceremony of *vidyarambha* (beginning of schooling) for a child in the house. This ceremony consists in guiding the child's fingers to write the first letter of the alphabet on a new slate. My grandfather was considered a most suitable "guru" for the ceremony of the "beginning of schooling." Both my mother and aunt had come to 31 George Town as teenage brides. My grandfather undertook to educate them himself. He taught them Bengali and Sanskrit and Miss McMurdoch, a Scottish governess, was appointed to teach them English.

31, George Town, Allahabad

On winter evenings, my aunt used to tell us stories from the books she read with her teachers. One winter we heard the exploits of the Count of Monte Cristo while we sat in a semi-circle round her for our dinner in the dining-room. I remember that when I was old enough to read the book, I found it rather insipid because my aunt's version of it had been much more hair-raising.

My Family

These years were a time of gracious living. We still remember enjoyable outings, visits to hill-stations during vacations or to Calcutta to meet other members of our family. Allahabad was a quiet university town in my grandfather's time. The High Court for the entire province was situated at Allahabad, so the main population all around the grand buildings of the court and University consisted of judges, advocates and their entourages, intermingling with professors of high repute. Prestigious schools and colleges abounded. In our home, an atmosphere of academic pursuits held sway. My grandfather was a focal point for students who came to seek his blessing before appearing at some crucial test or coming to him with their question-papers for a discussion afterwards. One such incident lives in the memory of all of us. A law student came in with his question-paper. My grandmother always took a keen interest in all the topics being discussed in the house. Now, she wanted to know what the student (a neighbour's son, Pramod Ganguly) meant by the law of torts. My grandfather, in order to simplify it for her said,

"Supposing you are building a house next to your neighbour's. You cannot put your washroom in front of his living room."

My grandmother said, "Why not? I shall put my washroom wherever convenient".

"You cannot, The Law prevents you from causing annoyance to your neighbour."

"The Law cannot dictate my convenience"

"Yes, it can!"

Pramod related to us later that he escaped with his paper before battle was truly joined!

We children were very fond of our grandparents, especially the older ones, who spent most of their time with them. We put up shows and plays on the occasion of my grandfather's birthday. My sister Renu had some histrionic talents. She instructed us and directed the shows. Allahabad, like many other towns, had a Ladies Club that sponsored literary and cultural activities. For its annual show this club gathered the children of members and sought to stage the dance-drama *Valmiki Pratibha* written by Tagore. Seeing their enthusiasm, my father, a star of amateur theatricals offered his help that was gratefully received. He produced and directed the play with a cast of children ranging in age from 8 to 16. The audience consisted of parents, close friends and family. It was pronounced a great success although a small mishap marred its perfection. Since the older children were doubling as bandits in one scene and wood nymphs in the next, they were required to be quick-change artists. My cousin Sidu forgot to take off the fierce-looking moustaches while she donned a sari and a crown of flowers. The spontaneous laughter of the audience and urgent whispers from the wings made her rectify the mistake. The audience was indulgent and kindly overlooked the mishap. The final curtain came down to tremendous applause. The music and lyrics are beautiful and a most convincing performance as Valmiki was given by Pari Chatterji, the oldest girl amongst us.

Into this happy-go-lucky world descended the simple yet majestic figure of Sri Ma Anandamayi. She was as benign as a gentle rainfall on green fields, unobtrusive but so precious. Within a short while we were ineluctably drawn into this new vista opening out for us. In fact our whole family entered the magic circle of Sri Ma's gracious and captivating influence. I attach here a chart to simplify the names and relationships.

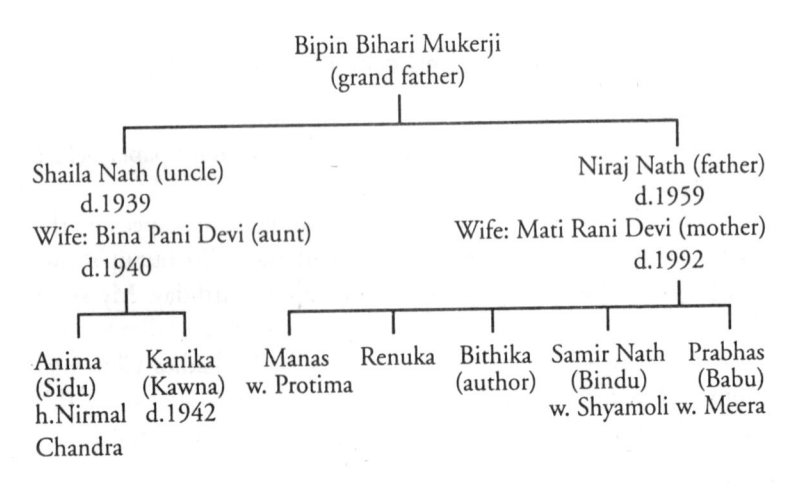

```
                    Bipin Bihari Mukerji
                       (grand father)
            ┌───────────────┴───────────────┐
   Shaila Nath (uncle)              Niraj Nath (father)
        d.1939                             d.1959
Wife: Bina Pani Devi (aunt)      Wife: Mati Rani Devi (mother)
        d.1940                             d.1992
   ┌─────┬─────┐          ┌──────┬──────┬──────┬──────┬──────┐
 Anima  Kanika         Manas  Renuka Bithika Samir Nath Prabhas
 (Sidu) (Kawna)       w. Protima    (author) (Bindu)   (Babu)
 h.Nirmal d.1942                           w. Shyamoli w. Meera
 Chandra
```

My Family

My uncle Shaila Nath Mukerji was an advocate practising law at the Allahabad High Court. My father had gone to Lucknow to join the Medical College. In the very first year, he had occasion to be insubordinate to his English Principal who had spoken some very abusive epithets to a group of late-returning students. My father, who was standing near him, was provoked into hitting the Englishman, for which offence he was rusticated from the college. My father was obliged to change the choice of his profession to law. He sat for the required examination and entered the judicial service like his father.

Ours was a joint family as was the custom of those times. My eldest brother Manu remained at 31 George Town with my grandparents and aunt and uncle, while my parents were travelling from town to town in accordance with my father's postings. We would visit 31 George Town on vacations. I remember that until much later, I had thought that my brother was my cousin along with the two daughters of my uncle, because I only used to see him when we came to Allahabad. In those days, it was considered the depth of bad manners to say "my wife" or "my children" or "my house" or call anything "mine", so strangers took time to sort out brothers, sisters and cousins from amongst a bunch of kids in the house.

As far as religious training was concerned we were taught prayers in Sanskrit to our own favourite deity and also to the Goddess of Learning, Devi Saraswati. My grandfather performed the "*Gayatri Japam*" every morning and evening as required of brahmins. My grandmother performed the *puja* (ritual worship) of the *Sivalingam* every Monday. There were other *pujas*, festivals and visits to temples.

It was all very traditional and orthodox. The main festival of Allahabad was the *Kumbha Mela*. The town was the venue of the *Kumbha Mela* held every 12 years at the site of the confluence of the sacred rivers, Ganga and Yamuna. A smaller event took place in between two major Kumbhas.

The festival of Kumbha enjoys a history of legendary fame. Even in written history the mammoth concourse of pilgrims at this site during the month of Magha (January/February) is mentioned as early as the 7th century A.D. The Chinese traveller Hwen Tsang wrote about the generous King Harshavardhana who gave donations to Hindus and Buddhists alike on the occasion of the Kumbha. Although the Kumbha Mela took place at an interval of 12 years the Magh-Mela was a yearly feature for the town of Allahabad. Pilgrims camped on the banks of the rivers in thatched shelters for a month, eschewing home comforts: a month of asceticism, listening to discourses on scriptures and performing *sadhana* in the seclusion of their own huts. My grandmother was keen on this month's *kalpavasa* as it was called. She however was not quite like other pilgrims. Her hut was quite elaborately constructed. It was furnished with chairs and a proper bed, carpets were spread on the straw-covered mud floor, and she had servants to wait on her. We used to visit her during the day and enjoy ourselves roaming round the *mela* grounds and eating snacks from the temporary stalls mushrooming all over the place. It was a marvellous meeting ground for people coming from all corners of the country, living simply and renewing their faith and commitment to their own tradition in an atmosphere of freedom and relaxation. In later years, we had occasion to live at the campsite of many Kumbha Melas in the company of Sri Ma. She attended nearly all the melas, even the 6-yearly half-Kumbhas. The experience of participating in the life of the people in an atmosphere of total commitment to a religious way of life and yet devoid of any kind of regimentation is indescribable and unforgettable. It is a marvellous opportunity not to be missed by anyone who can avail of it.

My father was posted away from his home town in 1925. My mother relates that when she left 31 George Town for the first time to go away with my father to Mirzapur, my grandfather advised her on the deportment of a gentlewoman in society. He told her that the ideal was to maintain a balance between familiarity and standing aloof. My mother lived up to this norm all the while she was away from the family circle. She never had any close friends but our house was always one of the centres for a friendly gathering of people in every town my father held office as Civil or Sessions Judge.

My Family

My grandfather died in September 1936 at the age of 82. He did not suffer a long illness, actually less than a week. It caused a major upheaval in our family. There was a great gathering of the clan. The people living on the estate at Uttarpara were grief stricken. My grandfather had kept in close touch with them, sending them monetary help when occasion demanded. Some of these pressing obligations devolved on my uncle as he now became the head of the family.

As written earlier, we were in Bareilly in the summer of 1937 when we had the great good fortune to come under the influence of Sri Ma. My mother used to write about her experiences to her sister-in-law, my aunt Binapani Devi in Allahabad. My aunt read out these lengthy descriptive letters to my cousins Sidu and Kawna. They were enthralled and began to yearn for a *darshan* of this marvellous personality.

When Sri Ma and her entourage left Bareilly on their way to Almora and Mount Kailasha my mother was as if bereft of the greatest joy in her life. My father was transferred to Moradabad in July 1937. My mother wanted to keep in touch with the travelling party. She entered into correspondence with Juthika Devi and Manik, two newly acquired friends who were travelling with Sri Ma.

During Sri Ma's sojourn in Bareilly, my father had used his camera frequently. We had visited the public gardens, where Bholanathji had given us great delight by playing with us in the mango-grove. He himself had posed for a photograph in front of a fruit-laden tree. When the photographs were printed my father posted a set of them to an address in Almora in my brother Bindu's name. Pitaji received this letter on his return from the pilgrimage to Kailasha. He immediately wrote back to Bindu, addressing him as "Samir".

I enclose here a translation of this letter that has been preserved in our family as a priceless possession:

My Days with Sri Ma Anandamayi

Almora 13.8.37
C/o Pandit Srinivasa Joshi
Teacher Almora

Kalyanvaresu [1] Dear Samir,

We arrived here on 10.8.37. Our companion Jyotish Babu (Bhaiji) is rather weak. His condition is not at all good. We are all worried about him. Well-known local doctors are treating him, we do not see any improvement. God's will will prevail. Give this news to your parents. Mrs. Jaspal has come from Bareilly to see Jyotish Babu. Tell everyone to pray for Jyotish Babu's recovery.

I have received the photographs sent by you (and your father); if possible send another set of the same to the address given below. In case you cannot then let me know.

Because we were travelling on the hazardous road to Kailash and as there is no postal service after Garbyang, I could not write to you. Do not take it to heart.

Dear boy, the scenic panorama of Kailash, Manas Sarovar, Ravana Hrada, Gouri Kunda and Mandhata Mountain is very beautiful. You have to see with your own eyes. It is impossible to express [its beauty] by writing or describing.

Some of the mountains are covered with snow, many others are bluish red or black as if covered by a tiger skin. All the mountains round Gauri Kunda itself are snow covered. One has to break through the ice to bathe in Gauri. The sight of swans riding the waves of the Manas Sarovar and Ravana Hrada, dancing along the ripples diving and honking is very captivating. The big swans are followed by lines of small ones — it looks very beautiful.

I am writing only a little. I am rather upset because of Jyotish Babu's illness. The rest are well. I hope all of you are well. With blessings.

Sd/- Ramapagla
(Bholanath)

The address where photos are to be sent:
Sashi Bhusan Dasgupta
Fine Art Gallery, Sadar Ghat
Chittagang (Bengal)

---

[1] In Bengali such Sanskrit words are used as forms of addresses indicating love and blessings toward a junior. Other words indicating respect and reverence are used toward elders by younger people.

My Family

Right after this letter, the grievous news of Bhaiji's death was received by all who had come close to Mataji and Pitaji. Letters were exchanged in worrying tones by all devotees regarding Sri Ma's strange inert condition at this time. Juthika Devi and Manik wrote regularly to my parents giving them news of Sri Ma. Exercising great care, the devotees brought her to the Kishenpur Ashram in Dehra Dun from Almora. My mother helped Bindu to write in reply to Pitaji's letter. He immediately wrote back a most loving note, which I translate below. It was a post card:

Ananda Mayee Ashram
Kishenpur
P.O. Rajpur, Dehradun
25.8.37

Kalyanvaresu Dearest Samir,
    I am very pleased to receive your letter. I have read out your letter to your Ma and others. Everybody has liked it. Your smiling face seems to come alive in your letter. Try to write regularly. Your Ma is quite all right. There is no reason for concern for her. Manik and Juthika left for Delhi yesterday. We send our blessings to all of you.
    Yours Sd/- Ramapagla

At this time in Kishenpur, Sri Ma hardly moved and barely took any food, excepting a few sips of water only. Nobody could understand the condition of her body because she was not ill. She spoke a little when necessary, but her natural radiance was quite eclipsed. Sri Ma had experienced the death of many near and dear ones in the worldly sense and never had she grieved over their loss, so nobody could think, at least not for long, that this was a manifestation of grief. Besides she had spoken calmly and serenely about the details of Bhaiji's *sanyasa* and death to his devotees and disciples. She had done a supra-human job of giving consolation to the almost inconsolable Hari Ram Joshiji, to grief-stricken Bholanathji. She had especially spent long hours talking tirelessly with Bhaiji's personal servant Khagen, who had come to Almora on receipt of the telegram conveying the sad news of Bhaiji's illness. He was in attendance when Bhaiji died. She told him in detail all that had transpired at the holy site of the Manas Sarovar, his spontaneous renunciation and the subsequent events of Bhaiji's illness and passing away. My parents heard about all this from Juthika Devi and Manikda.

In the light of the many strange events which occurred during the last years of Sri Ma's life, when she seemed to take on herself a lot of suffering due to negative attitudes coming from different directions, it is possible to construe the meaning of her apathy at the time of Bhaiji's passing away also. She may have been accepting totally the conspicuously negative attitude of Bhaiji's wife Manikuntala Devi, who must have been devastated by events. This may have been her way of lessening the burden of grief for the widow. Sri Ma herself suffered in order to ease that of the bereaved family. After all, Sri Ma had assumed full responsibility for Bhaiji and those who belonged to him. Manikuntala Devi had not wanted Bhaiji to go on this trek to the high mountains. Sri Ma had advised him to stay back, but his yearning to visit the Himalayan ranges was too overpowering. He had said to Sri Ma that he would write to his wife to reassure her that there would be no danger to his health. It is of course well known that both his wife and son were reconciled to Sri Ma later. Sri Ma's grace and compassion drew them in when they realised that Bhaiji was much more than merely a husband and father. I have seen Bhaiji's son Ramananda Rai in the ashram at Varanasi, but not his mother who by that time was no more.

My parents took the first opportunity they had to go to Dehradun. Renu, Bindu and my baby brother went with them. I had come to Allahabad for the academic year 1937-38 and was with my grandmother, uncle, aunt and cousins at the time. My mother used to write long letters to my aunt telling her about Sri Ma. My aunt would allow us to read these letters full of *matri-katha*. Thus she and my cousins Sidu and Kawna came to know a little about Sri Ma even before they had their first *darshan* a year later.

Renu says that Sri Ma used to lie quietly in her room. Bholanathji asked Renu and my mother to sit near her to keep watch or stay within call. He himself would come frequently just to see how things were. They would perform some little tasks if Sri Ma asked them to do so. From the very first day Sri Ma had permitted Renu to give her a little massage now and then. She would render Sri Ma other little personal services. Ruma Devi used to cook for Sri Ma but she as always ate almost next to nothing.

My Mother's Initiation (*diksha*)

My mother was given initiation at this time. None of us knew anything at all about this incident till a couple of years before my mother passed away. By this time, she had lost her eyesight completely. One day she asked me to read out to her the hymn in Sanskrit, which had issued from Sri Ma's lips and is printed in Bhaiji's book. I read it aloud, to which she gave close attention. After I had finished, she said, "Yes, that is right, I thought may be I had forgotten a syllable or two."

It came as a surprise to me that what we had heard her repeat sometimes under her breath were two lines from this hymn. I had not recognised the lines out of context, as it were. We came to hear the mantra only because we were in attendance on her while she lay bed-ridden in the last years of her life. Because a mantra is not to be revealed to another, she had asked me to read out the whole hymn, so that I would not know which portion was especially important to her. I was curious to know the background of this initiation. My mother then told me that one day in Dehradun almost fifty-four years ago, Sri Ma had told her to read aloud whatever was written on a piece of paper given to her by Pitaji. After she had read the two lines of the Sanskrit syllables, Sri Ma had told her to go down to the small basement room (under the verandah at the back of the ashram in Kishenpur) and do *japa* of this mantra. A specific number was given. It took a few hours for her to do this, but she did not remember them as such or that she was tired or restless. It was altogether a beautiful experience for her. At some specific hour Pitaji went down to the '*gufa*' (underground cell) and performed a *yajna* in a portable *kunda* (receptacle). The piece of paper was consigned to the flames and my mother was guided to offer some oblation to the *yajna*-fire. Sri Ma herself went down at the time of the final oblation (*purnahuti*). Both of them placed their hands on my mother's head and blessed her. Renu saw the comings and goings, but not what had transpired in the basement room.

Years later (in 1946), my mother was initiated formally by Didima [2] in Solan. She was one of Didima's early disciples, most probably the first among lay devotees. My mother's allegiance to her Guru (Didima) was undeviating and of transparent sincerity. Sri Ma herself paid my mother the highest compliment by saying once. "Like Guru, like disciple." I think it does summarise my mother's life of total dedication, one-pointed singleness of purpose through all the vicissitudes, which the fates had ordained for us. Before his retirement my father enjoyed a position of the highest respect in all the towns in which he held office as District Judge. My mother somehow never got involved in official circles. She lived her life like a lotus leaf in water. Our family went through bewildering ups and downs, but in retrospect we realised that our affairs were kept on an even keel by my mother's undeviating trust in Sri Ma's *kheyala* and faith that all is as it should be and not otherwise. Her gentle strength lay in taking no notice of the hardships while we were growing up. She was a friend, an unfailing source of support. Her care and concern were unobtrusive but always there to fall back upon. The more I think of Sri Ma's compliment, the more impressed I am to discover how truly comparable these two lives were.

My parents, Renu and Bindu visited Sri Ma again in Haradwar in the month of April in 1938. My father was very circumspect about these visits. First, he would write to ask if it would be convenient for us to come. When he received a reply he would rent rooms near the ashram and put up there. In the beginning we never just arrived at the ashram as other people did. Gradually we also learnt not to stand upon ceremony with the management, simply because there was no formal management as such. Whoever happened to be there made arrangements for the influx of visitors or the travel arrangements.

---

[2] Sri Ma's mother. We called her Didima but she was in ochre robes and her *sanyasa* name was Swami Muktananda Giri.

My Family

Some order always emerged somehow out of the seeming chaos created by Sri Ma's constant and unplanned travels. Her companions also were an apparently random collection of people. It was all very exciting and an enjoyable adventure. Bindu especially had a lovely time, being carried on the shoulders of Pitaji when he went out for *nagar-kirtana* (*kirtana* on the streets). We had always thought that Bindu was elevated so that people would see who was leading the *kirtana*. In later years, Bindu surprised me by telling me that the main reason why Pitaji had hoisted him up was so that Sri Ma would see and recognise him (Bholanathji) from her far off balcony. Bindu however, was needlessly modest. Bholanathji was fond of his voice and very often made him lead the *kirtana*. At this time, the party from Delhi frequently performed *kirtana*. All of them believed that *kirtana* was the panacea for all ills. Sri Ma was still not quite her own bright self. So the devotees took to singing *kirtana* to pray for her "recovery".

Baba Bholanath was certainly the moving spirit of the concourse of singers. He would frequently gather all the inmates of the ashram and go out on the streets of Haradwar leading them to the Ganges. His commanding figure easily attracted attention. Many people came over to pay their obeisance to him and swell his *kirtana* party. My father tended to keep away from these vigorous engagements, firstly because he was not an asset with regard to the *kirtana* and secondly, he wished to stay and converse with Sri Ma during the little time he had at his disposal. My father used to regale us with entertaining stories regarding the efforts of others to evade the vigilant eyes of Baba Bholanath. One day he saw the portly form of a devotee of Delhi, partially hidden behind a piece of furniture. My father kept a straight face till Baba Bholanath was safely out of the way.

It is difficult to recapture the marvellous atmosphere of those days. People of different towns, languages, religions came together naturally, as if it were one big happy family. Sri Ma's presence and Bholanathji's generous-hearted welcome to all and sundry made it a time of perennial festive rejoicing. Sardar Sadhu Singh, Sri Ma's Sikh devotee and Mia Talattuf Hussain, a Muslim devotee, were both in

Haradwar to attend on Sri Ma at this time. It is in retrospect that we think of them as Sikh or Muslim; for Ma they were as much her Pitajis (father) as any of her Bengali "Babas" from Dhaka or Calcutta. She could now talk in Hindi very fluently. Many interesting conversations, such as the one given below, took place daily.

A newcomer wanted to find out a little about Sri Ma. He asked her, "Describe to me a little of your own way of *sadhana*? What is the nature of your prayers?"

Sri Ma : Can you not understand anything about me, now that you are here?

Question : No I cannot!

Sri Ma : If you say your "prayers" then I would reply that I pray to myself!

Question : Who is your Guru?

Sri Ma : First my parents, then he to whom they gave me in marriage, after that all of you, even including animals, birds, trees, insects — everyone is a guru — because He alone is the Guru and all else that you see is He Himself and nothing else. Then, I myself am my Guru — there is naught else. Then again the question of Guru doesn't arise. Whatever is, is.

Question : Who do you worship? Rama, Krishna or the Goddess?

Sri Ma : The One alone appears differently; there is naught else but the One.

Question : I am referring to Dasaratha's son Rama or Nanda's son Krishna?

Sri Ma : But I know only Rama or only Krishna!

The interlocutor seemed pleased with this answer. After a pause he began again by saying,

> "You are saying that each one of us is That only, but we are not aware — just like fire, which is latent everywhere but is especially visible in a wood-fire. So you are the visible flame. Give us something of the plenum of bliss, which is your *svarupa* (essence).

Sri Ma : You also, Pitaji, must know something of this bliss, otherwise why should you look for it? It is already within you.

Question : But I am not aware of it, so it is as good as if it was not there. How should I attain it?

Sri Ma : See Pitaji, the only means of attainment is to be constantly engaged in its pursuit. An undeviating one-pointed and relentless effort is required. Consider how we live: we eat one morsel at a time, we walk step by step; we write one letter after another. Yet in this oneness there is infinity. See this flower: you will say it is beautiful, it is red etc., but never will you be able to express the entirety of the flower's impact on you. Much will remain unsaid, unsayable. So in the manifest the unmanifest remains hidden. Pitaji, the unmanifest, the infinite is within us. That is why I say that *ananda* (bliss) is within you also!

Chapter Three

My Cousins Meet Sri Ma

This chapter was written by my cousin Sidu

My cousin Bithu is writing about the family's contacts with Sri Ma Anandamayi beginning in the year 1937. Bithu asked me to help her out with my own reminiscences. This entailed a delightful journey down memory lane. My mother Bina Pani Devi, my sister Kawna and I came to know about Sri Ma from the vivid letters of my aunt, that is Bithu's mother. My aunt and her family had the good fortune to meet Sri Ma in Bareilly in the summer of 1937 and again in August / September of the same year at Kishenpur, Dehradun. We at 31 George Town, Allahabad had to wait a while for this magic moment to transform our lives too.

In the month of June 1938, my uncle Niraj Nath Mukerji was visiting us. I had just passed the Senior Cambridge Examination with some distinction. He was very pleased and asked what would I like as a present. I promptly answered that we would like to go to Dehradun to visit Sri Ma. As soon as he granted this wish we became excited and joyfully started to make plans and arrangements. Our family was conservative; it was not at all usual for young girls to go to an "ashram", especially when nothing much was known about Sri Ma at the time. My aunt persuaded my grandmother to allow us to go.

My uncle was posted in Agra where he had become friendly with Didi Gurupriya's eldest brother Birendra Chandra Mukherjee. Biren Babu was in Dehradun at this time and my uncle wrote to him to make arrangements for our visit.

My Cousins Meet Sri Ma

In those days travelling was easy. One just bought tickets and boarded trains. There was no need to make reservations etc. So one auspicious day we entrained for Dehradun arriving the next day at this beautiful hill-station which we had passed through years earlier on our way to Mussoorie for a summer vacation.

We were disappointed to hear from the *tongawallahs* (drivers of horse carriages) that Sri Ma was not at Kishenpur but at Raipur, a rather remote village at some distance from the town. My uncle was worried. We could

Clockwise: Bithu, Renu, Bindu, Kawna and Sidu

see that he hesitated to escort so many young girls to an unknown destination along lonely forest tracks. However, he was not immune to our eagerness, so we started off. In those days there was actually no road but just a rough track down which the horses stumbled. The June sun blazed down on us. But we were sustained by our hope that we would soon see Sri Ma. Consequently our disappointment was great when we at last arrived at Raipur and were told that Sri Ma had gone back to Kishenpur. The Brahamachariji (Bishu Maharaj) at the ashram made us welcome and offered refreshments, but we were too restive and decided to proceed straight on to Kishenpur. The *tongawallahs* retraced their steps back to Dehradun over the same mountainous track; we proceeded to Kishenpur, this time on the regular macadam road which goes right up to Mussoorie. Kishenpur is about 4 miles out of Dehradun on this road. We arrived around 4.p.m.

The ashram was very attractive but rather small, that is, there were no extra buildings for visitors. Birendra Chandra Mukherjee made us feel welcome. He had made arrangements for our stay in an adjacent cottage. We were able to unpack a little of our luggage, take baths, and change our clothes in readiness for the audience with Sri Ma. When we returned to the ashram, we found Sri Ma sitting on the verandah to the left of it.

Even today I can clearly visualise the divinely radiant form of Sri Ma which I saw nearly sixty years ago. We had never before visited any gurus or spiritual masters or mahatmas. We did not know how to greet her. We stood as if bewitched. Following the example of my aunt, Renu and Bithu, we also knelt down and touched the ground in front of her with our foreheads, in the manner of performing *pranam* in temples. Sri Ma looked beautiful. She was wearing a white *dhoti*; her black hair fell to her shoulders in soft, shining, tapering swathes. She had a large red *sindur* (colirium) mark on her forehead.

Four or five men were sitting with her. Sri Ma spoke to my uncle. He introduced my mother, my sister and myself to her. At about this time, two of the men got up to take their leave of Sri Ma. She asked them, "Must you go immediately?" They answered, "Yes, Ma, we cannot delay any more. There is much work to be done." So, bidding good-bye they departed. Right after, Sri Ma also stood up to go out for a stroll. We came to know that this was a daily practice and that she walked a little distance towards Mussoorie and back. On this day however, she turned left outside the gates to walk down towards Dehradun. We had hardly gone a furlong when we saw that the two visitors had met with an accident. One wheel of their tonga had come off and it lay tilted at an odd angle. One gentleman (Professor Phanibhushan Chakravarty of Varanasi) was evidently hurt and in pain and was lying at the roadside. His friend stood by helplessly. The tongawallah was looking to his horse.

Sri Ma approached them and said, "I had a *kheyala* that something untoward would happen, that is why I had asked if you could stay a while." Biren Babu, my uncle and others engaged in consultation as to what could be done. Sri Ma asked Bithu to squat down and

My Cousins Meet Sri Ma

Sri Ma in Dehra Dun in 1938

hold Phani Babu's head in her lap to ease his awkward position. My uncle, who had two years of medical training before he had changed over to the judicial service, examined the professor and said that the leg bone seemed broken, so he dared not disturb it.

At this point a car approached from Dehradun and stopped at our request. By a lucky chance, the owner of the car turned out to be a very close friend of my father's and also known to my uncle. They agreed to return to Dehradun in order to take the injured man to hospital. After the car left for Dehradun, all of us followed Sri Ma back to the ashram.

The time was about a month after Baba Bholanath had passed away. Sri Ma's regular companions were away at this time. An old lady named Ruma Devi used to cook for Sri Ma. Apart from Biren Babu, there was Manmotho Babu, Naresh Chakravarty, and a young man called Vyas who had just returned from Germany after qualifying as a dentist. We met Abhaya, a restless teenager, so mischievous and pert that Sri Ma had imposed a vow of silence on him. He was allowed to break the *maunam* (silence) in the evenings to sing *kirtana*. People listened to his melodious voice and forgave him his daily iniquities. Some local people would visit Ma for a short while, otherwise it was quiet and peaceful. When I recall those days, I marvel at our good fortune. We were constantly in Sri Ma's presence. Biren Babu suggested that my mother and aunt take up "*seva*" of Sri Ma, which delighted them. They cooked for her, served food, took care of her clothes and bedding and rendered small personal services. We became a very intimate group. Eating and sleeping became secondary with us. Most of the 24 hours were spent in Sri Ma's company.

We also witnessed one of the many miracles that nearly always happened in Sri Ma's vicinity. It came about like this:

The day after the accident recorded above, Dr. S. and the professor's friend came to the ashram. The patient's leg was broken in two places. The doctor had brought the X-ray plates with him. There were no facilities in Dehradun at the time for setting bones. The doctor wanted the patient Phani Babu to go to Delhi immediately because he needed a plaster cast for his leg. The patient, however,

My Cousins Meet Sri Ma

insisted on going to Calcutta although this long journey was contrary to the doctor's advice.

At their request, Sri Ma immediately went back with them to the hospital. Bithu and I accompanied Sri Ma. She stood near the bed of the patient and asked, "Are you in much pain?" The Professor was almost in tears! He said, "Yes Ma. Ask the doctors to let me go to Calcutta." Sri Ma touched his leg and passed her hand over the portion that had shown a break in the X-ray chart. After a while, he said in an easier tone, "All right, tell them, I shall go to Delhi."

The next day the doctor again came to the ashram in great excitement. He said, "We took a new X-ray before the professor's departure for Delhi to send to the doctor who would examine him there, but this one does not show any break whatsoever! How is this possible? I cannot understand it." My uncle and others also examined the two X-rays. One showed perceptible breaks and the later one a whole, unfractured leg bone.

Sri Ma smiled and said, "Well, in that case, Baba (the professor) may go to Calcutta, can't he? There is no obstacle now?" The Doctor readily agreed. Incidentally, this was the beginning of Dr. S.'s long association with Sri Ma. All of us were convinced that Sri Ma's gracious touch had been effective in healing the break.

There was another incident of a different kind, which revealed Sri Ma in a new light. One N. Babu had come from Calcutta. We were told that he also was a professor in Calcutta and well-known. Unfortunately, he had a most disconcerting manner. He would come out with very childish questions such as "Ma, what is taking place in Kailasha (Heaven) now? Describe it to me!" One day he went so far as to declare "You are my mother. I shall sit in your lap!" And indeed no sooner had he said so than he dumped himself on her lap. He was far from being a light-weight so it was a gross imposition. Everyone exclaimed aloud in annoyance. Biren Babu scolded him as if he were a child and he was made to get up immediately. Sri Ma remained unmoved throughout this incident but it was obvious that he was causing a disturbance. Next day again he asked a childish question, "Ma, tell me what is happening in the abode of God Vishnu?"

Sri Ma suddenly stood up on her *asana*. In a trice her whole demeanour changed. Her voice was also different. She spoke sharply, "You want to see? Do you indeed want to see?" Her countenance looked so forbidding that all of us were petrified; we had never seen her in this posture of wrath. We were so scared that we lowered our gaze because we could not bear to look at her blazing eyes. N. Babu lay down at her feet and wailed piteously, "Forgive me, Ma, forgive me."

Sri Ma resumed her seat and all was as before. She smiled at us so we could breathe again. We were thankful when N. Babu went back to Calcutta on the very next day.

These were unforgettably halcyon days for us. To us Sri Ma was a friend who fulfilled all our conscious and unconscious yearnings for happiness in life. We were content to be with her, to see her, to talk to her, or to walk around in her company. I do not think we had any particularly high-flown thoughts regarding spiritual discipline. Sri Ma, however, gave a good start. She said, the four of us, Renu, Kawna, Bithu and myself would sit in her room for half an hour each day and do *japa* or *dhyana* (meditation). We did not find this a difficult task. What could be more pleasant than to sit in her room and gaze upon her while she lay quietly in her bed.

One morning, Sri Ma asked us, "Can you cook?" My younger sisters did not speak, but I said proudly, "Yes, Ma, I can cook." Sri Ma asked again, "What dishes can you cook?" I answered, "I can cook all kinds of dishes." I was rather sure of myself because cooking was a hobby with me and I used to try out many dishes at home. Sri Ma then asked, "Do you know how to cook bamboo shoots or yam leaves?" I did not even know that these were edible things, so shook my head. Sri Ma laughed along with all the others who were listening to our conversation.

Sri Ma then asked for a brazier of soft coke and a few utensils. All preparations were made in a very short while. She said, "I shall teach you the dishes of East Bengal." Some potatoes and a green gourd were fetched from the kitchen store. Sri Ma said, "See, I shall show you how they prepare vegetables in East Bengal." She handled

My Cousins Meet Sri Ma

the cutter (an upright sharply honed iron blade fixed to a wooden stand, which is held steady by the foot, while both hands are used to cut the vegetables) like an expert. The soft green gourd was cut in circles and then shredded fine but held in one piece. Then she flicked it on to the plate and the half circle spread out in a lacy fan-like shape, quite beautiful to see. We had never seen such skill. Her movements were swift and sure. We learnt how to cook this vegetable that day, although none of us could ever shred it the way she had done. The inmates of the ashram had the good luck to sample Sri Ma's cooking and on other days too when she taught us more dishes.

I had the habit of snatching a nap in the evenings, so while the evening *kirtana* was going on, I would choose to lean against the wall behind everybody and enjoy a good nap. One day Sri Ma pointed her torch at my face and laughed. Everybody realised what I was up to and laughed also. Thereafter, whenever I was tempted to indulge in my bad habit I used to find the torch shining in my face.

Our little cousin Babu was just 2 1/2 years old at this time. He used to play around and became a general favourite. Ruma Devi especially took to regarding him as Bal-Gopal and would give him *lichies* (Indian fruit) to eat. One day we made a calculation and were horrified to discover that he had consumed more than 60 *lichies*. Visitors also used to give him this fruit. Sri Ma scolded us for not keeping better watch over him, but due to her *kripa*, he was not taken ill.

One day Sri Ma gave us new names. My mother was Shanti-Sudha and my aunt Achanchala. Sri Ma said, "Both imply the same state: both friends (sisters-in-law) are at the same stage. One keeps knocking on the door patiently, the other is shedding tears and praying for the door to be opened. She asked people to guess which was which but nobody was right because my mother had a shy temperament and my aunt was more forthright. Later in life, we realised that Ma had read their characters correctly after all. Some years ago, we had lost a small brother of two and a half years called Shanti. Although nobody had told her, Sri Ma probably named my mother "Shanti Sudha" with compassionate understanding of her sense of loss. My name was Siddha-Ma, Renu was Charan Renu, Kawna was

Ananda-Kawna and Bithy was Vedika. Renu and Bithu were given more than one name later. Renu became Anurag and Bithu, Sutapa, and also Brahmavit.

At the end of the vacation we returned to Agra and then back to Allahabad full of excited talk about what Sri Ma had said and what she had done in her *lila* with us. Some time, in late October 1938, Sri Ma came to our house at 31 George Town for the first time. Since then until January 1982 she continued to visit our home at regular intervals. Allahabad is a junction of several major routes. Sri Ma passed through Allahabad many times in the course of her ceaseless travels. Sometimes she broke her journey to stay overnight at 31 George Town, or just for the day or even for only a couple of hours. Before my young cousin Bindu built a small cottage for her in the compound under a *neem* (margosa) tree in 1956 she would most graciously abide by any makeshift arrangements that could be made for her. The *punya* (religious merit) of our saint-like forefathers must have created an aura in our house which brought us the blessing of Sri Ma's presence so often.

Sri Ma came to Allahabad once or twice in those days at the invitation of Sheo Prasad Sinha, an advocate who had become a devotee. Didi's elder cousin J.C. Mukerjee was a friend of Mr. Sinha. On one such visit he kindly suggested to my mother that she could ask Sri Ma to visit her home also. As written above, this was her first visit. My mother was delighted at the prospect and made elaborate arrangements for the reception. A small *samiyana* (marquee) was put up in the centre of the big lawn and decorated with flower garlands. We had a profusion of *shefali* flowers. My mother made a carpet like pattern of these small star-shaped white flowers on the green lawn. It took her almost the whole night to do this and it looked very beautiful.

It was my mother's wish that we sing a song of welcome (*agomoni*) when Sri Ma came to our house. Neither of us sisters was musical but we had a cousin, Mamata, staying with us who made us practice a song for the occasion. This, however, came to nothing because Kawna and myself were overcome by a fit of the giggles when the time came.

My Cousins Meet Sri Ma

Poor Mamata had to sing on her own while my mother greeted Sri Ma as she stepped on to the lawn. Sri Ma sat on the seat prepared for her. My father's personal servant Perag had made a huge garland of red hibiscus flowers. Sri Ma looked truly resplendent with this garland, which hung down in a graceful curve on to the lawn itself. We managed to sing the *arati* song while my mother performed it. Sweets and fruits were offered. Didi gave a little of it to Sri Ma, the rest being distributed to everyone else. My grandmother was helped to walk out on to the lawn and thus she had her first *darshan* of Sri Ma. My father stood at the gate of the gardens a little distance off and made a *namaskara* with folded hands. Sri Ma smiled at him.

My father was a devotee of Kali. His outward appearance did not reflect his commitment to an inner life of *sadhana*. It occurred to us in later life that he could have seen a vision of his *Ista-devata* in Sri Ma, radiant and smiling with a garland of hibiscus (flowers sacred to Kali) almost covering her entirely. It is also possible that Sri Ma came to our house at this very time to grant him this *darshan* because he himself would not have gone anywhere to visit her and these were the last days of his unexpectedly short life.

We had *darshan* of Sri Ma whenever she came to Allahabad. Once she stayed on a houseboat on the Yamuna across from the Ewing Christian College. I think she stayed twice at Sheo Prasad Sinha's house. Once, on being informed of Sri Ma's arrival we hastened to his house. We were told she was sitting in a tent. Till that time we had not known any restriction regarding Sri Ma's availability for *darshan*. My mother entered the tent but was told brusquely by an attendant to wait outside till sent for. She came out again at once. This was our first experience of the thoughtlessness of Sri Ma's attendants toward visitors. We were rather taken aback and embarrassed and wanted to leave immediately. My gentle mother, although almost trembling at this experience of uncalled for rudeness, displayed a degree of patience which was a lesson to us. She said we would wait till Sri Ma was free to receive us. Within a minute, however, J.C. Mukherjee came out and called us in, saying Sri Ma had sent him out to fetch my mother. Sri Ma put her hands on my mother's head and shoulders caressingly as if wiping away something. The hurt dissolved and we were as happy as ever.

The next few years of our family life were difficult. Without Sri Ma's constant *kheyala* and unremitting compassion we would not have survived the various ordeals as lightly as we did.

My father passed away on March 4, 1939 after a fortnight's illness at the age of 52. He, at that time was the leading advocate (in criminal law) of the Allahabad High Court. His wit and humour, and courtroom technique had made him a legend in his own lifetime; Allahabad was shocked at his sudden death. Our family was almost brought to a standstill because my uncle the younger son had never envisaged the possibility that such a responsibility would fall on his shoulders at short notice. He was just stunned. My aunt (Renu's mother), ever the pioneer, held everything together with courage and exemplary circumspection. She, in this as in every other crisis in her life, must have been sustained by Sri Ma's *kheyala* on her.

She and my mother were close friends. More than anybody, she knew what my mother was suffering. She prevailed upon my uncle to take herself and my mother to Vindhyachala by car to see Sri Ma, who was residing there at the time. The house was full of relations who had come to mourn our loss with us. From morning till night friends visited us to offer their condolences. Somehow, my aunt managed to whisk my mother away from all this just for a few hours.

As the car climbed up the hill, Sri Ma was seen coming out of her room and going down to the courtyard. She met my mother halfway, clasping her in her arms and speaking gentle words in her own inimitable style when consoling the bereaved. My mother said (later to my aunt) that all her anguish and the fearsome burden weighing on her heart had dissolved at Sri Ma's kind touch and words. On their return from Vindhyachala, my mother seemed more self-possessed and serene. In any case she was quiet and undemonstrative by nature. After things had settled down a bit we realised that my mother had lost interest in the world completely.

My Cousins Meet Sri Ma

We have heard many tales of sudden *vairagya* (dispassion) which leads to God-realisation. My mother seemed to make an easy transition from being one of the foremost ladies of the town to leading an almost ascetic way of life. Her friends pleaded with her not to withdraw from the world, to take an interest in the future careers of her daughters and so on. She listened to all such advice almost with amusement, saying calmly, "Mati (Mati Rani, my aunt, Renu's mother) is there, she will look after everybody."

In retrospect we realise that my mother just lived Sri Ma's *vani*; "To talk of God alone is worthwhile. All else is in vain and pain." Her renunciation of the world was total. She did not go away anywhere but continued to live with us and agreed to whatever plans my uncle suggested regarding our changed living conditions. She talked and laughed with us, met our visitors, spent some time with her own mother and younger brother who had come from Calcutta to be with her. She would also make an effort to tell stories to my youngest cousin Babu, a child, who was very fond of his *lal-mamma* (beautiful mother), as he called her.

All this, however, was on the surface as it were. Her inner life of constant *japa* and meditation slowly filled her entire life.

My mother became very ill after about 6 months after my father's death. She must have been praying humbly for Sri Ma's *darshan* because Sri Ma did visit her a few weeks before her death on April 5, 1940.

This incident, an answer to prayer, happened in this way:

Sri Ma passed through Allahabad some time in February 1940. She got off the train at Prayag station. She said to J.C. Mukherjee, who had gone to receive her, that she had a *kheyala* to visit Bina (my mother). J.C. Mukherjee said he was not sure if he could find the house as it was already night. Sri Ma was not dissuaded by this but said firmly that she had some idea and would locate it herself. So around 10 p.m. we heard Didi Gurupriya's voice saying "Open the door! Sri Ma is here!"[1] We tumbled out in great excitement and

---

[1] After leaving Dhaka in 1932, Sri Ma had not entered the houses of her devotees.

found Sri Ma sitting in a car and smiling at us. My mother, who was already bed-ridden, was lifted on to a chair. Renu and Kawna carried her frail weight very carefully to the portico. Sri Ma descended from the car and put her arms around my mother in a loving embrace, saying "See, I have come, have I not? (*ayee to ami eshechi*)" Then she added cheerfully, "Look Bina, these people did not know where to find you. I myself have directed them to your house." She spoke softly to my mother for some time while all of us stood back a little. Sri Ma then very gently bade her farewell, smiled at all of us and disappeared into the night. We were left standing as if bewitched by this sudden vision of Sri Ma. My grandmother had also been helped on to the portico to have *darshan* of Sri Ma.

It was clear that J.C. Mukherjee had not wanted Sri Ma to come to see my mother, because it is inconceivable that he did not know our house which is such a conspicuous landmark in this part of the town. He must have wanted to deflect Sri Ma's *kheyala* out of concern for her, because my mother was suffering from tuberculosis and in those days fear of this disease bordered on dread. All the same, Sri Ma came in answer to the mute prayers of her devotee, as it was clear from her opening words. In our ignorance we seek to protect a person, who truly protects us all.

Again in retrospect, we realise that my mother made the full turning around toward renunciation, which is the ideal ever held aloft by Sri Ma. She lived like a recluse in her own house. She made Renu and myself promise solemnly that we would not keep away from our exams in case anything happened to her. So it transpired that both Renu and myself continued to appear at our exams, (I.A. and B.A.), during the last days of her illness, even to the day when she breathed her last. It must have been her spirit that sustained us.

I am glad that I had this opportunity to write a little about my mother; now Bithika will continue with the tale of our association with Sri Ma.

(End of narration by Sidu, my cousin)

CHAPTER FOUR

Changing Times

In the summer of 1937, at Bareilly, we had come to know Didi Gurupriya and her father Swami Akhandanandaji rather well. Didi used to cook for them all and also serve the food. She sometimes took help from the visitors if they felt so inclined, otherwise she was highly competent and managed very well. When we came to Kishenpur Ashram in the summer of 1938, Didi and her father were away. Bholanath had passed away a few weeks earlier. My cousins had not met him but we who had, missed him very much. There was a strange, eerie atmosphere now of emptiness. We heard from the people in the ashtam how Sri Ma had tirelessly attended his sick-bed and nursed him till the end. Pitaji's last word was "*ananda*". It was evident that he experienced a blissful state before the end.

We had come from Agra where we were in close contact with Birendra Chandra Mukherjee, Swami Akhandananda's eldest son. From him we had heard an eyewitness's account of many of the *lilas* at Shahbagh and Dhaka. He had the privilege to be one of Pitaji's early disciples. He himself was a very grave mannered and dignified person. In the absence of Didi at Kishenpur he managed the ashram and also tried to look after Sri Ma as best as he could. When we arrived he had asked my mother and aunt to look to the personal needs of Sri Ma which pleased them very well.

After this summer vacation, my cousins and aunt returned to Allahabad. I stayed back at Agra for the new academic session of 1938-39. I joined the school Prem Vidyalaya at Dayalbagh. Dayalbagh was a well-run organisation established by a benevolent entrepreneur,

Swamiji Maharaj. He had aimed at the spiritual and pragmatic welfare of the entire community. I was in this school for almost 3 years and acquired a set of close friends.

During the Puja vacation (Oct. 1938) we went to Haradwar to be with Sri Ma who was staying in the house of Dr. Peetambar Panth. This house was situated on the banks of the main canal of the Ganges. The steps of the courtyard led right down to the river. Sri Ma's room was very spacious and it had a balcony projecting over the river. We noticed there were changes around Ma. Dr. Panth had instituted the first rules regarding hours of *darshan* and hours of rest for Sri Ma. But so far we had not been confronted by any closed doors.

The first day, however, around mid-morning we were told to leave Sri Ma's room, as Didi had prepared a light refreshment for her. Dr. Panth had decreed that no one should be in the room when Sri Ma was given any kind of food. We were taken aback but hastened to obey the new rules. Sri Ma said, "From tomorrow Renu and Bithu will give me whatever I have to eat in the morning!" I think she said this to lessen the impact of the changing order. With some ingenuity

Swami Akhandananda   Didi Gurupriya

Changing Times

I found out that Sri Ma used to have a little butter and *misri* (palm sugar) early in the morning and a dish of sprouted grains at midmorning. I told Didi that I would take charge of the first meal. I knew the other one would be too complicated for me. The next day, as I lifted the spoon of butter and *misri* to Sri Ma's mouth, she smiled at me and said, "You have chosen this because it is easier to do is it not?" I was embarrassed to have been found out but this little *seva* (service) became quite easy after all. My sister was more confident and competent also, so she must have managed all right[1].

One day there was an *akhanda-kirtana* for 24 hours. The *kirtana*-party from Delhi had come to sing *kirtana* near Sri Ma. I missed Pitaji. Without him there seemed no point in joining in the *kirtana*. The *kirtana* was planned for the whole night too. I made myself comfortable against a wall behind the chair that had been placed in a corner, in case Sri Ma came in during the night. Indeed she did eventually come and sit in this chair. When she pushed it back a little she saw me dozing peacefully. I was jerked awake when I found that Sri Ma had taken my long plait of hair in her hand and had draped it over her knees to the other side. My head now rested against her leg and I was perforce wide-awake. She sat with this plait of hair on her knees holding it firmly, so that I could not relax or doze off. Nobody else was aware of my predicament, at least not to my knowledge. Sri Ma released me after a while with a smile. I took a more active interest in the *kirtana* after that.

During Durga Puja, the inauguration ceremony of an ashram for women (which later become the Kanyapeeth) was celebrated in Sri Ma's presence. Two small girls, Shanti and Bhakti, were enrolled as the first inmates. At this time, I did not take much notice of this ritual, not knowing that in future I would become intimately connected with the institution.

---

[1] We had never seen Sri Ma eat with her own hands. We did not associate her with mundane enjoyments like relishing food. It seemed just right that the choice of food and the manner of serving it remained with Didi or anybody else who happened to substitute for Didi.

My Father's Initiation (*diksha*)

One day we were surprised to see that a *yajna* was being performed on the covered verandah adjoining the courtyard. My father seemed to be the main priest; he was assisted by Jogeshdada, Manmotho Babu and Dr. Panth. They were dressed in yellow silken *dhotis* and *chaddars* (shawls) and turbans. Although as a *brahmin* my father had the right to perform these rituals, so far we had never seen a *yajna* being solemnised by ordinary householders. Modern ways of living had departed considerably from the *vedic* norms. We did not know what the *yajna* was about. In Sri Ma's vicinity any religious rite seemed natural and seemly. Much later I came to know that Sri Ma had given initiation to my father in the manner in which she had earlier given it to my mother. Unlike my mother, my father was not given any other formal initiation by anyone else. I also came to know from my mother that my father had asked Sri Ma to speak in direct language to him. In general Sri Ma expressed her *kheyala* in tentative language which needed to be interpreted. My father had said, "If you wish me to do something, tell me straight out. I do not want to be confused by a lot of 'ifs' and 'buts'".

Sri Ma must have granted him this prayer because on more than one occasion we were surprised by the words Sri Ma had spoken to him. My father proved himself worthy of this privilege. He did not disregard her words even on the two occasions when this obedience must have cost him great pain and anguish. My father gave her implicit obedience, but Sri Ma showered her blessings a hundred-fold on him and all who belonged to him. Her *vani* that if you advance one step toward God, He comes ten steps toward you, is so endearingly true. The truth of it can be seen in the lives of these great devotees, who were worthy of the treasure they had found.

Sri Ma visited Agra once while we were there; she put up in a big cottage-type tent erected on our front lawn. Biren Babu introduced the newcomers to her. She quickly became the focal point of attraction for a large number of the well-to-do in the town. Sri Ma was not yet so well known in our part of the country that strangers would come crowding in wherever she was reported to be residing, as it happened in Dhaka, Calcutta, Jamshedpur and Varanasi. My mother used to write down conversations taking place around Sri Ma. I reproduce here some of this dialogue:

Haraprasad Bagchi, an eminent advocate of the town gave expression to his attitude toward religion, "We are busy in the world. We find fulfilment in working hard and enjoying the fruits of our labour. We are happy. What can religion give us that we do not already have?"

Sri Ma smiled her inimitable smile. "Baba, if this were indeed so, would you raise this question?"

Haraprasad Bagchi acknowledged the fairness of the comment and laughed to show his appreciation. Sri Ma continued, "I am also speaking of happiness! A happiness which is not counterbalanced by sorrow. A happiness which is your birthright. A happiness which can be yours when you are truly 'at home'. This is a wayside inn you are living in. Should you live in forgetfulness of your home? To be with God is true happiness."

Somebody asked, "Should we then renounce the world?"

Sri Ma, "No, why? The world is not apart from God. The natural way of life itself could be transformed into the religious way of life. There is nothing which can be 'other' to God, in fact, to live in the world is to be on the way to self-realisation. Since this perspective has been lost to us we perforce speak in the language of the world as apart from God. To realise one's self means to discover that there is naught else except God; God alone is and all else is God only."

At this time, I was a teenager and just old enough to appreciate such dialogue. I do remember clearly Sri Ma's conversations with a group of children, headed by Bindu. Sri Ma began by asking if they would accept her as a 'friend'. All the children eagerly accepted her as their friend. Then she said, "Now that I am your friend, will you mind the words I say to you? What do you say?" The children, looking upon her beautiful, radiant countenance, nodded assent. Who could disobey such a 'friend'!

Sri Ma, totally absorbed with the children said, "There are five points to remember: firstly, always speak the truth; secondly, you must obey your parents and teachers; thirdly, you must study as much as is expected of you". When the children had agreed to these more or less familiar points, Sri Ma said, "Fourthly, every morning after you have washed and are ready, you will pray to the Image of God you like best, that you should be a good boy or girl throughout the day. In case you have been bad you will beg pardon and promise not to be so again. Keep a diary, make a note of any misdemeanour so that you will not repeat it again. Now the fifth point, play as much as you can: if you have observed the four points then and then only you can be a little naughty too if you like!"

The children were very pleased with the last point. Looking at the apprehensive parents Sri Ma said, "Don't be afraid, if they truly observe the four points they will not have much scope for naughtiness!" Sri Ma was always close to children. As late as 1978, I have heard her talk to children from her high position on the rostrum and in language which could be understood by them. Indeed, she was ever the 'Friend'!

Changes at Allahabad

After Sri Ma's visit to Agra, we became a little involved in our own family affairs. Some account of this has been given in Sidu's narrative.

It so happened that our family sustained the loss of three members in quick succession. As written earlier, my uncle died in March 1939, my aunt in April 1940 and my grandmother in July of the same year. The summer vacation of 1940 we spent in Calcutta with our relatives, mostly with the mother and younger brother of my aunt in their large ancestral house in Khidhirpur. This sojourn was undertaken by my father to give some comfort to my grandmother and distract her from her sad thoughts. She had a nice time with her great-grand-nephews and nieces in Beleghata. It was good that she had this interlude to remember, since she passed away a few weeks after she returned to Allahabad.

My father was faced with monetary troubles at this time because, coming with a sudden shock of appalling news, he learned that my uncle had left behind nothing but a huge sum in debts. It was a strange tale of the expert committing the very mistake against which he warns others. My uncle had stood guarantor to a motor company which went into liquidation. The promoters, now his creditors, were the elite of Allahabad and personal friends as well. My uncle had carried the burden of this financial disaster all alone; evidently he had been confident that he would be able to discharge his liabilities soon. A man of his calibre, earning the top fees of his day, could have done just that had not providence stepped in to nullify his intent. After his sudden demise both my father and my aunt were saddened to think that had they known, they could have pooled resources to pay off this "debt" and so perhaps save a lot of tension for my uncle during the last days of his life.

My father and Sri Ram Babu, my uncle's assistant, set about the task of converting assets into money so that creditors could be paid off. The logistics of dismantling a large establishment were planned and undertaken by my parents after the death of my grandmother. We bade sad farewells to family servants or rather retainers of two generations. Perag and his family went back to Aligarh, their hometown. He continued to visit us very often and especially when there was need of his invaluable services in the house. My uncle's beloved garden of more than a thousand roses gradually began to show signs of neglect. His cars were sold and his drivers dismissed. These could have been very sad days but I have no recollection that we went through a traumatic experience. The four of us were a close group. We needed no outside help for our recreation or entertainment. Above all, the indomitable spirit of my mother was fully sustained by Sri Ma's *kheyala*. Her calm and dignified behaviour forestalled any pity or sympathy; she helped us to tide over the patch of hard times without difficulty.

Although, in a way, we did notice that the social house of cards was falling down all around us it never mattered too much because we were already disinterested in that aspect of our lives — so this period of transition was an adventure into new ways of life. Sidu, the eldest would think up practical and impractical ways of lessening the financial strain on the family. I recall one such experiment quite vividly.

Whenever Sri Ma came to Vindhyachala, we would persuade my mother to allow us to go to have her *darshan*. Sidu declared we would travel third class and make individual knapsacks of our baggage so that we would not need a porter and thus save a lot of money. My mother was always agreeable to all such impractical schemes thought up by my elder sisters toward easing her monetary difficulties. She was never a spoilsport. She only stipulated that we would take our night watchman (*chowkidar*) as escort.

So one fine morning, Sidu, Renu, Kawna, Bindu, the chowkidar and myself, descended on to the platform of Vindhyachala. We stood surrounded by miscellaneous bundles and small bags. Kawna started to giggle, soon we all joined in. We had never before carried our own baggage — the very idea seemed hilarious. So the inevitable coolies were engaged and we walked up to the hill-top ashram in good order. Sri Ma was kindness itself; we enjoyed a delightful week-end, not minding the primitive conditions of living obtaining at Vindhyachala in those days.

The only other girl of our age in the ashram was Bunidi. In the beginning we used to find it difficult to converse with the inmates. The dialect of East Bengal was unfamiliar and sounded funny to our ears. Sri Ma herself spoke in a manner which was not only easily understood but sounded softly musical. Nobody else spoke like her. Bindu became enamoured of Abhaya and the two of them spent a lot of time together singing and talking music.

Sri Ma spoke separately to all of us. To me she said, "Why do you keep so quiet? You might talk a little more." I do not know what she said to the others. I think, she taught us some simple *kriyas* at this time. We used to go for long walks with her. We learnt to raise the famous echo of Vindhyachala from the specific location, which was pointed out by Sri Ma herself.

After this happy interlude of living in close proximity with Sri Ma in surroundings which were peaceful and quiet, Allahabad was a bit of a come-down. But we were always buoyed up with hopes of our next visit. We became a bit different from other young girls of our time. With them we had no common topics of conversation excepting studies. Somehow we never felt called upon to "spread the glad news" to others. The coming together with Sri Ma was an experience to be shared only with those who were already held in thrall. When we looked up to her we saw the brilliant eyes embracing us in an all-knowing, deeply penetrating glance of total understanding. Nothing needed to be said. Very early we got used to her way of responding to unspoken thoughts or worries. A soothing touch, a kind and compassionate word lightened the burden of many childish problems. It seems amazing that Sri Ma, who dealt with grave errors and serious tragedies affecting the lives of grown-up people, would be so involved with the problems of youth. But she did not trivialise or brush aside the sorrows, which are endemic to the process of growing up. Many times she would say to me, "Never mind, forget it" and so I did. With humour, she lightened the sobriety of some natures unduly prone toward a grave attitude toward life; for the unduly effervescent types she provided a sheet anchor. To be with Sri Ma for us young people was like being with an unfailing friend who firmly guided us through the turbulence of rapidly changing times. The war in Europe was also affecting life in India. We could not but hear the rumbles of political upheavals that would soon sweep over our country.

For the academic year 1940-41, my mother stayed with us at 31 George Town, while my father went away to Agra, where he was posted at the time. His personal servant Dayaram looked after him faithfully during these times, when he was obliged to stay away from his family. My cousin Sidu persuaded my father to allow her to take up teaching in her own college for this year, a tremendous step forward in unconventionality.

Kawna and my brother Manuda were finishing their B.A. I was in the final year of Matriculation. My brothers Bindu and Babu were at school. Kawna was elected the president of the Women's Delegacy of the year. She was constantly busy with arranging academic and cultural functions for the women's college. (This building, incidentally, had been the home of Pramada Charan Banerjee our great grand uncle, where in our childhood we had attended garden parties). Kawna used to take me to listen to some of the famous professors of our day: R.K. Tripathi on Emperor Sher Shah Suri, Ishwari Prasad on the French Revolution, Amarnath Jha and S.C. Deb on English literature.

Kawna had a very striking appearance and a bright personality. Her mischievous sense of humour kept us in giggles at most awkward moments. Once when Sri Ma was visiting Allahabad we went to the hall where a reception had been arranged for her. During the *kirtana*, Kawna amused herself by singing entire strings of funny words to rhyme with the *kirtana*. However, she stopped before we could disgrace ourselves.

After the final exams of 1941, we gladly went off to Agra to join my father and from Agra, we went to Dehradun to be near Sri Ma who was staying at Raipur Ashram that summer. Raipur was not built up as it is now. Apart from Sri Ma's room and the satsang hall there were just a few rooms for visitors. There were no bathrooms or running water.

My father was embarrassed thinking that so many of us would be a burden on the ashram. He decreed that we should take it in turns to visit. He had rented a flat in Dehradun for us. All these scruples were abandoned very shortly because Sri Ma made us so welcome that none of us liked to stay away even for a day.

The simple living conditions were a novelty for us. Every morning we went down the hillside to the canal for our baths. In time we came to enjoy the freedom of the forest and even our occasional adventures with creepy-crawlies. Sri Ma knew how we felt. One day she said to Kawna and I, who had stayed on after the others had left, "If you feel nervous about going out at night, call me quietly and I will come with you."

We were at once sure that there was nothing to be nervous about and every aspect of this way of life became tremendously enjoyable. The food was simple — just one lightly cooked vegetable and rice or rotis. We had never tasted better food anywhere. Sometimes Sri Ma came and sat under the mango tree while we ate on the open terrace.

We came to know Didi and Swami Akhandanandaji quite well as well as Swami Paramanandaji. Swami Akhandanandaji had a dry sense of humour, which was very appealing. I used to spend a lot of time with him listening to his many anecdotes.

One day, I saw him talking to a village woman who was telling him how effective were the medicines which he had given her for her husband. After she had left with some more, Swamiji said to me, " I shall get beaten up by the villagers one day; what can you do with such simple people? I gave her quinine tablets to be given at specific intervals to her husband, as he seems to be suffering from malarial fever. She said that the first tablet did him so much good that she has administered all the rest in one dose and has come for more! Now if this man dies of an overdose, I'll be in trouble. I hope the antidotes work." Swamiji [2] always carried a supply of medicines with him and gave them to the people of the village when they suffered from ordinary ailments.

One day Sri Ma delighted us with a *lila* of behaving like a college girl. Sevaji had brought a white silk sari with coloured borders for Sri Ma. I forget what the occasion was. It was one of the days when all four of us were at the ashram. Sri Ma had a *kheyala* to put on the sari as we did in the modern style of taking the end of the sari over the left shoulder and letting it hang loose over the back. Sri Ma put on the silk sari in this manner; with our fascinated help she rolled up the full sleeves of her shirt-like garment, so that it would look like a blouse. Her hair was pinned up to shoulder length. She postured for us as if walking with books in her hand to a class like a college girl. She was perfect.

Sri Ma singled out Kawna for her special attention. She gave her the silk sari and also one of her own white cotton ones, saying it was an exchange. She had dressed like a college girl, that is, like Kawna and now Kawna would dress like her in white *dhotis*; some rules of diet were also prescribed. Sri Ma said it could be a *vrata* (observance) for one year. She also said that she would again talk about these rules

---

[2] Swamiji was the Principal of the Medical School in Dhaka before his retirement.

after a year. Kawna was very happy and we were proud of her. We thought Sri Ma was perhaps saving her from some future ill by making her undergo this slight regimentation of food and dress. We did not know at the time that Sri Ma had asked my father to leave Kawna with her for a year. My father had answered that had she requested one of his own daughters, he would not have hesitated but now that his brother and his wife had died people would say that he had abandoned the girl in an ashram. Sri Ma was quick to appreciate his dilemma and readily agreed. Ashram life was not recognised as viable in those days. Nobody had to argue any point with Sri Ma. She saw at a glance everything for and against a situation. My father could not know at the time that his beloved niece had only this one more year to live and that Sri Ma had offered Kawna a chance to spend it near her, for this young girl beloved of the gods died before her twentieth birthday.

But at this time our life at Raipur Ashram was one of unalloyed joy. We specially looked forward to the nights. Sri Ma's cot was placed in the centre of the terrace. Men spread their bed rolls on one side of the cot and women on the other; the older people created no problems but the younger set indulged in some squabbles over finding places as near to Sri Ma's cot as was seemly. Abhayda was the main culprit in this matter. He jealously guarded his place at the foot of the cot. My brother Bindu, a slim boy at the time, solved his own problem by simply slipping under the cot while disputes were going on all around him. Abhayada, although appreciative of this manoeuvre, said, "You are silly, you cannot see Ma at all". Bindu answered, "But I am nearest to her!"

On some nights Sri Ma would shine her torch to see if anyone was awake. I have vivid recollections of drawing close to Sri Ma's cot at night and holding whispered conversations with her. She would ask about our studies, tell us anecdotes, asked which god was favourite with us and many more things. It so happened that Abhayada came to know about these sessions one day. He professed himself very annoyed and decided to keep awake the next night. Sri Ma did not stir at all that night. It was all very light-hearted and great fun for us all. The bliss that radiated from Sri Ma's divine person permeated the whole ashram and filled all our hearts with joy. The words are inadequate. The reality was like a story in a classic work of literature to be perused again and again with ever-increasing appreciation and understanding.

We leave Agra

After we left Raipur at the end of the vacation we settled down happily at Agra. The Judge's house was situated in the midst of wide vacant lands. The Officers' Club was near by and here Renu and Kawna learnt to play tennis. Sidu and I were the lazy ones content to watch the other two. Sidu thought up various ways of amusing us. We invented an exclusive club of our own with Sidu as president and I as secretary. My mother was elected the treasurer for obvious reasons and was sometimes prevailed upon to attend our meetings. The minutes of these meetings are still with me.

In the new academic year of 1941-42 (July to March), I rejoined my old school Prem Vidyalaya at Dayalbagh. My sister also joined the new graduate classes. My brother Manu went to 31 George Town, Allahabad to enrol for his master's degree.

These arrangements did not last long. In December, my father was transferred to Ballia from Agra.

We came to know that Sri Ma was in Varanasi, residing at the house of Didi Gurupriya's eldest sister. On our way to Ballia we stopped at Varanasi. My father got permission to visit Sri Ma at this house. Didi's sister made us feel very welcome and we quickly became members of Sri Ma's large family of devotees. The large rambling house was full of guests. Sri Ma was staying in a small mud hut built in the midst of a very big garden. We were told that the owner of the house had this constructed for himself as a place of retreat. Sri Ma used to sit on the small verandah to give *darsana* to visitors.

We saw large crowds gathering round Sri Ma for the first time. She was very well known in Varanasi. Local visitors thronged to see her in the forenoon and evenings. We saw M.M. Pandit Gopinath Kaviraj and many of his colleagues engaging Sri Ma in philosophical discussions. They listened to her quick rejoinders with much appreciation. Sri Ma's style of answering questions was like quicksilver. Even profound and challenging themes acquired buoyancy when expressed in her words.

We came to know Nepalda (later Narayana Swamiji) quite well: also Swami Sankarananda. We met Bunidi again and many of her relatives.

After a very pleasant sojourn in Varanasi we went on to Ballia. Ballia at that time was a beautifully clean and peaceful township. Sidu and Kawna had obtained their graduations as brilliantly as was expected of them. My sister Renu and I had to stop midway when we left Agra because there were no suitable colleges for girls in Ballia. The four of us had a most enjoyable time there. The Judge's house was spacious, the surrounding gardens merged into orchards of big fruit trees; a rivulet of clear water flowed through the estate. There was no electricity or running water; scorpions, snakes and mosquitoes abounded, but the people were very friendly and helpful. In those days we had no problems regarding safety or any kind of threatening situation. All of us went for long walks in the evenings. We could sleep out under the stars without fear of night prowlers, man or beast. In retrospect it appears to have been the lull before a storm.

Bindu was now old enough to receive his sacred thread. It was my mother's wish that this ceremony should take place in the holy city of Varanasi. So we returned to Varanasi for this purpose but this time Sri Ma was not in town. It so happened that on the appointed day, the weather clouded over, the skies reverberated with thunderclaps and it rained heavily. The sacred rites could not take place. We returned to Ballia with another date fixed for the month of March. We were happy when we learnt that Sri Ma would be in Varanasi at this time because six other boys were also to be given the sacred thread on the same day.

On this occasion, when we entrained at Ballia, we met another Bengali family in the same compartment coming from Bihar. They were Kshamadi (Savitri Mitra), her mother and aunt and her cousin Durga. We soon came to know that we were heading in the same direction. Kshamadi was actually going to join the Mahila ashram now known as the Kanyapeeth. These girls were living in a house in Ramapura at the time. My sister and myself were in Haradwar in 1938 when the Kanyapeeth had formally come into existence and so we knew the little girls dressed in yellow clothes, but so far we had not realised their importance in the future scheme of things. Kshamadi became a friend. It may be recorded here that very soon people in attendance on Sri Ma got used to the names Buni, Renu and Kshama as the three girls who were especially close to her at this time. A little later they were joined by Udasji and Billoji. It may be said that Buni, Renu, and Kshama formed the nucleus of the ashram at Varanasi when it was established in 1944.

One day a lady from Atpara (Bholanathji's village) came to call on Sri Ma. While waiting with the gathering in front of Sri Ma's *kutia* (cottage) she proudly related to the other women how Sri Ma had come as a bride to their family at Atpara. Village families are very fluid in structure so no one actually disbelieved her although she was evidently not a close member of the family. Time passed. Sri Ma was found not to be inside the hut or in any other part of the garden. The women became restive. One nudged her neighbour saying, "Isn't Ma coming at all?" The one accosted replied with some impatience, "We don't know. Let us see what happens." Abhaya noticed the exchange of whispers. Looking from one to another he spotted Sri Ma's beautiful hands and the conch shell bangles on her wrists. He sprang right into the middle of the group and turned the edge of the sari which was drawn over her head and hiding her face. The laughing face of Sri Ma was revealed. Then she said to her neighbour (the lady from Atpara) "Why mother, I was sitting next to you for such a long time and spoke to you as well. How is it you did not "recognise" the bride of your family?"

On 13th Chaitra, (probably 30th March), the sacred thread was given to seven young brahmin boys: Hari Ramji's younger son Mohan, my brother Bindu, and five boys of the ashram, Navakumar, Tapan (Swami Nirmalananda), our well-known Dashu and two sons of Sri Ma's youngest sister, Kali Shankar and Gauri Shankar. The ceremony of invoking the presence of the most prestigious mantra of the Vedic tradition is always solemn and beautiful. Sri Ma's presence made it even more vibrant. Initiation of the *Gayatri* mantra is imparted to the son by the father. To the mother is given the role of acknowledging her son as a newly created brahmin. He approaches his mother with a begging bowl in his hand to say "*Ambā bhikṣām dehi*". ("Mother, give me alms") Fortunately, on this occasion, all the boys received their 'alms' from Sri Ma herself. In Sri Ma's presence the function became a general festival for all. The boys remained isolated for eleven days. They lived like ascetics, glimpsing the ideal way of life in order to retain a memory of this interlude throughout the period of growing up and eventually occupying their places in the world. These boys had a very pleasant time because Sri Ma visited them very often in their place of retreat.

Sri Ma asked the four of us to learn the ritual of Siva-*puja* one day from Swami Akhandanandaji. This simple form of *puja* is performed by young girls of Bengal. Our aunt had taught us also but we had got out of the way of it for many years.

Swamiji instructed us carefully. The ritual is simple: one pronounces mantras of self-purification and also the purification of the paraphernalia, flowers garlands, sweets, incense, lamps etc. One is to think that the very ground one is sitting on, the surroundings, are hallowed. Then one goes on to propitiate the elements, spirits, gods so that all may help the worshipper in his or her effort at invoking the presence of the great God himself. Thereafter, the mantras of invocation are pronounced. The worshipper is to imagine that God has revealed himself as seated on the lotus of the heart. Thereafter, one mentally goes through the details of the *puja*; to welcome, to wash the feet, offer a seat, seek to propitiate with flowers, sweets, lights, incense etc. Swamiji explained that this meditative *puja* (*manas puja*) was genuine *puja*. The outward ritual was a mere imitation of the real inner awakening to the reality of briefly living with God. He repeated the *panchaksara* mantra, which is special for Siva, with us during the *puja*. He spoke it aloud a few times saying with a touch of nostalgia, "It is a favourite mantra of mine but since I became a *sanyasi* I have no occasion to do its *japa*. Now thanks to all of you, I have this opportunity again."

Sri Ma received all of us in her *kutia* after the *puja* and spoke to each of us separately, explaining many things regarding the *puja*. That is, she did to me; I do not know what she said to the others.

I had known Swamiji in Raipur earlier. I very often sat near him under the *amloki* tree where he used to meditate for long hours. Once he said to me, "Just before you came a squirrel was running up and down my back. I thought to myself that had it been a snake I could not have maintained my *yogasana*." On another occasion, he said, "You are lucky to have found Ma at an early age. She has now withdrawn much of her majesty and splendour that we saw in Dhaka. She truly is the Incarnation of the Supreme Being."

Chapter Five

A Marriage and a Death in the Family

After these happy days in Varanasi, we returned to Ballia. I think we visited Varanasi a number of times, that is, whenever Sri Ma was in town. Once we stayed with her on a big houseboat on the river. The magic quality of Sri Ma's smiling presence was a fulfilment perhaps inexplicable to others but completely understood by those who have experienced it. One day Patalda (Satyendra Kumar Basu) said to Sri Ma, "My friends ask me, 'Why do you go to visit Sri Ma every evening? What do you get from her?'" Sri Ma said, "Why did you not say, I do not get just anything, that is why I visit her!"

Sidu gets married

In the summer of 1942 (June 19) my eldest cousin Sidu got married to Nirmal Chandra Motilal of Calcutta. His marriage was arranged by Sidu's maternal uncle who knew this family and was now living in Varanasi. The Motilals were also living in Varanasi at this time. Many families had been evacuated out of Calcutta because the threat of war was coming close on the Eastern Front. We also had a family of cousins staying with us for the same reason. My father found it convenient to come to Varanasi from Ballia. In his early career, he had been posted to Varanasi for a while so he had many friends who made all suitable arrangements for the ceremony of marriage. Apart from the heat, which was gruelling, we enjoyed the wedding festivities at both residences.

We left Sidu with her new family in Varanasi and returned again to Ballia. The long-time close knit quartet of cousins was broken. We

A Marriage and a Death in the Family

missed her but were happy for her. Our new brother-in-law was a most remarkable man. He came from a very different background. His aunt (father's sister) had been married to the Prince of Bhowal State, the richest state of Bengal. On his untimely death the second Prince inherited the state. An attempt was made on his life but he escaped miraculously and stayed away for 12 years in the entourage of his guru who had saved him. On his return, his wife denied his identity because her brother was implicated in the crime. The prince's sister and elder brother's widow, i.e. the elder Rani of Bhowal, supported his claim. This famous Bhowal *Sanyasi* case was in progress at the time. The heir-prince was living in Varanasi at the residence of his sister-in-law (our brother-in-law's aunt) who was one of the main supporters of his claim. The Rani received Sidu into her family after the marriage. The cultural background of these families was conservative in the extreme, far removed from any contact with ordinary people. They had most distinguished and polished manners. The men of the family were all tall and handsome, the women extraordinarily fair and beautiful. We were a little in awe of them initially, having lived away from our own ancestral roots for more than three generations. My brother-in-law bridged awkward gaps with great social poise and an endearing affection for all of us. In later years we stayed with them many times in Calcutta. Sidu also made great adjustments to conform to their ideas of proper deportment. Within a short while her new family was full of praise for her, admiring her adoption of their mode of behaviour in spite of her "modern education and habits of freedom of movement at all levels of society!" [1]

After the festivities of the marriage ceremonies we became increasingly troubled by the indisposition of Kawna. She had been running a temperature for some time. The fever persisted. The medical help available at Ballia was modest. Kawna had written to Sri Ma in Dehradun to seek her permission to visit her. She would tell my parents that only if she could be with Sri Ma she would get well. My

---

[1] Incidentally the Bhowal Sanyasi won his case from the Supreme Court, at that time situated in London.

father was in a quandary. He could not leave his post, although he had reconciled himself to allowing Kawna to go to Dehradun because he saw she was pining for Sri Ma's *darsana*. Sri Ma herself solved his problem. One fine morning Nepalda arrived in Ballia with a letter from Sri Ma saying that if my father permitted he would escort my mother and Kawna to Dehradun. So further separations among the family were put in train. It was decided that Renu and Babu would accompany the Dehradun party.

Sidu had now acquired some status as a married woman. On a visit to Ballia she persuaded my father to allow me to continue with my studies in my old school at Allahabad. My brother-in-law also leant his support and offered his escort for this project. I would leave home and stay in a girls' hostel. This was a major step in the process of breaking with tradition. My father however putting his trust in Sri Ma, accepted all this uprooting and our family was splintered into several groups; Renu, Kawna, Babu and my mother left for distant Dehradun. Kawna seemed restored to health and quite her normal cheerful self. Our cousins from Calcutta were still with us, so my father and Bindu had a family to live with while the rest of us went away. Nirmalda and Sidu and myself came to Allahabad. Sidu went with me to the College to meet the Principal, Miss C.R. Pooviah. I had already missed six months (January 1942 -July 1942) of college. Miss Pooviah was a very forceful lady but had a soft spot for those of her students who did well in their studies. She remembered both of us. She gave me a chance to continue, otherwise my career would have come to an end, there and then. I was admitted to the final year of Intermediate Arts (1942-43) and given a room in the hostel of the Crossthwaite Girls' College. My elder brother's name was put in the register as the local guardian and visitor. This did not amount to much because within a few weeks, the whole country experienced the disturbing situation following the call to join the Civil Disobedience Movement under the leadership of Gandhiji. My brother and his group of friends evidently became involved. 31 George Town, standing almost empty at the time, was probably used as the headquarters for printing "rebellious materials". In any case, my

A Marriage and a Death in the Family

brother and his friends were almost immediately detained under the Defence of India Rules and housed in Naini Jail. Schools and colleges were closed.

My hostel took on a deserted look because all parents fetched their daughters away. A few of us remained, those who had nowhere to go. Ballia had become completely isolated. I got no news from any member of my family for more than a month. From the windows and verandah of our hostel, we watched the destruction of government property. Telegraph wires were pulled down, mail boxes upturned. Gandhiji and other leaders had been imprisoned, so at some places, the populace got carried away by their enthusiasm. Later, I came to know how the agitators in Ballia had flown the Tricolour for three days on government buildings. Many exciting tales were related about the very disciplined uprising in Ballia. Some unscrupulous and ruthless officers fled the town. My father's house became a sanctuary for many who felt threatened, because he had gained some goodwill of the people by his policy of leniency regarding political offenders.

For the time being I remained in the hostel. The Principal came and chatted with us sometimes, otherwise we were on our own. There were no acts of terrorism during this uprising; it was singularly free from rioting or killings, so we were not afraid to stay quietly at the hostel. In the third week of September 1942, Sidu and Nirmalda came from Varanasi and fetched me home from the hostel. From Sidu I learnt that Kawna had passed away in Raipur near Sri Ma, on September 14, 1942. My father and Bindu arrived from Ballia. The depleted party from Dehradun came to Allahabad. We heard in detail from them about the last days of my cousin Kawna. Her death was so much more a mingling of spirits than an event of separation or bereavement.

Kawna attains the region of grace

Sri Gurupriya Didi has written about Kawna's last days in her Journal. It is given in Volume VIII of her published works. All of us at Allahabad heard the details from Renu and my mother on their return from Dehradun, at the end of the month (September 1942).

Renu recalled that when they arrived at the Raipur ashram, they immediately saw Sri Ma, who was standing at the edge of the open terrace looking down at them while they got out of their *tonga*. Kawna, without a backward glance walked forward and up the stairs (very steep) leading up to the terrace in three tiers. She seemed not to be ill at all. Sri Ma received all of them kindly and two rooms on the other side of the courtyard from the terrace were given to them for their use.

Sri Ma herself saw to every detail of Kawna's comfort, how the bed should be made, the room arranged, what food should be given her etc. Sri Ma's devotee Bharatbhai (of Jullandher) who was a doctor, examined her and prescribed medicines for her. Within a short while, the entire ashram became involved with Kawna's welfare. Since the fever persisted, Sri Ma asked Kawna to keep to her bed. She would visit Kawna's room every day and sit near the bed on a steel box over which Renu had put a folded blanket. Every evening when Sri Ma strolled on the terrace she would walk in one corner of it. After a few days people realised that she was walking along the spot which was visible to Kawna while she lay in her bed. So the few visitors who came took care not to stand in between.

Everyone became very fond of the young girl (she was not yet twenty) who suffered her illness so bravely and uncomplainingly. Sevaji came everyday to see Kawna, quite enamoured of her lotus-petal shaped big brilliant eyes and the lovely smile, which remained endearingly so till the last day.

As written earlier, these were difficult times. The "Quit India" Movement announced by Gandhiji had affected most of the country. The British Government suppressed it ruthlessly. For some time a reign of terror was superimposed on the euphoria of a sudden surge of spirit in a bid for independence. The mail service came to a standstill. Train services were desultory and used primarily for troop movements. But the devotees of Dehradun trekked to Raipur regularly.

They volunteered to do the little shopping that was required. Kawna seemed to become weaker everyday. My mother and sister were in constant attendance, especially my mother who hardly ever

A Marriage and a Death in the Family

left Kawna's bedside. Renu became friends with two other young girls staying in the ashram, Maronidi and Savitri Mamima. Apart from Didima, Didi and Ruma Devi, *sadhus* and *brahmacharis* only inhabited the Ashram. Swami Akhandananda, Swami Dharmeshananda, Swami Paramananda, Mukti Maharaj were in ochre robes. There were also *brahmacharis* such as Abhaya, Shobhan, Kanu (Maronidi's brother-in-law) Nepalda and perhaps one or two more.

During this time, my young brother Babu aged 7 years came into the limelight. He had nothing to do but play around in the sprawling premises. He was made to sit with his books for a while by my sister but there were too many distractions. He spent most of his time with the *sadhus*, mainly Mukti Maharaj. All those who remember Mukti Maharaj will understand readily the rest of the anecdote. Babu attached himself to Mukti Maharaj saying he also wanted to become a *sadhu* like him. Mukti Maharaj used to tell him rather sensational stories. Others also indulged him as he was the only child in their midst. Mukti Maharaj told Babu that he would have to behave like a disciple before becoming a *sadhu*. People were amused to see the boy fetch and carry for Mukti Maharaj who with his mischievous sense of humour, set him harder tasks every day. Babu persevered so well that Mukti Maharaj, at a loss as to how to stop the game told him he had to get his mother's permission before he could become a *sadhu*. Babu approached my mother while she was busy and formally asked for her permission, as taught by Mukti Maharaj. My mother, not attending to what he was saying, said, "Yes, yes, go and play somewhere else. I am busy now."

Now Mukti Maharaj was in difficulties. He said, "One last test. You have to carry my *kharau* (wooden sandals) on your head the whole day. If you can do this, then I shall initiate you." Mukti Maharaj had reckoned without the strong will power which characterised Babu even as a child. All residents were intrigued to see Babu walking behind Mukti Maharaj with the sandals held over his head.

In time, Sri Ma came to hear about this game. She called Babu to her in the hall. She spoke a few words in mild reproof to the *sadhus*, "Why do you tease the child like this!" Sri Ma asked Didi to fetch one of her new *dhotis*, which was dyed in the yellow colour worn by *brahmacharis*. She then tore up the *dhoti* in strips making a *bahirvasa* (*lungi*, or wrap-around) and *uttariya* (stole for the shoulders) and also loin cloths. While everyone looked on with a mixture of amazement and praise for Babu's good luck and fortune, Sri Ma herself took off his shirt and shorts and dressed him completely in the yellow cloths like a *brahmachari* — she patted him on the head and said, "Now you are a *sadhu*, isn't that so?"

Babu was delighted. The audience savoured Sri Ma's *lila* of granting the wishes of a child so beautifully. She remarked, "He has a well-shaped head. He will excel whichever line he chooses to adopt. If he becomes a *sadhu* in later life, in that also he will succeed."

Kawna, however, continued to be ill. Nothing seemed to do any good. An eminent doctor from Dehradun was fetched to examine her and diagnosed the disease as tuberculosis of the intestines. It will be remembered that at that time, there were no medicines for this terminal disease, except fresh air and good food. My mother and sister were not told that, in the doctor's opinion, Kawna had not more than 3 months at the most to live. Sri Ma herself supervised all meals. Once, at night she went out with a torch to the surrounding patches of dense jungle. Didi and Renu went along with her. Sri Ma pointed out certain herbs to Didi. Didi gathered them and prepared a medicinal dose under Sri Ma's direction. They came to Kawna's room. Didi put this spoon of herbs in her mouth and Kawna swallowed it with difficulty. Sri Ma sat with her for a long time, possibly watching for reactions. As soon as Sri Ma left the room, Kawna brought up the whole thing. Out of politeness, she was holding herself in with great difficulty. When Renu reported that the medicine had not been ingested, Sri Ma remarked in a soft voice, "You see, the body is rejecting any effort at reversing the process. It will not be long now."

Next day, Sri Ma brought one of her own robe-like garments (*alkhalla*) and an undergarment, saying to my mother, "You will find these clothes easier to manage while she remains bed-ridden." She herself helped my mother to change Kawna's dress. Sri Ma invited all the *sadhus* to come to Kawna's room and bless her by touching her head. After all of them had done so, Didi asked Sri Ma, if she also would not bless Kawna. Sri Ma said, "Shall I?" Thereupon, she passed her hands three times over Kawna from head to foot. Then she asked Kawna, "You are fond of *kirtana*. Would you like *kirtana* to be sung near your room?"

"Yes ", she replied with a big smile.

"Which name?"

Kawna hesitated because she thought everyone would expect her to say, "Ma-*nama*."

Sri Ma again said, "Speak the name of your choice"

"Krishna *nama*."

So Abhayda and his companions sang the *mahamantra nama* in front of Kawna's sickroom every evening. Abhayda was not the man to be commanded into regular routines but somehow every inmate of the ashram and the few visitors who came, went all out to be of service to this dedicated girl, who lay patiently with her eyes fixed on the door to watch out for Sri Ma's coming. She never demanded Sri Ma's presence nor did she seek to prolong her visits. Whenever, Sri Ma asked, "Shall I go now?" She would incline her head and smile.

After Sri Ma had changed her dress Kawna seemed to recover a little. It is my sister's impression that Sri Ma also gave her some mantra at this time because she was alone with Kawna for a few minutes while Renu and my mother waited outside the room. The persistent feeling of nausea and stomach-ache left her. She developed a little appetite. Sri Ma asked her if she would like anything special to eat. Kawna, with her frank smile, said, "Yes, bread!" Now bread (from bakeries) is not considered suitable food for people living in the ashram. Sri Ma, however, made no objection. Bharatbhai trekked all the way to Dehradun to fetch a loaf of bread. For three or four days Kawna ate every kind of unsuitable food and, moreover, digested it also. My sister made potato chips for her. She related that Kawna was full of reminiscences. She talked a lot about her college days and her particular friends, Savitri Sapru, Coral Caleb, Bhagya Gurha and other girls of Allahabad.

Then one day (Sept. 14, 1942) the nausea returned. She could not ingest any food. A few faint drops of blood were seen in the food she threw up. My sister used to report the least change in Kawna's condition to Sri Ma. When Sri Ma heard about this, she said a few words softly, "It is time. I hope they have made all the arrangements." She herself had kept aside a big garland which had been brought for her, earlier in the day. Sri Ma came to Kawna's room, bringing Swami Akhandananda with her. She talked to her in her usual interesting way, making Kawna laugh a lot. Then she said, "It is an honour to be initiated in the *sanyasa* mantra, in the holy precincts of the *uttarakhanda* (foothills of the Himalayas). How lucky you are that these *sadhus* are here to attend on you! There is the One only, is it not, *ekamevādvitīyam brahma*? All else is the One only." She spoke in this strain for a few minutes, because Kawna was a well-educated and intelligent girl. She listened carefully and inclined her head in agreement. Her luminous gaze was fixed on Sri Ma's face as usual. Sri Ma now asked everyone to leave the room. She herself remained there with Swamiji who, with a full heart, uttered the mantra of total renunciation to the patient who, unknown to everyone had only a few more minutes to live.

Sri Ma called everyone back to the bedside and normal conversation was resumed. Didi made *charanamrta* and quietly poured a few drops in to Kawna's mouth. Abhayda, Shobhanda, Kanu and another brahmachari sat outside the room singing the *mahanama mantra*. Kawna's room was full of *sadhus* in ochre robes. After a while, Kawna said a little hurriedly to Swamiji, "I think I have forgotten the mantra, will you say it again?" Everyone again prepared to leave the room, but before anyone had moved, Kawna said, "No, no. I have remembered. It is all right." She seemed to relax and looked her usual serene self. It was growing dark outside. Sri Ma got up and approached her, saying, "Shall I go now?" Kawna inclined her head. Sri Ma passed her hands over Kawna from head to toe thrice in a gesture of blessing and caress, which is inimitably her own. Sri Ma slowly walked to the door, looking back at the girl whose wide open eyes, looking extra brilliant, were fixed on her face. Then Sri Ma

A Marriage and a Death in the Family

went out of the door followed by Renu only. Everyone else, including Didi sat near Kawna's bedside. As soon as Sri Ma went out of the room the bright gaze became still. Didi, Swamiji and others said later that it was as if Sri Ma had taken Kawna away with her. Renu accompanied Sri Ma to her room. Sri Ma sat on her bed and spoke quietly, "Do not cry; lamentations for departed dear ones cause them distress." Renu understood from these words that Kawna was no more. There had been no indications that Kawna was appreciably sinking nor her usual self. Sri Ma said again, "The sound of the *mahanama-mantra*, so many ochre-robed *sadhus* gathered round — it seems that she has brought about a *mahotsava* (a great festival) for her moment of departure."

After a while, my mother also realised that Kawna had gone beyond her loving care. She went over to where Sri Ma was sitting in her room and sat quietly at her feet with Babu in her lap. Renu stood nearby. Everyone else was busy round Kawna's room. Swami Paramanandaji organised the funeral procession of brahmacharis and a few *sadhus*. In our tradition, cremation is expected to be performed as soon as possible. At that time, there was no question of informing my father or the possibility of his arriving in sufficient time. In any case Sri Ma, then and also later, took for granted his complete acquiescence in whatever way she might settle his affairs.

The sky became overcast and it started to rain a little. The little group of women near Ma watched as four *brahmacharis* picked up the wooden stretcher, on which Kawna's body had been laid. Didi had decorated it with new cloth and flower garlands provided by Sri Ma. She looked peacefully asleep. All the *sadhus* excepting Swami Akhandanandaji and Mukti Maharaj accompanied the cortege. The strains of the *mahanama* mantra rose in the air. As the men wended their way across the valley, they could be easily made out from the terrace of the ashram because of the swinging lanterns. The Raipur Ashram overlooks a vast stretch of scree interspersed by ribbons of mountain streams. Sri Ma said, "It is raining. Will they be able to light a fire under these conditions — let us see what God wills." Sri Ma continued to watch the flickering lights across the valley. For a while she sat on her cot, then again she would enter the hall and stand near the big windows on the valley side. They all saw the fire blazing high. In spite of the rain, the lonely mountainside became illuminated by the glow from the brightly burning fire. Mukti Maharaj was unwontedly overcome and his eyes filled with tears. In a rather uncharacteristically emotional voice he said, "What a glorious way to depart this world, Ma. Why only one? Why don't you help scores of us to cross over in this fashion?"

By the time the men returned it was morning. Sri Ma had little rest during the night. She talked intermittently of Kawna: Kawna's bright, open nature, her total self-surrender, her undemanding serenity and her good *samskaras* (predilections) which had brought about the confluence of so many auspicious factors — the holy *uttarakhanda* (Himalayas), only *brahmacharis* as pall-bearers, and *sadhus* to perform the last rites. But onlookers added the most important factor: Sri Ma's presence. Didi said that she had never seen Sri Ma so involved in anyone's death before, not even Bhaiji's. Paramanandaji, on his return, said they had been afraid that the damp wood would not burn adequately, but all were amazed to see such bright flames, as if they had a life and energy of their own. Sri Ma said, "The strict *brahmacharya* (celibacy) of many lives has created this energy (*brahmateja*), so no great outside help was needed to consume the body which was *sattvic* (pure) and therefore light and buoyant and ready to mingle with the elements."

Next day, the ashram seemed strangely empty. Visitors were shocked to hear of Kawna's death. Sevaji shed tears, saying she would miss the bright smile to which she had looked forward every day. Sri Ma continued to speak to everyone about Kawna during the next few days. Once, after doing their pranam to Sri Ma, some of the local women went over to my mother and put some flowers on her head and at her feet. Everyone was surprised. Sri Ma smiled and gave an explanation, "They have just learnt that Kawna was not her own daughter but a niece-in-law. All these days they had been noticing her dedicated nursing of Kawna."

A Marriage and a Death in the Family

My mother, Renu and Babu returned to Allahabad after a while. My father came from Ballia. At Allahabad, also, my father performed the ceremonial funeral rites, in accordance with traditional precepts (*sraddha*). Didi and Nirmalda had come from Varanasi already. After the ritual we again dispersed to our various destinations: my parents, Renu and Babu to Ballia, Sidudi and Nirmalda to Varanasi, and I to the hostel again. My brother remained in jail because my father, unlike a few other parents in similar circumstances, did not care to write a letter of apology to the British Government and give a promise of loyal behaviour in future, as advised by our family lawyer Sri Ram Babu.

My father was transferred to Kanpur before the year was out, bringing about more changes. The family of cousins staying at Ballia went back to Calcutta. Some time in February 1943, my eldest brother was released from jail along with his other friends. He looked very fit and happy. The young men had very good company in jail, in the persons of such stalwarts of the day as Lal Bahadur Sastri, Kamalapati Tripathi, Kailash Nath Katju, Keshava Deva Malaviya and other leaders. The University made allowances and permitted these young men to sit for their final examinations after an absence of about 6 months.

I had a special problem to face. The U.P. Board declined to condone my long absence from college (January 1942-July 1942). The Principal, Miss C.R. Pooviah sent for me and told me this news but said I was not to worry because she would try her best to get me permission to sit for the examination. I came home, as my mother had opened up the house for my brother.

Sri Ma used to visit Vindhyachala very often in those days. My sister being free had already joined her there. Bindu and I made frequent trips. Sidu and her husband came from Varanasi. Sri Ma was especially kind to her. Sidu saw Sri Ma now for the first time after her sister's death in Raipur. Saraswati Puja was performed at the hilltop ashram because Sidu had expressed a wish for this festival. Sri Ma said, "Since Sidu has uttered the wish for it, let it be performed." Sri Ma's *kheyala* was enough. As if a magic wand had been waved, all the elaborate paraphernalia of a *puja* festival were amassed in this remote region. The image was beautiful. Sri Atul Thakur of the Sadhana Samar Ashram performed the *puja* in a special collective way, in which all who liked could participate.

On February 1st, 1943, Sri Ma was observed performing elaborate *yogic kriyas* while pronouncing mantras in Sanskrit. This rare and beautiful occurrence was witnessed by Sidu, Renu, Savitri, Gola (Udasji) and Bunidi. Coming back to her normal everyday mode, she glanced at the girls and said "*pañca kanyā smaretnityam*" which is a part of a Sanskrit hymn to five virgins.

A very important event took place in Vindhyachala at the beginning of March 1943. Sri Prabhudattaji Maharaj, a well-known saint of Jhunsi, came to visit Sri Ma. Protima Devi of Allahabad had brought him to the hilltop ashram. Although Sri Ma was well known in Bengal, she had not as yet come in direct contact with the *sadhu-samaj* in Northern India. In our religion all renunciates belong to well-defined ascetic orders. They profess special schools of thought and preserve their identities as distinct brotherhoods. Sri Ma was none of these things. *Sadhus* are also forbidden a familiarity with women, and Sri Ma was a woman in ordinary white clothes, leading an ordinary life of living simply in the world.

Prabhudatta Maharaj (as later events proved) recognised Sri Ma through all her disguises. He prostrated himself in front of her. He was also a very fun-loving person. He brought an atmosphere of jollification to the ashram. Sri Ma responded by appreciating his sense of fun and adding many of her own ruses. At his midday meal he started eating enormous quantities so that Didi, who was serving the food, would be forced to say, "There is no more!" As soon as Sri Ma realised what he was up to, she amassed so much food from various sources, that he had to give up and acknowledge defeat, much to everyone's amusement.

This meeting was the beginning of a history of fruitful associations between the ochre-robed ascetics of our country and Sri Ma. In subsequent years, at Prabhudattaji's invitation, Sri Ma came to Jhunsi many times much to our great delight. Bindu and his friends made innumerable trips on their bicycles, while we crossed the river by

A Marriage and a Death in the Family

train, tonga, *ekka* (horse carriages), or by boat and once even by wading through the shallow waters of the Ganga to the other shore.

I seem to remember that it was the 8th of March when Prabhudattaji came to Vindhyachala. I have a personal reason for remembering this date. My final exams were to be held in the last week of March. Our principal, Miss Pooviah, sent for me and told me that I should meet her again on 9th March to find out whether I had permission to take my exams because the Board Meeting would be held on the 8th.

I took a couple of books and with my mother's ready permission went to Vindhyachala with Bindu. On the platform at Vindhyachala, we met four young men and their father who were also going to visit Sri Ma. These were Shaileshda, Kusumda, Subodhda, Bhupen and their father. Together we trekked up to the hilltop ashram. Sri Ma asked me about my examination. I told her what the principal had said and that I would return on the 8th to Allahabad. This time we met Chhabi and Mani Chowdhary, the two daughters of the long-time devotees Sri Naren and Srimati Juthika. We became great friends. Mani and I would talk about college subjects. Abhayda, Mani, Bindu and Bhupen formed a good group for singing *kirtana* in the evenings.

On the 8th, I thought to myself that after all I shall not get permission, so why should I miss this opportunity of staying with Sri Ma? Bindu went back alone, I stayed back and thus was present when Brahmachariji came to visit Sri Ma. Sri Ma was staying in Sri Mahesh Bhattacharya's house at the time. At night, she asked me, "What day is it today?" On hearing the answer, she said, "Aren't you supposed to go to your college tomorrow to meet the Principal?"

I made a feeble excuse, "Bindu has left already." Sri Ma said "Never mind, go with Shris Babu and his sons." So early next morning, I descended the hill in the company of Saileshda and his brothers and so returned to Allahabad.

Miss Pooviah had no news for me. She said, "Go home and study for the examination. I am going to fight the whole School Board to get you through!" This she must have done because on 17th March

I received my Admit Card and permission to appear at the I.A. Examination. Her faith in me was justified because I did very well in these exams, passing with honours. I was glad not to have let her down. The summer vacation was spent in Kanpur with my father. This year all of us children remained at Kanpur while my parents and their friends paid a visit to Sri Ma at Almora. At the end of the vacation Bindu, Babu and myself returned to Allahabad. My mother came with us so that we could enrol for the fresh academic year July 1943. This was my first year at the University and Bindu's first year in college. Babu was still in school. Renu joined the Art School and her skill was much appreciated by her teacher. Her watercolours were exhibited in the town. We were very proud when a stranger bought one of these paintings from the Art Gallery.

CHAPTER SIX

Our Entry into the World of *Sadhus*

Jhunsi (a village on the other side of Ganga from Allahabad)

The *sadhu-sammelan* at Jhunsi in January 1944 was a watershed event in Sri Ma's way of being in the world. Here, for the first time, she was given full recognition as the very personification of Upanishadic wisdom, that is *brahmavidya*. The ochre-robed *sadhus* unanimously came forward to accord her the highest respect it lay within their power to give. Sri Ma had come into contact with Haribabaji Maharaj, Udiya Babaji, Swami Sharananandaji and others in the previous year but this was the first time that she was being entertained by Prabhudattaji Maharaj as a very special guest of honour in Jhunsi.

In those days, Sri Ma used to sit in front of the group of women to one side of the hall. The ochre-robed *sadhus* occupied the slightly raised seats at the back of the hall, so that the congregation faced them directly. One day there was some discussion about a festival of *nama-samkirtan*a. Prabhudattaji opined that it was the duty of *sadhus* to keep in close touch with the people during these difficult times. The political leaders had been put behind bars to curb the Civil Disobedience Movement — so the *sadhus* should come forward to give encouragement and to keep alight the torch of hope for the masses. All big towns were put under Rule 144, that is, all kinds of assemblies were prohibited under the Defence of India Rules. Prabhudattaji conjectured that a religious festival would be exempt from such Rules. Everyone agreed with him. He then asked Sri Ma to choose a place where this big celebration involving thousands of people might take place.

Sri Ma broke into an *attahasa* (loud laughter). It is not possible to find adequate words to describe this peal of ringing laughter. It sounded like 'hah-hah-hah' in a very high tone of voice, a petrifying experience — like a sudden clap of unexpected thunder. Sri Ma's entire body radiated this sound, her whole aspect glowing and resplendent. She was no longer one of us, nor someone we could even begin to understand. In general, when anybody laughs others at least tend to smile, even if they do not understand the original cause of amusement. This was a different phenomenon. There was no question of hilarity or a sympathetic sharing of merriment. There was total silence in the hall, while the waves of this resonant sound eddied away. When later in life, I read in the *Durgasaptasati* about the divine *attahasa* of Devi, I immediately cognised that it would have sounded like this.

In the hall, there was utter stillness. No one spoke or even moved for quite a while. The blind *sadhu* Swami Sharananandaji, a man of great intellectual ability and much revered by all the other mahatmas, eventually broke the silence by saying that he now understood somewhat Sri Ma's *svarupa* (nature) of *ananda* (bliss). He had not "seen" Sri Ma but now heard the *attahasa* as the audible *svarupa* (essence) of bliss. Maybe she had laughed for him to "know" her! Who can tell?

Sri Ma now quietly answered their question in her normal gentle voice, saying the place which met with the approval of all of them, should be considered her choice. Jhunsi itself was chosen as the venue for this large scale function, which Sri Ma attended in due course. We had a great time. Every day we managed to cross the river to go to Jhunsi, staying overnight and then returning home to go to college.

At about this time Didi Gurupriya acquired the new site for an ashram at Varanasi. She used to come and go from Jhunsi very often. The consecration of the site was enacted by the performance of *Vasanti Puja* (April 1944) on it. All of us went over to Varanasi to attend this festival. Sri Ma was staying in the adjacent Jaina Temple. The visitors were billeted in nearby houses. This was our first experience of *puja* on a large scale under Sri Ma's aegis. Being Bengalis, we were familiar with the annual Durga Puja festival but nothing had prepared us for the observance of this religious rite in all its meticulous details. The composite icon for this *puja* is itself magnificent but became awe-inspiring in Sri Ma's presence.

Renu got her first lessons in cooking *bhoga* and I my first lessons from Nepalda (Narayana Swamiji) in preparing *naivedya*, that is, the offerings of fruits and sweets. Learning from him the importance of colour arrangements, I was one day creating a design with red pomegranate seeds and white coconut powder when Sri Ma came into the room. She said, "The designs should be agreeable no doubt, but you must always keep in mind that this is food you are offering to the deity. Fruit, if arranged on a copper plate, will spoil and not remain edible at all". She then taught me how to cut out shapes from banana leaves and line the metal plates before arranging fruits and sweets on them. Fine designs were not possible on the uneven surface, but naturally that was not the whole point of the decoration either. So I learnt to combine beauty with practicality.

On the day of *dashami* (the last day, on which the image is immersed in a river) we were all overcome by a feeling of bereavement. Sri Ma then had the *kheyala* to spend the night on the *vedi* (platform) which stood so empty now. We at once became cheerful. The small number of us who were staying around the site gathered by her with our simple bedrolls. Swami Paramananda and one or two more took up their positions at the not-too-secure main entrance. The site at that time was open on the side of the Ganges and the ghats. Around 2 a.m. a peculiar kind of man came in from somewhere right up to where we were sleeping. We woke up when Sri Ma accosted him. We called Swamiji, who managed to talk him into backing away by degrees and so out of the grounds. It is a nice incident to remember, demonstrating that those who think they can protect instead need the protection of the ever vigilant *kheyala*.

In the meantime, my father was transferred from Kanpur to Aligarh. During the summer vacation, we went to stay with him.

Renu and Bindu went on to Almora to be with Sri Ma, Babu and I remained with my parents, till it was time for my mother and us to return to Allahabad at the beginning of the term July 1944-March 1945.

Durgapuja at Krishna-Kunja

For a long time Sri Ma had been paying a number of visits to Krishna-Kunja, a big *satsang* hall in the heart of Allahabad. The owner of this property was known to all of us as Bucchun Bhaiya. He and his wife were devoted to Sri Ma. The hall was hung on all sides with replicas of the same painting depicting Sri Krishna with a flute in his hand standing under a tree, leaning slightly against a beautiful white cow. There was one big painting in the centre of the hall. We were told that the owner had a vision of this scene and he had commissioned an artist to paint it. This is why the hall was known as Krishna-Kunja (Bower of Krishna).

We were very happy to learn that Durga Puja would be performed in Krishna-Kunja that year. Such anomalies [1] never disturbed people near Sri Ma. To us it meant we would be able to stay with her for a number of days. We moved bag and baggage to Krishna-Kunja. We were free to go in whenever we arrived from home. In fact, Sri Ma's life was lived publicly. The restrictions imposed by Dr. Panth had proved to be of short duration. We slept in her room, attended her *bhoga*, sat with her in *satsangs* and read out letters to her. When I recall those days, I am overwhelmed by the magnanimity and naturalness of her presence which kept in thrall all those who came near her. We looked to Didi to tell us what to do, because Sri Ma would sit there in utter beauty and grace, for many hours till she was bidden to take a rest for a while, or a meal, or a glass of water. There was no outer or inner circle as far as Sri Ma was concerned. Didi knew this in her heart of hearts, as everyone else did who had the privilege to serve her. At times she would take any kind of service from the merest stranger or the most awkward of her retinue, such as myself. What I liked best was to wield the fan from a distance!

Preparations for the Puja were made on a grand scale. Buchhun Bhaiya's wife took days to clean, wash and dry out the various grains, cereals and *masala* (condiments) for the cooking of *bhoga* (cooked

---

[1] In general the worshippers of Krishna (Vaisnavas) do not offer puja to the different images of the Goddess Durga.

Our Entry into the World of Sadhus

Durga Puja at Krishna Kunja

meals for the deity). Fruits, vegetables, dry fruits etc., were stored with scrupulous care. Sri Ma guided us everywhere, where to put what, how to arrange things so that everything should be at hand for all the three days from morning till night. Unknown to us there was another important Durga Puja taking place in another part of the town. The Satya Gopal ashram in Allenganj was the venue of the annual Durga Puja for many years. Sri Gopal Thakur of this ashram had sent an invitation to Sri Ma to come to his Puja also.

During the three days of this Puja Sri Ma went out twice to visit Satya Gopal Ashram. Sri Gopal Thakur received Sri Ma as the living goddess he had been worshipping all his life. Theirs is a system of *puja*, which enjoins the opening of the heart in an intensely emotional outpouring of devotion and adoration. Sri Gopal Thakur himself used to become ecstatic and his considerable entourage was affected by the surge of religious fervour.

This meeting was the beginning of an era of association between the two Ashrams. Whenever Sri Ma came to stay at Allenganj we also flocked there and were made welcome by the family of Sri Gopal Thakur.

The memory of my university days are shadowy compared to the memory of our life with Sri Ma. I did take part in such activities as were required of me, like debates and writing in journals or acting in plays at annual functions, even in sports, which definitely was my weak point. Five other girls and I had more or less been together since our school days so we were a close-knit group but I do not recall that we talked about Sri Ma at any time. My friends knew about my allegiance but although respectful and understanding they did not share in my sentiments regarding Sri Ma. I remember one interesting incident, which took place at this time. We had gone to the railway station to receive Sri Ma on one of her visits to Allahabad. Here, I met a classmate Shivani who had come to see someone off by the same train. While we were waiting for the train, she expressed her doubts to me about paying such exaggerated respects to a person who, after all, was only a human being. She was very sceptical about our devotion to Sri Ma. The train came, Sri Ma alighted on to the platform. I was amused to see Shivani bowing very low to do *pranam* when Sri Ma passed us on her way toward the exit. When I asked Shivani as to why she had bowed so low to another human being, she said, "Well, it was involuntary — she truly has a majestic presence!"

For us the real everyday world of college activities, social engagements, household routines became insubstantial and unimportant. We counted the hours and days to our next visit to Sri Ma. Other families who were close to Sri Ma became as if kith and kin, whereas people who had claims of blood relationships, due to lack of reciprocity gradually became strangers.

My mother's deep one-pointed allegiance to Sri Ma was like a benign aura of approval and sustenance. My father would at times express his misgivings regarding the breaking of too many conventions. Nobody went to live in ashrams in those days. To be running after "a Mataji" was behaviour bordering on the outrageous. The orthodox ways of worship included visits to temples, the celebration of religious festivals and the occasional observance of rites and ceremonies at home presided over by the family-priest. But my father was himself truly devoted. He did not visit the ashram very often but would listen to the accounts of our visits with keen interest. His deep commitment and surrender at the feet of Sri Ma were proved up to the hilt as time went by. He was undemonstrative, but it could be seen that Sri Ma would call upon him for any service without any hesitation, just as she could her long-term devotees from Dhaka.

We came to know Prabhudattaji Maharaj quite well. He was very agreeable company for young people. His exuberant out-going nature could galvanise the most staid group of people. He had a way of landing heavy thumps on the backs of unwary young men, so everyone learnt to be very agile whenever he came by. Once, he playfully landed a fist on my back between the shoulders. I think he did not know his own strength. I nearly fell to my knees. I was standing near Sri Ma's *chowki*. I held on to it and quietly crept away to the back of it kneeling behind Sri Ma, who was talking to Prabhudattaji. I suddenly found Sri Ma's hand on my head. She had put back her arm inside her *chaddar* (shawl) to touch me, so that nobody else noticed anything amiss. It stopped my trembling and sense of shock. Some people will remember that I used to be a very thin girl at this time. Only Sri Ma had noticed my predicament and unobtrusively taken care of it.

Before coming into contact with Prabhudattaji Maharaj we, as a family, knew very little about *sadhus*. As a matter of fact, due to our westernised education we had acquired some modern values. We had been taught that to turn away from the world was a form of escapism and cowardice. Religious beliefs should not be automatically accepted, but tested with the touchstone of reason. At this time, however, there was no awareness of conflict in our joyous participation in all that happened near Sri Ma. If Sri Ma graciously accepted the hospitality of *sadhus* like Prabhudattaji at Jhunsi or Udiya Babaji and Haribabaji at Vrindaban, then we were only too happy to trail along behind her and also to sit quietly for many hours in *satsangs* listening to discourses. *Sadhus* no longer remained an unknown category but became an integral part of our growing-up because Sri Ma was increasingly involved with them. We were too young at the time to understand or appreciate all the implications of events as they happened. I was myself forcibly awakened to this aspect of Sri Ma's *lila* once in Vrindaban (January 1947). We were staying in Udiya Babaji's ashram where Sri Ma was an honoured guest. One day, while we were preparing to accompany her to the satsang hall, she remarked to me in a rather amused voice, "Now they give this body such V.I.P. treatment! This body passed through the lanes of Vrindaban so many times; then nobody (the *sadhus*) took the slightest notice."

I was none too articulate in her presence, otherwise I could have responded by saying, "Unless you reveal yourself, who can recognise you? Previously, perhaps, you came to see how it was in Vrindaban, but now it is time for the *sadhana* of the *sadhus* to bear fruit. They needed to overcome their negative attitude toward a 'woman' and cease to see you as a female." For Haribabaji Maharaj Sri Ma was the personification of his *Ista-devata*, that is, Gauranga Mahaprabhu. We were told that he had seen her as such when he was given a few photographs of Sri Ma taken in a state of *samadhi*. He had recognised the

Our Entry into the World of Sadhus

ecstatic states in her as similar to those described in Vaishnava sacred literature. Udiya Babaji admired her endorsement of unsullied asceticism. He knew her to be a *sthitaprajna* (*Gita*, II).

In retrospect, I realise that these were crucial times for our country in more ways than one. The world war (1939-1945) brought about radical changes not only in Europe but in India as well. Some time before the partition of India in 1947 Sri Ma had indicated that all those who were able, should leave East Bengal and come to Varanasi to make new beginnings. Thus we came to know such men as Amulya Kumar Dattagupta and Man Mohan Ghosh quite well. We were by this time quite conversant with the dialects of East Bengal and made friends easily with the girls in these families. They were unused to the heat and the narrow lanes of Varanasi. Sri Ma's visits to the *sadhus* were also an unfamiliar environment for them. Amulya Kumar wrote in his journal, "It is so painful to sit through a *satsang*. We do not understand Hindi; moreover, Haribabaji's voice is so soft as to be quite inaudible — but because of Sri Ma's presence every ordeal is bearable. She gives her full attention to whatever is going on; no doubt the whole thing is an exercise in fortitude for us."

So satsang became increasingly a part of ashram life. I think that not enough thought has been given to the coming together of the mahatmas under Sri Ma's aegis at this time. Also, in retrospect, I realise that Sri Ma, by commanding so naturally and so endearingly the allegiance of the ascetic orders, diverse and distinct in themselves, created a composite platform for the guidance of our country. While the *sadhus* are the guardians and repositories of our heritage, they were not close to the people, neither did they speak in a harmonious voice. Doctrinal differences had kept them apart in their own well-defined grooves for centuries. We have no central institution of religion, which had authority to direct the spiritual aspirations of congregations. The individual is free to believe to whatever degree it may suit him, or not to believe at all. He remains a Hindu by virtue of being born to Hindu parents. Hinduism is an undemanding religion in the sense that if one has no aptitude for the religious way of life, one need not suffer any tension or anxiety regarding one's destiny.

One will not attain salvation but return again and again to the theatre of action, that is the world. According to many people of the modern era, that is not at all such a bad prospect!

The seething cauldron of changing political, social, intellectual and religious values of these decades needed the steadying influence of a teacher of exemplary presence. What is called Renaissance in other traditions is built into ours. There is always a pincer movement, a simultaneous recovery of the ancient heritage together with an impulse toward appropriating the contemporary. Our country was lucky to find itself being guided toward the future by Sri Ma. I think later generations will appreciate the role Sri Ma played at this time in shoring up the *Upanishadic* tradition of our country. It was no doubt a turning point in the history of our nation, but we who lived through it did not think of it as such; we were having a marvellous time as if we were on a perpetual picnic.

My eldest brother Manu gets married

On November 29th of this year, my eldest brother Manu got married. This occasion saw the gathering of our family. Our house was full of guests for weeks. There was much feasting and many celebrations, which mark the performance of a conventional marriage ceremony.

Our new sister-in-law's name was Protima. When she was taken to have Sri Ma's *darshan* in Vindhyachala, Sri Ma said, "She, who was with your family earlier, has come again (*Je cchillo seyi esecche*)." We interpreted this to mean that one of our ancestors had returned to the family. In time, she became close to Sri Ma and received her initiation from Didima some years later.

Protima with her guru Didima

Our Entry into the World of Sadhus

After the Durga Puja of 1944, Sri Ma went to Baandh at the invitation of Haribabaji Maharaj. His envoy Sri Premraj had come to fetch her. But she returned very soon to Vindhyachala.

Sri Ma remained in Vindhyachala for some time. Even if she visited other places, she would come back to Vindhyachala, making it possible for us to be with her again and again.

During this winter the girls of the Kanyapeeth had also come to Vindhyachala for a change of air. Sri Ma would often go out walking with them to distant flat grounds on the hilltop so that they could play games or run around. Once Maunima challenged Sri Ma to a race. Maunima being so much lighter, we expected her to win easily but we were delighted and surprised as well when Sri Ma outdistanced her quite effortlessly. She did not even run, just walked very fast!

The winter vacation came to an end but we stayed on with Sri Ma, missing classes for a while. Didi kept coming and going to Varanasi, Lucknow etc. to see to the paper work for the new ashram at Bhadaini. Buni, Renu and Kshama were around to see to Sri Ma's simple needs. We met other devotees from other towns. I remember I stayed in the guest room with Kanti-kakima (wife of Jiten Datta of New Delhi) and Kalyanidi (wife of Nani Gopal Bhattacharya of Varanasi) and a few others. The cold was excruciating. There were no amenities or facilities in Vindhyachala. The rocky hillside slopes sufficed as washrooms. The little mountain spring half way down the hill did duty for a bath and washing of clothes. Sometimes my hands were so cold that I did not feel the water but just saw it when I poured it over my hands. I recall the discomforts with an effort and some wonder because we did not experience them as such. It was all a very great adventure.

This is the time when we saw Sri Ma take *maunam* (silence). It was an unfortunate series of incidents, which led up to this. Narayana Swamiji has himself written about this, so there is no need to go into it here. In short, he had expressed his opinion against some proposed food for Sri Ma as not congenial to health. Some new devotee, who had meant well, had suggested this food. Thereafter, Swamiji was annoyed with himself for his gratuitous advice and decided to become *mauni* (silent) as a gesture of self-discipline. After some time, we all realised that Sri Ma was not answering questions or speaking at all. We were all taken aback by this outcome of a rather trifling incident. Didi was away. The older girls did their best. One day Sri Ma's entire body became cold and still. Buni started crying. They assembled braziers and applied warm towels against Sri Ma's hands and feet. For many hours there was no response at all — then Sri Ma with some difficulty lisped a few words in a rather peculiar fashion to dissuade the girls from trying to restore circulation in her limbs. She made an effort to put everyone at their ease. She was kindness itself in reaching out to the girls, who were at their wits' end to know what to do. Sri Ma then indicated that preparations should be made for leaving Vindhyachala the same day.

It was cloudy and it looked like rain. J.C. Mukerjee talked to Sri Ma saying that it would be difficult to make arrangements immediately, but that he would fetch a car the next day from either Allahabad or Varanasi. There was no change in Sri Ma's expression. Just at this point Didi arrived from Varanasi. All the girls immediately surrounded her and the tale of Sri Ma's *maunam* (silence) poured from their lips. Didi knew Sri Ma's *kheyala* would not be diverted, so she set about packing up things with the help of the girls. We also packed our belongings. Sri Ma, I think, waited for Didi and others to have their midday meal. It became very cloudy and a storm seemed imminent. J.C. Mukerjee was just thinking that Sri Ma had agreed to his suggestion of travelling next day when she calmly walked out of the ashram gates and continued down the hill-slope. We ran to tell Didi. Didi was ready. So we all picked up our own bundles and set off behind Sri Ma. At the foot of the hills, we caught the Roadways bus for the town. At Mirzapur railway station we took up our quarters in the Waiting Rooms. Sri Ma was with us and everything was pure joy! The train arrived and we all got in. Sri Ma used to travel class-III in those days. She had spoken one word: "Vrindaban", so we knew she was going there. Sadly Bindu and I got off at Allahabad station to go home while Renu went off with Sri Ma on her travels.

CHAPTER SEVEN

Renu's Marriage with N.P. Chatterji

The very controversial incident of my sister Renu's marriage with N.P. Chatterjee took place in early March, 1945 (17th Phalgun to be exact) in Bahrampur, West Bengal. At this point in time not many people remember much about it and many of the persons concerned are no more.

As far as I know, this was the only *kheyala* for which Sri Ma had to give (or 'chose' to give) explanation after explanation all over the country to her oldest devotees as well as to mere strangers. Didi's Journal (V-VIII) gives a detailed record of this event. Sri Ma was continuing her *maunam* which she had adopted in Vindhyachala at the beginning of the same year. She used to speak on Thursdays and part of Fridays. By evening, she became silent again. Surprisingly, Didi could interpret her glances and the slight movement of her fingers. Didi herself did not know how she was able to do this!

I shall write about this account from the point of view of my own family. Renu had been travelling with Sri Ma for a month or so. Sri Ma was in Bahrampur by invitation of the devotees of the town. The latter also made elaborate arrangements for the mahatmas who were travelling with Sri Ma. My father was in Etawah as District Judge. He was there by himself because my mother was in Allahabad to see us through our various final examinations.

One evening in late February my father arrived in Allahabad unexpectedly and took my mother aside and talked to her for a long time. After a while they called me in to join their discussion. I was given a letter to read. This was from Didi Gurupriya with an enclosure from Sri Prabhudattaji Maharaj. The gist of both letters (as far as I can remember now) was that it was Sri Ma's *kheyala* that Renu would get married on a specific date (17th Phalgun) and that my father should come to Bahrampur to bless his daughter on this auspicious occasion.

My father was very upset. He was grappling with dozens of conjectures and questions, "Why should anybody talk of marriage without previously consulting Renu's parents? Who was the bridegroom? Why at this time? Was he one of the brahmacharis in the ashram?" And so on and so on.

I, strangely, had no misgivings. I spoke spontaneously to my father, "But, why should you worry? Didi writes quite clearly that this is Sri Ma's *kheyala*. So nothing can go wrong. After all, Ma herself is there, so whatever happens will be the right thing to take place." My conviction had some effect on my father's agitation. He calmed down and decided to travel down to Bahrampur as desired by Didi. He asked me if I would go with them. This was a serious question to ask because my final exams were looming ahead. I felt very grown-up and flattered that I would be playing a supportive role in this crisis. My father then sent word to J.C. Mukherjee (Didi Gurupriya's cousin) who had become a family friend. We called him Jiten Kaka (uncle). He was very familiar with the people in the ashram, and my father hoped to obtain from him a fresh angle on the state of affairs. When he came over and learnt about the messages from Bahrampur, he expressed his displeasure in strong terms. He was very fond of my sister, as were many other people connected with the ashram. Since Renu used to help Didi in cooking marvellous food for a large number of people and serving them also, a big circle of devotees knew her. Her smiling and pleasant expression made even strangers approach her with confidence. Jiten Kaka saw no reason why the ashram should involve itself in the question of her marriage without any reference to her parents. He offered to accompany my father to Bahrampur. My father was very grateful for his support.

We arrived in Bahrampur and by dint of asking people for directions came to Sri Ma's place of residence. The whole town seemed to

Renu's Marriage with N.P. Chatterji

be celebrating a big festival. There were many comings and goings on the streets. We passed a huge open-air arena with tiers of seats where later in the week we watched the notable *yatras* "Nader Nimai" and "Nimai sanyasa", a memorable experience. For the time being we were rather preoccupied with the personal drama taking place in our family. Sri Ma received us graciously. She seemed pleased that I had come. I ran up an open staircase to meet my sister who was engaged in cooking the midday meal. She seemed quite her normal self but I could have no private speech with her.

Renu and Gini with Sri Ma

We were introduced to a prestigious citizen of Bahrampur, Anil Chandra Chatterjee, who had kindly made arrangements for our stay in his palatial house. I had never seen a house like that before. It contained numerous courtyards with rooms arranged round them. After some conversation my father and Anilda discovered a relationship which was not remote. So we were happy to be billeted with them. There was a girl of my age, with whom I became friendly.

After we had settled in, my parents had a long private interview with Sri Ma. This was Thursday, so she spoke to them. I came to know the details of this talk much later. Sri Ma's *vani* was something like this: Prabhudattaji Maharaj had elicited her *kheyala* regarding Renu's marriage. (All the mahatmas were also in Bahrampur at this time, at the invitation of the townspeople). One day, when Renu was serving him his meal, he had said to Sri Ma that such well-educated, cultured girls from good families should not remain unmarried without some definite aim in life. It came to her *kheyala* spontaneously "But Renu is already married."

The background of her *kheyala* was as follows:

Years earlier, when we had met Sri Ma in Bareilly, the devotees from New Delhi had come to our town to perform one of their *nama yajnas* for her. Many other devotees had come from nearby towns. One such was N.P. Chatterjee from Mathura where he was teaching at a college at that time. My mother happened to take note of the tall handsome young man and liked his deportment toward Sri Ma. My mother asked Sri Ma, if she should approach the father of the young man, Manmotho Nath Chatterjee of Dehradun (as other devotees from New Delhi informed her) proposing their daughter Renu's name in marriage for his son. Sri Ma readily gave her approval saying, "Why not? It seems a very good match." In Sri Ma's *kheyala* the marriage of Renu and Jyotida (N.P. Chatterjee) was accomplished right then.

In point of fact, nothing came of this matter for two reasons: one, because my father had set his sights higher than a college teacher. Second, because my parents were informed by their common friends that Manmotho Babu was *kulina brahmin* (see infra page 110) and he would not entertain any proposal of marriage from non *kulina brahmin* families. In any case, it was no more than a passing thought in my mother's mind, because unless Sidu, the eldest daughter of the house, got married first, the question of Renu's marriage would not arise at all.

We, as a family, came across father and son in Dehradun where we had gone for the summer vacation of 1937. We came to know each other in the ashram, just as we did dozens of other families. My father and Manmotho Babu became friends. We found that Jyotida (N.P. Chatterjee) had a very special relationship with Sri Ma. Sri Ma's given name to him was Jyotivikasa, so we became used to calling him Jyotida. The ashram knew him as Narsingda, his name being Narsimha Prasada. We learnt that Jyotida's mother had died when he was a child; consequently, he and his father were very close companions. Jyotida did not like his father's increasing bent toward asceticism, so he kept guard, so to speak, whenever Manmotho Babu came to stay

Renu's Marriage with N. P. Chatterji

with Sri Ma. He would turn up as soon as he could and fetch his father away. Sri Ma indulged Jyotida in many ways. She had said that his own destiny was toward an ascetic way of life and in time, he would be a Yogiraj! Jyotida was not pleased with such talk, and said he would rather be a *bhogiraj*, that is, enjoyer of worldly pleasures. He would entreat her privately to grant him the boon of worldly success.

We heard all this from Sevaji (Dr. Sarada Sarma) who was like a mother to Jyotida. Sri Ma, evidently to compensate the absence of the indulgence of a mother's selfless love in Jyotida's life, had presented him as a spiritual son to Sevaji. Sevaji and her friend Mahalakshmiji were both very fond of Jyotida. Jyotida on his part, throughout his life was very loyal and dutiful toward her. My aunt, who was with us (Sidu and Kawna's mother), also became rather indulgent toward him. I think the idea of a mother-less boy being brought up by a recluse of a father, fired the imagination of elderly women, who at once wanted to shower their affections on him. Jyotida was very well behaved and not at all like an over-indulged young man. Shortly after this meeting at Dehradun we met them again at Delhi where we had gone from Agra to attend another *nama yajna*. Jyotida was married at this time; we were introduced to his wife, Shanti Devi, who became Shanti-bowdi (brother's wife) for us. Manmotho Babu was rather at a loss to know how to guide his daughter-in-law in the confusing state of affairs which prevailed during a big function happening near Sri Ma. He asked us to take her around with us and make her known to other people as well.

A short while after his marriage, Jyotida was granted his wish to enter the prestigious Indian Civil Service by a chain of circumstances, which he believed to have been set in motion by Sri Ma's *kheyala*. In March 1945, he was posted to Assam as Deputy-Collector. We had met him and Shanti Bowdi and the two children born to them in due course off and on over the years. My parents were uncle and aunt to them.

Now in Bahrampur, Sri Ma said to my parents that she had asked Prabhudattaji if he himself would participate in the marriage ceremony of Renu. To this the Mahatma had replied in the affirmative, saying, if the marriage were performed in the vicinity of Sri Ma, it would be quite like a marriage in a rishi-ashram of ancient times, and he would claim the privilege of giving away the bride. It seems, he really had a great affection for Renu and was ready to assume this role for her sake. Up to now, my parents were listening carefully to Sri Ma's words, and were almost on the point of even accepting the Mahatma's involvement in worldly affairs. Then Sri Ma stunned them by naming the bridegroom of her *kheyala*, that is to say, Jyotida. She said, even *rishis* (seers) of Vedic times sometimes had more than one wife, as for example *rishi* (seer) Yajnavalkya. Continuing with the simile, she said that if her *kheyala* for this ceremony way back in Bareilly was taken note of, then Renu was actually Jyoti's first wife like Maitreyi, while Shanti was the second like Katyayani. It will be remembered that when the *rishi* was about to leave his hermitage, he divided his possessions equally between the two of them. Katyayani professed herself satisfied, but Maitreyi wanted to know if these worldly goods would lead to Supreme Bliss. She thus became the famous interlocutor for *brahmavidya*. This story is given in the *Brhadaranyakopanishad*.

Sri Ma continued in this strain for some time, but my parents were unable to accept the spiritual overtones of this proposed marriage. They were appalled at the idea of Renu marrying an already happily married man with two children. It was a shocking blow to absorb. My father expressed his utter rejection of the idea in vehement language. Sri Ma then became grave and quiet. She said her *kheyala* regarding the date of the marriage should be considered irrevocable; my father could look around and arrange for a suitable bridegroom before this date. My father grasping at this respite spoke to Jiten Kaka, Anilda and others he had come to know in Bahrampur. Didi herself told influential people to gather information regarding eligible bachelors. Dozens of men were mobilised and my father paid many courtesy calls on the families of prospective candidates. I think he even went to Calcutta once to meet a few families, but all to no avail. He could not present an eligible bachelor for Sri Ma's consid-

Renu's Marriage with N.P. Chatterji

eration. He was under great mental stress and his wrath fell on Prabhudattaji. He spoke sharply to the mahatma regarding the inadvisability of *sadhus* interfering in worldly affairs. The Mahatma was very hurt. He said he had thought Renu belonged to Sri Ma and so he had felt concern for her welfare. Had he known that she was only a visitor he would not have said anything.

In the meantime, Sri Ma had already sent for Jyotida and told him to come with his family. I happened to be standing outside on the road when they arrived from the station. Looking at Jyotida's usual imperious demeanour, I suddenly felt like laughing, thinking that he does not know what is in store for him here. I went in and told Sri Ma about their arrival. She looked questioningly at my amused expression. When I explained, she also smiled a little. Jyotida and Shanti Bowdi came in and paid their respects to Sri Ma. Thereafter, I took them to Anilda's house, who was ready to extend his hospitality to a family known to us and who were Sri Ma's guests. On his way out of Sri Ma's residence, Jyotida saw Renu at a distance and called out loudly, "Renu, do you know why I have been called here?" My sister till then had not been told by Sri Ma, so she replied truthfully that she did not. This is a truly amazing demonstration of unquestioning dependence on Sri Ma's *kheyala*. She just knew that she would be married, but in name only, because Sri Ma had acknowledged her yearning for a life of non-attachment lived in the aura of Sri Ma's *kripa* (grace).

I think my father, meeting Jyotida and his family breathed a sigh of relief. He counted fully upon Shanti-bowdi to nullify the whole project. He said to Sri Ma that he was ready to obey her *kheyala* but only if Shanti would give her wholehearted consent to the idea. It was impossible for him to give her cause for unhappiness. Sri Ma agreed to his condition because in any case, she was herself ready to explain her *kheyala* to Jyotida and his wife.

To this day, none of us knows the exact words she had with Renu, Jyotida and Shanti-Bowdi separately, one by one. Jyotida told me later a small part of this conversation. To him Sri Ma's first question was "Are you willing to go through a second marriage ceremony if I say so?" To this, he had replied promptly, "Why one only! I can go through ten of them if you say so!" There were one or two excuses for this levity on his part. For one, he had that easy friendly relationship with Sri Ma. He knew that whatever he had gained in life had been due to her *kripa*, so if she should call upon him to render some service, he would be more than willing to obey. This bizarre request for a second marriage he took in his stride because he did happen to be a *kulina*-brahmin, something of a rarity in modern times. Perhaps, people of other provinces are not familiar with the *kulinapratha* of Bengal. The *kulina* is a special sect among brahmins. Sometimes a *kulina* brahmin was required to enter into polygamous marriages because parents of *kulina* girls were too orthodox to settle for a non-*kulina* bridegroom, preferring a marriage in name only rather than the stigma of spinsterhood for their daughters. All this had become obsolete in our own time but we were aware that such customs had been observed earlier. He had at once thought that he was being asked to confer his name nominally upon some female who Sri Ma thought would benefit by it.

The concurrence of Shanti-bowdi came as a surprise to many. Her whole-hearted endorsement of the marriage she herself communicated to my father in unequivocal terms. She said, "Uncle, do not be disturbed on my account, I am convinced that this marriage is for the good of the three of us and I am happy about it."

My father hugged her and blessed her; he had no more objections to raise. Jiten Kaka reacted very sharply when the decision was finally taken. He was most displeased by my father's acquiescence. He said that if Renu had been his daughter he would have taken her away to Allahabad in double quick time. He was so disgusted that he left us and went away saying he would have nothing further to do with such a bad business. I was also becoming a little restive because the B.A Exams were just weeks ahead. I asked Sri Ma if I should go back to Allahabad with Jiten Kaka. She raised three fingers of her left hand. I interpreted this to mean that she was asking me to wait for another three days. I readily agreed to this. Needless to say, within this time all of us were back in Allahabad, including Renu. Sri Ma

Renu's Marriage with N.P. Chatterji

had made it clear to Jyotida, Shanti and Renu that the marriage would just be a spiritual bond. Renu would remain with her parents or in the ashram as she was in the habit of doing. Neither she nor Jyotida would have any rights or duty toward each other.

In the meantime, other events had taken place. Prabhudattaji had left town. Before his departure, Sri Ma had prevailed upon my father to go and apologise to him. The Mahatma had graciously accepted my father's apology. It may be stated here that he continued to be very kind to our family and we always had a special place in Jhunsi whenever Sri Ma came to visit him.

For my father, it must have been a very difficult decision to take: Renu was his elder daughter for whom he was planning a good match like all parents, but by this deed he would be pre-empting her from leading an ordinary happy life in the world. The kaleidoscope of the experiences of our family, of life and death, illness and health, success and failure, joy and sorrow and so on, in retrospect assumes shadowy lines, but my father's great moment of rising to the occasion of Sri Ma's expectations of him remains undimmed in my memory. By this act of loyalty and faith he bound her *kheyala* forever and ever to all members of our family down to nieces and nephews. Whether, individually, we were deserving of this *kheyala* or not, I do not know, but we did inherit this priceless treasure as each one of us will acknowledge if asked. We were never alone, never afraid of what might happen, because we always felt protected by the aura of Sri Ma's presence in our lives.

Another event that paralleled Renu's marriage was Abhayda's marriage also at this time. We heard about it after we arrived in Bahrampur. We knew Abhayada to be a rather wayward but charming young man completely given over to the life of asceticism. He was quite close to our family. In a way, the news of his forthcoming marriage was more shocking for us than my sister's. A girl from the Kanyapeeth, Jamuna, had been chosen as his bride-to-be. Sri Ma had first suggested another girl, but her mother obviously was of the genre of Jiten Kaka because she had immediately whisked her daughter away to Calcutta. I hope nobody will take offence if I write that for us Abhayda's marriage was a sort of comic relief from the serious drama of the other episode. My father one day met Abhayda carrying a couple of colourful saris, which he had been asked to purchase by Didi. This was such an astonishing sight that my father's sombre mood underwent a complete change. He laughed aloud delightedly, saying, "Truly, Sri Ma can achieve the impossible. If Abhay is going to become a householder then anything is possible."

On 17th *Phalgun* (some time in March), we moved down to a place a little away from Bahrampur for the wedding ceremony. One of the devotees, a zamindar of some importance, had made all arrangements for the ceremony. It was a labour of love and devotion on his part; a *mandap* (a marquee) had been erected, all the things which are necessary for the rites had been most carefully bought by him. We were given comfortable quarters to stay in. My father and Jyotida separately and individually became engaged in performing the pre-marriage religious rites obligatory in Hindu marriages. Shanti-bowdi and the two children had remained at Anilda's. My mother, Renu and I could at last sit together for a little while and talk about the events taking place. There was no question of a midday meal because my parents, Jyotida and Renu were obliged to keep fast, only I could eat something.

In those days, no legal ratification of Hindu marriages was required. A bigamous marriage was not forbidden in Hindu Law, but it was not the convention either. In our section of society it was altogether unheard of. When evening drew near the priest made preparations for the ceremony of marriage. The zamindar's family and a few women from the village took matters in their own hands. At first, Renu had wanted to keep to her ordinary everyday clothes but the women who were clustering round the 'bride' would not hear of it. They brought out a bridal Banarsi sari, which had been purchased for the purpose. They did their best to make everything look like on an ordinary marriage. My mother and I sat around giving support where necessary. My father, after the giving-away ceremony, retired to the men's quarters. He had brought a large amount of cash with

Renu's Marriage with N.P. Chatterji

him from Allahabad. He now took the opportunity of reimbursing his kind host for all the expenses incurred by him and made such payments as were due to others. He expressed his gratitude and appreciation for all efforts made on his behalf.

After the marriage rites, the few people sitting around dispersed. My sister had been working hard all these days, helping Didi to look after the guests and all the mahatmas. She was dropping with fatigue and very thankfully lay down next to my mother and went to sleep. That left Jyotida and myself to while away the few hours remaining before dawn. In our society of arranged marriages, the wedding night is spent wakefully by everyone. It is a night of music or just hilarious merry-making. In this case, Jyotida and I stayed awake talking desultorily; there were companionable silences broken by him to do some thinking aloud. He had always treated me like a younger sister, so I was used to his ways of thinking. He now explained to me his answer to Sri Ma about the "ten marriages". He said it was such a relief to him when Sri Ma revealed the identity of the girl concerned. His reaction was that at least no stranger was involved. Our two families were so well known to each other that chances of misunderstandings were nil. Then he mused aloud, "Shanti cannot quite envisage the repercussions of this event. She is so proud that she thinks it is quite our own affair; why should anyone pass judgement on our private lives? It will not work out that way. I can almost 'see' the smirks hidden suddenly when I enter the office. The junior officers will avert their gaze when I speak to them. Oh well! What has to be, has to be!" "How will they know so soon?", I asked. Jyotida smiled ruefully, "I guess such a scandalous titbit will make the rounds of official circles within a matter of hours."

When dawn broke Jyotida and I strolled round the countryside for a little while. I for the first time felt a little sad for him. His role in this drama had definitely been the most difficult one. My sister, after all, expected nothing from this marriage so she was not headed toward any disappointment. Jyotida also gained nothing but lost a great deal, because throughout his life the whispering and gossip would follow him to all his higher postings and his career of worldly success.

He had shown me clearly that no one would understand his motive, or rather lack of motive in this affair. Even his children later on in life might perhaps find fault with him. I now understood why Sri Ma had said he would be a 'yogiraj' in future. The future was now for him. It seemed that the marriage Sri Ma had ordained for him, was, in fact, the gift of ochre-robes in spirit if not in reality.

Sri Ma arrived with her entourage a little later in the morning. With her coming, the whole atmosphere changed. The big household became involved in joyous activity. Jyotida, my sister and my parents, made their *pranams* to Sri Ma. She had brought Shanti-bowdi and the children with her. Sri Ma asked the children to do *pranam* to my sister. My sister was embraced by Shanti-Bowdi so they had a semblance of a single family.

At this time, we heard about the events that had taken place in town the previous evening. Jyotida's premonition had been right. A group of young men had entered Sri Ma's room rather belligerently, saying they had come to stop the anti-social activities going on there. They had heard that one of her devotees had abandoned his wife and children and was even now getting married to another girl. Men like Anilda and others tried to pacify them. Sri Ma herself sought to explain her *kheyala* to them. Their aggressive attitude created a very uncomfortable atmosphere. Somebody went and informed Shanti-bowdi, who rushed to Sri Ma's room and by all accounts put to rout these well wishers by a few well-chosen remarks. Matching their hostility, she retorted in anger, saying that she was perfectly capable of looking after her own interests, and that they had no business to tell her whether her husband should or should not marry a second time; for their information, he had her permission and complete approval for this event, etc. etc.

Didi has given a graphic description of this encounter in her Journal. It was the first of many unpleasant repercussions that arose as a backlash of this event. The second came from our family. All of us, following Sri Ma's instructions, left Bahrampur the same day, travelling together to Calcutta where we put up at a cousin's house in Beleghata. They were not devotees of Sri Ma but knew about our

Renu's Marriage with N.P. Chatterji

loyalty to her. They were appalled at our news but managed not to react too sharply. This cousin had a great regard for my mother, so she accepted the situation very gracefully. We sent word to my cousin Sidu, who was now residing in her husband's house in Bowbazar. She came with great joy to meet us. She was happy to see Jyotida and his family too. When eventually, she was told about our adventures in Bahrampur, she was aghast and incredulous. Her later reaction was to feel devastating sorrow on my sister's account, who was especially close to her. She wept and lamented, "Renu, Renu, why did you not die, rather than this?" (*tui more gelina keno?*) We did not know whether to laugh at her extravagant reaction or point out the infelicitous nature of her remarks in the presence of Jyotida and Shanti-bowdi.

By this time everyone was feeling harassed and we were glad for the parting of ways. Jyotida and family left for Alipur Duar in Assam. My parents, Renu and I returned to Allahabad to face the music of considerable social disfavour. The charitable amongst our friends and family opined that my mother had become crazy with religion, the non-charitable came to such conclusions as their own natures demanded.

My eldest brother Manu was in service in Kanpur. He now wrote to ask if all the rumours regarding Renu's marriage were true! So I sat myself down and wrote a long letter describing things as they had happened. He was loyal to Sri Ma but naturally it was not easy to understand this *kheyala* which seemingly transformed so many lives. Very gradually friends and family came to realise that the marriage was in name only.

The brunt of the opprobrium was borne by Sri Ma herself. Wherever she went, she was questioned about this marriage. When she came to Varanasi, Mukti Maharaj expressed his disagreement in the non-too polite language that was typically his own. Since my sister was seen to be dedicated to the service of the ashram, everyone was well disposed toward her. Mukti Maharaj upbraided Sri Ma for ruining the life of a young girl. Sri Ma explained her *kheyala* again and yet again to Mukti Maharaj. With tears in her eyes, she said, "Baba, believe me, infelicity (*amangala*) can not come to anybody through this body. (*Ai sarirer duara, karur, amangala hoi na*) Whatever has been done is for the benefit of all concerned. You do not see the beginnings or the ends of things, only the little which is in between. Whereas, the stretch of *samskaras* is vast indeed, linking many lives together." Sri Ma, in general, did not give explanations of her doings. She had said once to Abhayda, "*kaifiyat dewa na*" that is "do not expect any explanations from this body." In this case, Sri Ma went on giving her full attention to all questions raised in her presence, mostly adverse and repetitive, till the nine-days-wonder began to lose its hold on the imagination of people.

Renu returned thankfully to Sri Ma's company when she went toward Dehradun and Almora after leaving Bengal. At this time, Sri Ma, raising her arms in the manner of balancing something on her head said to Renu these remarkable words, "For your sake, I carry this bundle of thorns on my head!" (*tomar janne ai kantar bhojha mathai chapiechi*).

I would like to write the epilogue to this affair also. Next year, that is, in 1946, we happened to visit Bahrampur and Navadweep again in the company of Sri Ma. I was appalled to read a pamphlet published locally describing the marriage in sensational terms. I was very angry and told Sri Ma that I would ask my father to start legal action against the writer. Sri Ma spoke gently, patting my head and shoulders, "Do not get agitated. All these things are very short-lived. Left alone, people will forget the whole thing very soon. Let time pass, let time pass." And so it happened.

CHAPTER EIGHT

The Break in my University Career

After my final examination in March 1945, we were again free to be with Sri Ma, who had come to Varanasi to attend the second Vasanti Puja being celebrated in the new ashram. My mother, sister and I and our two brothers attended it. We witnessed the fire-dance *arati* which used to be performed by Jotu-bhai so beautifully. This second *puja* was better organised and many buildings had come up. The girls in the Kanyapeeth were now settled near the ashram. As the years passed, I became more and more involved, to the exclusion of any other major interest in my life.

During the long summer vacation, we joined my parents in Shahjahanpur, my father's new place of posting. My father, mother, Babu and I spent some weeks in Shahjahanpur, till it was time to return to Allahabad and enrol ourselves for the new academic year 1945-46. I was enrolling for M.A. in Philosophy. My professor A.C. Mukerji effected the change over from my original idea of doing M.A. in Sanskrit. Philosophy was one of my subjects in B.A.

A.C. Mukerji (no relation with us, in spite of the common name) was a marvellous teacher. He made the problems come alive — metaphysics seemed the most worthwhile pursuit in the world of academia. Sanskrit, however, remained my first choice, even at the time of the valedictory function for the passing out graduate class. Professor Mukerji said to me, "I hope you will offer Philosophy in your M.A.?" I answered, "Well, Philosophy seems to be a futile subject. It raises more questions than it answers! You yourself propounded so many problems in our metaphysics class, but I do not feel that you have resolved any of them!" Professor Mukerji, in a very conspiratorial manner bent towards me and said, "You come and join my class and I promise I shall resolve all your doubts!"

This promise made me give up my first choice, Sanskrit. I thought to myself that after all I could take the Sanskrit Exams later on, but probably never again have the chance of studying Philosophy under one of the great teachers of the day. Not that any problems were ever resolved — they only became more complicated and all encompassing; but I never regretted this changeover. In a way, I got the training to understand a little of Sri Ma's *vani* (utterances) from an early age. I would marvel at the philosophic undergirding of even her lightest statement. She never put forward an argument which did not have an inner coherence. When she dictated a long letter, this interlocking became very apparent. She would ask the writer (one of us) to read the letter again and again, changing one word here, a punctuation mark there, so that the meaning stood out as clear as crystal.

My parents agreed to my staying in the University Hostel for young women, so that my mother and Babu could join my father at Fatehpur, the town where he was posted after Shahjahanpur. Bindu went to Kanpur to enrol in a college again and be with my brother and Bowdi (his wife). Bindu unfortunately had failed to pass the I.A. Examination.

Bindu and his studies

Bindu had a love-hate relationship with his studies. He had quite a brilliant mind, was always well up in the current literature, but the discipline of studies was beyond him. He had chosen science subjects so his lack of application took a heavy toll. He failed twice in his Intermediate Sciences and twice before his graduation. His overall demeanour was such that he did not remain downcast for very long. His versatile genius made a minor problem of his studies. He was the captain of the cricket team of his college. He played tennis quite well till he hurt his back in a crushing fall. Very tragically this initiated the history of arthritis, later to become a real burden which overshadowed his life. His ebullient spirits made nothing of these problems.

The Break in my University Career

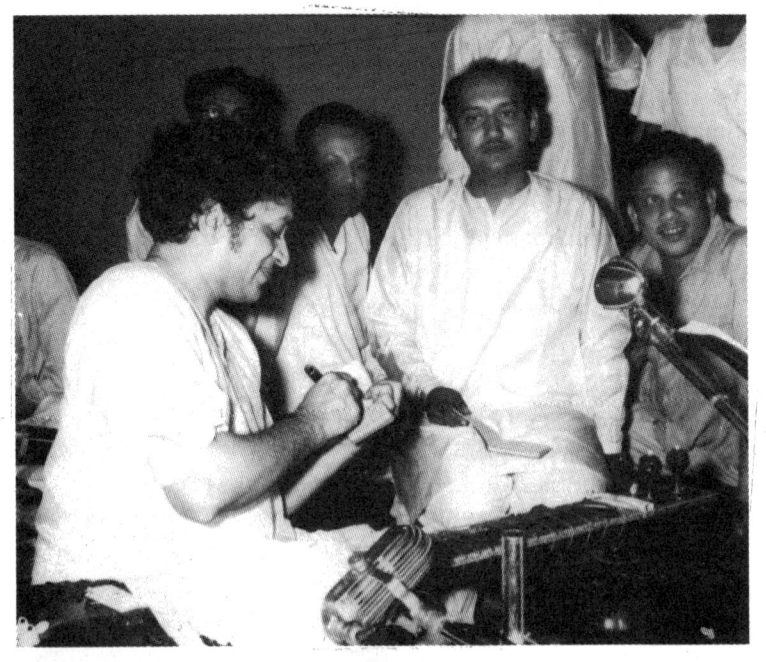

Pandit Ravi Shankar at 31 George Town with Bindu and friends after a concert

His overwhelming interest in music kept him busy with every related activity in town. All concerts, musical sittings or conferences found him at the forefront of the management. He had an unerring ear for spotting new talent. Sometimes he would say, "This young artist will become a star, you will see!" And so it always happened. His friends, such as Rajeev Dave, Vijay Kichloo or Sarvesh Mathur etc. would be able to testify to his musical talents.

My sister-in-law, Protima, used to play the sarod before her marriage. Seeing Bindu's tremendous interest in music she gave him the instrument because she did not play it any more. Bindu's natural talent found ready expression in this direction. He began to play as if he had been taking lessons for years. He did put himself under the tutelage of Suprobhat Pal, a noted sarod player and a disciple of Ustad Ali Akbar Khan. The highlight of his musical career came when Ustad Ali Akbar Khan formally initiated him as one of his disciples.

Thus, Bindu's interests remained varied. He spent two extra years in college and two more in the University before graduation. At one time, somebody had asked him, "How is it that you seem to know intimately all the top-people of our part of the country, who all seem to have been your class-mates?" Bindu had smiled with some embarrassment, replying "You see, I had so many extra years which meant a new batch of students; so my circle of friends is naturally much wider than usual!"

After graduation, he at last gave up science and offered International Law for his Master's degree. At the first opportunity, he sailed over this hurdle obtaining a 1st Division. My mother was so thrilled that she went to the university to see his name in the list posted outside the Senate Hall.

All this happened in due time. I write about Bindu at length because he, I think, was one of those rare people who were born with a natural devotion toward Sri Ma. As I wrote earlier, in religious literature they are called *lila parsada* (companion of divine *lila*). Sri Ma always treated him as a friend and confidante — talking to him about ashram affairs or about problems relating to their inmates. To this day it is my regret and a matter of deep remorse that I did not learn this lesson from Bindu, that is, how to listen to Sri Ma. Just to take one example: somebody had reported to Sri Ma about an affair, which I was in a position to know, was a tissue of lies. But the tale-carrier was close to her and she had no reason to disbelieve this person. In any case, she never doubted anyone to begin with. The other party to the incident was well known to me.

Sri Ma and Bindu

The Break in my University Career

Bindu and I were sitting in front of Sri Ma when she started talking about the other party saying, "Do you think, it was right for this person to behave in this manner? Is it proper conduct?..." I was on the point of protesting that she had been told lies, when Bindu gave me a sharp nudge, so I swallowed and kept quiet. When we came out of the room, I said to Bindu, "But Bindu, our friend is not to blame. Should not Ma be told the rights of the case?" Bindu answered, "What difference does it make? She evidently believes this person who is so close to her. It would have been an obstruction to her *kheyala* of speaking out in defence of this person to us *(bhave badha)*. After all, truth is never hidden from her; this is a superficial level from where she is responding like one of us. She always knows, it is not for us to set her right!"

This attitude came naturally to him, whereas I always got diverted into offering defences or finding excuses for the persons under discussion. This also resulted in a funny incident. A whole bunch of us were standing around in Sri Ma's room. My cousin Tara was singing in the hall below us. We could hear the strains of this music very faintly. Sri Ma spoke about Tara's timbre of voice and certain other characteristics of her singing. She glanced at me standing against the wall in her room, while she spoke to Bindu who was sitting in front of her. Remembering Bindu's lesson of not offering obstruction to her *kheyala*, I said, "Yes Ma, yes Ma," two or three times.

Sri Ma looked at me sharply and said, "Say what you want to say, do not go on saying, yes Ma, yes Ma, like Bindu." Everyone burst out laughing, so I could never acquire this quality of allegiance, which was innate with him.

In the latter half of the year 1945, the war came close to India. So far we had not been touched too closely by it — only to the extent of practising blackouts and getting used to the system of ration-books etc. The horrors, which had swept over European countries, were quite unknown at the time. In retrospect and in reading Didi's diaries again, it occurs to me, that throughout these years Sri Ma underwent sufferings from no known causes. Very frequently, she would be seen to perform *yogic kriyas* and pronounce mantras, sometimes for more than two hours. Once she exclaimed, "Stop the fight! Stop the fight! *(vivada band karo, vivada band karo)*" Yet again she said, "I see a terrifying sight!" Didi connected this to a death which happened in a nearby village, but would Sri Ma use the word "terrifying" (*bhayankara*) to describe a death? It occurs to me that if research is undertaken then a correlation between events in the world and Sri Ma's autonomic responses could be established. I have no doubt that these instances of excruciating suffering she underwent at times, which were unaccountable and mysterious to her devoted entourage, were reflexes to the sufferings of people elsewhere in the world.

India was galvanised in the winter of 1945 when the country came to know about the Indian National Army of Subhash Chandra Bose. The first that we knew of this Army operating at the Eastern borders of India, was when the British Government arrested a few of the officers and brought them to the Red Fort in New Delhi. They were to stand trial for desertion from the British Army to join up with Subhash Chandra Bose. Among other officers of the I.N.A. were Capt. Laxmi Sahgal, Colonel Dhillon and Colonel Shah Nawaz Khan. Students in Calcutta went on strike and organised processions to protest against these trials. The movement spread like wild fire. Before we knew fully the rights of the case, we became involved in protest in Allahabad also. The British Government had expected to make an example of these officers to the rest of the Army. But this proved to have been a major error of judgement.

The Indian Army was well equipped and they had fought in all the major theatres of the war on behalf of the Allies. They were not enamoured of the British Government and reacted with great sympathy toward the officers of the I.N.A. The British made the further mistake of firing upon the student processions in Calcutta, killing a few. I remember the first name which came through was "Rameshwar Banerjee." The students marching along added this name to their slogans of "*Dilli chalo* (March to Delhi), *Lal-Kila tod do*" (Break down the Red Fort), and then "*Rameshwar Banerjee zindabad.*"

The Break in my University Career

I was, in spirit, one with my friends who got involved in this political upheaval, but was not so keen on marching or attending rallies. One of my friends who was in the Hostel with me was Hem Kakkar. She became very enthusiastic. Whenever she heard the shouted slogans which acted as rally cries, she would throw her books under any convenient hedge or tree and run off to join the crowd of insurgent students. I would pick up her books and follow. In this way, one long hot day, we joined a procession, which marched from the Banyan Tree in the University Square to the Muhammal Ali Park in Chowk (City). To this day, I do not know how I did this. The boys were very gallant. They allowed us to stand under shady trees from time to time, fetched us *kulharas* (earthen cups) of water to drink from and guarded us from being jostled by the crowds when we entered the city precincts.

When we returned to the hostel in the evening we were lined up in front of the Warden's quarters and heard in silence admonitions against our conduct, warning of expulsions and fines etc. The warden was our much beloved Miss Lalita Pathak (Buaji, to the ashram) who more or less, we felt, went through the motions as desired by the authorities, so we did not heed her seriously.

The student movement became so strong that the British Government hastily brought the trial to a finish and released the officers, who had become national heroes. The War had come to an end but much time passed before the story of horrors perpetrated on the hapless people of Europe filtered into India. Very soon we were to become involved in the terrifying events of a calamity on our own soil.

The examination of M.A. 1st year (March 1946) drew near. It has been my experience that I am unable to look after myself properly. My health was never robust — now it suffered under adverse conditions. We did not have hot water facilities in the hostel. The early morning baths in ice-cold water took their toll. I contracted a fever and was soon bed-ridden. The doctor diagnosed pleurisy. In those days the treatments were all simple; antiphlogistine fomentation and rubbing with an iodine ointment. My parents were informed and I was bundled off home to Fatehpur. My friends in the hostel, Sarala Bhatnagar, Raj Kumari Aga and of course Hem Kakkar, had looked after me very methodically. I was rather sad to have to part from them.

In Fatehpur, I recovered after a while. As soon as I felt in possession of my health I requested my parents to allow me to go to Allahabad so that I could sit for my examination. The doctor, seeing my one-pointed resolution, chose not to object. With great misgiving my mother brought me to Allahabad. I sent for my friends, who came round with their lecture-notes and other papers to help me to make last-minute preparations.

At this time, we came to know that Sri Ma had come to Varanasi. I at once suggested to my mother that we go there. My mother said, "The doctor gave his permission for Allahabad only. Your father will be displeased if you disobey him." But I was persuasive, saying that nothing could go wrong if we went for Sri Ma's *darshan*; my preparation for the examination was so sketchy to begin with, that the loss of a couple of days would not matter at all.

We arrived in Varanasi, much to my sister's surprise. When I did my *pranam* to Sri Ma she said, "Have you just arrived? I saw you this very morning bowing here, and your hair falling at my feet!" (*payer kachhe chulguli jhur jhur kore parchhe*)

Sri Ma was told about my illness and also my determination to sit for the examination. Sri Ma looked grave and said, "It is not my *kheyala* that you appear at the examination now." (*amar kheyala hoina*). This came as a tremendous shock to me because up to that time, I had not thought of any alternative at all. I blurted out, "If I cannot sit for the examination, I shall come with you!" Sri Ma looked at me for a few moments in silence, then said, "If you promise to stay quietly and not strain yourself in any way and eat at proper times the food which has been prescribed for you." Renu was put in charge. Renu, however, was always so busy with attending to Sri Ma's V.I.P. guests and a hundred and one things which happened all the time near Sri Ma, that she did not have time to look after me. Kshamadi who almost never let me out of her sight assumed this duty.

The Break in my University Career

I take this opportunity to record my gratitude and appreciation of Kshamadi's spirit of *seva* (service) not only in this case but for all ill people, young or old (or animals) who came within the orbit of her ministrations. She was a born Florence Nightingale, and a sort of "elderly-aunt" figure to all the girls travelling in Sri Ma's entourage. Buni and Renu would find their beds made when they returned late at night from Sri Ma's rooms. She organised the putting up of mosquito nets, always a difficult job in a bare hall, which was generally at the disposal of the womenfolk. I have many such clear memories of Kshamadi, managing for everybody at very unlikely places. Once in Rajpipla we were billeted, as usual, in a hall. It was very cold, for which we were rather unprepared because the weather had been mild on the other side of the river Narmada from where we had come. Moreover, Buni suddenly suffered an attack of asthma. Kshamadi commandeered all extra bed clothes, made up a couch with a high head-rest. Buni was unable to lie flat when the attack was on and would sit up with her back and head resting on a bank of pillows. After she made Buni comfortable Kshamadi dealt with each one of us, providing Tara, Buba Sati, myself and a few others with an assorted jumble of bedclothes. When everybody had settled down, it was found that Kshamadi had nothing for herself!

We would have laughed at her predicament, but this night we were too uncomfortable to be amused. I think it was Buni who told Kshamadi to extract one or two blankets from the pile erected round her; and so ended a memorable night. I have happy recollections of a spirit of sharing and togetherness, which added to the fun of these impromptu gatherings. The older girls, Bunidi, Renudi, Kshamadi, Billoji, Chhabidi (Didu) were good to us. We the second generation, as it were, of Sri Ma's retinue, Tara, Buba, Sati, Moni, Gini, myself etc. were happy to fetch and carry and make ourselves useful in as many ways as possible.

In Bahrampur with Sri Ma

In February 1946 Sri Ma was preparing to travel down to Bahrampur accompanied by Haribabaji Maharaj, and a large number of his followers from the villages around Baandh. Haribabaji was on a pilgrimage to the towns in Bengal sacred to the memory of Sri Gauranga Mahaprabhu. This turned out to be quite a coincidence as far as I was concerned. When I had asked Sri Ma's permission to accompany her I had not known about her destination. When I was ill in Fatehpur I had read the six volumes of Sisir Kumar Ghose's *Amiya Nimai Charita*, a marvellous biography of Lord Gauranga. I also had a keen desire to see all the places so vividly described by the author. Now, unexpectedly my desire was going to be fulfilled.

My mother went back to Allahabad and then on to Fatehpur. She must have borne the brunt of my father's displeasure at this irresponsible behaviour on my part. But he could not have been too angry since Sri Ma herself had assumed charge. Like all thoughtless children we had taken our parents for granted. It was very late in life that I learnt to appreciate their extraordinariness. I do not recall that my father ever raised his voice in anger against anybody, not even a servant. He never said a word to Bindu when he failed his exams. He may have expressed himself to my mother, but as this never filtered down to us, we knew nothing of it.

I travelled down with Sri Ma's party trying to forget my disappointment. This, in effect, was quite easy because the confusion created by this unwieldy motley crowd bordered on pandemonium. The Hindi-speaking villagers were absolutely terrified of going into Bengal — allegedly the home of Tantric esoteric practices! Haribabaji Maharaj had brought them on this pilgrimage. They had not dared to say "No" to him. We were told that their womenfolk had literally cried at parting, convinced that their husbands, brothers or fathers as the case may be, were destined to be turned into a "herd of sheep" in darkest-Bengal! Only Haribabaji's presence and Sri Ma's radiant smile gave them the fortitude to disregard the rumours of black magic!

Our hosts in Navadweep were competent and willing. They provided dozens of mosquito nets and other facilities to their rural guests who did not speak a word of Bengali nor even the Hindi of common usage. The village dialect had to be interpreted. Only the *Hari-nama-samkirtana* broke down all barriers. I found that what I

The Break in my University Career

had read about Navadweep was true. From any corner of the town, one would hear strains of *Hari-nama-samkirtana* being sung in some house, or temple or satsang hall. The town seemed saturated in this heart-warming music! The names of the Lord composed in couplets were sung in beautiful ragas to the rhythm of a special percussion instrument (*khole*). We paid visits to all the famous temples. Everywhere Sri Ma was received with special honours. She was already well known in Navadweep. The Vaishnavas treated her as their Istadevata Lord Gauranga. Every visit was hailed as the advent of the Lord himself.

The strain of the travel found me unequal to it. I took to my bed for a couple of days. On the third day, I felt better. I took a refreshing bath and then stood outside the guesthouse, where we were staying, watching Sri Haribabaji proceed on his way singing *kirtana* with his entire retinue. A horse-drawn carriage stood at the gate with Sri Ma and Didi inside, about to follow the *kirtana*-party. Sri Ma saw me from the window of the carriage and beckoned me closer. "Are you well?" she asked; "Yes", I answered. She then said "Climb in". The carriage was quite small, just enough for her and Didi. Seeing me hesitate, she said, "Sit on my lap." I got in and trying to put my weight on my feet sat on Sri Ma's knees as lightly as I could. Sri Ma said "Do not perch like that, sit properly." Didi said, "Sit on my lap." So obeying both, I sat in the middle. We went to see a very beautiful temple that day. Haribabaji used to walk backward, whenever he saw Sri Ma's carriage. He never turned his back on the vehicle she would be riding. He himself hardly ever used a car or a carriage, preferring to walk with his people.

From Navadweep we travelled to Bahrampur. The previous year about the same time we had lived through the drama of the two marriages under Sri Ma's aegis. Many people recognised my sister. There were some whisperings and odd glances, which was a bit unpleasant but all washed away in the sustaining graciousness of Sri Ma's company. She kept Renu close to her. I was under orders to go to bed not later than 10 p.m. no matter what was happening near Sri Ma. Kshamadi and I walked back to our quarters at quarter to ten, sometimes leaving everyone else enjoying a conversation with Sri Ma in her room. Kshamadi herself lay down on her bedroll pretending to be relieved from attending *satsang*. I remember that she used to tell me stories from her own childhood, village customs in Bihar and funny incidents, till I fell asleep. I did realise that I was being taken care of by Kshamadi so that I would not feel left out of all the activities happening near Sri Ma, but I never thought to tell her so. We took such things from her pretty well for granted.

Off and on, I had Sri Ma's company quite unexpectedly. One day we visited the Ganges for an outing. Sri Ma's car was seen to be out of order when the time came for us to return to the town. A *riksha* was fetched for her. Sitting in the *riksha* she stretched out her hand for mine and obeying the gesture I climbed up and squatted in the foot-space beside her. On our way back, she held on to me in a protective way, so that I would not fall off. All the others walked behind the *riksha*. She evidently saved me the long walk.

If all the people who spent some time with Sri Ma were to write about themselves and Sri Ma, then perhaps some measure of understanding may dawn as to the vast inclusiveness of her attention-span, her extraordinary command of the events eddying round her in endless continuity. Hundreds of people from all walks of life and from all corners of the world came to her with their own very individual points of view. Yet, one glance from Sri Ma and one knew that one could belong to her forever. In retrospect, I realise that remarkable changes were taking place in our society under Sri Ma's influence. She was recognised as a teacher of great spiritual power, yet she did nothing to reveal herself. She did not give discourses or claim any privileges, yet her presence was sought ardently by all those who had seen her even once. They came to know that they could invite Sri Ma to attend a religious festival. A revival of religious rites was witnessed in places Sri Ma visited because the people would want her to revisit them. In turn, this brought people together for organisational work. Since Sri Ma paid such respect to mahatmas they were also invited. A confluence of various religious groups, the laity, the ascetic denominations, the many levels of society, happened as a matter of course. At the

The Break in my University Career

time, we took all this for granted, not really appreciating the magnitude of the phenomenon taking place all around us. Just as a great symphony is created out of hundreds of diverse instruments under the expert guidance of a brilliant conductor so Sri Ma raised the consciousness of our own understanding of the traditional wisdom, a new pride and joy in our heritage of the Upanishadic teachings. There were no discordant notes or alien resonances. The beautiful and inimitable gesture of the slightly raised right hand seemed to encourage and inspire everyone, literally, everyone, to tread the razor's-edge-path: the same gesture promised the fulfilment of the supreme joy of arriving home at last.

From Bahrampur we came to Calcutta and stayed at Prankumar Babu's (Bunidi's grandfather's) house. Amidst all the activities going on all around her, Sri Ma found time to talk to Renu and me privately. She said that it was not right for me to travel with her at this time because everything was so uncertain and she could not ensure any degree of comfort or watchful care, which I needed. Softening the impact of her words, she said, that I would be able to join her later when she would stay in one place for the summer holidays. She then told my sister to consult a good doctor and arrange for me to go home to Fatehpur. It was Sri Ma who elicited the name of my own uncle (mother's only brother) from us as a possible escort. We would not have thought of him by ourselves because, he lived rather like a recluse and we were not close to him.

So I left Sri Ma's party and went with my cousin Sidu to her home in Bowbazar. I had a nice restful time, made much of by my brother-in-law and his people. My cousin now had a baby son. She said she had prayed to Sri Ma for a son, the previous year on the occasion of Sivaratri, which had been celebrated in Calcutta. Just one year later, the son was born on this year's (1946) Sivaratri day.

Sidu got in touch with my uncle and also their family physician. The doctor prescribed some tonics and rest. My uncle was pleased at the idea of visiting his sister after such a long time. So I came home to Fatehpur. My mother also was very happy to see her brother so unexpectedly.

From Calcutta, Sri Ma went on a long over-due visit to Dhaka. Haribabaji was still on a pilgrimage. He wished to see the places where Sri Ma had spent her earlier life. Renu was with Sri Ma. She also had the opportunity to see these hallowed sites, Ramna Ashram, the *panchavati*, Siddheshwari and also Shahbagh. She said that it was like coming to a forest hermitage after the noise and bustle of Calcutta. The devotees of Dhaka surrounded Sri Ma. She talked to them almost the entire day and throughout most of the night. Renu remembers that she was sitting behind Sri Ma. At one stage Sri Ma leant back and reclined on Renu's knees. It was a very awkward position for her but Renu did not want to shift because she felt Sri Ma would then sit up. Sri Ma had already been sitting for long hours, and it was necessary that she should be a little comfortable. Renu also recalls with great wonder that although she held this position for more than two or three hours, she had no sense of aches and pains or fatigue. Sri Ma talked to the people of Dhaka till it was almost dawn. One of the main interlocutors was Biren Babu (Didi's eldest brother). We had known him at Agra. This was Sri Ma's last visit to Dhaka. The partition of Bengal was looming ahead. In another couple of years East Pakistan was to destroy the ashram and all its Hindu temples, even the ancient and famous Rama Kali temple. Only Siddheshwari remained. Sri Ma told all those who came to her for advice that if possible they should come away from East Bengal. This is how the devotees of Dhaka found asylum in India before the horrors of partition got underway.

Chapter Nine

In Solon with Sri Ma (1946)

On leaving Bengal, Sri Ma travelled right across the northern regions and went up to Solon, the capital of Baghat State. Raja Sri Durga Singh of Baghat State, or Yogibhai as he was known to us, had made elaborate arrangements for her stay along with that of all the mahatmas who wished to stay where she did. A very spacious tennis court with its adjoining clubhouse were made available to Sri Ma. My mother, Babu and I joined Sri Ma's party at Fatehpur. My sister was already with her. Quite a number of Sri Ma's devotees gathered in Solon as this was the summer vacation. The schoolhouse in the middle of the bazaar was given over to us. Here I met Gini again and we resumed our close friendship. I had met her earlier in Bahrampur.

Raja Sri Durga Singh

We shared a room in the schoolhouse, which had no amenities. We were obliged to use the hillside as our washrooms. Within a week, we realised that all our quarters were termite-infested — a kind of invisible insect called *"pisshu"* which got inside clothes and made life miserable by creating itches. The skin began to show red patches. Poor Babu was so bitten that he ran a fever. Others also were badly affected. Sri Ma persuaded all these people to leave for home. She would not have liked us to complain to our hosts about our discomforts. Gini and I tried desperate means to control this itching so that we could answer truthfully that we were not very uncomfortable. I think we used to rub D.D.T. powder on our skins. I do not know why nothing untoward happened to us. Anyway, our rashes were on our backs and legs, which were not visible to Sri Ma, so she allowed us to stay on.

There were other problems. When it rained the roof leaked so badly that there was hardly a dry spot in the room. So I have memories (and Gini has them also, no doubt) of Gini and myself moving our bed rolls from spot to spot at night or sitting huddled up, trying to manage the leaks as well as the dreaded "*pisshu*". We devised a method of passing such sleepless nights. We used to tell stories to each other. This led to another problem. One night I told one of the spooky tales of Algernon Blackwood, a favourite author of that time. After listening to this story, each time Gini went out to the hillside I had to accompany her, because she was too afraid to go out alone!

All this was forgotten when morning dawned and we went over to the clubhouse and saw Sri Ma. She strolled on the Tennis Court while we stood by. There were very few people around and local visitors were circumspect and well behaved. They did not create problems by crowding round her.

These were marvellous days replete with many incidents. We went up to Simla for three days and yet again witnessed the famous *namayajna* of the Delhi party. Gini and I were always with Sri Ma while Renu and Didi were busy in the kitchen. Once while the *kirtana* was in progress, Sri Ma left her seat on the verandah and entered the ring of the singers, raising her right hand in her inimitable gesture during a *nama samkirtana*. Gini and I had heard that Didi always stood behind Sri Ma whenever she was moving about in a *kirtana* party, so we sent someone to fetch Didi and both of us slipped inside the ring of men to stand behind Sri Ma. Almost the next second we found our hands gripped by Sri Ma; she simply took us right back to the verandah and then re-entered the *kirtana*-group. She was so fast that they had not noticed her absence and we had the impression that we just walked in and out in the same movement. We realised later that Sri Ma would not permit two young girls to mingle in the crowd. Her ecstatic mood in the *kirtana* was not pretence either; she was always such a harmonious blend of the supra-natural and the practical that we forever lived in a wonderland where any marvel was possible.

On the next day of the *namayajna* in Simla Sri Ma went out for a walk on the Mall. We also ran out and followed her for a while. It had rained in the night and was very cold. We had no time to put on our sandals or shawls. Bhupen out of sheer mischievousness pointed this out to Sri Ma. She stood still looking back at us. Gini and I were sent back to the Kalibari in disgrace. Although we were annoyed with Bhupen to begin with, we were thankful also, because it was not really advisable for either Gini or myself to expose ourselves to the cold. We were shivering with cold after walking on the icy road barefoot. On our return to the Kalibari, we found a chowkidar making tea in his guardroom over a log fire. We requested him to allow us to sit in front of the fire for a while. He not only did this but gave us a *kulhar* of tea each. I still remember the warmth and comfort of that *kulhar* of tea.

I do not remember the exact date of our arrival in Solon but noted we happened to be there on 2nd June 1946. Both my sister and I remembered an incident, which had happened in our lives, ten years earlier. The whole family had been together in Bareilly. The four of us — Sidu, Renu, Kawna and myself — were a happy group, enjoying each other's company and very conscious of the agreeableness of our circumstances. On 2nd June 1936 while we had been in the garden we were overcome by an unusual feeling of nostalgia. The elder sisters wondered where we would be, say, after 10 years and how life would have treated us meanwhile? So we made a promise to each other that we would come together on this day and at this place from wherever we were and compare notes.

This promise was half fulfilled since Renu and I were together but not in Bareilly. In some disquietude of mind regarding this broken promise, we took Sri Ma into our confidence. She, at once, entered fully into our thoughts. She said, "One has gone forever out of your reach (Kawna) and another is married and settled in her own family (Sidu). The two of you may now remember them and be together in spirit." I do not recall her exact words but it was our belief that she absolved us from the promise, because she gave us some little *kriya* to do in commemoration of the day of togetherness. Sri Ma never trivialised the problems of the young. When she said to young people to look upon her as their Friend truly she was that to them, because she gave of herself to them unfailingly in sympathy and understanding.

A rather beautiful incident occurred in Solon at this time. Haribabaji had begun to read from a book called *Gopihrdaya* written by Rehana Tyabji. The author was recalling previous lives, and she seemed to remember that she was one of the *gopis* at the time of Krishna *avatara*. She wrote in such a vivid style that Krishna-*lila* became alive during the satsang hour. Haribabaji's devout way of holding the book and his unqualified faith in the narrative added to the spiritual atmosphere.

When Haribabaji had finished the book, I asked to be given it for a day, so that I could read it myself. I kept it in the drawer of a dressing table, which was in the dressing room of the clubhouse. We used to use it more or less as a lumber-room, to deposit all our extra things. After lunch at the schoolhouse, I returned to the clubhouse to find Sri Ma describing what she had just "seen". She was describing a *rasamandala*. Beautifully dressed young women were dancing in a ring holding hands, to a lively rhythm, which went like this 1-2, 1-2-3. They were advancing toward a point and retreating again like the ebb and tide of sea-movements. Sri Ma gestured toward the dressing room to indicate the focal point of the dance. She had asked at first if the book *Gopihrdaya* was in the clubhouse. Nobody knew because they had thought that I had taken it away with me to our schoolhouse. On being asked about the whereabouts of the book I said, "It is in the drawer of the dressing table". So everyone realised the remarkable nature of this coincidence. Sri Ma then asked me if my *Istadevata* was Krishna, but before I could answer in the negative she continued, "No, I remember, you have a different image as Ista." She then described the dance of a small dark-hued lad who was moving around me while I slept in the dressing room. It was true that I had been lying in this room for some time as I was permitted to do sometimes. The book was also there. Next day, Sri Ma was asked to describe this scene at the time of the satsang. Haribabaji asked, "Was there a person at the focal point of the dance?"

"Yes"

"Who?"

"I have no *kheyala* to say now!"

The blind Mahatma Sharanandadaji said with a smile, "Who else but Sri Ma could herself be the focal point". Everyone was pleased at this solution.

In the evening, the Rani Saheba came to visit Sri Ma. While she was with Sri Ma, only women visitors were allowed. She was very stylish. She talked to Sri Ma very informally and like a friend of long standing. The whole clubhouse was made out of bounds for menfolk by guards while she remained with Sri Ma. We saw that she observed strict purdah while she was in her State.

Haribabaji was a stickler for routine. He came to the clubhouse at 10 a.m. every day to begin the satsang. Haribabaji read from Bhaiji's book *Matridarshana*. Sri Ma spoke at length answering the many questions put to her by the mahatmas. We too had the opportunity to hear directly from her the accounts written by Didi as well.

The mahatmas wanted to know about Sri Ma's life of *sadhana*. In answer to the questions Sri Ma obviously had the *kheyala* to go into the depths and details of the *lila* of *sadhana* almost every day. Once she said, "It all happened naturally. All of you know that this body had not learnt about such matters from books or other people. Moreover seeing my absorption in meditation, many people thought they would help me by talking about *sadhana* or reading to me a work of spiritual endeavour. Such efforts were rejected absolutely by this body as if they were bricks thrown at a solid wall. Sometimes extraneous advice was disturbing like an electric shock — it would dissipate the inner inspiration for the time being.

"Everything came from within. The manifestations of the Vedic mantra, and its rhythm, how beautiful they are! In *sadhana*, there are levels; there are stages at which the mantra would reveal itself. Some of you have seen how this body would be affected? When Vedic mantras came pouring forth from this body, it assumed the right postures while the hands moved in appropriate gestures; the flow of breath was in consonance with these pronouncements, even the gaze would be altered. All mantras have their special form of manifestation. When the manifestations are self-generated, or the outer aspect of the inner being is revealed, then all kinds of phenomena are possible. As far as this body is concerned, there is no question of a later or an earlier stage. Whatever came to pass happened in its entirety as if fully revealing itself and then made way for another. The natural process has its own splendour. You plant a seed or a sapling and then start tending it — the tree emerges in all its glory of leaves, flowers and fruits. One doesn't need to pull at the buds. It will all happen in due course and display a beauty of its own. Unremitting care alone is required."

Question: "Would you say some ways of *sadhana* are better than others?"

Sri Ma: "From where to choose? And what is there to discard? There are infinite ways with infinite variations. I have heard people refer to the Vedic, Puranic and Tantric traditions, and also other traditions which are considered alien to these. This body has gone through all these manifestations and they have revealed themselves fully — this is why everyone finds this body understands him. *Sadhana* brought about no changes in this body — it remains as it is. You may compare it to a lump of dough — you may make anything out of it, a bird, an animal, a tree, a doll, then again pat it back to shapelessness".

I recall another rather strange incident of these times of a different type. One gentleman, N., had accompanied Sri Ma from Barhrampur. He was very quiet, but Sri Ma showed some special attention every now and then. Sri Ma told us one day that his wife used to come to her frequently. Seeing a fresh scar on her arm one day, Sri Ma asked her if she had been hurt. Then this lady told her a harrowing tale of her drunkard husband. This gentleman, a rich zamindar, used to indulge in drinking sessions at times quite oblivious of his status and duties in the world. When he came out of his drunken stupor, his wife would inflict a wound on her own body to remonstrate with him against his way of life. He would be very repentant, promising never to drink again but another bout inevitably occurred. The lady showed Sri Ma how her arms and legs were full of these self-inflicted wounds, now turned into scars.

N. was prevailed upon to visit Sri Ma. She asked him if he would come away with her wherever she might go. He must have been aware of her graciousness and compassion because she said no word of blame about his weakness. He obeyed and came away from home to be with her. Thus he was in Solon leading a quiet life. One day he said to Sri Ma that he had a great desire to touch her feet. He knew that a sinner like him should not aspire to this privilege but he felt this touch alone would save him, or some words to that effect. Sri Ma was sitting on her *chowki*, with her feet a few inches from the ground. Since Sri Ma did not say anything, N. knelt down and with much trembling and trepidation touched her feet, taking them in both his hands.

At this moment, Dr. Girin Mitra [1] entered the room and took in the scene at a glance. Sri Ma's expression was indescribable. In general, everyone in her retinue is expected to stop newcomers from their attempts to touch her feet. Girinda smiled and looking at Bhupen, said, "I am too old to start out on the path of dissipation, which could bring about this great privilege. But you are in the right age, so start from now!" Everyone laughed. Sri Ma was understood to say that her *kheyala* remained so constantly on N., because of his wife in distant Bahrampur.

On the eve of her departure from Solon, she sent for my sister and myself. Didi also was there. Sri Ma said that it was her *kheyala*

---

[1] Kshamadi's father, who was one of Sri Ma's long-standing devotees.

that I should remain in the cool atmosphere of the hills, instead of travelling around in the heat of the plains. We should ask our parents to come up so that I could stay with them in a rented cottage. Sri Ma herself told the Rani Saheba that I would remain in Solon, till she herself returned after a couple of months to attend the Durga Puja which would be observed in Solon that year.

Yogibhai's people assumed charge of us from the day Sri Ma left for Vrindaban, leaving Renu, Blancaji and one or two others who would follow as soon as my parents were able to come up to Solon. Our depleted party was accommodated in a furnished house, while a suitable flat was searched for. Ram Singhji came every day to ask Renu for her requirements regarding vegetables and other foodstuffs. He would express his surprise at the meagre list, saying, "Didi, are you people living on air?" Since Yogibhai's people would not consider taking money from us, my sister made do with as little as possible. I take this opportunity to record our appreciation and gratitude to the princely household of Raja Sri Durga Singh, or our Yogibhai. They knew us as Sri Ma's devotees and that was enough. They looked after us as very honoured guests. Very soon, a big flat was found for us near the market and not too far from the palace. My parents and Babu arrived from Fatehpur. My sister and the rest of Sri Ma's retinue left for Vrindaban. In Solon I came to know Atmanandaji (Blancaji) quite well. She and I used to go for long walks on the mountain paths. At the time she was struggling with her own problems.

We had a restful time in Solon. The Rani Saheba used to send for me at times to tell her if her preparations for the Durga Puja were right. There was nothing for me to say. All was perfection. She herself, dressed in silken clothes and accompanied by a batch of maidservants, would sit for hours cleaning the grain and cereals required for bhoga. The spices also, were cleaned, washed and dried under guard so that birds or other animals would not defile them. The *pandal* (marquee) was constructed under her direction. This time the big terrace just below the palace had been allocated for this purpose. Yogibhai had made ready a lovely single-storied bungalow for Sri Ma adjoining the terrace. It had a long verandah encircling the entire five or six-room building. It was beautifully furnished with attached bathrooms and a kitchen for cooking Sri Ma's *bhoga*.

On Yogibhai's Birthday, the entire state mounted a big celebration in his honour. In the Durbar hall, which previously I had seen at the time of the *namayajna*, all was pomp and splendour. The Raja Saheb, dressed formally in brocade and jewels, sat on his throne, while the elite of the State brought him presents. A musician of good reputation gave a recital on the occasion. I had been sent for. On arrival at the hall, I found everything changed and the atmosphere very formal. I was ushered in by a relay of maidservants to the presence of the Rani Saheba, who was sitting in a sort of balcony overlooking the hall. There was a sheer screen in front of her so that she was not visible from the auditorium. She beckoned me to sit beside her, but I realised the formality of the occasion and sat down beyond the special costly square of carpet on which she was seated. I knew I had done right when the chief lady-in-waiting also sat down next to me. We had a good view of the Durbar. The musician sent a message to the Rani Saheba, if she would like to hear any particular raga. She answered "Tilak-kamoda", I remember.

A vignette of days gone by. It is good to remember how happy she was during these days because she passed away very shortly afterwards.

When the time for Durga Puja drew near, Sri Ma arrived in Solon, transforming the hill state into one huge *puja-mandap* as it were. Guests arrived in big batches. There were all the mahatmas who usually came to stay with Sri Ma, if she was not travelling for a few weeks. This was reciprocal. If the mahatmas came, then Sri Ma stayed put as long as they themselves were not ready to leave the place. Many nearby houses were made available to guests from faraway Bombay, Calcutta, Jamshedpur, Varanasi etc. The Kanyapeeth and the Vidyapeeth also came. The arrangements for board and lodging were perfect; everyone marvelled at the standard of hospitality established by Yogibhai's people. One rich business magnate from Calcutta said, "It is a lesson to be learnt by all towns who invite Sri Ma to come to them."

On occasions such as these, Sri Ma's entourage became a mixed crowd. Sometimes, it was amusing to see the juxtaposition of incompatibles: a son of the soil, a villager from the hinterland of the Gangetic plain and a sophisticated lawyer, or judge from the metropolitan cities. It no doubt resulted in a widening of horizons for everybody.

The *puja* was celebrated on a grand scale. We have seen many Durga Pujas being performed in Sri Ma's presence, but I think no one will disagree that the *puja* at Solon surpassed every one of them. The main reason was the one-pointed devotion of the people of Bhagat State. The Himalayan States worship the Devi in her various images. The Durga-image was new to them but they took her to heart immediately. The matchless splendour of this icon on the one hand and the inimitable smile of compassion rendered by the sculptor are always an unforgettable experience.

Renu was busy in the *puja* kitchen for the duration of the function. I helped Nepalda on the other side of the main *puja*-room in preparing gorgeous *thalis* (large plates) of fruit, dry fruits, sweets and soaked grains (*naivedya*). Sri Ma came in everyday to see and admire his works of art. I also earned my share of approval. On the day of Mahashtami (October 2nd 1946), my sister came in hurriedly and told me to go to Sri Ma's room on the completion of my work and not to eat or drink anything as I would be initiated. Initiated! Before I could ask for any further information, she vanished.

I was not at all prepared for this contingency. A dozen questions rose automatically. Who would initiate me? I thought of all the ascetics of the ashram one by one and could not reconcile myself to an initiation by any of them. Perhaps Sri Ma herself? But she never gave initiations! Prey to such doubts and misgivings, I, after all the *naivedya* had been taken into the *puja* mandap, slowly approached Sri Ma's room. I found Didima, my mother and my sister with her. To me Sri Ma said, "Sit here next to your mother. She knows what to do. Today is a very auspicious day — the Mahashtami. The *Shastras* opine that to be initiated by your mother is to gain 14 times more merit than from any other guru". She may have said other things also but my relief was so great that I did not take in anything else except that the Guru would not be somebody I would not be able to accept. I thankfully occupied the seat already set out for me near my mother.

My Initiation

My mother, always serene and calm, seemed to be especially so; there was a stillness about her which struck me as unusual. Sri Ma took my sister away, leaving Didima, my mother and myself in the room. Sri Ma was very busy on this important day and she could hardly spare more than a few moments, but she kept coming and going and I think she came in when my mother actually gave me my mantra. In any case, she was there to accept my *pushpanjali* (offering of flowers) at her feet on the conclusion of the ritual.

Later, I could piece together the happenings of the day. First, Sri Ma had asked Didima to give initiation to my mother. Sri Ma made all arrangements because my mother, not expecting all this, was helplessly at a loss to provide the proper facilities like an asana, fruits, sweets and flowers. After my mother had received her initiation, she was in a position to impart a mantra to others. My sister came first. Sri Ma sat with them the whole while, guiding them. Sri Ma through

Sri Ma and Swami Muktananda Giri

Didima also disclosed the mantras to my mother. My mother knew nothing of these rites and rituals. Didima painstakingly taught us what to do and how to go through the ritual of evening-*puja* (*sandhya*). Lastly Didima said to me, "Sri Ma herself is your Guru. Your Guru and she are the same — always meditate on this truth."

It is now just a little over 50 years since that day! The predominant thought in my mind is, with such overwhelming *kripa* constantly being showered on us, how is it that we have remained the same without becoming totally transformed. My consolation must be that Sri Ma knew fully what recalcitrant material she was dealing with!

At the conclusion of the prolonged festivities, Sri Ma left Solon with her entire retinue. My sister and I remained with her. My parents and Babu returned to Fatehpur.

After Solon, Delhi was a tale of crowds and confusions. We came to Dr. J.K. Sen's house, where a small new annexe had been built for Sri Ma. Sri Ma was very mindful about the conveniences of her hosts everywhere. Here, in Delhi where one household could not have provided for her large retinue, she allotted them to the houses of willing devotees. I think I stayed for one or two days at Gini's. Her parents, her three sisters, and brother Buddhu became well-known to us. Her house was full of Sri Ma's photographs. Her father was in the habit of doing a *namaskara* in front of all the photographs before he started for his office. I remember the children teasing him by saying that if they ever wanted him to delay departure for his office or not to catch a train, they would simply add a dozen more photographs all over the house! They were a marvellous family.

Haribabaji was also in Delhi. He wished to meet Gandhiji who was in town at this time. Sri Ma's name was enough for opening all doors. We arrived at Gandhiji's residence in a motorcade because all who were at hand wanted to go with her wherever she went. Gandhiji received her with great affection and pleasure. He talked of her visit to Sevagram and how she would not stay with him and was against her wandering around so much. Sri Ma with some emphasis said, "Pitaji, I do not go anywhere away from you, I am ever with you. Believe this. This daughter never speaks an untruth."

In Solon with Sri Ma

Gandhiji did believe her, but was reluctant to let her go away, quite like everyone else from mahatmas to the merest child. He put his arm round her and led the way to the prayer meeting. It was obvious that he was not interested in the mahatmas who had come to visit him. Sri Ma held back till he had acknowledged their presence and it was arranged that the mahatmas also would be accommodated on the dais. Upadhyayaji (a close friend of the Nehru family) who knew Sri Ma since the days of Smt. Kamala Nehru was there; he made all the arrangements most satisfactorily. Gandhiji made Sri Ma sit close to him. He was in a happy mood. He would talk to her, and then he would talk about her to the congregation. I think he was asking for some donation or other. I remember him saying, "Do give generously; see, my daughter (*bachhi*) is here. What will she think of you if you behave in a miserly way!" He made the congregation laugh a number of times.

This was their last meeting. The tragic date of 30th January 1948 was not far away.

I think we visited Vrindaban also at this time and then the majority of us came away to Varanasi, leaving Sri Ma with a depleted party. My link with my academic life being broken, I was at a loose end, so I continued to be with Sri Ma's entourage. The years 1946 and 1947 were very lucky for us. Sri Ma came to Allahabad (Krishna-Kunja and Sri Satya Gopal Ashram), Jhunsi, Vindhyachala and Varanasi repeatedly, sometimes at an interval of a few days only.

Buchhun Bhaiya and his wife invited Sri Ma to come to Allahabad for this year's Kali Puja (late October or early November) so I came to Allahabad again after leaving it so abruptly at the beginning of the year. My family was at home. My brother Manuda and his wife had a little daughter born to them in May. This baby was brought to Sri Ma for the ceremony of *annaprasana* (the first intake of rice as solid food). The Kalipuja was performed with the usual meticulous care, which we had come to associate with Sri Ma.

One day a *sadhu* came to Krishna-Kunja and began a conversation with Sri Ma about the practice of yoga. He told her that he was an adept at *anandasana*.

"Is that so?" Sri Ma asked, "Can you show us this asana now?"

We understood the name to mean a yogic posture which enables the yogi to leave behind his body and move about freely, in fact the asana in which the Adi Samkaracarya is said to have left his own body to enter that of the king. The yogi promised to show her this asana at night. When all visitors had left, he lay down in the hall and seemed to assume what we knew as the *shavasana*. Sri Ma strolled up and down the hall a few times and then said, "So this is his *anandasana*!" He was very obviously sleeping very peacefully. Nobody disturbed him.

Sri Ma left for Faizabad for a couple of days and then returned to Krishna-Kunja for almost a week. I did some heart-searching. I told my parents that since my academic life had come to end, and I had not the least desire to enter the married state, I would go to join my sister at the ashram in Varanasi. The Kanyapeeth was well established by this time and we were well acquainted with the girls, since they also had been with us at Solon.

My father looked stunned but he did not say anything. Much later, actually years after his death, my mother told me of a conversation he had about me with Sri Ma at about this time. He had expressed his anguish about my future, which seemed so uncertain to him. He had said, "I shall not be here to look after her." Sri Ma, then, had spoken these reassuring words, at once allaying his entire anxiety regarding me, "But I am here!" (*ami to achhi*); so Sri Ma stayed with me through all the vicissitudes of life. Even on occasions which are considered devastating by other people, I have not known fear, or felt inadequate; Sri Ma was always and is ever with me.

Now, quite happily, I went to Varanasi. Sri Ma sent Didi to escort me to the Kanyapeeth. Didi returned the next day to Allahabad to either Jhunsi or Krishna-Kunja. At Allahabad, Sri Ma travelled back and forth across the river many times. My parents and Babu returned to Etawah where he was posted at this time. Bindu remained alone at Allahabad to appear at his examination. Unknown to me, Sri Ma had told him to get my admission papers from the Allahabad University so that I could sit for the M.A. examination of 1947.

On one occasion, Bindu went with Sri Ma from Krishna-Kunja to Jhunsi and from there, he came on to Varanasi with her. On arrival Sri Ma had gone on to the river and had spent the night on a houseboat, coming to the ashram next morning, much to our delight. My sister and I were pleased to see Bindu so unexpectedly. One of his reasons for coming to Varanasi was to tell me that the University had no provisions for a case such as mine. I had not submitted any medical certificate, I had not failed the exam, I had simply dropped out. Now almost at the end of the session 1946-47, I could not be admitted at all. Sri Ma said to me, "It is not right to leave an undertaking unfinished." Since I had begun to study for the Master's degree I should complete it. She further said, that I was to consider myself part of the ashram even if I was at home for some time, for the sake of finishing my education.

Thereupon I told Bindu that since Sri Ma had the *kheyala* that I should finish my educational career, he should try once more on my behalf, because I was sure permission would be forthcoming. In December of the same year, 1946, Sri Gopal Thakur performed the Gita Jayanti Utsava at Varanasi Ashram. This ceremony is quite elaborate, comprising *puja*, recitation of the text, devotional music and then commentary on the text in the evening. These were very disturbed times in the country. News of riots and the massacre of Hindus by Mussalmans were heard from all sides. Sri Ma listened quietly to tales of woe. She once exclaimed, "God in the form of devastation and screams of terror!" *(hahakar rupe Bhagavan).* One could not but feel that in the presence of God evil is the greatest mystery on earth.

Sri Ma returned again to Jhunsi at the invitation of Prabhudattaji Maharaj. My sister and I also came with her. I remember we spent one whole day on the Ganges, on a houseboat. The riverside was crowded. Once in the afternoon Sri Ma, Renu and I got off the boat and walked a little way away from the crowds. Sri Ma asked us to hold up our shawls in the manner of a teppee. There had been no washroom facilities on the boat. After coming out of this tepee she asked us to use it also one by one while she held up the sheets at one end. Sri Ma never made a fuss regarding these creature comforts. We have seen her devise ingenious ways and means of managing these necessities, under conditions of maximum discomfort.

I recall that during these days Dr. Pannalal was very close to her, nearly always with her, wherever she went. Now we went with Sri Ma to his big and spacious house. He had himself designed the house and he showed the many architectural styles incorporated in it. He had become rather fond of me and used to say I was his favourite granddaughter. Once he said in Sri Ma's presence, "I feel envious of these young people. They have a lifetime of enjoying Sri Ma's company. I am old and have arrived too late to derive full benefit from *matri satsanga*." I said, "Why Doctor Sahab, I feel envious of you!"

"Why? Why?"

"Because, you have lived your life and are now free to devote yourself to Sri Ma without a thought to distract you toward other things. Look at us! The future is so uncertain, we don't know where destiny will take us and whether we will be able to live lives worthy of Sri Ma's *kheyala* for us."

Dr. Pannalal was very happy with this answer and said, "You are very right!"

At the confluence of the rivers a temporary township of straw cottages and canvas tents had come into existence, a yearly phenomenon at Prayaga. Dr. Pannalal had made some arrangements for an elaborate camp, so that Sri Ma could come and stay there with some of her people. Another officer of the Kumbha Mela, K.C. Banerjee also had cottages made for Sri Ma. Sri Ma travelled back and forth from Varanasi, Vindhyachala to Jhunsi and also Allahabad at Krishna-Kunja, where the Delhi Party celebrated a *namayajna*.

Since, I had not heard anything from the university. I stayed with Sri Ma. At the beginning of 1947, we gathered at Varanasi Ashram. On 14th January a *mahayajna* was begun with the *samkalpa* of *vishvakalyana*, that is, "the welfare of humankind". We watched with great fascination the re-creation of the times of Vedic rituals. Under Sri Ma's guidance, perfection was achieved regarding the least detail of Vedic *karmakanda*. We decorated the temporary *yajna-mandapa* with flowers, flags and buntings. The beginnings were small.

Only three *brahmacharis* were initiated as priests: Narayana Swamiji, Kamalakanta and Sadananda. In time, it grew to major proportions. It ended as a magnificent function in 1950.

In those times, Didi was always short of money. Sri Ma herself told us the following story. One day Sri Ma was sitting in her balcony-room (on the west side of the ashram), and only Didi was with her. Didi was saying, "I have started this big affair, I do not know from where I am to get tomorrow's expenses!" In the meantime, my mother had approached the door and was hesitating to enter it. Sri Ma said, "Come in, what is it?" My mother had some money with her, which she had brought as a contribution toward the *yajna*. She was hesitating to offer this sum in front of Sri Ma. Now she placed it in Didi's hands, who accepted it with great relief. Sri Ma used to relate this story to people later by saying, "When Didi was in despair, this Lakshmi (my mother) came with money for the morrow, and after that, money simply flowed in and Didi never had to feel anxious about the expenses of the *yajna* anymore."

Sri Ma's appreciation of the little that anybody might do was truly phenomenal. A compilation of such anecdotes would easily fill a volume.

After the inauguration of the *yajna* Sri Ma again travelled to Vrindaban at Haribabaji's invitation. I was permitted to go with her, as still there was no news from the university. At this time Udiyababaji also was very drawn toward Sri Ma. Both Mahatmas made her welcome in many ways. The few of us who were with Sri Ma had a very good time. We first went to Delhi and from there by train to Mathura and then to Vrindaban. At Delhi railway station all the women who had come to see her off could not bear to part from her and boarded the train, much to the confusion of the ticket-checkers, as well as their husbands who were left standing on the platform. Sri Ma laughed, thoroughly enjoying the few minutes of chaos. She sang a couplet from an old Bengali ballad, namely, "A bride-catching black crocodile has appeared in the Yamuna — he is taking away all the brides." (*boudhara aik ka lo kumbhira elo re jamunai* etc.) The menfolk searched their pockets and, pooling their resources, handed over this money to one of the women just as we steamed out of the station. I had heard about such events in Sri Ma's vicinity elsewhere, now I experienced the carefree jollity of the adventures. Everyone was gay and without a thought for the morrow. We *bonafide* travellers shared our saris, so everything worked out well.

Sri Ma, Haribabaji and another mahatma

Haribabaji Maharaj was very fond of one of the young villagers of Vrindaban. This was Manohar. He had a good voice and took a leading part in *kirtanas*. Otherwise, he was a bit wayward and caused Haribabaji a lot of trouble by his irresponsible ways. This time he was being very good. He had taken up regular work in the fields and had earned some money. He bought some cereals with his first pay and brought them to Sri Ma. He wanted Didi to cook a pot of Tahri (fried rice with vegetables) which Sri Ma would distribute to everyone.

When ready the pot of rice was brought to Ma. She started to distribute the *prasad* with a big spoon. As soon as people came to know that Sri Ma was giving *prasad*, they came running from all corners of the ashram. Sri Ma moved out on to a step. I picked up the pot and held it up for her. She had become very quiet and there was an ethereal look on her face. I sensed that something wonderful was happening with the pot of rice. It seemed to have an unending supply. It was not a big pot. I could easily hold it up in one hand. Other people also had the same thought — one person came up to peer inside the pot. I gestured to him not to do so and drew the pot away from him. More than 200 people must have received the *prasad* that day. Sri Ma stood with the spoon in her hand till the last person had come and gone. When she dropped the spoon in the pot, it was quite empty. I have always found the word "miracle" a misnomer, as far as Sri Ma was concerned. We saw no line of demarcation between the normal and what could be called the supra normal. Her understanding, her compassion made nought of human frailties — to ask was to be given a hundred fold; if one advanced one step, she came forward ten. She herself was the miracle. Her glance could create, metamorphose or establish bonds of allegiance with everyone. There was no "other" for her. What Manohar evinced that day (January 30, 1947) was one of many such incidents, but still it was in itself a thing of beauty and all-encompassing generosity.

From Vrindaban we returned to the Sangam at Allahabad. When Sri Ma went away to Varanasi this time I stayed back to see if I could do something about my enrolment. I went to see Professor A.C. Mukerji, who wrote a strong letter of recommendation, which the vice-chancellor endorsed and so a special case (not to be used as a precedent) was made out for me. Sri Ma's *kheyala* was fulfilled, I sat for the Examination and got through, just making first division. I had passed B.A. with some distinction and had obtained two scholarships, one for being in the merit list and Sri Ganganath Jha Fellowship for obtaining the highest marks in Sanskrit. I had taken the first month's scholarship money and had put it on Sri Ma's bed, explaining what it was. Sri Ma said, "Put the envelope inside the pillow case", which I did. Nobody else was in the room. I mention this small incident because it would have a sequel.

Chapter Ten

Summer Vacation at Kishenpur Ashram (1947)

The birthday celebrations of 1947

In May 1947, all the mahatmas were invited to this most important event in our ashram. The terrace extending in a round circle was newly constructed and a beautiful site fit for Sri Ma's decorated *chowki*. With the help of the boys from the Vidyapeeth and the girls from the Kanyapeeth Renu and myself made up festoons of garlands and greenery. Renu always had artistic ideas, which were carried out by us to the best of our ability. Swamiji was a source of help, supplying wire constructions or other oddments. For many years mainly Renu and her helpers did the decorations.

I take this opportunity to record an endearing comment made by Sri Ma on one such occasion. *Janmotsava* was again being celebrated in Varanasi, this time in 1956. Lots of changes had taken place during those years. Sri Ma had become well known all over India. The ashram was full of V.I.P. guests from all corners of India and beyond. The large compound of an as yet to be constructed hospital was the venue of this *utsava*. Sri Krishnananda Avadhutaji had taken upon himself the job of decorating the rostrum where *puja* would be performed. Panuda with his team of workers was in charge of the accommodation of guests.

One day, I happened to be walking with Sri Ma when she entered the *pandal* (marquee). I said, "How expertly the decorators are transforming the whole place. All these years, Renu and I were so

Summer Vacation at Kishenpur Ashram

inadequate with our amateurish efforts." Sri Ma looked at me and said, "The decorations that you did were much better!" I puzzled over these words for some time and came to the conclusion that our own efforts were more meaningful than the professional expertise of the outsider. Renu had worked with the girls of the Kanyapeeth. In time, Bishuddha came to be recognised as possessing great talent in this field. Later on, Guneeta and her contemporaries easily rose to a level of artistic display, which did not fall short of any professional standard.

All this, however, lay in the future. In 1947, we joyfully did our best. Although May is a hot month, we did not experience any great discomfort.

After the festivities of the *utsava*, Sri Ma travelled to Dehradun.

On the eve of our departure, Sri Ma sent for me and asked if I would undertake to teach a little girl, called Durga, some Hindi and a little bit of arithmetic and some general knowledge. Durga was the youngest of the girls in the Kanyapeeth at this time. Someone had rescued her as an infant from the riot-torn outskirts of Dhaka at the time of the partition of Bengal. She was an orphan; Didi had given her asylum in the Kanyapeeth. The trouble was that this child had the strangest predisposition to unbridled mischief. Nobody knew how to control such an imp. Kshamadi was very good for the girls, loving them as her own, and maintaining rules and regulations strictly but impartially and justly. She was well liked by the girls as well as all the inmates of the ashram. But Durga was beyond her powers of ministrations. She was consistently defiant, disobedient, non-co-operative, and unmindful of her lessons. Sri Ma now told me that the Rani of Kalakankar, who was a devotee of long standing, on listening to Didi's woes regarding Durga, had offered to take her away with her, provided the girl knew a little Hindi. So would I assume responsibility for this child for a month or so? I said I would, thus unknowingly embarking on a career of futility in child-education. Sri Ma smiled and said, "Well, Durga will be established on the Vedika (platform for the image of the Deity)". I was amazed that Sri Ma should recall that she had given this name to me almost 10 years ago. It was truly astonishing because even I only remembered when it was thus recalled to my memory.

The little goddess, however, was a free spirit. Kanti Kakima, who used to watch my efforts at teaching Durga, complimented me on my patience and perseverance. To complete the story of Durga: the Rani of Kalakankar took her away and must have tried her best to make a young lady out of her. Durga, however, came back to the Kanyapeeth after a while. The Rani Saheba had failed in her purpose. Strangely, one of the women who worked in the ashram took a liking to Durga. Didi, with a sigh of relief arranged a marriage for her with the only son of this woman and so Durga had a home at last.

In Kishenpur, I met Gini (Sujata Sen) again. We became inseparable companions as before. Gini and I were given the job of preparing the hall for the satsang every evening. Haribabaji was there with a large retinue and also many important people were staying in and around the ashram. Every evening Gini and I swept out the hall and adjacent verandas. We spread out the duree (cotton carpet) in the hall. Lastly we arranged the *asanas* for the mahatmas as well as Sri Ma who always sat against the jamb of the west door. Haribabaji's chowki to hold his book was placed in front and his *asana* behind it. Thus, Sri Ma was visible to the men sitting inside the hall as well as the women sitting in the verandah on the west side of it.

Flowers are abundant in Dehradun, especially during summer. The range of colours seemed unending. Finding some bluish-grey star-like flowers one day, it came to my mind that I would make a *satchakra* on Haribabaji's chowki. All other colours are easily available, so I arranged them in lotus shapes with the right number of petals in appropriate colours in proper order, depicting a serpent-like spinal cord ending in the white thousand-petal (in this case, just a large number) white lotus. Haribabaji was very pleased and said many nice things about it. Sri Ma was surprised that I knew the details of the *satchakra*. The same evening, she, in private, taught me a *kriya* involving the *chakras*. If we had all obeyed her instructions regarding these little ways of *yogic kriyas*, I am sure our lives would have taken on a different direction, but alas, the temptation to avoid discipline was always a force to be reckoned with where I was concerned.

Pandit Sundarlal of Vrindaban was a *Vaishnava*, impatient of any references to Advaita philosophy. He would challenge any speaker who talked about any subject beyond duality. Sometimes, Sri Ma had to intervene if the debate became too acrimonious. She always adopted a position which would be acceptable to both contenders.

It could be summarised thus: "The One is the 'many' or the 'two'. If it is said that the One *appears* as many then there arises a question of reality and that which is not real.

"Where is the scope of that which is not? Even to say that the One only is, is inadequate, because it indicates a distinction. Whatever is, is (*Ja ta*). All is He and He is all.

"What is He not and where is He not? Where the *lila* of duality is a hindrance in understanding (*badhaka*), know that it is a stage of the *sadhaka*. What the scriptures describe as the plenum of bliss is not a stage or state but it is what it is, on gaining which all is fulfilled at once!"

Pandit Sunderlal would demur at this resolution of the debate, more for the sake of arguing with Sri Ma than anything else. Once he said to her, "You do not pay any attention to what I am saying; you have glanced away from me to other people 10 times during my talk." Sri Ma smiled and said, "Pitaji, please continue, I shall be fully attentive!" When Pandit Sunderlal finished his discourse, Sri Ma said, "Pitaji, you have not been addressing me only; you have glanced away at others 117 times!" Everyone burst out laughing much to the discomfiture of the old man.

These scholars were pleased to read the scriptures or give discourses in Sri Ma's presence. She was the auditor *par excellence*. The audience at large was content to look upon her and glad of the opportunity to sit for many hours in her presence. At first, we used to be rather impatient whenever mahatmas came to the ashram. It entailed a lot of work, hours of boring (to most of us) satsang and the lessening of Sri Ma's attention on us. But gradually, we came to understand and appreciate what Sri Ma was doing. As Didi expressed her thoughts once, "May Ma's Pitajis live forever. They anchor her *kheyala* to this world — we are quite unworthy to do so!" The mahatmas in appearance or in reality were given over to the quest for truth, "the one and only duty worthy of man" as Sri Ma said so often. So it was just that they should come first in her attention, or rather that her *kheyala* should automatically be drawn to them.

Another change happened by imperceptibly slow degrees. Sri Ma would stay in one place for longer spans of time. Larger and larger numbers of people could come and have her *darshan* publicly in *satsang*. They could then communicate with her during question-and-answer sessions, the high point of *satsang*.

One day Sri Ma spoke a little on the off-repeated question: How is the realisation of the One only possible? She said, "Do you want to know about the significance of direct perception with regard to brahman-realisation (*brahma-jnana*)?... The plane or dimension of brahman-realisation is not where the triad of seeing, seer and the seen operates. I use the words 'plane' or 'dimension', but brahman or self-realisation is not a state. Where the question of action (any kind of doing) or non-action (abstaining from activity) does not arise, when there is neither a state nor a non-state, that is supreme-realisation.

"If the path of worship is followed, then for the *sadhaka* Name and Form are important. Even so, One-ness is achieved by seeing your own Ista (the Name/Form dear to you) everywhere; whoever you see, whatever you hear about is your own Adored one. The *sadhaka* sees his Ista everywhere and in everyone. This devotional attitude also leads to the realisation of the One only. Another *sadhaka* may proceed by way of knowledge. He asks, 'Who am I? Am I distinct from Thou? Or, Who is He? Is he distinct from myself?' The I is absorbed in the Thou or the Thou annihilates the I; it is One only — the Atma.

"It is difficult to understand; if one tries to understand (*bojha*)[1] then one crumbles under the load of words (*bojha*)! The thing to do

---

[1] Bojha in Begali means 1) understanding 2) load.

is to open the door and step out on to the path. Whether it is an approach from the position of duality, non-duality or duality-cum-non duality, is immaterial; keep walking. You will meet fellow wayfarers who will give help and guidance. From you nothing but effort is required. Revelation or realisation happens at its proper moment."

Question: "Why should I not simply wait for it to happen?"

Sri Ma, "Certainly, if you can! That itself should be *tapasya* (austerity) of a high order. I speak of making an effort because you are usually busy in the world, striving after practical things, therefore the will needs to be engaged on the path to self-realisation also. Is it not just convenient to become dependent on God's grace when it comes to effort toward self-enlightenment? If you are busy in the world, you should also devote some time and effort toward self-inquiry!"

During this summer vacation, we witnessed the miracle of Ramlal's recovery from a fatal illness. Ramlal was a small boy, very attached to his friend Sri Ma. He was visiting with his parents, Ranadeva and Lila Ghosh of New Delhi. One day, little Ramlal started running a temperature. Doctors were called in. Soon the fever became very high and would not respond to the best treatments of the day. The doctors said it was pneumonia and from their attitude the parents gathered that the child had no chance of recovery. Sri Ma was sitting in the *satsang*, while Haribabaji was reading aloud from a book. Liladi came to the west verandah and bowed down to Sri Ma, weeping helplessly. She kept on saying, "Ma, grant me Ramlal's life, Ma, grant me Ramlal's life." Liladi's heart-rending sobs brought tears to the eyes of the entire audience. Haribabaji was visibly moved. Only Sri Ma sat still like a statue, her serene expression quite undisturbed.

After a while Liladi, out of sheer exhaustion, quietened down. Haribabaji said that all of us should pray for Ramlal's recovery. He chose the special mantra from the *Durgasaptasati* 11.29 and had it written out on slips of paper and distributed to all the inmates of the ashram. An *akhanda japa* of this mantra was begun near the room of the patient. I think the crisis came a couple of days later. Sri Ma used to visit Ramlal's room very often, pointing out how best to look to his needs. Haribaba himself took part in the *akhanda japa*. On the night of the crisis, a pall of gloom descended on the entire ashram. The fever had a strangle-hold on the little boy; ice packs and other such remedies as were available in those days proved ineffective. We came to know later that under Sri Ma's instructions Didi had kept vigil in Ramlal's room during the dead of night. Following Sri Ma's privately-given directions, Didi had held the boy's heel with her left hand while doing *japa* of her own Ista mantra. Around pre-dawn Didi suddenly felt afraid, as if something dreadful was at hand — then she collected herself and settled into Sri Ma's *dhyana*. Next to the room, Gini and I were sleeping on the east verandah. Gini woke up at this time almost trembling with fear; then she told herself it must have been a nightmare. Next morning the fever broke.

By slow degrees Ramlal turned the corner and recovered after this night of crisis. We all believed that death had been averted by Sri Ma's *kheyala* alone.

Haribaba and his people

Sri Ma said to me one day, "Do you remember the money you put in my pillow case in Varanasi?"

"Yes", I said.

Sri Ma smiled and said, "Haribaba has agreed to sponsor the planting of a *panchavati* on the piece of land which was bought and donated to the ashram by Shachibabu. Didi was worried about how to make a clearing and clean up the area, knowing full well how Haribaba is keen on cleanliness and proper arrangements. Didi said that she should engage a team of labourers to clear the tangled undergrowth and make it possible for Haribaba to approach the land in reasonable comfort, but she had no ready cash for the purpose. Then I said to her, put your hand inside my pillowcase! Didi was happy to find sufficient cash for her purpose. So your scholarship has come in useful for the planting of the *panchavati* (grove of five specific trees)."

How kind of Sri Ma to have found such a use for it, and coincidentally, I happened to be right there at the time. Bindu used to tease me about this later, when both he and Babu were earning good salaries.

Summer Vacation at Kishenpur Ashram

He would say, "See, you gave your first earnings to Sri Ma and so you are always short of ready cash. Babu and I were clever enough to give our first salaries to our mother, so are now affluent and hope to improve day by day. Worldly affairs and spiritual grace do not mix well!"

On this visit, Haribabaji was quite alone to begin with and without his usual retinue, excepting for Ghanshyam, his personal attendant. We came to know that he had walked away from Baandh without informing anyone. He told Sri Ma that nobody there was serious in their quest for spiritual felicity. They just paid lip service to him. In any case, his dream of crossing the river of life (*bhavanadi*) holding hands with all his followers was unrealistic. On the spiritual path, one must travel alone.

Sri Ma made arrangements for his stay in the ashram. My sister used to cook for him and Paramanandaji served this food to him. One day Swamiji happened to pass by when Sri Ma was sitting in the kitchen directing my sister to arrange the food on the *thali* (plate). Swamiji remarked, "Do not take so much trouble. Your Baba is going to mix up all the items together before eating." Sri Ma was taken aback, "What? Even the chutney and sweet dish?" Swamiji nodded assent. So Sri Ma then said, "Let Baba do what he likes; we must arrange the food properly."

Some of the important villagers and landlords of Baandh came to Dehradun in search of their revered Haribabaji. They knew he would have gone to Sri Ma. They came to plead with him to return to Baandh. They told Sri Ma their side of the story. They said, "Baba does not understand that we try our best and yet fail to keep to his standards. We have work to do in the fields, at home and elsewhere. We sometimes miss the *satsang* or fall asleep. Baba is disappointed in us." They asked for Haribabaji's indulgence once more. He agreed to return. He invited Sri Ma to visit the village too.

After the summer months spent in Kishenpur, I returned to Allahabad for the new academic session 1947-48. Sri Ma asked me to enrol myself for the final examination. Bindu and Babu came with me. My father had been on his own for long stretches of time. This time my parents decided to put me in charge at 31 George Town. All our regular servants were there to look after us; there were other people in the servants' quarters, who were on call for any service in the house if necessary. I spent my time in the library upstairs. I was a very conscientious guardian to the two boys. But I think my own tendency toward quietude was not a very inspiring condition at home. I wish now that I had been more like my mother who was ever young at heart and ready to enter into all adventures as a companion. Even my sister would have provided a livelier atmosphere, but she was in the ashram in Varanasi. Babu was a quiet boy and very regular in his habits. He always had a fund of stories to relate about his school and friends. Bindu, however, was erratic. He spent much of his time away from the house in hectic activities all over the town.

Sri Ma continued in and around Allahabad throughout this year and the next few years. Whenever possible, the three of us would go to visit her at Jhunsi or Vindhyachala or Varanasi. At about this time, more than one foreigner, who later became inmates of the ashram, came from different parts of the world to be with Ma. The first was Henri Petit, a Frenchman who was attached to the Embassy of Ethiopia. We saw him in Jhunsi and also elsewhere since he travelled with Sri Ma's entourage. I came to know Blancaji quite well on one of our visits to Vindhyachala. Over the years, we became very close friends. It is one of the friendships that I value most highly. Colin Turnbull was staying in the ashram at Varanasi. Sri Ma called him Premananda. She treated him just like the other *brahmacharis*, sometimes visiting his room and showing him how to arrange his things more neatly and effectively. Jack Unger came from America and was put in Colin's room. In the ashram, all white-skinned people were put together; they did not see any difference between an American and a Scottish graduate from Oxford. Perhaps, it was good that Jack had Colin to guide him over the first hurdles of the Indian way of life.

Vijayanandaji (Dr. Weintrob) came quietly and as quietly merged into the background of Sri Ma's colourful following. He learnt Hindi very fast so that he could dispense with an interpreter. I came into contact with him because I very often translated for Sri Ma. I remember one incident in this connection, of which I am rather ashamed.

Summer Vacation at Kishenpur Ashram

Sri Ma came to Vindhyachala once with 6 or 7 foreigners. She wanted to give the visitors some respite from the chaotic conditions which prevailed in general near and around Sri Ma in the major Ashrams. The morning hours were spent in quiet meditation in Sri Ma's room. The first day Sri Ma sat on her *chowki* looking like a beautiful carved figure in ivory but palpitating with an inner radiance. I have yet to see another person who could be so still and yet so vibrant when sitting in meditation. The devotees from the other lands sat before her quietly. We closed the door and came out. Didi thought this was a good opportunity for her to snatch an hour's sleep. So, she lay down in the tiny lobby outside Sri Ma's room while I sat close by. Unfortunately Didi started to snore after a while. I shook her awake but then again she would go off and start to snore. It became an exercise in futility on my part. I breathed a sigh of relief when the time came to open Sri Ma's door and re-enter her room. The devotees looked happy; they did their *pranams* and left in their own orderly fashion to go to their own rooms. Sri Ma did not say a word to Didi, but to me she gave one of her "scoldings." Smiling all the while, she said, "How could you allow this to happen? How is one to meditate with this awful sound in the next room? I am reminded of the names that they called me in my childhood, *atela* (inattentive) *bedisha* (ineffective). Could you not be firm and keep Didi awake?" and more words to this effect, making it sound humorous rather than severe. Didi was very remorseful and apologised. I, of course, deserved all the epithets Sri Ma remembered to call me, but maybe the meditators had not been disturbed; after all, they had the opportunity to sit in the presence of Sri Ma and to gaze at her.

On 14th August 1947, Sri Ma happened to be in Varanaṣi. We all sat around her on the terrace of the ashram. We had decided to meditate during the midnight hour of the transference of power from the British to India. A colourful garland, made up of tiny national flags, was put on Sri Ma's lap. We prayed that the new nation might survive the innumerable problems that loomed ahead. It was not too joyful an event; the riotings, killings and uprooting of thousands of people marred the final achievement of independence.

Sri Ma passed through Allahabad many times. She once stayed in Krishna-Kunja just for the day. Only Swami Paramananda was with her. She sent word to me so I, very happily, went over and stayed with her the whole day. I remember it was hot. Sri Ma was resting on some simple matting on the floor. I sat close by wielding the hand fan. After some desultory conversation, she asked me what I had done on a specific date. I could not remember immediately, but by dint of association of ideas recalled that a visiting friend had taken Bindu and myself to the cinema.

Sri Ma asked me, "What was the cinema about?"

Surprised, I said, "You want me to tell you the story of the cinema?"

"Yes."

I then related to her the story of "Rage in Heaven". It was a story of a madman who appeared to be sane; he committed suicide, but so arranged the clues that his best friend would be arrested for his murder. It was an all-star cast, although, I now forget their names. Sri Ma listened to the story with close attention. Then she spoke to me about the futility of wasting time in a manner which could add nothing to my chosen way of life. I said immediately and rather unthinkingly, "Ma, I will not see films any more!"

Sri Ma seemed pleased. She must have had a *kheyala* about this because ever since that day, I have been totally free from all desire to go to the pictures; so much so that I lost interest in the doings of cinema stars, a fascinating pastime of my youth. Film magazines held no interest for me; cinema posters and hoardings left me quite indifferent. It was as if a slate had been wiped clean. It was not that I never saw a film again. Bindu first made me break my word to Sri Ma. While he was in service in Kanpur, he once came to Allahabad and took me to see "Jhanak Jhanak Payal Baje" a musical film of beautiful songs and dances. He said, "You must see this film even if you commit a sin by breaking your word to Ma!"

I had no sense of committing a sin, only some wrongdoing for which I hoped to be forgiven. Somehow I never felt any renewal of interest in films and continued to obey her advice in the spirit, if not

Summer Vacation at Kishenpur Ashram

in the letter. In later years, I saw "The Sound of Music", and also "Shatranja Ke Khilari".

This brings to my mind another piece of advice but one that I could not at all abide by. Somebody had reported to Sri Ma that I was fond of reading mystery novels. Sri Ma asked me about this and suggested that I should not be addicted to them. I was appalled. I said, "Ma, I am terribly fond of reading mystery novels and I am afraid I will not be able to give it up easily." Sri Ma dismissed the matter lightly and I breathed a sigh of relief. Evidently, she did not have a *kheyala* for eradicating this interest, because I continued to enjoy them and still do. I do not think she ever said anything to anyone, which could not be complied with easily.

As far as I can remember, it was during this time that Sri Ma went very often to Sarnath and stayed in one of the *dharamshalas*. She would talk to a few scholars who visited her specially to engage her in discussion. Dr. Pannalal and J.C. Mukherjee were there to interpret for Blancaji and Lewis Thompson. Sri Ma did not take any of her regular attendants with her. Gini who was staying in the ashram, and I were detailed to accompany her. We were to serve her the evening meal of milk and *roti* that we took with us. The Ashram girls also packed our meal for us. Babu and Bindu also came with us. These were marvellous evenings. The first night, Gini and I inexpertly made Sri Ma's bed on the open verandah and put up the mosquito net. The men were sleeping on the terrace a little way off. Sri Ma said to Babu, "Your brother (Bindu) used to sleep under my *chowki* — would you like to do the same?" Babu happily slipped under the *chowki*. Gini and I held a whispered consultation. Supposing Sri Ma got up during the night? There were no amenities like attached bathrooms in the *dharamshala*. We were required to go down a long verandah and staircase and then reach a set of washrooms. Sri Ma, unfortunately, could be given no special facilities. She would go down to them before retiring for the night. I got up the courage to say, "Ma, please wake us up if you get up during the night."

Before retiring, Gini would serve Sri Ma the *roti* and milk we had brought with us. I was always too nervous to render any such service to Sri Ma. Gini was not very much better, but she managed. We then lay down, I at the side of Sri Ma's cot and Gini at the foot of it. During the first night Sri Ma put her hand out of the mosquito net and touched my head lightly. I woke up with a tremendous start, which brought a smile to Sri Ma's face. I woke up Gini and both of us accompanied Sri Ma the long trek down to the washrooms.

Next morning Sri Ma described how I had started and laughed pleasantly — I was a bit embarrassed — perhaps I had been too tense. It never happened again. I learnt to come awake as soon as Sri Ma stirred on her bed. We used to go back to the ashram in Varanasi in the mornings and return again in the evenings. Dr. Pannalal allowed Bindu to drive his big car. Although he did not have a licence, being below age, he was even then a good driver.

Sri Ma and my hair

In Sarnath, we used to go on long walks with Sri Ma. Once, Sri Ma looking at my hair hanging down my back asked Bindu to measure its length. I was told to stand up straight. It was found that my hair reached just below my knees. Sri Ma said that she too had very long hair and at one time it used to get in her way when she would be assuming *asanas* (in Bajitpur). The hair would get entangled and got torn out by the roots but she had no sense of pain or discomfort.

There was of course no comparison between Sri Ma's soft smooth silken black tresses and my heavy mane of hair, which was the bane of my life. Since childhood I had a tremendous head of hair. My mother used to make 5 fat little plaits and pin them up on my head. Two squarish plaits could be made when the hair came down below the shoulders. It remained a cross to be borne by me. Washing my hair was a major operation[2]. As I grew up I could make one long plait but it took all my strength to accomplish this simplest of hairstyles.

After we had joined the University we went back for a college reunion at Crossthwaite Girls' College. Our Principal, Miss. C.R.

---

[2] In later years, in Canada, my hairdresser used to demand double payment for an ordinary shampoo!

Summer Vacation at Kishenpur Ashram

Pooviah talked to us pleasantly but found fault with our appearance. She said, "What is this?" You are looking like schoolgirls with your hair in plaits. At least you can put it up to look more like university students!"

Our group of six took this to heart and at our next joint meeting (which used to be either over ice cream at Guzder's or at the cinema), we decided to put up our hair in as many styles as we could contrive. I, of course, was no good at this, neither was Hem. Uma, Rajkumari and Vijay Lakshmi (Babni) set about arranging everyone's hair. Sumitra opted out, preferring her plait. I did not enjoy the cinema at all because I could hardly move my head and after a while the whole contraption came down scattering pins all over the laps of the people sitting behind us. In great embarrassment, I pulled the *pallava* of my sari over my hair hanging down my back. Raj Kumari was annoyed at the destruction of her work of art. She said nobody had any business to have such heavy hair.

Another incident comes to mind. In Agra, I was once chosen to enact the part of a king in the annual school drama. There were two scenes. One court scene and another in a garden where an assassination attempt was to be made. On the final night, our English Teacher Miss Bindre came to the dressing room to supervise the make-up etc. She was aghast to see my loose hair, that a senior girl was trying to pin up unsuccessfully. When the crown was put on my head, it somehow held in my hair, but without the crown it flopped down round my shoulders. Miss Bindre said in annoyance, "Well, you will have to wear the crown for the garden scene also. You will look very silly but it cannot be helped."

So this hair was one of the burdens of my life which Sri Ma lightened for me by various means. Once in Varanasi ashram, a group of us were propping up the walls as usual, or rather the railings in front of the upstairs room. Sri Ma said that since leaving East Bengal she had not seen any of the hair styles which were popular there. She beckoned me inside and asked me to sit with my back to her. I knelt down, while all the other girls crowded round us. That day Sri Ma demonstrated five or six different ways of plaiting the hair and arranging these around the head. One of them consisted of two intricately plaited paisley shapes facing away from each other at the back of the head. I of course, could not see anything, but heard the exclamations and gasps of wonderment at Sri Ma's skill in beautifying such unwieldy material. One style was called "palm leaf" I remember. Lastly, she made a hairdo that stayed up on my head much to my own amazement. I think it lasted two or three days before it had to be taken down for combing and brushing.

Another incident comes to mind. Once in Varanasi, Sri Ma was sitting out on the terrace to receive a very important sadhu Ma. As usual, we were standing around at a distance eagerly waiting for a glimpse of this lady, about whom we had heard many strange tales. She arrived with a few attendants; she was quite young and good-looking and had long beautiful hair falling over her shoulders and back. She and Sri Ma had some speech together. After a while, I thought Sri Ma was beckoning me to approach her. Hesitatingly, I went and knelt in front of her; she told me to perform some errand but added softly and very surprisingly, "Do not cover your hair with your *sari-pallava*." So, I very self-consciously walked down the terrace to perform Sri Ma's errand. All my friends assured me later that Sri Ma had only demonstrated how a greater profusion of hair may look — a tongue-in-cheek sense of humour which she indulged in on occasions.

There were numerous occasions when Sri Ma took special note of my hair. It remains a mystery to me to this day. Some time, during this period, I cut off a big shank of hair from the back of my head and made two long plaits, threading them with a silver ribbon. These were made out into straps for a pair of white satin sandals for Sri Ma. She could walk only five or six steps in these *chappals* because the hair-strap slipped out of its moorings. It was a silly idea to begin with. I was almost relieved when they gave way. As far as I remember, Sri Ma gave away the pair to Babydi who was standing near her at the time.

CHAPTER ELEVEN

Raipur and Solon Revisited

January 1948 saw the first Kumbha Mela after independence at Prayaga. Sri Ma came to the campsite of the *sangam*. Dr. Pannalal had made arrangements for her and a few of her party as well. Sri Ma did not stay anywhere at a stretch. The camp not being big enough to house local people, I stayed at home. My mother had come to Allahabad to stay with us during the final examination.

On 30th January, I was studying in the library upstairs when I heard my mother at the foot of the staircase. She called out to me, saying nervously, "The radio is relaying strange bulletins, I have switched it off!" I came down and switched it on again, and heard the terrible news of Mahatma Gandhi's assassination. Bindu came home after a while, bringing more details about it which he had got from other sources.

Next morning, we went to the camp and heard Sri Ma talking again and again about Gandhiji. The whole camp was plunged in gloom. We heard that Sri Ma had said, on the news being broken to her, "Just like Jesus Christ! Just as Jesus Christ had appropriated the violence of his people totally and so had forgiven them."[1] We all kept fast till the news announced that the funeral services were over. A chapter of the history of India ended with a needless tragic death.

I appeared at my final exams. I remember one rather endearing incident occurring at this time. Babu and I were sitting opposite each

---

[1] Sri Ma was referring to the exemplification of *ahimsa* only. She did not mean any other comparison.

other at my study table. I had made a pile of my notebooks for next day's paper along with about a dozen books. Babu was studying some school book. I realised that he had been watching me for some time. He asked suddenly, "What is the subject of your examination tomorrow?" Not knowing how to explain things to him, I said simply, "Immanuel Kant".

"Is it the name of a book or a man?"

"A man."

"Oh good! It is only a biography. Learn it by heart, Didi (elder sister)!" After a pause while he contemplated the books and files on the table, he said, "He must have had a very long life!" I said to myself, yes indeed, and a longer shadow dominating the western intellectual world to this day.

I had worked very hard for this examination. My choice of optional papers had been the unpopular combination of Morphology of Knowledge and Immanuel Kant. I also studied Neo-Vedanta with Professor A.C. Mukerji who was of course a marvellous teacher. I audited his entire course just for the pleasure of it. As far as I was concerned this was the only examination I had taken seriously. I wanted to stay home and sleep for a week. But, I remembered Sri Ma's words that I should consider myself an Ashramite, living at home only for the sake of the studies. After the *viva voce* examination, the last hurdle, I took leave of my mother and brothers and went away to the ashram at Varanasi. When the boys finished, they and my mother went to Etawah to be with my father.

Sri Ma seemed pleased to see me. After a few days we started on our travels. We went to Kishenpur. This time among others Didu (Chhabi Chowdhury) was with us. The older girls always took care of me so I was looked after very well by Didu. In those days I weighed considerably less than 100 lbs. and was suffering somewhat from the strain of the examination.

In Kishenpur life was quiet and Sri Ma available to us throughout the day. One day, I happened to be standing near the door of Sri Ma's room. I saw one of the local ladies had arrived with a basket of flower-ornaments. With great care, she was putting them on Sri Ma's wrists, upper arms, neck and head. I thought she was shedding tears of joy and devotion. Sri Ma looked very aloof; she continued to look beyond the door to the distant hills. Her limbs remained limp like those of a rag-doll. The thought came into my mind unbidden "How indifferent Ma is. Here is this poor woman pouring her heart out, but she is not paying the least heed!" No sooner had I thought this than I found Sri Ma's full gaze on my face. She had turned from the other door and was looking straight at me. She said, "She is not doing all this for me. Her little boy is ill. She wants me to make him well". I was ashamed of my thoughts. Sri Ma paused a while and then said, "You have a spare bottle of Horlicks haven't you? Give her the bottle for her boy."

I ran to my room to fetch the bottle of Horlicks. It never occurred to me to wonder as to how Sri Ma knew about my stock of Horlicks. Nobody else did. My mother had packed in a couple of them knowing my habit of going hungry rather than make arrangements for some nourishing food. In the after-years of the war, such foreign commodities had become very rare. Neither did I wonder about Sri Ma's reaction to my unspoken thoughts. That she could see into our minds and thoughts we took for granted.

After a few days, Sri Ma told Didi that she would go to Raipur and Didu, Bhupen and myself could accompany her provided we could get ready in ten minutes. Didi Gurupriya asked if food should be taken along because at Raipur we would not be able to cook anything at such short notice. Sri Ma said quite nonchalantly, "All those who need to eat the evening meal need not come with me but stay back here". Didu and I hastily rejoined that we would not require anything.

We arrived in Raipur in the evening. There were only three inmates — Swami Shashwatanandaji, Bishu Maharaj and another ascetic. There was as yet no electricity — but the ashram was very big and sprawling now. I had seen it in the summer vacation of 1941. Renu of course had been here with my cousin who passed away in 1942. I now looked at the set of rooms that Renu had described so vividly and where Sejdi (Kawna) had breathed her last. I was overcome by a terrible feeling of desolation.

Just as Renu and Sidu had formed a natural pair, I was a close companion of my brilliant cousin Kawna who was just two years older than me. I went around Sri Ma's room and sat on a rock to be alone with my thoughts. To my great surprise I suddenly found Sri Ma standing in front of me with her hand held out with something (probably dried fruits) in it. I put both of my hands together to take it, so that it would not spill over. Sri Ma clasped my joined palms in both her hands and looked steadily at me for a few moments. I at once knew that she knew. It was a beautiful moment. The upsurge of tears vanished completely. I was quietly happy and at peace. By this time there were other people behind Sri Ma, but nobody had noticed anything unusual. Even Didi did not think that I could be remembering my cousin's death, only Sri Ma remembered, knew and was with me in my sorrow. Who can gauge this compassion which encompasses us forever and ever.

Sri Ma strolled on the wide terrace. We stood at a distance and watched entranced the beauty and majesty of her gait and movements. The village women flocked to her side. They were well known to her. Amongst them was the woman who had cut off Sri Ma's matted locks when she had come to live at Raipur in 1932. The woman had close-cropped the hair, lifting the *jata* (matted hair) like a crown off the head. These women eddied around Sri Ma exchanging reminiscences. After a while, we saw one woman arrive with a big receptacle in her hands. This turned out to be *parathas* (pancakes) and vegetables for all of us. Didi was happy to receive this food and immediately took out a little of it for Sri Ma. Sri Ma beckoned me forward and told me how to make individual servings in the leaf bowls (*donas*) for Didu, Bhupen, Kamalda, myself and one or two others. The food was just sufficient. We ate standing around and then washed our hands. The leafy *thalis* (plates) and bowls were disposable. In ten minutes or so everything was as before.

Sri Ma said with a laugh, "See how simple it all was! Left to Didi we would still be waiting for a dinner being elaborately cooked by her; then we would have had to clean the utensils etc. etc.! This is a place for ascetics. It is good to be *karapatris* (ascetics who just eat only what can be held in one hand only)." Only then did we realise that Sri Ma herself had sent word to the village to prepare this simple dish for us, so actually we had good food and did not have to work for it!

Next, we came to know that Sri Ma would be going to Solon. The Rani Saheba of Solon had passed away about a month and a half earlier. Yogibhai, being in mourning, would not be able to leave his state for one year, otherwise, perhaps, he would have come to Sri Ma. Sri Ma herself saw to the packing of our luggage. Didu and I were to take just one bed-roll between the two of us containing blankets and sheets for both. Bhupen and Kamalda were also directed to take small packs. Poor Didi was in difficulty. She generally carried Sri Ma's entire effects along with her own because of the uncertain nature of Sri Ma's movements. The utensils for cooking, a big bag of letters, her own writing equipment, Sri Ma's simple clothes and bedding, a black fitted box containing a variety of ayurvedic medicines, prepared carefully for Sri Ma, and a great many other things she thought may come in useful at odd moments. Sri Ma did not, as a rule, supervise Didi's accumulation of baggage, but now she sat in her room directing Didi to discard 90% of all this paraphernalia. Didi's beloved "black box" became the first casualty. Sri Ma so simplified the entire packing that when we started on our journey just two porters were able to carry the entire baggage belonging to 6 people — Sri Ma, Didi, Kamalda, Bhupen, Didu and myself. It must be borne in mind that Didi preferred to take sufficient utensils and foodstuffs for Sri Ma, so that she could cook and offer *bhoga* to her, without waiting to be given anything or being obliged to ask for anything from people who came to have *darshan*. Apart from fruit and milk, no foodstuffs were bought from shops for Sri Ma. Didi never made any fuss about Sri Ma's meals. It was done very quietly and unobtrusively.

Dehradun and Solon are on different mountain ranges. We travelled down to Moradabad. Changing railway lines at Moradabad we went up again to Kalka and then by the smaller gauge on to Solon. Sri Ma had not let anyone inform Yogibhai of her visit. Now, coming out of the railway station, we slowly walked up the gentle incline of the road to the palace. I recalled Sri Ma's earlier visits when she had been received with elaborate arrangements sponsored by a high-powered reception committee. An atmosphere of jubilation had pervaded the entire market place. Now nobody took any notice of us. Sri Ma had come on a visit of condolence, so she was keeping a very low profile. Her behaviour was always so correct even in such matters that one marvelled at her understanding of worldly norms.

The Raja Saheb's personal attendant Rupram happened to be coming down the road; he halted in amazement when he saw Sri Ma. He could hardly believe his eyes. After making his *pranam*, he ran to a roadside shop and rang up the palace. Within a few minutes a big car came down from the hilltop and all of us climbed in. In another few minutes the car drew up in front of the palace gates. It was our time to be shocked. Yogibhai was standing in front of the gates. He was dressed simply in a long silk *kurta* (shirt-like garment) and *dhoti*. His head was uncovered and his feet bare. We had never before seen him in such informal attire. Sri Ma advanced toward him while we kept in the background. Yogibhai did his *pranam* and asked why she had not announced her coming etc. Deviram Bhai and others then escorted Sri Ma to her own cottage just below the palace grounds. After some time, Yogibhai came and sat in her room and talked to her for a long while. For the next two or three days, he was seen to spend as much time as he could spare from his other duties in Sri Ma's room. None of us disturbed him while he was there. Even Didi stayed in her own room, so that he could talk with Sri Ma alone.

After three or four days, when we were sitting together before retiring to bed, Sri Ma herself told us, "He has been talking about his wife all these days. Now, I think his reminiscences and memories are all exhausted and his heart is emptied of the burden of grief for the time being. It is time for me now to insert my word into this vacuum. He has talked himself out — now he will listen to me!"

For the rest of her stay Sri Ma talked to him for many long hours. Soon after the Rani Saheba's death, the annexation of the many kingdoms and principalities of India had taken place. This was an added tragedy. Devirambhai, Ramsinghji and Ruparam related to us how Yogibhai had been completely indifferent to this outrage. He was just thankful that the Rani Saheba had passed away before the orders for annexation had been received. The Rani Saheba was the sister of the reigning prince of Tehri Garhwal, a much bigger state. She was very mindful of the dignities of royalty and we had seen that during her lifetime, all proper observances had been carried out with due care. We saw the changes that were already visible in this household. Yogibhai's people related the story of the Government takeover. They had heard stories of the looting of other treasuries and tried to persuade Yogibhai to have his own treasures and valuables removed to safer places, but he was not interested. He said, "Let them take whatever they want." His entourage, on their own initiative, had removed his special personal belongings to other places before the take-over party came to Solon. The officers, it was rumoured, misappropriated the treasures of the various states which they came to annex for the Government of India. Ruparam said events turned out as predicted and that the rumours were true. It was more like a raiding party than a Government manoeuvre for the greater good of the people. Yogibhai proved himself to be as truly an ascetic in reality as he was in name.

I received the result of my M.A. Examination while I was in Solon. I had passed in the 2nd Division. This was truly a traumatic experience for me. I had made an effort this time. All the other examinations that I had passed in 1st Division with honours and scholarships had not been taken too seriously by me. Sri Ma said some words of consolation.

From Solon, we came down to the plains again, to climb up a third mountain range, this time to Nainital. Dr. Pannalal had invited Sri Ma to visit his home in Nainital. We were the same small party. Dr. Pannalal's eldest daughter Lila and her husband Rameshwar Sahai were in Nainital at this time. We were accommodated in their house. Didi and Sri Ma had a big tent in the compound. The weather was mild, the surroundings beautiful. Sri Ma had visitors even in this remote retreat. One day a man dressed as a yogi came to visit her. He sat quietly, not asking any questions but his very sad and defeated countenance drew everyone's attention to him. Sri Ma herself engaged him in conversation and elicited the story of his life. He and five other friends had left home 15 years ago to follow the path of asceticism. They had practised rigorous *sadhana* for many years but gradually the group had dwindled. Two of his friends had gone back to their villages, two others had fallen victim to severe illness, one had died. He alone remained on the path, more or less as a habit rather than with hope of any achievement in the future. Sri Ma asked him if he would like to talk to her about his sadhana in private. He seemed not to be interested. But Dr. Pannalal sensing Sri Ma's *kheyala* for him, immediately arranged for a private interview. All of us came away leaving them together. After an hour or so, this man was seen to emerge from Sri Ma's tent, his manner completely changed. He looked a different person. He bowed to Dr. Pannalal, saying he had received inspiration for his ongoing *sadhana*. On being questioned later Sri Ma said to the small group of people round her, that she had gone into the details of his *sadhana*. She had pointed out the many mistakes the group had committed which had led to illness. She said "The body is a finely tuned instrument, these yogic paths are dangerous unless one is guided by a competent teacher. Yoga as *sadhana* is different from yogic exercises. One performs exercises, but in *sadhana*, the yogic states happen automatically at their proper time. There is no need to strive for these attainments."

1948 was the first year after independence. One of our noted leaders, a great scholar and a lady of remarkable achievements, Mrs. Sarojini Naidu, had been appointed the first Indian Governor of our province. She was in her summer residence in Nainital at this time. The British had ruled India in style. The Governor's house in Nainital was a spectacular estate. Dr. Pannalal, who was well known to the Governor, received an invitation for Sri Ma to visit her at the Governor's residence. Mrs. Naidu wrote that she would have come herself but she was in bad health and could not undertake the journey. She would be grateful if Sri Ma kindly came to her to give *darshan*.

This letter raised a controversy. One group of people said it was very high-handed on the part of the Governor to ask Sri Ma to go to her. The other group maintained, that Sri Ma did visit ordinary people at their invitation, so why should Mrs. Naidu be deprived of her *darsana* just because she happened to be the Governor! In the end, Dr. Pannalal accepted this invitation on Sri Ma's behalf. On the appointed day about a dozen *dandees* arrived from Government House. The *dandees* looked very elegant and were carried by smartly liveried coolies. It was quite a distance up and down hills from the Priory (Dr. Pannalal's residence).

We arrived at Government House. My first impression was of wide stretches of green lawns edged with colourful flowerbeds. Under a marquee in the centre of one of the lawns, there was a slightly raised platform, which was covered with a magnificent tiger-skin. The Governor was sitting in front of it to receive Sri Ma. Sri Ma went up to her and spoke in Bengali, *"Hari kathai katha aur sab vrtha vyatha, ki balo ma? Tomar bangla bhasa mone achhe?"* (To talk of God alone is worth while, all else is in vain and pain, isn't it so? Do you remember Bengali?) The Governor held her hands for a while, she inclined her head and said that she understood very well but could not speak the language (Bengali) fluently any more, being out of practice for so long. Sri Ma sat on the tiger skin looking regal and radiant. The various officials stood about in formal attitudes. I walked around the group to a quiet spot behind the Governor's chair and sat on the grass, disliking the idea of standing around for any length of time. Mrs. Sahai, Didi and Didu and the others stood behind Sri Ma's seat. Dr. Pannalal tried to initiate a conversation between Mrs. Naidu and Sri Ma. After some desultory talk, he began to describe the gardens of the Governor's house. Mrs. Naidu added that the zoological menagerie was worth seeing, so if Sri Ma wanted she could walk around to see a "bird of paradise", a much-appreciated denizen of the forest.

Sri Ma got up and walked away, surrounded by her entourage and many of the officials. After a while, I realised that only the Governor and I were sitting and everyone else was standing about. As I was almost hidden behind the high backed chair, I stayed where I was. Mrs. Naidu's younger daughter, Miss Lila Naidu (I recognised her from her newspapers photographs), approached her mother and asked her in some wonder, "Who is she? How is it that Pannalal of all people is in attendance on her?"

Mrs. Naidu gave a short account of Sri Ma. Her language, as usual, was elegant and expressive; she had just seen Sri Ma for a very short while, but these few minutes seemed to have sufficed for her. I write from memory the words she spoke about Sri Ma. They may not be accurate and certainly were spoken in better English, but the meaning is correct, I think:

"She is the quintessence of the spirit of India. She is the tuning fork, the touchstone, the ultimate criterion for distinguishing between what is our tradition and what is not. She is just perfect as she is. It is only possible in India to experience perfection personified."

Sri Ma and her party returned after a while. Farewells were spoken and we came away after some refreshments were served.

From Nainital, we proceeded to Almora by car. Sri Ma halted at the sanatorium in Bhowali to visit her youngest sister who was an inmate at this time. This sanatorium was well known to her because in earlier years she had come here to visit Kamla Nehru more than once. The ashram at Almora was beautiful. The Vidyapeeth was housed here under the charge of Saileshada. We met the other teachers Mrnmayda and Swarupbhai. I do not remember Panuda, who must have come immediately after this visit or may have been away at the time.

One day, the *swamijis* from the Ramakrishna ashram came to have lunch at our ashram by invitation. Didi cooked an elaborate meal. The big room was turned into a dining hall. Sri Ma's *asana* was placed at a little distance in front of the *asanas* laid down for the *swamijis*. When the *sadhus* sat down to their meal, Sri Ma also sat in her place, while Didi waited with the bowl of rice for serving which would mark the beginning of the feast. All the other dishes were already arranged beforehand as is the custom with us. The *sadhus* looked at Didi and said, "But how is this? We must have a little *prasada* before we begin!" What they meant was that Sri Ma should begin

Raipur and Solon Revisited

first. Didi did not know what to do. She could not feed Sri Ma and serve the *sadhus* at the same time. Sri Ma beckoned to me to come and sit beside her. She gestured to me to serve her the food, that is, feed her. I was taken aback. I had never done this *seva* before. My hands were not even washed but Sri Ma gave me no time to feel nervous or inadequate! She said, "Quick, quick, a little of the rice!" I somehow made a rice-ball with some vegetable and put it in her mouth. Didi then took some rice and vegetables from her plate and served morsels of this to the *swamijis*. When they began their meal Didi wanted to come back and take her place near Sri Ma to feed her, but she was prevented from doing so. Sri Ma went on giving directions to Didi about looking after the requirement of the guests. I continued to feed Sri Ma. There is a ritual about Bengali cuisine; a method of procedure obtains regarding different items of food. All such rules became hazy in my mind. I do not know what I did with all the artistically displayed dishes arranged in front of Ma. Ma herself in her infinite compassion for the unworthy never glanced down at her plate or at me. She just swallowed whatever I put in her mouth. She had a good meal probably because Didi was glancing at us from time to time. Had she not, I would have been justifiably blamed for being clumsy or inept. Ma's kindness in accepting the food that day I alone could appreciate fully.

After the very pleasant sojourns in Nainital and Almora we descended to the raging heat of New Delhi. Sri Ma's Birthday Celebrations were held in Dr. J.K. Sen's house. The festivities went ahead in spite of the gruelling weather. Sri Ma sat for hours in the *satsang pandal*. The mahatmas who had come to attend the function did likewise.

We were in the habit of keeping a total fast on the eve of Sri Ma's Birthday. The *puja* takes place at pre-dawn. By the time the entire congregation exercises its privilege of touching Sri Ma's feet or the *chowki* on which she is lying in *samadhi*, it is mid-morning of the next day. As usual I kept a fast. By evening I was in a state of near-collapse because of the heat I think. I was sitting in a chair in the front room, telling myself that I should get up and help with the work of arranging for the *puja*: suddenly, I found myself being propped up by Udasji. She was holding some receptacle at my lips and urging me to drink immediately. I found it was lemon-water with sugar. I tried to protest saying I could not as I was fasting. She said, "No, No, Ma has sent this for you, you are to drink the whole lot." After she had carried out Sri Ma's instructions, she vanished as suddenly as she had come. To this day, I do not know how she located me in the busy household, because I had not been near Sri Ma for a long time. Nobody else noticed anything, but evidently Sri Ma's *kheyala* had been on me and she prevented me from disgracing myself completely by my foolish attempt at *tapasya* when I was not in good health. Thereafter, I was able to take part in the celebration normally.

A *nama-yajna* was celebrated as part of the festivities. On its eve Sri Ma asked Bindu and myself to procure two hand-sprayers such as are used on the occasion of *Holi* in March. She asked somebody else to procure blocks of ice. Next day around noon, when the *kirtan* was crowded and everybody was feeling the heat, Sri Ma sprinkled them with cold, rose-scented water much to their relief and enjoyment. Even the heat became bearable.

After all the functions were over, Sri Ma travelled back to Nainital again. She called me to her one day and said, "I 'saw' your father in a very unhappy and angry mood [because I had come away to the ashram without seeing him first]. Go back home now. Come back when it is more convenient and he is more reconciled to the idea." I went home to Mainpuri with Bindu. He and my sister had joined us in New Delhi for the celebrations. Bindu went back to be with Sri Ma during the rest of the vacation.

My father was very pleased that Sri Ma had sent me back to be with him at this time. He was 55 years old and was to retire on July 13, 1948. This was a major transition in his life. We began the work of dismantling our establishment. He had taught me how to pack glassware and delicate ornaments. We worked together much of the time. In those days, there were no professional packers and removers. One had to do all the household packing personally. Servants helped with the big items and with the nailing and binding of crates. I remember one interesting incident, which happened at Mainpuri. One day my father sent for me to come outside where he was sitting with a visitor, who was introduced to me by name, which I now forget. The visitor was a tall, handsome young man dressed impeccably in a white silk *kurta* with the traditional gold chain-buttons and white *dhoti*. Some refreshments were served and then he took his departure, touching my father's feet very respectfully. My father seemed amused. He said, "This young man is the son of the most famous dacoit who had ruled unopposed in this area for a very long time [Mainpuri/Etawah are districts where dacoits hold sway even in these days]. His father was the client of your uncle. Now that he knows I am his father's lawyer's brother, he has come to pay his respects to me."

I was aghast. "Is he a bandit chief?"

"No, no, not now. They are landlords (*zamindars*) but the aura of undisputed power comes naturally to them."

"How did they meet my uncle? And why could not the police arrest them when they came to the town openly?"

"They did not come to the town openly. Your uncle would come to Etawah and put up at the P.W.D. Inspection House. As you see, during summer, we all sleep outside in the open. At dead of night, the dacoits would come in on horseback and stop near his bed to consult with him about their cases. Then they would as quietly slip away to their village hideaways. The *chowkidar* (caretaker) evidently did not dare to raise any alarm." — an interesting dimension of the lawyer's business. In those days, there were no boundary walls, or barbed wire round Government Houses. The Judge's House in Mainpuri was situated amidst rolling green fields, which belonged to the neighbouring villages. We slept out under the skies with no fear of anything untoward taking place during the night apart from a sudden shower or a thunderstorm.

My father handed over charge on July 13 to his successor. He kept his equanimity and did not seem to be experiencing any kind of mental stress. I was inexperienced and did not understand the finality of retirement from a long service and a way of life. In later years, I appreciated my father's quiet changeover from the status of a 1st officer of the District to the position of a private citizen. He had a big Chevrolet car with a canvas top and red wheels. Babu had many friends in the villages and felt a bit sad when they came and stood around the car. My parents, Babu and I got in. Farewells were spoken and Ibrahim, our driver, set off in style. I think we spent three days on the road, because we drove very slowly.

We arrived at 31 George Town on July 16, I think. The house had been shut down. Now, we opened it up and my father started on a new routine in his daily life. The gardens were extensive. He and the gardener Jagdeo started on the task of making something out of it. Bindu was in college and Babu in school. After my parents had settled in, I again left for Varanasi because Sri Ma was there.

My parents

CHAPTER TWELVE

One Year of my Life as an Ashramite

Durga Puja in Calcutta (1948)

Sri Ma was invited to visit Bishtupur (district Birbhum) in Bengal by a zamindar, Ram Bahu, before the Durga Puja, which would be performed in Calcutta. Sri Ma allowed me to accompany her small party. I had not previously seen the interior of Bengal. The celebrated scenic beauty of Birbhum district was exactly as we had read in books and heard in songs. The lyric *"gram chhara oi ranga matir patha"* (My heart remembers the red lane meandering away from the village etc) came vividly to mind while we approached our destination. The red track led us along wide stretches of water, which looked almost black, where they reflected the surrounding dark blue hills rising on all sides. The immense lakes were profuse with white and pink lotuses. I almost fell off my carriage when I saw the wealth of lotuses so near at hand. The carriage driver was amused at my excitement. He stopped and waded into the lake to pluck an armful of the glorious flowers for me. Bunidi scolded me for getting us all wet but we now had flowers worthy of being placed at Sri Ma's feet. Sri Ma also was a little amused to see my excitement with the flowers and scenery. One other person who was bewitched by the scenery was Maunima. The zamindar took Sri Ma and all of us to visit the ruins of ancient temples situated within the heart of the *sal* forest. The dark and sombre *sal* trees rising to immense heights seemed to provide a fitting background to the ruins. The temples must have been beautiful and on a grand scale in their time. Sri Ma took a keen interest in their architecture. We heard with interest Ram Babu's description of the bygone history of the place. Birbhum was Swami Paramanandaji's district. He was pleased to find us so fascinated by the beauty, hospitality and quality of food of this district.

Maunima was so enamoured of these outskirts of the town that she told Sri Ma that she would like to remain there for the rest of her life. Sri Ma at once endorsed her views, suggesting various practical ways and means whereby Maunima could be made comfortable in one of the many guest houses surrounding a lake in the village where we ourselves were putting up for the time being. I listened to this conversation with some scepticism. It was well known that Maunima could never stay anywhere for more than a few days. She often travelled with Sri Ma and soon selected her place of residence. Sri Ma always made elaborate arrangements for her comfort and security every time she showed a preference to stay behind in a garden room or safe place. But lo and behold! Maunima was back in Sri Ma's entourage within a few days, having met with some insurmountable difficulty at her place of stay.

Listening to Sri Ma's enthusiastic endorsement of Maunima's resolve, I felt a little uneasy at the exercise in unreality, as it were. I approached Didi and said, "Does Sri Ma deal with us also in this fashion? How are we ever to know if she is not indulging our passing whims? How are we to distinguish her own *kheyala* from this acquiescence to our desires?" Didi had no doubt, and replied in robust tones, "Ma never deals with us like this. You will know what is her *kheyala* or what is not when the occasion arises!"

Didi was very positive but my doubts remained undispelled because I had never seen Sri Ma apply double standards at any time. If one could transform the mind into a crystal wherein Sri Ma's *kheyala* would be reflected without being flawed, then perhaps one would know for sure, but that in itself is an impossibility!

Incidentally, it may be recorded here that the very next day after this conversation with Ma, Maunima said sadly, "Ma, everything is very beautiful but the mosquitoes are intolerable!" And so once again she came away with us.

One Year of my Life as an Ashramite

Durga Pūja this year took place in Calcutta. This was my first real encounter with crowds in Calcutta. The sheer overpowering press of people, their totally unreasonable demands regarding free access to Sri Ma's rooms at all hours was a nerve-racking experience. Sri Ma hardly had time to take rest, spare a few minutes for light refreshments or even just to drink a glass of water! It was incredible. It was not that they were impelled by devotion; the true devotees got shoved to the back and watched helplessly as pandemonium swirled round Sri Ma. Incredibly, she always remained the same, serenely managing to exchange a few words with those closest to her, smiling at those who stood at the back of the crowd, and acknowledging the presence of those who were too timid to push themselves forward. Amidst the seething press of humanity she was as undisturbed as if alone and in peaceful surroundings, as in Nainital or Solon. Bunidi made herculean efforts to guard her door; as a result she came in for much abuse. Some women even pulled her hair — amazing violence when one considered the context in which this occurred. On many such occasions Sri Ma would head straight into the melee and make her way to the hall and sit there for a while, till everybody had quietened down and were pleased to have had their way. I tried a few times to help Bunidi and others, but I was no match for these aggressive women who apparently believed it their right to approach Sri Ma come what may whenever they came for *darshan*. We heard them mutter, "Sri Ma is all right and kindness itself. It is these girls who want to keep Ma away from ordinary folk like us!" Another allegation was that Sri Ma was for the rich and important people only. Nothing could be further from the truth. If they only knew the kind of talk that went on in Sri Ma's room and the problems she dealt with, they would know that richness and worldly importance played no part in Sri Ma's granting of her grace (*kripa*). But the rich were not excluded either. I have not known any rich or important person to take Sri Ma for granted in any way whatsoever. They approached her with as much homage and adoration as the humblest of her retinue. I have not known anyone, not even Prime Ministers, or Ambassadors, or business magnates to look upon her countenance with any degree of familiarity or presumption of acceptance as a matter of course. It needed Sri Ma's look of kindliness or a friendly smile to dissipate the initial diffidence with which everyone approached her. It is true however, that there was a lack of discipline and organisation near Sri Ma. Sri Ma was never disturbed by the chaos all around her. Much later, I heard from Didi that they had met with ideal disciplined crowds in South India. Sri Ma went on a tour of the South in 1952. Didi said she wished the people of Calcutta could come and see a crowd of 10,000 sitting quietly waiting for Sri Ma. Moreover, they did not break ranks to rush to her as soon as she appeared. It was not that they were less devoted. In Madurai she was looked upon as Meenakshi Devi, the presiding Deity of the town and so it was to be all along the route. But in Calcutta and Dhaka they behaved like "brats" with their indulgent mother. Perhaps, they thought it was their privilege! Having known her when she was unknown, they wanted to demonstrate their superiority over crowds in other towns.

During the three days of the Durga Puja, I was away from the ashram and its unmanageable crowds. I was busy in the *Puja-pandal* working with the ashram people, where Kusumda (Nirvanandaji) and I were in charge of the *naivedya* room. My sister was in the shed where the cooking for the *puja* was being done. Sri Ma used to come and give suggestions and guidance wherever needed. The park where the *puja pandal* had been put up was soaking wet and muddy under foot. Sri Ma asked us to carpet the whole floor with banana leaves to lessen the discomfort of working under such conditions.

Cooking on such occasions was done on a large scale, so that hundreds of devotees could have *prasad* after *puja*. The cooking pot or *kadhai* was of an immense size and there were about 100 kgs. of vegetables in it. When it was bubbling and ready my sister did not know how to take it off the fire, which was a veritable gigantic grate. She came to ask Sri Ma, who accompanied her back to the kitchen. Sri Ma stood with her right hand touching my sister's shoulder, teaching her how to empty the big cauldron little by little into smaller vessels, how to pull away the logs so that the fire would simmer down gradually and many other manoeuvres which were commensurate with such large scale cooking operations. In time, my sister became an adept.

I am sure it was a grand function and a rewarding experience for many but I had a feeling of tiredness and exhaustion all the time. On the last evening, returning to the ashram, I tried to find a quiet corner for myself. I ended up in Sri Ma's kitchen and lay down in one corner and fell asleep. After a while, I heard Bunidi's voice whispering, " Get up, Ma is here!" I opened my eyes to see Sri Ma's feet and also Bunidi's. Bunidi had evidently persuaded Sri Ma to come in for a minute so that she could be served with a glass of lemon-water, before she went back to the crowds for unpredictable lengths of time. Bunidi always took care of Sri Ma in these little ways. I was too spent to muster up energy to rise to my feet and was glad to hear Sri Ma whisper back, "Let her be, let her be!"

It was during this *puja* festival that we met Sri Ma's elder sister-in-law Pramoda Devi. We knew that she was a V.I.P. guest who had been billeted in the hall with us but discovered her identity only when Sri Ma came to her bedside one late night and began a conversation with her in a village dialect not understood by us. Those of us who had not gone to bed gathered round them. The hall was now empty of local people. I could imagine that Pramoda Devi must have been feeling a little lost in the mammoth crowd of devotees. She had only caught glimpses of Sri Ma as she had passed though the hall on a few occasions. Sri Ma now sat on her bed. She held her (Pramoda's) hands with both of hers. She reminded her of many incidents and many experiences of Narundi, Sripur, Atpara etc. Pramoda Devi, taken aback a little at first, soon regained her poise. She seemed to recognise in the august personality of these days, the young Nirmala who had served her so well. Sri Ma translated the dialect for us. Her narration of many incidents was funny in the extreme and evoked hilarious laughter. This brought in other women who were sleeping in other rooms. We became quite a crowd. In answer to a question, Pramoda Devi spoke words of loving praise for her young sister-in-law. She said very gravely, "Such *sevabhava* (spirit of service) is not possible in any other person. In all the years that she was with me I never had occasion to find any fault with her."

I do not know about other auditors to this testimony but I was astonished by Sri Ma's look of gratitude. She looked a little embarrassed but highly pleased that Pramoda Devi spoke such words of praise for her services. She had not taken for granted that her behaviour would be perfect, nor was there any pretence or make believe in her role of a young bride in the house of her eldest brother-in-law. I was surprised by this look of gratitude on other occasions also. Sometimes at the request of some older devotees she sang songs which she had learnt in her childhood. If anybody spoke admiringly of her voice and singing Sri Ma would be as gratified as a child who is trying to please its elders. To me as to many others, Sri Ma's singing was an enthralling experience. We would sit bemused but it did not occur to us to speak words of praise to Sri Ma. However, I have heard Bunidi and Chhabi Banerjee and one or two others speak admiringly and say how beautiful the singing had been. Sri Ma would say, "Yes, yes, go on. You must encourage this little child, what else!" or similar words. I used to be surprised at this *lila*. Sri Ma's deportment as a housewife had been perfection itself, so was her singing, so was her behaviour with ordinary folk, old and young, scholars, politicians, musicians, in fact anybody and everybody. To say as much to her seemed to border on the inane. This phenomenon, however, gave me an understanding of the religious hymns (*stotras*) which are spoken in praise of different deities. I always used to wonder, why does God need all this flattery. The extolling of His auspicious qualities, magnificence, His compassion, it all seemed like stating the obvious. Does God need man to say all this to Him? Apparently He does, because He takes nothing for granted. He waits for man to turn to Him out of his own free will and so welcomes words of adoration. So spoken adoration, although sounding silly at times did perhaps have an important place in *sadhana* !

During this sojourn in Calcutta, one day Sri Ma found time to scold me for non-observance of orthodoxy in matters of food habits. Actually what she said was, "Does it never occur to you that you should follow the orthodox system?" Very reluctantly, I gave up my freedom to sit with my friends and eat in public. This stage of my life did not last long because the symptoms of the illness, which was soon to take me out of the ashram, were already imminent. I came away from Calcutta with a bad cough, which resisted all known remedies of the time.

We came back to Varanasi. I think Gopal Thakur came from Allahabad to celebrate the function of Gita Jayanti. The new ashram saw a synthesis of different forms of worship demonstrating Sri Ma's *vani*, "All forms of worship are rendered to the One only". Gopal Thakur belonged to a school of thought which emphasised full-hearted emotional commitment to the deity; the ritualistic undergirding of this *puja* of adoration remained at a minimal level. Gopal Thakur led the prayers and songs; his disciples and mainly his daughters took up the refrains and also sang beautiful hymns, creating an atmosphere suffused with spirituality.

In the same ashram, a few yards away, the *Savitri Yajna* was being conducted in an atmosphere of scrupulous obedience to injunctions laid down in scriptures regarding ritualistic performance. The rhythmic, sonorous sound of the Gayatri mantra pronounced in unison by many voices to the accompaniment of the flickering light of the leaping flames from the central *yajna-kunda*, created another kind of atmosphere of no less religious significance than an emotional outpouring of the heart. Sri Ma's presence leant magnificence and splendour equally to both groups; at the time it all seemed very natural and just as it should be.

In the beginning of 1949, I was left in the Kanyapeeth, when Sri Ma went away on her travels.

In February, my youngest brother Babu was to receive his sacred thread in Allahabad. I came home to attend this function. The ceremony went off with its usual accompaniments of religious rites and feasts for relatives and friends of the town. Babu spent the scheduled three days in retreat. On the fourth day all of us repaired to the River Ganga. This is the minimal ritual now obtaining for the Upanishadic tradition of living as a *brahmachari* for 12 years in the ashram of the guru. The new *brahmachari*, however, must observe certain restrictions regarding his diet for one year at least and he is supposed to adhere to the recitations of his Gayatri mantra all his life.

My illness

At this time my father began to suffer some discomfort in his eyes. It was decided that he would go to Lucknow to consult Dr. Mitra, the eminent eye-doctor of those days. I offered to accompany my father. So we first travelled to Kanpur to be with my brother who was posted there as Deputy Superintendent of Police.

After independence in August 1947, Sri B.N. Lahiri had become the first Indian Inspector General of Police in U.P. He was a man of remarkable abilities with a sense of commitment to his profession. He had inaugurated a new policy regarding police personnel. He wished to give a new image to the police as servants of the public and not tyrants over them, which had been the case during the British regime. To facilitate this new policy he recruited directly a group of young men from well-known prestigious families and sent them to be trained as officers. My brother was in this first group and Kanpur was his first place of posting.

I had been suffering from a persistent cough all these months. Now, at Kanpur I succumbed to a raging fever. The doctor (Dr. Banwarilal Rohatgi) who came to see me, told my father that it looked like tuberculosis but since we were going to Lucknow he should consult a specialist. My sister-in-law with her little daughter, Mimi, also came along since I was by then rather helpless with the fever. We came to the house of the friend who had invited us to stay with him in Lucknow. The specialist Dr Tandon confirmed the earlier diagnosis.

Tuberculosis was a dreaded disease — almost like having plague in the house. I persuaded my father who wanted to take me home, instead to make arrangements for my hospitalisation in Lucknow. My mother came from Allahabad.

Mother and I settled down to a quiet routine. The doctor had prescribed "complete rest". I was very obedient, lying as still as a doll in my bed the whole day. My mother wrote to Sri Ma about my illness and why I did not return to the ashram from Allahabad after Babu's sacred thread ceremony. Sri Ma wrote back to say I was to follow medical advice with regard to diet as well. I suppose she said this to release me from the rules of orthodoxy, which she had imposed on me a few months earlier in Calcutta. By the luckiest of chances, the wonder drug streptomycin had just come on to the market. Dr. Tandon started me on this. When the fever left me he advised me to go to a sanatorium for three months because no matter what was promised by a family, the patient would be sure to take risks by over-exertion and lack of dietary prudence.

So my mother and I spent another three months in a cottage in Gethia Sanatorium. My mother had risen to the occasion of my hospitalization with her usual calm spirit. This was the first time in her life when she was obliged to go alone to the vegetable market and buy groceries and fruits. She was without a servant who could help her to cook and clean afterwards. However, she took all this in her stride. In Gethia she also managed competently, this time with the help of a servant who did her shopping and fetched water from a lower level. The sanatorium was a series of cottages and flats scattered over the hillside amidst great trees and well-planned flowerbeds.

The memories of my illness are extremely interesting for me. Apart from the fact, that I caused so much distress to my family, especially my father, I rather enjoyed the interlude. When I read Thomas Mann's *The Magic Mountain* I appreciated it greatly because my life in the sanatorium had familiarised me with this routine. I had not suffered any of the distressing symptoms of the disease, excepting the dry coughs, which did not last very long. Gethia was a private sanatorium built by Hem's father Dr. Kakkar. Their house was close by. She came home for part of the holidays and we went for walks along mountain paths. Bindu also came after his exams and in one day disrupted the entire routine of the sanatorium. He visited the house of a group of convalescents and arranged a musical evening that lasted well into the night. Bindu brought a wave of cheerfulness, which transformed the staid and sombre atmosphere. A dinner party for all inmates was arranged at a central place. Even the staff participated.

Dr. Tandon had said that I should avoid the heat and dust of the plains for at least three consecutive years. So I spent another 3 months in Nainital where my father and Babu from Allahabad and Bowdi and Mimi from Kanpur joined me. So we actually had a nice holiday in Nainital. I had made many friends in Gethia also, especially a Muslim girl who was attending on her husband by special permission of Dr. Dalal, who in general did not allow husband and wife teams in the sanatorium. This young woman used to come to my room and we spent many pleasant hours together talking about a wide variety of subjects.

We left Nainital in November. During this time, I put on a lot of weight. Dr. Tandon was aghast when he saw me in Lucknow. He pronounced me free of the disease and assured me that I would be of no danger to my family or the people with whom I came in contact. Everybody would smile when they saw me because I was evidently a funny sight. I am not in the habit of looking at myself in a mirror, so I had not realised that I was overdoing the weight-gaining regimen. If overweight people become thin, they look nice, but if thin people become fat they certainly cause amusement. Anyway, I subsequently managed to lose weight but I was never down to my original 96 lbs.

We returned from the mountains to 31 George Town to the welcome of servants and friends. Sri Ma was in Varanasi so I lost no time in presenting myself to her after almost one year. She was not rude like my friends and family who had made personal remarks quite mercilessly, but she did smile and say I looked very well. Sri Ma was about to take a tour of Gujarat at the invitation of Kantibhai Munshaw of Ahmedabad. I got permission to join Sri Ma's party. This was a very enjoyable trip in the company of a part of our wall-propping-up group [1], that is, Tara, Buba, Sati and myself. I remember the four of us with Kshamadi and Ganga travelled down to Ahmedabad under the escort of Sadhanda of our ashram. Sadhanda was an easy-going person and apart from asking us if we needed anything at all the big junctions, he left us to our own devices. We arrived in Ahmedabad almost at the same time as Sri Ma who came from New Delhi. Sri Ma had told us that on arrival we must abide by

---

[1] Whenever Sri Ma came to Varanasi, a group of young girls would be standing around or sitting surrounding her *chowki*. If asked to vacate their places for other visitors they would remove themselves to the farthest walls. In time they came to be known as 'the-wall-propping-up-party'.

One Year of my Life as an Ashramite

The wall-propping up party. From left to right:
Rama, Chitra, Buba, Gini, myself (almost hidden), Renu, Didi Gurupriya, Sati, Agamoni, Tara.

Kantibhai's arrangements and not take matters in our own hands and thus create confusion. It was a big party of people. Kantibhai was a man of great organisational powers. The bulk of the party was housed in his own residence, a huge building furnished and decorated in the first style of affluence and elegance. Tara, Buba, Sati and myself were billeted to a friend's house. Our hosts received us kindly and showed us to a guestroom. It was already late at night and we had been told that we would be able to go to Sri Ma's place of residence the next morning. When we were travelling in Sri Ma's company, we did not bother with our appearance, thinking nobody would be taking any notice of us. We were already tired by our long journey in a crowded compartment and wanted to get into our equally travel stained bed-rolls as quickly as possible. But the guestroom gave us pause; we looked at the beautifully furnished room with its four made-up beds, with snow-white sheets and fresh blankets and then at each other. Without a word, we unpacked and took out freshly laundered clothes;

instead of a quick wash we took proper baths, washed our hair and scrubbed our hands and feet; all this just to lie in the gleaming beds prepared for us!

Next day, we were treated to a lavish breakfast at a horse-shoe shaped table which we found very intriguing. Within days we became close friends. They were especially enchanted with the singing of Tara and Buba. This family had a large collection of records; later in the week, we enjoyed many a music session with them, when we returned from Sri Ma's residence late at nights.

After breakfast, we walked to Kantibhai Munshaw's house. For Sri Ma, Kantibhai had set up a big tent on a side-lawn. It was like a spacious house. We found Sri Ma sitting in the big audience-room and went in to do our *pranams*. We were surprised when we found Sadhanda already there, telling Sri Ma something about us, "Ma, please never again ask me to escort these girls on their journeys!" In great consternation we looked at each other! Now, what have we done! Sri Ma looked enquiringly at Sadhanda. He said, "Ma, the men in my compartment told me that I looked like a *sadhu*, so what was I doing with 6 young girls and where was I taking them! I realised that it did look very odd to them that I was going over to the women's compartment at every big station, so I beg to be excused from such a duty in future!"

Sri Ma did not seem to pay any serious attention to Sadhanda's complaint. She dismissed him saying lightly, "We will see." Then she asked us about our place of residence and how far it was from Kantibhai's house. She said. "It seems to be a walkable distance. Do not use their cars even if they offer them." So, although we had cars at our disposal, we walked everywhere throughout our stay in Ahmedabad.

The business community of Gujarat was extremely rich, yet the simplicity of their deportment disarmed us. Kantibhai's wife Kundan Ben was humility personified. The couple waited till their last guest had been fed before they took their own meals. The crowds, which assembled for Sri Ma's *darshan*, were well behaved and patient. Sri Ma answered their questions in Hindi. This was a cadre of society which would have remained unknown to us had we not been in Sri

One Year of my Life as an Ashramite

Ma's entourage. It amused us to see that they had the haziest notions regarding people from the north. Kashmiri (Udasji), Punjabi (Billoji), Bengali (ourselves), or people from U.P. and Bihar were just North-Indians to them. The vastness of our country and the variety of its languages became a reality when we travelled with Sri Ma.

Sri Ma arranged for groups of our party to go on pilgrimages to Dwarka and Dakore. When we showed reluctance to leave her even for a few days, she said, "One should visit the residing deities of the places where you go as a mark of respect". We did enjoy these short trips and had many agreeable experiences.

Nama yajna was performed by the Delhi party at the invitation of the devotees of Ahmedabad. We were sitting in Sri Ma's room awaiting the arrival of the Delhi Party from the station. Sri Ma described their mode of *samkirtana* and their backgrounds to Kantibhai and to Mrs. Talyarkhan and other dignitaries of the town. She said, "The name is for them God Himself. They live with Him while they sing. I have been told that Haran Babu was so attuned to this music

Namayajna (Abhaya with harmonium)

that if he heard the strains of *kirtan* coming from anywhere, he would just follow the sound and even enter a stranger's house and join in. You will meet his sons, Lal and Nani, who are quite as dedicated as their father was." While Sri Ma was speaking about the group, they arrived from the station and came in to do their *pranams* before retiring to their allotted rooms. Sri Ma said, "If you are not too tired, will you sing a few lines of a *kirtana* now? I have been describing to these people a little of the ritual of a *namayajna*." Nanida unpacked his harmonium and in his deep melodious voice began, "Radhe Govinda, Radhe Govinda, Radhe." I vividly remember the utter stillness which enveloped the entire congregation; they sat in rapt attention listening to this sound of the music of just the Names. Whatever Sri Ma had just said became a reality.

The *Namayajna* exceeded all our expectations of an ennobling spiritual experience. In those days, the Delhi Party was at the peak of their much-celebrated reputation. Birenda was the guiding spirit. His inimitable way of dancing around the altar of pictures and flowers with a pair of cymbals in his hands captivated the hearts of the people of Ahmedabad. Mrs. Talyarkhan, a Parsi lady, was especially enchanted by this music and became a great fan of the *nama yajna*. She

With Sri Ma in Ahmedabad. Clockwise: Buba, Didi, Ganga, Buni, Renu; Tara, myself, Kshama and Sati.

One Year of my Life as an Ashramite

was a disciple of Ramana Maharshi but became very close to Sri Ma after her own Guru was no more. We were told that it was the great Maharshi himself who had told some of his disciples that they could go to Sri Ma if they felt the need of spiritual guidance in his absence. During the Fifties we saw many groups and individuals from South India visit Sri Ma in Varanasi, no doubt in response to this behest of the Maharshi.

From Ahmedabad, we went on to Rajpipla, Bhimpura and other places on the banks of the hallowed river Narmada. It was a truly joyous experience. The beautiful river, second only to the Ganges, has attracted great ascetics to her banks for centuries. We saw many sacred sites where yogis of high reputation had practised *sadhana*. The Mahant of the prestigious local temple welcomed Sri Ma with every sign of respect and devotion. As members of Sri Ma's entourage we also came in for our share of due recognition.

The story of my acquisition of an image of Siva at this time is rather interesting. We had heard the legend that in the Narmada "*Jitne kankar utne Samkara*", that is, all riverbed rock-pebbles are images of Siva. We used to go to the river for our daily bath. The first day, all of us were fascinated by the sight of the sparkling waters rippling over a variegated bed of coloured rocks of all shapes and sizes. The girls started picking up one or two pretty ones; soon everybody had a collection of beautiful rocks big and small. I was not interested and looked with amusement at the growing heap of rocks in the arms of my friends. At the very last moment of leaving the river bed I looked down and picked up a tiny white translucent rock, beautifully smooth and a little smaller than my thumb. Nobody saw me do this; I wanted to drop it back but somehow did not do so. We arrived back at the ashram and crowded into Sri Ma's room to show her our finds. Sri Ma took each rock in her hands, admired its colour, at times pointed out special markings and in general seemed very pleased. She put all of them in her lap. I as usual was standing at the fringe of the crowd, and just as I was about to go forward with my little rock I heard her say, "Yes, all these rocks are very beautiful; but as you know, it is believed that they are not to be considered so but as the images of

Siva himself. They are not playthings or items of decoration. You must take them back tomorrow and return them to the river-bed." A sigh of disappointment went up but the rocks were restored to the river as directed by Sri Ma. Only mine remained because on hearing her statement I stayed where I was and did not show her my rock, telling myself that since Sri Ma had not seen it her words did not apply to it. I just did not want to part with it.

We returned from Gujarat and dispersed to different towns. After some months Sri Ma went back to Gujarat on her way to Bhimpura. We went to the railway station to meet her train. Although I had brought away the little rock from Narmada, I was not quite easy in my mind, thinking that I had disobeyed Sri Ma's spoken words. So, I took the rock with me to the station to give it to her to be taken back to the river. As chance would have it, there was no crowd at the station. I stood at the window of her compartment and confessed to my surreptitious acquisition of a stone from the Narmada. Sri Ma said quite calmly, as if she knew about it all along. "Since you have Narmadeshwara (Siva) himself you are required to do *puja* everyday. The minimal form of worship is to offer 3 *bilva*-leaves in the morning, daily." I was relieved that she did not ask me to give it back. Later, when we had installed the Image properly in a silver *peetha* and got used to its worship by offering *bilva*-leaves I realised and appreciated Sri Ma's great indulgence and graciousness because Siva himself seemed to have come to stay, conferring *ahetuka kripa* on us. More than twelve years later, Sri Ma happened to tell my brother Bindu's wife Shyamoli to worship Siva on some occasion or other. Shyamoli said that it would be difficult for her to go to a temple because there were none in their vicinity. Sri Ma said, "Why, there is Siva in your own family house." Shyamoli could make nothing of this. When she told me about Sri Ma's statement I explained to her the history of the little image at home. I was amazed that Sri Ma had remembered. Perhaps she said it to strengthen our faith in what we were doing. I am struck by the similarity of Sri Narmadeshwara's entering our home in this way and Sri Ma's statement that she had made to my father in Bareilly that she had come to his house uninvited!

CHAPTER THIRTEEN

The Best Years of the Ashram in Varanasi

For nearly thirty years Sri Ma continued to pay frequent visits to Varanasi. In the beginning many functions were celebrated, on a simple scale; they grew in scope and magnificence as the years went by. The completion of *Savitri-yajna* January 14, 1950 was one of the best we witnessed. It had begun on 14th January 1947. A small square shed-like building with sloping roofs had been erected for this purpose in the middle of the courtyard. Sri Ma's *kheyala* about a *mahayajna* spoken in Dhaka nearly twenty years earlier was fulfilled by a strange bunch of coincidences. Didi, who was at the forefront of all organisation at the time, never thought to take credit for its accomplishment. She has written a book about this *mahayajna* which explains how a concatenation of events inspired her to proceed toward the undertaking of a vedic *yajna* at a time when the country seemed poised on the brink of a war-like situation of massacre. The *samkalpa* (aim, intention) of the *yajna* was written out very carefully by Didi. She had repeatedly asked Sri Ma and understood her to say, "To please Him who is the most adored one (*Istadevata*) of all creation and thus the good of humanity (*visvakalyana*)."

For three years we had become used to the sound and smell of the *yajna*. The oblations put in the fire gave out a very agreeable aroma. As Didi had hoped, the wherewithal for this gigantic undertaking poured into her coffers from unlooked-for sources. Sri Ma's *kheyala* brought about congenial conditions; not only sufficient money, but also suitable men and women who lightened Didi's task. All the ramifications of the *yajna* were of profound significance; every detail was carried out with circumspection and consummate artistry. The small structure that contained the *kunda* had corrugated sheets of galvanised iron as a four-sided sloping roof. Ten pairs of banners and flags decorated the edges representing the ten chiefs (*dikpalas*) of the ten directions. Each flag and standard was marked by the special *astra* (weapon) and *vahana* (mount) of the god. As, for example, elephant and *vajra* for Indra, bull and trident for Siva, buffalo and mace for Yama; swan and *kamandala* for Brahma; Garuda and *cakra* for Narayana etc. Like everyone else I had noticed the flags fluttering in the air all these years. But this particular year I had a special role to play in this matter. When I arrived in Varanasi a little ahead of time for this festival, Sri Ma said, "So you have come. Didi, bring out the satins which have been purchased for the flags." Didi laughed and said, "I see that Ma was waiting for you. I said to her so many times that the flags should be marked but every time Ma said, 'Later!' Now I know why!"

Sri Ma had commissioned Renu to make sketches of the mounts and weapons. I was given the 20 sketches, a room to work in, and the bundle of satins of many colours, cut out and stitched to specific lengths and shapes. The flags were triangular and the banners rectangular. I and one or two girls from the Kanyapeeth settled down to a lengthy sewing session. The sketches we traced out on pieces of satin and then we appliqued them on to the flags. Previously Kamalakanta had cut out the shapes and had attached them to the flags with running stitches. We had not noticed that there were different animals, they had all looked rather alike. Now, Renu's beautiful sketches embroidered on to shiny surfaces looked quite attractive. This set was made for the function of *purnahuti*, that is, the completion of the *yajna*.

Sri Ma looked *prasanna* when we brought our handiwork for her inspection. I do not know how to translate the word *prasanna*. The words, 'pleased', 'satisfied' etc. do not apply to Sri Ma but sometimes, she definitely allowed her approbation to delight the heart of the recipient.

The Best Years of the Ashram in Varanasi

The Varanasi Ashram at its best

Guests started arriving for the function. The VVIP guests, of course, were the mahatmas who were quartered with their groups of disciples. The royal families who were devoted to Sri Ma, I think, made their own arrangements. Yogibhai and his people came to the ashram as usual. Then there were business magnates from Bombay, Ahmedabad, Calcutta and other parts of India. Above all, were the scholars who would give learned discourses and the singers of devotional music, especially the Ramayana. Haribabaji came with his troupe of Raslila performers. The gaps in this great mosaic of the populace were filled by the common people belonging to various provinces, professions or walks of life. Sri Ma's *asta sakhis* (eight friends), the eight village women from Almora, mingled with the highly sophisticated and stylish ladies from metropolitan cities. A miniature India was created in and around the ashram. The ashram at this time was at its most spacious. The whole building constructed over the pillars rising out of the Ganges was in full use. The great hall projecting onto the river was the venue of daily satsangs. The middle of the hall was circular which was just below the circular terrace adjoining the courtyard of the ashram. The hall was flanked by sets of rooms. There was a complete story below this level duplicating the upper structure. The kitchens for the entire gathering of guests were located here. The middle space could accommodate more than two hundred people at a time. From morning till night, it was the venue for the gathering of stores, preparation of vegetables and a hundred and one details for providing food for the concourse of people gathered in and around the ashram. A young teacher of the Vidyapeeth, Mrnmayda (who later became Swami Chinmayananda) was in charge. I do not remember having seen him come up out of these premises to the level of the courtyard during the entire duration of the festival. Another person who stood like the rock of Gibraltar at the main gates of the ashram was Panuda, a colleague of Mrnmayda. Panuda was in charge of reception. He allocated rooms and hotels and rented houses to people pouring in at all hours of the day and sometimes night. We do not know when he left his post to eat or sleep. My father was so struck by his seemingly immovable stance at the gates that he used to describe him as "Kumara Angada" (Angada, it is said, so positioned himself in the court of Ravana that nobody could dislodge him; subsequently this posture came to be known as the "Angada stance"). Even as early as this in his life Panuda had impressed people by his organisational capabilities; he acquired great expertise in the matter of receiving the mahatmas, arranging for their accommodation and in preparing the hall for the daily satsangs. The days of Gini's and my amateur efforts were over. With the help of servants Panuda did an impressive job of placing carpets, asanas, bolsters, microphone etc., on the dais for formal occasions, and also for the more homely meeting in the hall of the ashram every day.

In every corner of the sprawling ashram people were busy with some aspect of the coming solemnities. Many celebrations were happening at the same time. Sri Ma would find time to attend each one of them and so add to the enthusiasm of the convenor. I remember Didi and I happened to be in one of the upstairs rooms doing something when a girl came running with a message from Sri Ma, "Didi, Ma wants a presentation tray prepared for a bride with all suitable items; bring it to the hall." Saying this she ran back from where she had come. Didi looked quite bewildered, "Who is getting married? I cannot recall that we have been told of any marriages!" However, she assembled a sari, a pair of white conch shell bangles and sundry other items of a bride's decorative getup and we hurried to the hall carrying these things on trays. What a surprise it was when we realised that these offerings were to be dedicated to Rukmini, the bride of Krishna! The narrator of the Bhagavat Purana had come to the incident of Krishna's marriage that day and he had asked for a bridal gift for the occasion. There was much blowing of conch shells; the audience reacted suitably with *jayadhvanis* and a general air of rejoicing prevailed. The remarkable fact was that Didi would not have been surprised at anything that may have been happening near Sri Ma. The ashram was ever a bubbling fountain of mirth and joy, each person had his share not quite knowing what the others were busy with! It was a fairground where one could discover the multiple nature of religious enterprise.

The day of *purnahuti* dawned crisp and clear. Amidst joyous scenes the solemn ritual of offering the final oblation to the fire was accomplished. Sri Ma herself directed all arrangements. She had very thoughtfully provided for pails of milk and water and a hand spray beforehand. As in Delhi earlier, Bindu and I brought her this hand-spray not knowing what she wanted it for. When the flames leapt up, the wooden rafters caught fire and started smouldering, Sri Ma indicated the presence of the pail of milk and water and the sprayer. Batuda, the Panditji in charge of the *yajna*, most thankfully utilised it to put out the fire in the beams.

The sound of the solemn Gayatri Mantra recited every morning for the last three years ceased. We almost felt bereaved as if somebody dear to the heart had departed forever. Since Sri Ma was there, the mood of nostalgia was short-lived. We became busy with the other events as they occurred in the ashram.

Since my illness, I had not been staying in the ashram. Sri Ma had made me understand that the ashram was a public institution and if I were to be allowed to stay, other patients suffering from infectious diseases would claim accommodation. As a residential school, the Kanyapeeth could not be exposed to any possibility of danger from such diseases. I very readily agreed to these notions about general safety. The doctors had told me that I had never reached the stage of showing positive reaction to all the tests but such things could not be explained. I was happy that I spelt no danger to my family and friends and was content to return to 31 George Town with a clear conscience. Evidently I was not cut out for an ascetic way of life in a convent. In later years Sri Ma arranged for a *chowki* for me in the office of the Kanyapeeth and told me that it was for my use in case I came to spend the nights in the Kanyapeeth.

My illness brought about another change. The summer vacations could not be spent in Sri Ma's company. Pursuant of Dr. Tandon's orders, my father arranged for me to go to the hills at the very commencement of the summer of 1950. One of his friends in Dehradun, Darshanlalji, arranged for a rented house for us near the main road in

The Best Years of the Ashram in Varanasi

Mussoorie. My sister Renu, Bindu Babu and myself went up to the hill station at the beginning of summer.

I had taken all the volumes of Didi's diaries that were available at the time. I spent a major part of my time reading them again and again and writing out a biography of Sri Ma in English. The idea of undertaking this project had come from Atmanandaji who was very keen that I should write in English about Sri Ma. At that time there was hardly any informative literature. Non-Bengali devotees felt the lack of suitable literature very keenly. I quickly became engrossed in my task; it gave me great satisfaction to read and write about Sri Ma.

Darshanlalji used to visit us to see how we got on. I requested him to take me to the prestigious Mussoorie Library so that I could enlist as a member. He walked with me to the Library. When we arrived at the impressive gate of the magnificent building, he unfolded a newspaper that he was carrying under his arm and prepared to read it standing in the sun. He said, "You go in and sign the papers; I shall not enter these gates." A bit puzzled, I walked in. The receptionist was helpful; I became a member and in later months used the Library frequently. It was very well stocked and the reading facilities were old-world and charming. When I spoke enthusiastically to Darshanlalji, he smiled and said, "I am glad for you. You see child, I remember the days when there used to be a notice posted at these gates, 'Dogs and Indians not allowed'. The building evokes bad memories for old-timers like myself." I was truly appalled and offered to get my membership cancelled but he laughed and said "No, no, the management is changed now; very soon nobody will remember that this building was out of bounds for us." Darshanlalji was a very well educated barrister of his day and belonged to a family of wealthy landowners. It always came as a shock to me that the English had ruled India for more than a hundred years without really understanding anything about Indian society and with so much disdain for it.

We spent another long summer in Mussoorie and Dehradun in 1951. Thereafter, all my doctors pronounced me fit for a normal way of life. Most thankfully, I resumed my studies at Allahabad University. In the winter of 1951, I enrolled as a research scholar under Professor A.C. Mukerji. He was very pleased to see that I was again about to follow academic studies. He never asked me about my allegiance to Sri Ma or my illness or why I had interrupted my studies for about 3 years. As I myself was not a talkative type it suited me very well. The beautiful library of the University was a haven of peace for me for the next three years. As a research scholar I was free to leave town off and on. The guide and I came to an understanding regarding assignments; he was not exacting and I was conscientious about my work, so it all worked out well. During these years I went to Varanasi, Vindhyachala or more distant towns to be with Sri Ma whenever possible. This is how I became more and more involved with the Kanyapeeth.

We lived in an atmosphere of home away from home in the ashram. I remember Gini and I were standing on a second story balcony watching Renu performing some task on the terrace of the ashram in Varanasi. Gini remarked "I cannot imagine the Kanyapeeth without Renudi and Kshamadi!" These young women were not only good with the girls under their charge but they looked after all the elderly women who were residents of the ashram. Kshama and Renu would look after their small needs. During a festival or whenever Sri Ma was in residence, huge amounts of foodstuff were prepared, served and disposed of day after day. The elderly women like Sushila Mashima, Hemididi, Matori Pishima, Thakuma and many others hardly had time to be away from the kitchen for long. Kshama would quietly gather their clothes for washing and drying. Renu has said that she learnt to be especially thoughtful of this irreplaceable cadre of Sri Ma's devotees, who for years cooked *bhoga* with great affection for all.

A Management Committee was created at the time of the *purnahuti* of the *Savitri Yajna* called Sri Ma Anandamayi Sangha. Yogibhai was asked to become the first President of the Sangha. He was eminently suitable, not only because he was a devotee of long standing, but also a *krpa-patra* (protege) of Bhaiji as well as Bholanathji. He had espoused Sri Ma's concerns about the mahatmas and was always ready to provide hospitality to all and sundry. Everyone looked upon him as a person of great integrity and of unquestioning devotion to Sri Ma. Renu recalls that when the question of Presidentship was raised, Yogibhai had demurred, saying that in the presence of the Rajmata of Tehri Garhwal it would not be seemly for him to put himself forward, as it were, for this post. So Rajmata Anandapriya was elected the first President of the Sangha. She resigned after a while in favour of Yogibhai who held the post till his death in 1977.

All the Princes of our country who were close to Sri Ma were men of exemplary character. Their devotion to Sri Ma and their concern for her people was felt and experienced by the common people. Raja Saheb of Mandi and his family were as close to Sri Ma as any of the families from Dhaka. Maharaja Manavendra Shah of Tehri Garhwal was Yogibhai's nephew; their entire family remained very close to Sri Ma. There were many states of Madhya Pradesh where Sri Ma was made welcome and received as the presiding deity of the palaces. I never had the occasion to accompany her on these visits but I have heard about them from those who did. In this connection, I am reminded of a story told to me by Vijay Ratanji Vyas. Vyas had accompanied Sri Ma to one of the smaller states in Saurashtra. He and one or two others were sitting in the hall in front of Sri Ma's room while one after another of the royal family came and entered her room. These private interviews went on for long hours. At last Sri Ma was free to leave her room and take a stroll in the hall. Vyas muttered in an audible whisper "I wish my fate had decreed royalty on me." Vyas was known for his somewhat irresponsible statements and in general Sri Ma took no notice of them. This time, Vyas recalls that Sri Ma halted in front of him and in a very uncharacteristically stern voice said, "Tell me, do you wish for the same sort of fate that these people are labouring under? Do you have any idea what they are telling me and how they are suffering? If you want to assume their destiny, tell me now!" Vyas was completely taken aback. He said he had no doubt whatsoever that Sri Ma was in earnest regarding a change in his destiny. He hastened to beg pardon and said, "No Ma, I am perfectly happy as I am. I do not want to change roles with anyone!" Vyasji was always a delightful companion. Bindu, Bhupen and other young men in those days had merry times with Vyasji, who lived in Varanasi for many years before he settled in Bombay.

After the *purnahuti* of the *Savitri Yajna*, things became more settled. Sri Ma of course was not bound by any rules; she continued to travel in her own haphazard manner, sometimes cutting short her journey at unexpected places and sometimes proceeding beyond where she was expected to alight. Didi was always quick to gauge her *kheyala* and moved like quicksilver from one set of circumstances to another. Once in Varanasi, Sri Ma said she would go to Vindhyachala. Didi knew that wherever Sri Ma was people were sure to follow. Since she got some notice of Sri Ma's plan, she thoughtfully assembled some cooking utensils to take with her. The Secretary of the Varanasi Ashram came with a notebook and pencil. He said "Didi, you have to sign out these items and return them to this ashram." Didi was astounded. She said, "Rubbish! All these utensils were bought by me and are to be used in the service of Sri Ma wherever she may reside. I need them in Vindhyachala now!" The secretary although respectful was firm. He said, "All assets have been entered into stock-books; now I am accountable for them." Didi adjusted fast; she even expressed some pleasure that a system seemed to be emerging which would be supportive of her almost single-handed efforts at organising all the ashrams. She said, "All right, bring your book — I shall sign for the utensils I am taking out".

Those who have seen Didi in later years cannot imagine her terrific energy and capacity for multifarious activities. For many years, she looked after Sri Ma's personal needs along with performing all the required public relations tasks. She wrote innumerable letters and also her Diary every day. She would get up early in the morning, clean and scrub the pails and utensils in use for Sri Ma. Pails of water needed to be stored in most ashrams in those days. She would cook the midday *bhoga* that generally was a big feast-like meal because there were usually many people to partake of the *prasad*. She was required to serve this meal also. She was up till all hours in the night busy with Sri Ma's affairs. The only time during which she could rest or even sleep was when Sri Ma sat in the evening *satsanga*. Didi was never an enthusiast for satsangs, but she was very mindful of the role of the mahatmas near Sri Ma. Didi used to say that she was very grateful to Sri Ma's "Pitajis" and "Babas" for keeping her *kheyala* anchored to the world. Sri Ma's constantly reiterated *vanis* regarding dispassion and one-pointed search for Truth seemed to be exemplified by the renunciates in ochre-robes, especially Haribabaji Maharaj, who truly strove to live in God-remembrance all the twenty four hours of the day.

It was very delightful to work with Didi. In my small way, I helped her sometimes in the kitchen, sometimes in writing letters and other odd jobs. Didi was a good raconteur. Her stories of Sri Ma's early life in Dhaka were fascinating. Her own account of her young days at her parental home was almost as interesting. She had a good sense of humour, there were no emotional or sentimental overtones to her stories. She was very matter of fact. Sometimes, we saw some young men and women become transported during *kirtanas* or devotional singing. These spectacles were always distasteful to me. I was happy when Didi endorsed my reaction, saying "I have never felt even a twinge of *bhava*, although I have supported Sri Ma's body so many times when she was in ecstatic states. Other people seem overcome by the devotional atmosphere but I seem impervious to spiritual influence!" I liked Didi's robust outlook on life. She was totally devoid of what is called *dosa drsti* (fault finding). Interested persons always pointed out faults in other people to her. I wish she also had the capacity to evaluate the tales carried to her, but she was too straightforward herself to doubt or see beyond the obvious. She, therefore, was not a good administrator. She had genuine love and affection for the young women and men who were around and accepted all devoted families as extensions of her own.

The first Samyam Saptah

Yogibhai, after becoming the President of the Sangha, mooted the idea of a celebration which would be based on Sri Ma's teachings and which would be special and peculiar to our own ashram. Many discussions were held about the manner and duration of this observ-

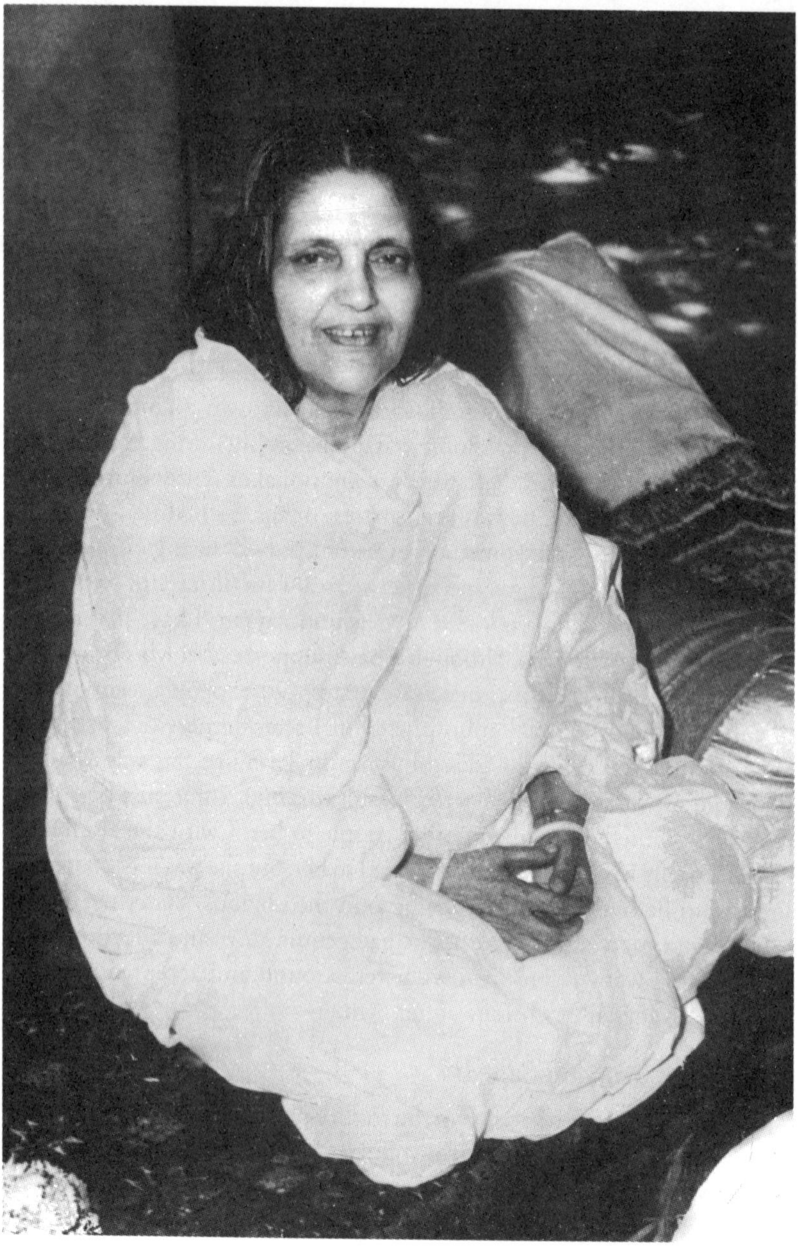

The Best Years of the Ashram in Varanasi

ance. It was Yogibhai's suggestion that since Sri Ma always spoke of restraint and discipline in daily life and a one-pointed dedication toward self-enlightenment, how would it be if we chalked out the ideal manner of daily routines for maybe a week or a fortnight? This disciplined regimen would be practised in Sri Ma's vicinity, so that she would guide and help our efforts. The idea met with great enthusiasm. Plans were drawn up, invitations sent out to devotees in other towns. The ideal duration was accepted as that of one week.

Sri Ma had come to Varanasi for the festival of Jhoolan (end of July 1952) and Janmastami. Varanasi ashram was selected as the venue of the first venture and the week between Jhoolan (full moon night) and Janmastami (the eighth day), the right time for it. A rather strict schedule of daily routine was drawn up. Time was allowed for personal *sadhana*, meals, a little rest, otherwise the whole day was divided up into durations of *japa*, *dhyana* (meditation), *kirtan*, listening to readings from scriptures and talks by eminent speakers in the evening *satsang*. The best part of the day came at 9.30 in the evening when Sri Ma would answer questions from the audience.

The *vratis* (those who enrolled themselves for the week of regimen) were divided into three groups as far as meals were concerned. The A class would keep fast on the 1st and 7th days. On the other five days, they would have a light lunch at midday and milk at night. For their lunches, Sri Ma devised very interesting meals. She herself came to the kitchens, supervised the preparation of the dish of milk and fruit which she named *payphal*. She put in it many exotic ingredients like various kinds of dried fruit and aromatic herbs like rose leaves etc. In the opinion of the devotees, the previous day's fast was made worthwhile by this extra-ordinarily satisfying lunch. For the other four days, they had similarly tasty but light cereal meals, also supervised by Sri Ma. The Group-B could have light cereal meals on all the days, but once a day only. Group-C was allowed two meals a day. Strange as it may seem, the largest number opted for Group-A.

Sri Ma attended all the sessions. Nobody complained of tiredness, boredom or hunger. People seemed to be enjoying themselves; they were so alert and keen that many wanted to keep it up for a fortnight. I was one of the volunteers who had charge of guarding doors during the hour of meditation. No one was to enter or leave during this time. The ashram itself needed to be made silent so that random noise would not penetrate to the satsang hall. At this time, Varanasi ashram was at its magnificent best. The venue of the *samyam saptah* sessions was the spacious hall under the terrace adjoining the main courtyard. The circular pillared hall projected right on to the river. Sometimes one could even hear the lapping of the waves below the windows.

Sri Ma asked Renu to make four sketches of the stages of *sadhana*. She herself adopted the poses, which Renu tried her best to portray on paper. The first was that of a man sitting up straight and doing *japa*. The second of a man sitting in meditation, the third of a man in a state of renunciation or *sanyasa*; the fourth was the most difficult and which Sri Ma named *sahaja,* that is to say "natural", a *sadhu* who looked at ease and blissful. She herself posed for all the portraits and Renu did her best. Her drawings were always clear and expressive. Sri Ma had these portraits framed and hung on the wall of the satsang hall. This set of pictures travelled to Vindhyachala, Calcutta and then Bombay on the occasion of subsequent *samyam saptahs*.

Saporybhai, a Bombay devotee, acquired them, saying he wanted to keep them as mementos. Sri Ma asked Renu to make another set of the same portraits. The second set remained at Pilani with the family of the Birlas. The set which is in use at present was created by Sushilbhai, now known as Sri Satyananda (who lives in Assisi, Italy)

The first *samyam saptah* was an unqualified success. It began with the celebrations on the occasion of Jhoolan Purnima and ended with the equally festive rites of Sri Krishna Janmastami. So the period of rigorous discipline was crowned by joyous activities. By tradition the next day to Janmastami is observed as the day of Nandotsava, that is, villagers come to Nanda's house to congratulate him on the birth of a son. Sri Ma's long-term devotees, Kamalaji, Ramaji and other matrons dressed up as village women, the dairy-maids of Vrindaban, and with pots of curds balanced on their heads danced in a group around Sri Ma. Sri Ma joined in, putting her left arm around

The Best Years of the Ashram in Varanasi

one woman after another. She moved gracefully from one to the other; eventually the pots were dropped to break and scatter the contents. Sri Ma picked out lumps of curds which were held up to her in the shards of the pots and fed them to the people surrounding her. She also smeared the faces of all her companions. The men who were keeping their distance from the dancing group suddenly found Sri Ma in their midst and could not escape being smeared with curds. But even during this general scene of chaos and confusion Sri Ma was just what she was. I remember clearly how I hid at the back of the crowd because I somehow did not particularly relish being caught up in this messy affair spreading by leaps and bounds. Sri Ma, however, found her way to the back row. I prepared myself for a drenching but no, she held her hand poised in front of me. I opened my mouth and was given an infinitesimal speck of curd so neatly that there was absolutely no mess! Later *samyam vratas* were held in November, so the Nandotsava never became a feature of it. So ended a function, which in time assumed mammoth proportions. Over the years, *samyam saptah* took on a very special character of its own. Sri Ma's *Vani*, "To talk of God alone is worthwhile, all else is in vain and pain" was brought to fruition for a short while in the lives of a cross-section of people who could never have dreamed of accomplishing it except in her presence.

    The mahatmas, who were invited to give orations on the occasion, were delighted with this function. They were used to the noise and hectic activities of the various festivals and celebrations they attended in different ashrams but the *samyam saptah* proved to be an event after their own hearts. In an atmosphere of quietude, a large number of people practised rigorous *sadhana* and seemed to be enjoying themselves. The main reason for this was that they were almost constantly in Sri Ma's presence. She attended almost all the programmes from early morning till late at night. During the hour of *maunam* (silence) she sat straight and still with eyes sometimes closed and sometimes open with a steady gaze, a perfect figure of meditation. I always took the job of a volunteer because I could not sincerely obey all the austerities expected of a participant. I sometimes observed Sri Ma carefully during the hour of *maunam*. It was a very interesting phenomenon. Without moving at all, she somehow watched each and every one sitting in the hall. Her eyes seemed to encompass all directions. It was not that she moved her head or eyes but from any corner of the hall someone would open his eyes and meet her bright gaze.

Sri Ma and mahatmas

CHAPTER FOURTEEN

Sri Ma and the Kanyapeeth

Sri Ma took a very close interest in the Kanyapeeth. From the date of its inauguration in Haradwar in 1938, it could always evoke her *kheyala*. In the beginning, the aims and ideals were slightly different from what they are now. Didi had experienced some difficulty in her own life regarding her overriding commitment to religion. In her own home, she had lived like a recluse till she met Sri Ma and found fulfilment. Didi had nursed some ideas about founding an institution, which would cater to young women who wished to devote their lives to spiritual endeavour. In our cross-section of society, young girls were only considered safely housed either in their parents' or husbands' households. There were a few who took up a profession, mostly teaching, but to live away from home and its environment was not possible without giving rise to much adverse comment. So Didi thought she would set up a Mahila Ashram where such young women who wished to follow a spiritual path could stay in comfort and safety away from their homes. Sri Ma spoke words of encouragement at all stages of the development of this small institution. She detailed a daily routine for the inmates. Her teaching in this respect was that to dedicate oneself to the quest for enlightenment was the only one goal worthy of man or woman. One should try for an undeviating, consistent and honest line of approach toward the goal. All such activities which are conducive toward this end are to be adopted, and such tasks as are irrelevant to the issue are to be eschewed. She was always practical about the daily routine she drew up for the girls. It was comfortable; apart from the hours of sleep and personal chores, some time was also set aside for recreational purposes. Such congenial work could be undertaken as would be conducive to the development of a spirit of service. Sri Ma laid emphasis on the purification of the mind. She said *seva*, or service, was the easiest way to achieve this. Any work done in a spirit of service did not add to the burden of karma and could not assume the character of chores. She would say, "I have heard people say that this body was obliged to work very hard when young, but since all work was done in a spirit of *seva*, it was never irksome or difficult. Everything was joy". She had encouraged Didi to take in small girls for her Mahila Ashram. Young women would have the congenial task of looking after these *kumaris* and so engage in *kumari-seva*. The teaching of these children would also be a fruitful way of spending some hours of the day. Although Sri Ma laid emphasis on routine and regular practice, she was always ready to make allowances for legitimate difficulties. Her teachings had a fluidity which catered to individual requirements.

The Kanyapeeth was accommodated in the South Wing of the ashram in 1944. Swami Paramanandaji was in charge of the construction of the buildings. Gradually, wing after wing was added, till the Kanyapeeth building became a conglomerate of dormitories, *puja* rooms, study rooms, a library, a music room, kitchens and dining rooms and rows of washrooms. The red-cemented verandah that gave access to the building saw hundreds of occasions when Sri Ma gave *darshan* to crowds of people. It was also the venue of innumerable feasts for devotees on the occasion of Vasantipuja or other festivals celebrated in the ashram. Sri Ma's room on the ground floor was the focal point of many gatherings. In the formative years of the Kanyapeeth, the girls had the good luck to have Sri Ma reside in their building many times. She took interest in their curriculum, their daily food and every detail of life spent in the ashram. Gradually, the character of the institution underwent changes. With the coming of a number of small girls, attention went to them. The older girls preferred to join the entourage round Sri Ma. Hardly anyone wished to stay in the "Mahila Ashram" and devote herself to *sadhana* when she had the chance of travelling in Sri Ma's company. Kshama of course, preferred to be with the small girls in her charge: she and Renu for many years formed a good team in Varanasi.

With time, many changes moulded the shape and aims of the institution. In 1947, Ganga Devi was put in charge in place of Kshama, who was detailed to help the management of the Savitri Yajna. Ganga Devi was herself a *panchatirtha* from Calcutta University. She started the girls on their course of study. Kshama used to teach the girls arithmetic and Bengali, Renudi dealt with miscellaneous subjects like history, geography and English. The question of a systematic way of education arose from time to time. Ganga Devi coached the older girls so that they could appear at their matriculation examination in Calcutta. Unfortunately, the entire batch failed their examination. The preparations had simply been too sketchy. At about this time, I had joined Allahabad University again to finish my Masters Degree. On one of Sri Ma's visits to the Satya Gopal Ashram in Allahabad, I expressed my dissatisfaction with the curriculum of the Kanyapeeth. I told Didi that since they were living in Varanasi, they should adopt the educational system of the United Provinces. To learn Sanskrit in the Bengali script would be to restrict its use severely. At this time Miss Lalita Pathak had become a devotee. Miss Pathak was Professor of English at the Allahabad University. She had been our teacher during our graduation years. Miss Pathak also supported me in my views. Didi raised the problem of proper teachers for the Kanyapeeth. Lalita Pathak said, "I know a young lady in Varanasi, Padma Misra, who could be approached on this matter. She is teaching Sanskrit in Banaras Hindu University. I am sure she can tell us about suitable teachers for the girls." Didi, as was her custom, asked us to go to Varanasi immediately and talk to Padma Misra. Sri Ma was herself going to Varanasi so Miss Pathak and I had no objection to this scheme. I remember this visit very vividly. Miss Pathak and I went to B.H.U. in a riksha, and searched for the quarters of Dr. Padma Mishra. So many times over the years I had approached the ashram by going round the Vizianagaram Palace toward Bhadaini. I had sometimes wondered about the road that went straight off toward an unknown destination. Now, I knew it went to B.H.U. B.H.U. was very shortly going to be my home for the next thirty years or so. Here were Lalita Pathak and I happily bowling along asking sundry people if they knew where Dr. Padma Mishra lived.

We arrived at the beautiful staff-quarters pointed out to us by passers-by. I remember that her servant Bhola (whom I came to know very well later), received us and showed us into a well-appointed sitting room.

Padmaji came in; I immediately thought that, yes, she is the right person for us. Miss Pathak introduced me. She explained a little about the Kanyapeeth. Padmaji had heard about Sri Ma, but so far had not visited the ashram. I was impressed when Padmaji said "Yes, I shall come to teach whenever it is convenient for them." There was no hesitation or wonderment about the project. It was as if she were just waiting for the call. So we settled it that she would come to the ashram in the evening to have *darshan* of Sri Ma and came away very well satisfied with our expedition.

Sri Ma used to sit out in the courtyard in the evenings. When Padmaji approached her, Sri Ma picked out a garland of red-roses from the heap of marigold ones at her side and put it on her neck. This was the beginning. All of us of the wall-propping-up-party from then on would watch interestedly whenever Padmaji approached Sri Ma. She always got the best available garland.

I took Padmaji to the Kanyapeeth and introduced her to the girls. Didi made her welcome and explained our problems regarding courses of study. Padmaji somehow adopted the Kanyapeeth as a matter of course. She took me with her to meet T.A. Bhandarkarji, a retired teacher of Sanskrit who agreed to come to the ashram to teach some classes. Classes were organised according to the curriculum of the Sanskrit University. Padmaji seemed to breathe life into the educational programme. Studies and examinations became things of joy rather than impossible tasks.

The Kanyapeeth never looked back. In time, it became affiliated to the Sanskrit University and received recognition from the Government. With donations from the Government, more competent teachers could be employed. The students grew up to appear at the higher examinations, namely *Shastri* and *Acharya*. Geeta and Gunita achieved the added distinction of qualifying for the research degree of *Vidyavaridhi*. Padmaji guided the education of the little institution through all its stages of growth and expansion. She could easily prevail upon noted scholars to give some time to the Kanyapeeth.

Today the Kanyapeeth is recognised as a reputed institution where girls are taught impeccable Sanskrit. Many of them can speak fluently in Sanskrit and give discourses on philosophical subjects. Gita made us all proud by rising to the stature of a Speaker entitled to the Vyasasana on the occasion of a Bhagavat-Saptah in Varanasi Ashram.

The facility with which seemingly impossible things were achieved in Sri Ma's vicinity bordered on the miraculous, or rather it would be more proper to say that the miraculous was the norm where she was concerned. We saw no straining after any aims; she would express a *kheyala* and sooner or later it would be fulfilled. Sri Ma had the *kheyala* that the young girls should have a good education in Sanskrit and so all facilities arranged themselves toward this end.

In time, the Kanyapeeth became self-reliant, there was a sufficient number of teachers, the senior girls themselves assumed charge of the hostel arrangements, school curriculum, play and recreation music and arts, and lastly, the most important aspect of *puja* and yogic discipline.

For many years the institution depended upon outside help for carrying out a considerable amount of the office-work. At Padmaji's suggestion I went to request Bharadwajji, who had retired from the post of Chief Accountant at B.H.U. to come and help us out. In the beginning, he was not prepared to work for a privately run institution, expressing his doubts regarding mismanagement of funds. I was provoked into saying, "I do not know about auditors but we are more afraid of Sri Ma's disapproval regarding improper use of donations received in charity. She does not like even one rupee to be spent in a way which is not according to the wishes of the donor. We have to be very circumspect with the money which is received for the Kanyapeeth. We do the best we can but our lack of knowledge creates muddles all around".

Sri Ma with the Kanyapeeth and its teachers. Last row (from left to right): Vani, Vijaya, Kanti, Vimala, Nirmala Handoo, Geeta, Miss Pathak (Buaji), Miss Padma Mishra, Udasji, Sati, myself, Pushpa, Renu.

Bharadwaji was amused as well as convinced that we were a proper institution. He came and was captivated by Sri Ma. He and his wife became devotees. They attended every *samyam saptah* in the ashram. He remained close to the Kanyapeeth till the day of his death. I take this opportunity to record our great appreciation of his dedicated service, his total espousal of the cause of the Kanyapeeth, his generous giving of time and leisure to us beyond the call of duty. His service was a labour of love. His officework was faultless and the older girls became adepts in book-keeping and the management of their finances.

Not the least contribution of Padmaji to the Kanyapeeth was this introduction of devoted upright men and women who served the institution all their lives. Padmaji's recommendation was enough. She was so admired and looked up to in the academic world of Varanasi, that her sponsorship of the Kanyapeeth gave it prestige as an educational enterprise.

In 1988 the Kanyapeeth celebrated its Golden Jubilee. It was a great occasion. The girls organised an entertaining programme for the distinguished guests. Kashi Nareshji and many mahatmas came to grace the occasion. Swami Chidanandaji presided over the function. Many scholars of Varanasi congratulated the girls for so meticulously maintaining the ideals of non-attachment, selfless service and dedication to the spiritual quest which had come to be associated with Sri Ma. All guests, from the mahatmas to the assembly of more than a dozen old alumni of the Kanyapeeth, stated unequivocally that they felt the presence of Sri Ma in the Kanyapeeth.

The *lilas* performed by the students

During the regime of Ganga Devi the festivals of Jhoolan and Janmashtami acquired some importance in the Kanyapeeth. Ganga Devi was a Vaisnava and had brought images of Radha and Krishna with her. The devotees of Gujarat had presented Sri Ma with a typical *jhoola* (swing) which is to be found in every household. This *jhoola* (swing) was given to the Kanyapeeth. It used to be put up on these occasions and decorated with fruit, flowers and garlands. On Sravana

Purnima (some time in July) Sri Ma was requested to sit on it for a little while. The Janmashtami (Birthday of Krishna) came on the eighth day after the festival of the swing. Ganga Devi would invite Sri Ma to come to the hall of the Kanyapeeth every evening of this week. Sri Ma would be entertained by a variety programme put on by the students of the Kanyapeeth.

A stage was put up at one end of the hall where the girls enacted small plays. A curtain separated the stage side of the hall from the auditorium. Sri Ma sat surrounded by women devotees of the town and those residing in the ashram. On a few occasions, some men especially invited by Sri Ma came on to the verandah from where they could see the play. Among these were Dr. Pannalal, Patalda and one or two others.

Sri Ma being invited by me to the hall where the lilas were performed

Renu used to look up suitable books and dramatise their stories with a view to casting the available girls in the various parts. We had come to know that Sri Ma did not approve of elaborate dresses. Whatever we could assemble easily in the ashram was used; so much was left to the imagination of the audience. Renu directed and produced dozens of plays, meriting praise and acclaim from the audience. I shall write about a few only, the few which have lingered in my memory for some reason or other.

Once the girls enacted the life of Sri Ramanujacarya. It was an abbreviated version of his biography written out in dramatic form by

Renu. At that time, we had a girl called Rama with us. She truly was superb in the role of the young acarya (teacher) who became the great Ramanujacarya, the author of "Sri Bhasya". The following year Sri Ma asked if we could do a repeat performance of the play. Since this had to be done almost extempore, the older girls were commandeered into the cast by Renu. I became the guru who would die before the arrival of the disciple. Rama, alas, had left the ashram so the star role was given to Bishuddha because she alone could memorise the part within a day.

The story was that the three fingers of the guru's hand were seen to be curled inside the palm. When Ramanujacarya arrived, he lamented his misfortune but interpreted the guru's message to him. As he made his promises to do as directed, the fingers opened out one by one and the hands remained normal and still. Sri Ma sometimes referred to this play as the one with the curled-in fingers of the guru.

Another play, which was enacted by teachers and students, was the story of Naciketa from the Kathopanisad. Renu had some trouble with the rehearsals because Kshama, who had the part of the father, could not bring herself to say her line "Go to the abode of death" to Naciketa, that is, Bishuddha. Kshama however promised to say her lines on the final night. We engineered some light effects to give dramatic force to the scene of enlightenment. Sarojudidi, another teacher, in the role of Yama drew a lot of applause.

One year Renu wrote out a short play on the life of Christ. The scene of the crucifixion was so powerful that Blancaji, who was in the audience, unable to watch it, just left the room. The actor Pavitra, a very talented girl, played the role of Christ. She stood on her crossed toes like a ballerina with out-stretched arms and looked very realistic. We did not have stage props. It was all done by acting and postures. After the *lila* was over, it was seen that there was a drop of blood on Sri Ma's tongue where it had got bitten by her tooth. Dr. Pannalal thought that this slight trace of blood may have been because Sri Ma had momentarily merged into Christ.

In this connection, another incident should be recorded which helps us to understand Sri Ma's attitude toward this world of play-acting. Dr. Pannalal had been reading the biography of Milarepa, the

Tibetan ascetic of great repute. He used to tell Sri Ma about the hardships endured by Milarepa in search of enlightenment, how his guru tested him severely again and again before he was ready to consider him worthy of discipleship. Renu borrowed this book from him and wrote out a dramatic version in consultation with Sri Ma. Sri Ma was keenly interested; she would suggest scenes and dialogues! Renu would carry her notebook and pencil all the time. Whenever Sri Ma had an opportunity, she would speak a few words regarding the play. The time came for rehearsals. Renu came with her notebook to Sri Ma's room. While talking about the attitude of a disciple Sri Ma slipped down to a kneeling posture in front of Renu who was standing in the role of the guru near her *chowki*. Sri Ma's whole aspect underwent a change; she shed tears of supplication and almost bowed at Renu's feet, who hurriedly stepped back out of Sri Ma's reach. Didi quickly spoke in ordinary tones about the play, to dispel the mood of ecstatic *bhava*. She helped Sri Ma on to her *chowki*. Sri Ma lay down obviously still in a state of total self-surrender to the guru.

Also on other occasions we came to realise that there were no lines of demarcation between appearance and reality for Sri Ma. Whatever was presented to her was true; there was no lie, make-believe or evil. Everything was a divine manifestation of Him who alone is, everywhere and forever.

Milarepa was enacted a few times in the Kanyapeeth by different casts, as it was very pleasing to Sri Ma. Once even Didi and Ganga Devi were prevailed upon to take parts. Since clothes were not changed it was easy for a spectator to become an actor for a while. We had learnt the unimportance of props and acoutrements from watching Haribabaji's villagers perform elaborate *lilas* without any at their command. A fiercely moustached villager would cover his head and face with an *angoccha* (the indigenous red towelling cloth), and convincingly enact the role of Radha or a Sakhi in Vrindaban. One of the best performances I have seen is that by a boy dressed in an ordinary red-bordered sari playing the role of Vishnupriya. He moved the entire audience to tears by his deportment in anguish at the separation and his quiet acceptance of a life of asceticism.

Sri Ma and the Kanyapeeth

One of our very successful plays was "Shishupalavadha". The last scene was very dramatic. While Krishna was still in the attitude of majestic wrath, the assembled kings started on a *stotra* of adoration, while Shishupala lay dead at his feet. I as usual was in the wings. Somebody came and hurriedly called me to Sri Ma sitting in the hall. I bent down to listen to her whisper. She said "Ask Shishupala also to get up and join in the prayer to Krishna!" I returned to the wings and inched my way behind some of the "kings" to whisper to the fallen hero, "Get up and join in the prayer." Shishupala was played by Manmohanda's daughter Agamoni. She took some time to understand such a strange cue from the wings, but did get up and join in as directed. The audience probably thought it a miracle — written into the text.

Sri Ma later gave me an explanation. She said, "You see, her mother and sisters were in the audience; they would not have liked the sight of Agamoni lying lifeless on the stage, while the other girls were singing hymns to Krishna". Sri Ma's compassion reached out to all participants. The authenticity of the tableau on stage was not more real than of the audience. How blissful those festivals were. The girls of the Kanyapeeth were joined by many youngsters from the families of devotees living nearby. It was a glorious week of celebrations.

Once a devotee brought a set of silver ornaments for Sri Ma from Vindyachala. When she was decked in these villager-type ornaments, she had a *kheyala* for performing a *lila* herself. Only the older girls knew about Sri Ma's project. The whole day Renu and I were in and out of Sri Ma's room showing her the different props as requested by her. The evening programmes started as usual. While one of the plays was being performed, Sri Ma quietly left her seat and entered the green-room. She put on the blue sari and silver ornaments given by the devotee. We were to enact the story of Chhadmayogi. The story tells how Krishna enters Radha's bower in disguise because she, feeling hurt (*maana*) through Krishna's inattention, would not give permission for him to come in. Sri Ma chose Buba to play the role of Radha. Sati, Tara and myself were the different sakhis (friends of Radha). Sri Ma would whisper lines, which we were to speak from time to time. She had no opportunity for a rehearsal or even to tell us how to set about the enactment of the story. I had a difficult time dressing Buba to her satisfaction. Sri Ma said, "Couldn't you get a nicer sari for her? I want a gauze-like veil over her head and back through which the long black plait of hair (*veni*) will be shimmeringly visible." Buba has fine textured brownish hair. We added dark tassels to it to make it long and black. Sri Ma took great care with the appearance of Radha but alas, nothing was quite up to her standard; she kept on asking "Don't you have anything prettier than this?"

At last we were ready. The scene opened with Radha sitting with her *sakhis* in the forest grove. Sri Ma as the disguised yogi entered with a conch-shell held to her mouth. The sound was a playback from the green-room. She had wrapped herself in a tiger skin and marched up and down the small stage uttering the words, "I am hungry!" The *sakhis* engage the yogi in conversation. He begins to abuse Krishna to which Radha takes exception and orders him to be evicted from the bower. The yogi reveals himself and all is joy and celebration.

I cannot quite recall if we could systematically work our way through this scenario, because the audience went ecstatic to see Sri Ma decked out as she was and raised shouts of "Jai Ma," "Jai Ma". They were happy to see Sri Ma since they had missed her in the auditorium. I do not think they paid any attention to the dialogue or to us. Sri Ma then walked into the auditorium to the delight of the women and so the play came to a happy end.

Pushpa was a great asset with her musical talent. She provided all the songs, *kirtanas*, hymns needed for the plays and also the background music. One of her very beautiful musical presentations was the dance-drama "Mahisasuramardini" performed by Jaya and Tara, both very young and slim at the time. Jaya looked beautiful as the Goddess and Tara was very convincing as the *asura* (demon). The martial rhythm of the famous *stotra* sung as accompaniment created a truly uplifting atmosphere.

We gained so much prestige by our performances that once we were asked to do a play in public, in the hall of the Gopal Mandir on the occasion of the annual Sanskrit Divas in the presence of Sri Ma and Gauri Nath Shastri, the guest of honour. The Kanyapeeth certainly rose to the occasion. The guest of honour was profuse in his appreciation of the purity and simplicity of the presentation. Since those times the young girls themselves, now more competent than we had been, carry on the tradition very effectively. Km. Geeta Banerji now writes, produces and directs plays which are appreciated by the discriminating Varanasi audience every year. Swami Chidanandaji was once invited by Sri Ma to sit in with her while a group photograph of the Kanyapeeth was taken. He was the guest of honour many times at the annual prize-giving function. He has become so identified with the aims and ideals of the Kanyapeeth that he graciously comes to attend this function every year, from wherever he may be. The ultimate compliment was paid to the Kanyapeeth by a distinguished Varanasi scholar. After participating in one of the Sanskrit-Divas programmes, he said, "It is said that if one dies in Varanasi there is no rebirth but salvation; however, if I should be reborn I would like to come as one of the *kanyas* (girls) of the Kanyapeeth!"

Sri Ma's *vani* that "little girls (or boys) are like fresh unsullied flowers worthy of God; for them to be in touch with the ever present Grace is easy and natural", sustained the small institution. Sri Ma's *kheyala* was always with the Kanyapeeth. Perhaps it was right that when Sri Ma's *kheyala* was directed toward the performing of a *lila*, the venue should happen to be the Kanyapeeth.

Sri Ma's *Lila*

During one of our dramatic evenings Mauni Ma said to Sri Ma, "Ma, why don't you perform a *lila* yourself?" Sri Ma said at once "Should I do so? Will all of you act in it if I direct a *lila*?" Everyone agreed enthusiastically.

The next day, Sri Ma sent for me and gave expression to her *kheyala* regarding this *lila* to be performed in the evening. In retrospect I realise that on this occasion Sri Ma revealed herself fully. The *lila*, simple enough in itself, would need pages of exegesis to study its meaning fully. At the start Sri Ma called for a stage where actors and audience would form a homogeneous group. Sri Ma never had time to instruct me fully. I would follow her around with a notebook and pencil and write down whatever she could manage to say from time to time, sometimes even while going from one meeting to another. I understood her instructions as follows:

The hall was to be divided into eight or more sections. These divisions were to be fluid and arranged without disturbing the audience, who were to fill the whole room inclusive of the space generally set aside for a stage. There would be two central figures in each of the main section. One, depicting an image of God and the other a worshipper. The entire hall would be like a congregation where people would sit in groups round a certain image. Groups could merge into each other but a discernible narrow path would lead from group to group. This was indicated by flower garlands on the floor. The groups detailed by Sri Ma were as follows, as far as my memory goes: The first two groups at one end of the hall would be those of Vaishnavas and Saivas. In the first square two small girls from the Kanyapeeth would stand in front of Ganga Devi in the classical pose of Radha and Krishna. In the second Didi would sit in meditation in front of Siva. Other *tolis*, or groups, depicted devotees of Rama and the Goddess Durga. In one section, we had the worshippers of Buddha and in the next some ascetics who looked up at the calm and serene figure of the Adi Samkaracarya. In a less clearly defined section there were yogis, Ganapatyas with Hanumanji enacted by Vishudda. I think there were other figures, not very clearly defined, but who could represent images or worshippers of non-Hindu forms of religion.

There was a small balcony on the other side of the hall. The many simple adjuncts to this *lila* were assembled here: a book, a pair of cymbals, a *rudraksha mala*, a flower garland, *tulasi* petals, *bilva* petals and other items. The whole day Sri Ma would dictate snatches of the lines to be spoken by me. The idea was that I would describe the various images, extolling their majesty and grandeur, but also their particular captivating qualities which kept their devotees enthralled. Then I would call upon an attendant (Sri Ma, in disguise) to provide them with some item which would be of use to them in their

Sri Ma and the Kanyapeeth

mode of worship of their chosen *Ista devata*. Sri Ma said, "You are to say, "Hey! you *dasi* (servant woman!), come here!" I was astonished. I said, "Whom am I to call a 'servant woman'?"

"This body, of course!"

"But I cannot say 'servant woman' (*dasi*) to you!"

"Can't you?"

"No, absolutely not!"

Sri Ma looked a little non-plussed, but Didi who was nearby supported me. She then overcame this check to her *kheyala* by saying, "Well, I had many nicknames as a child. One of them was Tirthavasini. How about '*Tirthavasini Mai*'?" I had no objection to *Tirthavasini Mai* which I thought was very apt.

Thus, I was to call upon her, saying something like this, "O *Tirthavasini Mai*! Come here, see how beautiful this grove of trees is; how captivating are the images of Radha and Krishna. See with what dedication people are gathered here for a *kirtana*. Truly one is transported to another world in such an atmosphere."

After my commentary Sri Ma, so heavily veiled that she hoped she would not be recognised, would emerge from the balcony carrying a pair of cymbals which she would place in the hands of a worshipper. Then she would go back to the balcony and become invisible to the audience. Sri Ma very painstakingly dictated lines for each group in the hall for me to utter. Her words constituted a paean of praise, a hymn of ecstatic adoration in every case. There were neither special nor marginal groups. All were equally important. She wove such a rich tapestry of words signifying man's upsurge toward the divine that it seemed to encompass all possible attitudes, which bind God and man together. It was an acknowledgement of variety and a celebration of unity. Only Sri Ma could create this *lila* and "enact" it with such magnetic intensity.

After the *lila* was over we discovered that Didi had missed the entire performance. In the beginning Sri Ma had instructed Didi and the other worshippers to close their eyes and meditate. When they heard my voice calling out to *Tirthavasini Mai*, everyone had opened their eyes to look at Sri Ma. Since Didi was not told to do so by Sri

Ma she did not open her eyes and thus missed the entire presentation. We all laughed at Didi but it was undoubtedly a remarkable example of unquestioning obedience.

In my desk drawer, I still have a few pages of my original notes; Atmanandaji published her account of this *lila*. I think she was one of the very few who really appreciated the presentation. The rest were looking adoringly at Sri Ma as she moved up and down the hall absorbed in what she was doing. Although her face was hidden, the beautiful hands were unmistakable. The audience was content to look upon her to the accompaniment of devotional music. I do not think anyone bothered to listen to my commentary upon Sri Ma's movements. Such was always the effect of this fantastic personality. She commanded total attention. We never paid true heed to what she was saying but were interested only in being in close proximity to her, to see her, to be near her and generally bask in the luminosity of her magic presence.

Sri Ma, in a later year, directed another *lila*, this time in Dehradun. I was not there but heard about it from others. This time Sri Ma herself did not take part but directed others in their performances, again a *lila* of divine images and their worshippers. The players were Chhabidi, Chitra, Bishuddha and other young girls who formed Sri Ma's entourage at that time. It was acted in public in the satsang hall of Dehradun Ashram. Sri Ma took delight in such extemporised arrangements and also a type of simple artifice which makes do with whatever is to hand. She was never at a loss or discouraged by lack of facilities; on the contrary, she understood the potency of minimal stage props to achieve "suspension of disbelief" in a spellbound audience. It must also be recorded that her *kheyala* itself brought about a concatenation of circumstances which covered all contingencies.

CHAPTER FIFTEEN

The Message of Sri Ma Anandamayi

It is as true to say that Sri Ma had no message to give to the world, as that she spoke on every topic which is of interest to human beings. She spoke tirelessly, for countless hours, discussing, answering questions, discoursing upon themes raised by scholars or simple people; the refrain of her talks, however, became clear as years went by. She repeated a pithy statement again and again, anywhere and everywhere,

To talk of God alone is worthwhile,
All else is, verily, in vain and pain!

Once, a successful man of the world posed the question,
"What harm is there if we are happy in our way of life? If we are satisfied as we are?"

Sri Ma: "I am not saying there is any harm, if you can remain happy in the world. If one can remain immersed in it then it is all to the good. But actually, no one can do that. If anyone tries to immerse himself in worldly pleasures, they begin to choke him. As for example, you put on nice clothes and go out on a pleasure trip; as soon as you return home, you want to take off all the restrictive items of dress and wish to relax in your everyday simple garments. It is man's nature to seek freedom. This is why even if a man busies himself in the world he seeks relief from it after a while. The coercion chafes him. Everyone seeks peace and happiness because man is of the nature of bliss. There is the possibility of eternal bliss in him, that is why he becomes impatient with worldly ties. Creaturehood means limitations; when he gains freedom from all limitations, he becomes established in supreme bliss.

"Pitaji, how much pleasure can this world contain? If you get even a taste of the happiness in that dimension then you will not care for any pleasures of this world. This is the absolute truth. Keeping company with *sadhus*, attending *satsangs*, reading of elevating books etc., brings about an interest in that other world. It is not necessary to eschew anything (any pleasures of this world). Only try to establish contact and hold on to the other dimension. Whatever is redundant will fall off of its own accord."

Once a modern young man very boldly told Sri Ma that bliss could be experienced easily by taking appropriate drugs, so why should one go in for a lot of *tapasya*?

Sri Ma answered, "Yes, but such experiences are temporary and not unalloyed — there are unpleasant repercussions. The bliss (*ananda*) the scriptures are talking about cannot be induced artificially because it is not related to the physical or the mental or even the intellectual plane. In fact one cannot do anything to bring it about. One just prepares oneself and awaits its happening as a realization. It is not a state, but one becomes of the nature of bliss." Sri Ma was in general heard to steer clear of modern terminology regarding higher consciousness. I heard her once say emphatically, "To talk of expansions of consciousness without reference to faith and devotion is mere euphoric indulgence (*vilasa*). If you leave God out of your concerns in life then you opt out of the way to the ultimate gain of peace."

Just as Sri Ma did not brook any trivialisation of the life of devotion, she bracketed all emotional outpourings and overtly physical displays of religious sentiments. I have heard her say to contemporaries who were prone to such displays, "One should always keep control over one's behaviour and emotions. If you lose yourself in these waves of feelings the result may not be auspicious — why? Because some onlookers may pass adverse remarks which you do not need. Others may become genuinely impressed and begin to admire you.

This also is not conducive to a life of *sadhana*. One must proceed on one's way, without being distracted by extraneous matters."

Sri Ma always stressed the need for privacy and inner strength. *Sadhana* should be practiced away from public gaze, she would say, and it should not cause inconvenience to others either. A woman said to her, "Ma, I get no time to sit quietly even for 10 minutes. Something or the other, someone or the other will make demands whenever I am hoping that at last I am on my own". Sri Ma smiled and said, "Such is the nature of households — but let things and family keep you busy during the days; the nights are your own."

To another person who posed a similar problem she said, "Can a man stand at the sea-shore thinking he will go in for a bathe when the waves have subsided? He has to plunge in facing the oncoming breakers."

Another point which Sri Ma stressed was relentless constancy. She would say, "Do not give up your effort. If you feel overcome by sleep, take a nap; if you feel a great thirst, get up and take a drink; but come back again and again to your *nama japa*. Tell yourself that I must, I must finish my *nama japa*, no matter how many times I am disturbed."

A young man asked her, "Ma, if somebody feels like wandering around all the time, what should he do?" Sri Ma asked "Why does he feel like wandering around?"

Questioner : "No special reason, just a random wish for roaming around."

Sri Ma : "That is not possible. There must be a reason, although it may not be clear to him. This thought that there is no aim beyond the fact of wandering around, itself is a reason. Well, if you do feel such a desire, go ahead and fulfill it; perhaps, after wandering round aimlessly, you may feel like settling down at a particular place. Constant movement is not conducive to *sadhana*. If you keep shaking an ewer of water, it cannot become still. So the mind". (Sri Ma seemed to know that it was his own question and not asked on behalf of someone else).

My Days with Sri Ma Anandamayi

Sri Ma surrounded by devotees (photo by Richard Lannoy)

Sri Ma always focussed on God-remembrance. "In very truth, the offspring of immortality (human beings) must focus their thoughts on God. Divorced from God there cannot be even a chance of peace, never — never — never ! By abiding in God-remembrance alone, man will find peace! The veil will be rent and the remover of sorrow will stand revealed. He alone is the conqueror of evil; He is the innermost being, the sole treasure of the human heart.

"Everyone without exception will have to put in immense effort. Men and women are equally endowed with the capacity for realizing God. It is the supreme duty of each human being to impart full worth to this birth which is such a rare boon (by engaging in God-remembrance), otherwise they will continue uselessly in the round of births and deaths."

During one of the very popular satsangs in Varanasi, a question was raised regarding rebirths. Pandit Vaidyanath said, "Ma, we believe in rebirths according to karmic laws." Sri Ma, "Yes, that is so."

Question: "But Christians believe in one birth only. After death they are to wait for the Day of Judgment when God will decide their destinies."

Sri Ma: "Yes, that is the truth."

Everyone laughed to hear Sri Ma endorse two seemingly opposite points of view. Sri Ma also joined in saying, "Bholanath used to call me queen of the Appellate Court *(Appealeshwari)*, because I seem to agree with everyone. The fact is that I truly see the interconnections between statements; the singulars one by one lead to the totality or infinity. What is there to reject and what is there to accept? Beliefs belong to the plane of the mind; the mind is shaped and determined by untold predilections. The proneness toward a set of beliefs rises from predilections which are not known to you. I see that whoever is expressing a belief is convinced that it is so and from his point of view that is so indeed!"

Sri Ma had a way of diffusing doctrinal disputations. She laid stress on the quest for knowledge which alone could resolve all doubts.

A God-oriented attitude of mind was needed. Unless and until man takes the path toward the supreme, he cannot find peace; therefore, the remembrance of God must be sustained under all conditions and circumstances.

She would say, "You ask, how to achieve peace? I say to you, if you constantly live with things which are unquiet and disturbing, how can you hope for tranquility? Sitting near a fire, you cannot feel cool. To attain God is to attain peace. All that is helpful toward this end is of the nature of serenity. There is no other way to peace."

When I contemplate the overwhelming variety, depth and flow of Sri Ma's *vani* (words) I feel like comparing it with the advent of the holy Ganga in our country. No set of simple words could do justice to the mystery of the mighty river's first majestic appearance, the beauty of the deep blue waters cascading down reverberating gorges; the playful dancing progress through mountain ravines to the plains at the foothills of the Himalayas. Here she takes on a new role. The scintillating shining waters become serene; the river flows deep and wide and gracious so that her people may derive as much benefit as they can from her bounteous presence. She allows them to take advantage of her generosity, even to exploit and to impose. She then silently withdraws into the ocean. Even in the act of withdrawal she divides herself in immeasurable ways for the benefit of her ever-demanding children. She comes in majesty and grace flows in abounding plenitude mile upon mile till she reaches the ocean for a mingling of the manifest into the anonymity of vastness. Through all the changes of her journey she uniformly maintains her purity. From Gomukh to Gangasagar the waters are holy and confer peace on all those who come to her. To the Hindu, she is the mother Ganga but she denies herself to no one; all are equally welcome to come to her shores to find holiness, peace and tranquility.

I remember a conversation between a *sadhu* from the Sri Ramakrishna Mission and Sri Ma regarding the future of India. The Swamiji tried for a long time to elicit some pronouncement regarding the future but Sri Ma parried his questions. To his question "Shall we ever achieve the glories of the past and again rise to new heights in the future?" Sri Ma said, "If so many of you feel that such should be the case, then perhaps such an atmosphere will prevail and your dreams will come true". The Swamiji was pessimistic. He said, "People are heedless. They are busy copying the West. And they (the Westerners) are coming to learn our ways and taking away the best of the East with them". Sri Ma said, "Why do you say 'they'? They are also you, isn't it?" This answer gave the Swamiji pause and food for thought.

Sri Ma's dialogues were full of puns alliterations and anagrams. All topics were dealt with lightly but profoundly. To a gentleman who asked her "How can union (*yoga*) be achieved?" She promptly replied, "Can you say you are experiencing disunion (*viyoga*)? The very thought, however, that I must be united with God or how may I be united with Him, will open up ways; yearning itself is the means to union."

Listening to her talks, discourses, casual conversations over the years, I realized that she was recalling to our attention the ancient Upanishadic thought of discrimination between that which is pleasant (*preyas*) and that which is good-in-itself (*sreyas*). All aims in life, all values guiding conduct, she would subsume under the one rubric of quest for ultimate truth. The donation of 10 minutes, each day, or one day in a one week program of *samyam* (restraint, abstention) formed parts of the same overall pattern of a life devoted to God-remembrance.

She seemed to gauge to a nicety the aura of anyone who approached her for guidance; she would start them off from wherever they were; she could fill with hope even the most pessimistic of interlocutors. Sometimes she met with indifference — this was also acceptable to her. Once she said, "If you have no interest and do not need to ask anything, then I have nothing to say but if you ask, and, if it is my *kheyala*, then certainly I shall tell you the *sreyas*, the ultimate worthwhile aim of life for every human being."

The ideal of renunciation permeated her discourses like the thread stringing many flowers together. Not that she asked anyone to renounce anything, not the world, society, a career, family, a home or friends. She would say that if one could abandon the mind at the feet of the Lord, then nothing more needs to be done. All will happen in its own time. She did, however, give the highest respect to anyone who looked to be a renunciate, a man in saffron clothes. Gradually, people of our generation came round to this new way of looking at our *sadhu-samaj*. It must be acknowledged that previously we had rather looked askance at ochre-robed people. It must also be said that Sri Ma herself was disappointed by many of these people innumerable times over the years, but she never lessened even an iota of her reverential attitude in the presence of a *sanyasi* (renunciate). These men and women were committed to the highest calling and thus deserving of respect.

An oft-repeated question in Sri Ma's vicinity was, "Can a man see God?"

Sri Ma: "Certainly, one can; He appears before the human eyes. Just as you see me before you and talking to you, so can one see God and hold conversations with him."

Sri Ma said many times that she was an onlooker only; she was not here to do anything or to teach anyone. In fact where was the "other"? She herself was all that there is, in fact there was no space even for her to turn over, so what was there for her to do or say? But if asked to give advice she would repeat her *vani* — "To talk of God alone is worthwhile. All else is in vain and pain."

CHAPTER SIXTEEN

Bindu and I Take Up Jobs

The illness which laid Didi low for nearly twenty years had first reared its head around 1953; Sri Ma came to Varanasi from Bombay just before Sivaratri in March 1955. We knew that Didi had been ill and under treatment in Bombay. Bindu and I went over to Varanasi to meet the party from Bombay. We found Didi lying on a mobile trolley in Sri Ma's room known as the red-verandah-room of the Kanyapeeth. Bindu and I did our *pranams* and greeted her asking her about her well being. She replied suitably and then introduced us to a gentleman sitting quietly in one corner of the room, saying, "They have come from Allahabad, they are Renu's younger sister and brother." We greeted him but took no further notice of him. We were in a hurry to go back to Sri Ma who was sitting out in the courtyard. Later, in the day, we heard from our sister the details of Sri Ma's *kheyala* regarding Didi's illness. Didi had been suffering from a backache for a long time. She had been treated for this backache for some while in Calcutta and also in Delhi, but it persisted till she became bed-ridden. Sri Ma was in Vrindaban at the time. She sent for Renu from Varanasi and explained to her that Didi would be left in her charge. Renu expressed her willingness to assume the *seva* of Didi. Gini was already in attendance on Didi. They both remained with her for many months thereafter. Sri Ma used to send one or the other of the ascetics living in the ashram to escort the party on their travels.

In 1954, the Samyam Saptah was celebrated in Bombay. The enthusiast for this function was S.N. Sopory. Soporybhai brought many of his new acquaintances to Sri Ma. The first names to be remembered in this connection are those of Dr. Surabhai Seth and B.K. Shah. Renu recalls that B.K.Shah, or Bhaiya (brother) as he came to be known in the ashram, seemed to have been watching the activities round Didi for a few days. One day he spoke to Ma, "I am addressed as Bhaiya by Didi, so I should be allowed to assume charge of her affairs; I claim it as my privilege to take care of my sister!" Sri Ma immediately told him to do as he thought fit. To begin with he called in the best orthopaedic surgeons of the town. Dr. Surabhai Seth was in overall charge of Didi's treatment. Many surgeons of good reputation came for consultations. The doctors diagnosed bone-tuberculosis. In order to immobilise the spine completely, they advised using a plaster-cast and wanted Didi to stay in Bombay for the duration of her treatment. Bhaiya vacated his Breech Candy Flat for Didi and her attendants. Renu recalls that there were groups of Gujarati ladies near Sri Ma. They were all very devout and ready to carry out her *kheyala*. Although Renu and Gini admired the richly-appointed flat with its magnificent view of the ocean, for many days they did not know who actually was the mistress of the household. It was an extraordinary example of self-effacement. Bhaiya's wife, Lilaben was totally identified with Bhaiya's attitude toward the devotees of Sri Ma. In time, we all came to admire her expertise in all household matters, her generosity, and her dedication to Sri Ma. Their house in Villeparle became an extension of the ashram, as it were. Relays of devotees came to Sunayana House for various reasons. Anybody in need of medical treatment was sent to Bombay and put under the care of Dr. Surabhai Seth who was the medical officer of the Nanawati Hospital at Villeparle. For more than forty years these great devotees continued to render the kind of service to Sri Ma that ordinary people can hardly imagine. Sri Ma came to depend upon Bhaiya as an unfailing support of her many-faceted *kheyala*. He would quietly assume charge of her many commitments regarding personnel, projects or travels that others might regard as burdensome. Not that anything was a burden to Sri Ma, but Bhaiya had a way of defusing a situation before it could reach the status of a problem. He was famous for this in his own line of business. At this time, he was the Chairman of New India

Bindu and I Take up Jobs

Insurance Company. A very big undertaking spoken of highly by those who knew about such affairs.

Bhaiya understood Didi's dilemma. She was in the habit of accompanying Sri Ma on her travels. With the help of the doctors and physiotherapists, he had a special cast made for Didi. When she lay in this cast, she was immobilised. She could be put on a trolley specially designed for her while she was in the cast, and thus could travel in vans or trains. The trolley was so constructed that it could be slid into 1st class carriages on the railways. The physiotherapist taught Renu how to lift Didi out of the cast, should the necessity arise. Incidentally, only Renu could do this, being taller than the other girls and also stronger.

When we saw Didi in Varanasi, she was on the trolley. Thanks to Bhaiya, Didi continued to travel with Sri Ma for many months till she was well enough to move on her own, her back supported by a stiffened jacket.

Bhaiya brought about changes in the ways of many families, especially ours. Sri Ma and her party went to Vrindaban after Sivaratri while Bindu and I returned to Allahabad. After a few days, we received a telegram from Swami Paramanandaji that Bindu should come to Vrindaban immediately. We thought that he was being summoned to take part in either a *namayajna* or a similar musical function. He returned to Allahabad after a few days, looking rather troubled. The story he told us was this:

During the Sivaratri in Varanasi Bhaiya had taken note of Bindu, his devotion to Sri Ma, as well as his general deportment in the ashram. He had told Didi that he wanted such intelligent young men from families of devotees for his company. He would welcome them as officers and train them in their job. Didi had immediately consulted with Swamiji and had sent for Bindu. Bindu had an adventure on the way. At a small station, he had got down for a cup of tea. He did not notice when the train quietly moved on out of the station. Nothing daunted, he made the railway staff ring up the next station to take off his baggage from the train. He caught a later train, collected his baggage at the next station and arrived in good order in Vrindaban, although a couple of hours later than expected. Bindu said that he went to see Didi first and related his adventure in high good humour. Didi signalled in vain to him to keep quiet about his silly mistake, as Bhaiya was sitting with her. Bhaiya said, "Never mind, Didi, you must see to the final results; he has got his baggage back and has arrived as expected!"

Thereafter, Bindu had a formal interview with Bhaiya. We did not know at the time that this was a rare opportunity. We were quite ignorant about the business world and singularly ill-informed about Bhaiya's importance and position in that world. We had also not encountered till then his particular quality of persuasiveness which sets at naught all difficulties. Bindu explained to him that his career had been mapped out in his family. His initials were S.N.M. My grandfather had so named him because he intended that Bindu should inherit the practice of my well-reputed uncle Saila Nath Mukerji. With this aim in view, Bindu had passed his law examinations and had recently been admitted to the Bar of the High Court. He had joined the profession as a junior to Babu Jagadish Swaroop, an eminent advocate. Bindu tried to explain to Bhaiya that he knew nothing about "insurance", except that people closed their doors when they saw an agent approaching!

Bhaiya smiled; starting from scratch, he disposed of all objections one by one till Bindu had no more to raise. Many years later we came to know about his ways of conducting difficult board meetings. One of the senior general managers related the story that once they had spent two hours in fruitless discussion and were about to embark on a collision course. Bhaiya was not at the meeting. He came in at the last minute; he heard what everyone had to say and laid down a policy, which met with instant approval from all members. Poor Bindu

Bindu and I Take up Jobs

was no match for this man, who was known for his dynamic leadership. When Bindu saw no way out, he said he was used to Allahabad and his home and would never dream of leaving 31 George Town. Bhaiya said that after his training, he could be posted in Allahabad.

Bindu then went in to see Sri Ma and asked for her *kheyala* regarding this new job. Sri Ma said, "If the Goddess of Wealth (*Lakshmi*) is gracious toward you, should you not make her welcome?" This *vani* was interpreted by Swamiji and Didi to mean that Bindu should accept the offer. My parents also thought the same when we heard about the entire episode. Ours was a family of lawyers, judges and teachers. Our elder brother was a police officer, that is to say a government servant. Bindu now entered the new world of finance. Actually, he was very good in this profession because of his marvellous range of contacts in every cadre of society. His numerous talents together with complete integrity and loyalty toward his company, made him rise quite rapidly in this profession.

Bindu prepared to leave Allahabad for the company training school in Dehradun. The farewell parties he was obliged to attend soon got out of hand. He had to fit in breakfasts, lunches and dinners, each day for many days. We hardly ever saw him unless we went to the parties with him. I remember one such dinner at the house of Professor A.C. Banerjee, Vice-Chancellor of Allahabad University. His son Milan Banerjee was a close friend. Milan's mother, Prabha Mashima (Auntie Prabha as we called her) brought out a gorgeous-looking sweet dish, saying lovingly, "Bindu, I have made this specially for you!" I was sitting next to Bindu and I knew that most probably he could not even bear to look at another sweet dish. He, however, expressed his pleasure and took a large helping of it. He then whispered to me "The worst that can happen is that I shall die of this. So be it!"

He survived his parties and left for Dehradun, leaving us a little sad. His lawyer's black gown was folded and put away. He had made his debut at the High Court in pleading for a writ petition which had been admitted by the Judge in accordance with the unwritten code which prevailed in Allahabad that a maiden effort should not be rejected. The judge, moreover, had spoken words of welcome, saying he hoped that he would revive the famous technique of his uncle and reintroduce wit and humour to the courtrooms. The Bar Association also gave him a farewell party.

During Bindu's absence, Babu and I continued with our studies. Babu steadily went through his graduation and enrolled for his Master's degree in Economics. The first General Elections were held in 1948 in our country. The only important party then was the Congress, which was elected to rule the country. There were fierce rivalries however, between some candidates and allegations of malpractice. The Government appointed a tribunal of 3 judges to hear election cases. My father was invited to be one of the judges of this tribunal in Allahabad. He was very glad to be of some service at this time because after retirement he was rather at a loose end. The three years of this tribunal tided over the transitional period for him.

During these years, I had very interesting experiences at the University. Allahabad University at the time was dominated by a non-brahmin faction, which was very powerful. My guide, Professor A.C. Mukerji, was not proof against the dictates of this group. When a post fell vacant in the Women's College, my guide in spite of his earlier promise that he would appoint me to it as the most qualified research student under his charge, gave it to another student, who was a little junior to me but she happened to be the daughter of the virtual 'King-Maker" of the university. When I met him next he said, "Do not be disappointed; when the post is advertised, and a Selection Board takes interviews, you are sure to come in. This is a temporary measure."

The post was advertised after one year. When I appeared at my first Selection Board interview, I was asked just one question, "Do you have any teaching experience?" to which I was obliged to answer in the negative. The Board recommended that the status quo be maintained for the time being. During the next 3 years I and my rival, who was also a friend, appeared at 4 interviews. My name came up first at each but for some reason or other it did not get through the Senate. But this also prevented my friend from being confirmed in

Bindu and I Take up Jobs

her appointment. In the meantime, I completed my research and also took up a job in one of the local colleges. This job was very low-paid but it would give me the experience of teaching graduate classes, the one qualification I did not have.

In early 1957, another Selection Board came to decide this long-drawn out case under the vice-chancellorship of B.N. Jha. My rival and I used to meet at these interviews; we would chat together before and after and compare notes. After this particular interview, which had gone specially well for me, she said to me, "I know you deserve to get this job; I have applied for a post in Pilani and I shall be happy to go and take up a job there."

I answered, I remember, "Let us not decide anything now, although it looks as if I have done well; one never can foretell the future!"

The next day, I was recalled to the University and to the interview room. It appeared to me that the whole Board was sitting just as they were the previous afternoon. Only the Vice-Chancellor spoke. He said, "A question has arisen about your expertise in teaching in Hindi, since it is not your mother-tongue. Will you please speak in Hindi today". This was easy for me because by that year I had been teaching graduate classes in Hindi for 3 years. I was the only candidate. I naturally came to the conclusion that at last the matter had been settled finally. But no. The Senate referred the question back to another Selection Board for a review.

In 1957, a post became available at the Women's College of the Banaras Hindu University. My friends in Varanasi put in an application on my behalf. I first came to know about it when I received a call for appearing at a Selection Board in B.H.U. I went to Varanasi and appeared at the interview, which I did not take too seriously because I had no intention of leaving Allahabad, but Providence is not that easy to deal with. I received a letter of appointment after a couple of months.

I had taught at the Prayag Mahila Vidyapeeth for 3 years. I had become very close to my colleagues and especially to my students. This is not the story of my experiments with education, otherwise I could write an account of how I and my colleague Dr. Laxmi Gurha (Political Science) worked together to reorganise the entire college from school classes to graduate classes. When we had joined it in 1954 it was in a mess. Assembly was just a rowdy group of youngsters and I was appalled to see the general air of lackadaisical management. Laxmi and I set our hands to establishing order and discipline, ably helped by Sujata Sen, the Vice-Principal Manorama Agarwala, Shanta Joshi and Mithilesh Kumari. We were a good solid group in charge of senior classes. The Principal kindly gave me a free hand to introduce such order and method as I saw fit. We became so successful that we were able to take some 200 of the students on a picnic. The girls were good and helpful and behaved in a perfectly responsible manner. It was most rewarding work for us. In all subsequent matters where the questions of student unrest came up, I for one never blamed the students. In my long career as a teacher, I have always found the students appreciative of good governance, fair and just dealings, hard efforts undertaken on their behalf and most of all competence in one's chosen field of work. I have always felt very rewarded by the response that I have met with from my students. I take this opportunity to record my appreciation of all the love and allegiance that I have received from my students in Allahabad and Varanasi. It was with deep regret, then, that I left my graduate class in Prayag Mahila Vidyapeeth and joined the Women's College in Banaras Hindu University.

I discovered that Dr. Padma Mishra, whom I had met earlier in connection with the Kanyapeeth, was very popular on the campus and very much appreciated amongst her colleagues. B.H.U. at that time had 14 autonomous colleges. The campus was laid out in broad semi-circular sweeps comprising central offices, colleges, playing fields, hostels for students while the outer ring consisted of quarters for the staff. It was a magnificent layout, the beautiful buildings vying in beauty with majestic trees lining all the avenues. Once or twice, I had to stay back on the campus during the summer vacation. This was worthwhile just to be able to walk along avenues of golden-orange flowering *gulmohars* and purple blossom laden *kachnars*.

Bindu and I Take up Jobs

Sri Ma came to Varanasi soon after I had joined B.H.U. She seemed pleased to see me. Giving me a garland of small fragrant white flowers, she spoke these strange words, "Keep visiting as usual; a sense of duty comes to the fore (when one is in service)". I pondered these words for a long time. Now, I realise that she was perfectly right. There were two types of people in service near her. One group was to be seen everywhere and so often with Ma that we used to wonder how they managed to stay in service also. Foremost among these is definitely dear Patun (S.K. Datta) who not only continued in his service but also steadily rose to higher and higher positions. Yet he was one of the very closest companions of Sri Ma, forever at her side to discharge her *kheyala* and assume many responsibilities. I definitely belonged to the second group. I became involved in my professional career. I loved to teach and took it very seriously. I was concerned about the students under my charge and devoted myself to their affairs. I got involved in extra-curricular activities with some success. When we had leave or during short vacations, I went home to Allahabad. My visits to Sri Ma became infrequent. Luckily, she came very often to Varanasi so that I continued to be close to her, but I saw more and more significance in the words she had spoken to me at the start of my career.

While Sri Ma was in Varanasi, a notice came from Allahabad University asking me to appear at yet another Selection Board. I came to the ashram after college and told Sri Ma about this notice and that I would have to go to Allahabad for the interview. Sri Ma said, "Repeatedly they have overlooked your claim, it will be like laying yourself open to a further insult, would it not?" I said, "Ma, times have changed a little. My case has acquired some notoriety; it is believed that this time they mean to set things right. My father is keen that I should return to Allahabad. I cannot just say to him that I will not come for the interview!" Sri Ma then spoke these decisive words, just for my father, "Tell Baba that I have said so."

In all my days with Sri Ma, I have seldom heard her make such a positive statement without qualifications. She always hemmed in her *kheyala* by many phrases, such as, "Is it not better? Do you think so? If you consider it right", etc., etc. But this time she spoke as if directly to him and in unequivocal terms.

I wrote back home that I would not come for the interview. In my absence my colleague and friend after all these years was confirmed in her post at last, so that was all right too. Sri Ma had asked me once if there was any difference between these two University posts. I had answered that B.H.U. paid a lesser salary than Allahabad, otherwise, they were the same. Strangely, after 3 months or so my starting salary was increased by Rs. 50 as special recognition of the research degree. Now it was exactly the same as the starting salary of Allahabad University which in those years used to be Rs. 300. B.H.U. however, provided spacious quarters with a garden on the campus together with all service facilities, so it was one of the most coveted jobs in those days.

I used to return to Allahabad every weekend. I had so arranged my classes that I could leave by an evening train and return on Monday morning by an early one. This was my first experience of living alone in a house. It used to feel strange in the beginning. I remember one day I was reading the newspaper late at night. I was taking care not to make loud rustling noises when I suddenly realised that there was nobody else in the house and that I would not wake anyone up. Such small things brought home to me the fact that I was strictly on my own. Our old family servant Antu had been sent to set up household for me. He was bored with nothing to do the whole day. Very speedily he engaged a young female companion housekeeper for me and left for Allahabad. This young girl, Ramkali, and I carried on for a couple of years, then she left to join her husband. Thereafter, I had the good fortune to be served by an elderly Nepali woman, Gangabajai, who became well known to all my friends and family. She was a great soul, imbued with a spirit of service, devout, hard working and with an exemplary temper which was most disarming.

1957 saw the beginning of student uprisings in B.H.U. I became involved from the very first day, as it were, but that would be another story. Some of my colleagues came to the ashram with me sometimes. Strangely, not many became involved, at least not as much

Bindu and I Take up Jobs

as Padmaji and I were. I was always amazed by the indifference shown by the bulk of the people who gathered round Sri Ma. They treated her as the Movable Image (*chalanta vigraha*) of a temple. They paid her obeisance, received a garland or sweets and went home to carry on as before. She was recognised as a Divine Presence, and thus a source of blessings and *kripa*. A daily visit to do *pranam*, like a daily visit to the temple, sufficed for most people crowding round her. She was beautiful, gracious, talked in a delightful manner, distributed flowers, fruit and sweets and made absolutely no demands. Sometimes, if asked for advice she would say, "Give me 15 minutes of your time, everyday at a chosen hour; try to think only of God. You may do *japa*, or meditate or just keep silence. This slot of 15 minutes is a thin wedge to insert into the ever-revolving cycle of preoccupation with the world. Maybe this little break can be expanded. By God's grace it will influence the rhythm of your whole life!"

Sri Ma's *vani* that she was an onlooker was certainly true. She had repeated often that she had not come to do anything but just to see how everything was, just as a gardener strolls down his garden path and observes the various plants and creepers that enhance the beauty of the premises.

In the winter of 1958, Banaras Hindu University hosted the annual meeting of the Indian Philosophical Congress. Amongst others, I saw Professor J.N. Chubb of Elphinstone College of Bombay who had come as an expert to Allahabad for the last Selection Board I had attended. He knew me at once and thought I was a delegate from Allahabad. He was astonished to hear that I was teaching in Varanasi instead.

I came to know him quite well. From him I came to know the details of University politics which had kept me out of its teaching cadre. He had been specially appointed by the Chancellor to rectify the omission. Apparently he had not succeeded. But he told me about another incident which was of more significance to me. He told me about the interview that the delegates of the Indian Philosophical Congress (Dhaka, 1929) had with Sri Ma at Shahbagh. He had been the youngest member of the group. The academicians had put searching questions to Sri Ma. She had answered each one brilliantly. Her answers had been spontaneous, in simple language but of profound implication. He specially remembered one question and its prompt rejoinder. Someone from the group had asked, "If everyone were to work toward achieving goodness, would the world become perfect in future?" Sri Ma said, "But it is that already!"

Professor Chubb said that he had been struck by the spontaneity of the answer. He had glimpsed an understanding which truly saw the world as an expression of the Good.

The last years of my father's life

After many upheavals in my father's personal life, as well as the political changes which had affected us rather closely, he had leisure to enjoy the peace and tranquillity of 31 George Town for a few years. My eldest brother was settled in Government service. Bindu had come back to Allahabad after his training. He had opened the first office of New India Insurance Company with a staff of two.

I had gone away to Varanasi but I came to Allahabad very often and my father knew I was happy in my job. He was reconciled to my sister's sojourn in the ashram. My cousin Sidudi came every year with her two sons during summer vacations. The children (Sidudi's sons Prabhat and Protap and my brother's daughter Mimi) grew to love the extensive grounds of the house, just as we had done in our childhood. Lastly, my brother Babu, after getting his Master's degree, appeared for the examination for the banking services. We were very glad when he was selected for the officer's grade by the Bank of India, but a little saddened too, as he would now leave home for training and posting.

As written earlier, Sri Ma visited Allahabad quite often during these years. She would stay at Satya Gopal Ashram or in a house-boat on the river, or a tent pitched on the lawn of some devotee.

Once Sri Ma came to Jhunsi. The mahatmas were also with her. She told my father that the evening *satsang* would be held in our house. She gave directions to enclose the portico and put up a rostrum for Haribabaji facing the house. She herself would sit at the side

Bindu and I Take up Jobs

(Northeast). The audience could be accommodated on the steps going up to the entrance lobby and then the drawing room itself. All these specific arrangements were for the mahatmas. We knew that had she been on her own she would not have said anything. All was done as she directed but the rains came in the form of a deluge. We now realised that she had so positioned Haribaba that he remained away from the slanting rain which drenched Sri Ma. Haribaba went on reading his text. We held up umbrellas behind Sri Ma's chowki. The rainwater washed over the carpets on the floor of the portico. But the festive air prevailed. All devotees were entertained to the midday meal. The whole house was filled to capacity with local visitors and guests from out of town. Sri Ma's presence made it a gala occasion. She went away with her entourage by the late evening train to some other destination, plunging us into sadness. An account of this *satsang* is written in Amulyada's book also; he praises my father's hospitality toward all devotees.

On an earlier visit Sri Ma had said to Bindu, "I come here to Allahabad, but there is no place for me to stay! I have to manage somehow or other." This was a very unusual statement on her part, but perhaps Bindu was deserving of this *kheyala*. He responded by saying that as soon as he was old enough he would build a little cottage for her in our compound.

Many years passed. Bindu now had a job. When Sri Ma came to Allahabad she still made the best of impromptu arrangements. But now she reminded Bindu of his promise of a cottage at 31 George Town. Due to Sri Ma's *kheyala*, Bindu was able to build a cottage for her under a huge neem (margosa) tree a short distance from the main house. We furnished and decorated the little house in anticipation of her next visit to Allahabad. Renu had asked our gardeners to build a set of village-type tiled mud-walled rooms at the side of the cottage, where *bhoga* could be cooked. Actually, Sri Ma used to spend afternoons in one of the rooms as it was cool and quiet. Many functions were held at our house in later years but, somehow, Sri Ma came less often to our house after the cottage was built than earlier, or so it seems to me. At this point in time, I realise that Sri Ma had this cottage built so that it would later on become for our family a temple where she had resided, once we were deprived of her *darshan*. The worship of her Image installed in the little building has become an important part of our daily life now.

My father's last *darsana* of Sri Ma was in Varanasi during the Durga Puja of 1959 in October. This festival is always a big occasion for Bengalis. Sri Ma's presence enhanced its magnificence a thousand fold. My parents came from Allahabad to attend this Puja. They stayed with me in my quarters from where they visited the ashram to attend the *puja* for the 3 days of its duration. Throughout the *puja*, the public participates by offering flowers to the Goddess to the accompaniment of mantras in Sanskrit. After the priests have formally accomplished their ritual *puja*, some time is given to the feature known as *pushpanjali*. The devotees keep a fast till it is time, hold flowers in their cupped hands and repeat mantras after the priest; then they throw the flowers toward the image while standing outside the inner sanctum. Some devotees remembered that my father could recite beautiful mantras to the Devi. His voice and enunciation of Sanskrit were very good and especially heartfelt in this case, as he was a Shakta. We had organised a Durga Puja in Allahabad a year earlier; people remembered that he had recited these beautiful mantras for the public for 3 days. Now, in Varanasi by popular demand, he took over this job of the priest and led batch after batch of devotees in their worship of the Goddess with *pushpanjali* (flower offering) for all the three days. On Navami Tithi (the 3rd day), after the last batch of worshippers had finished, his voice sounded a bit hoarse. He was in the inner sanctum while I was standing just outside. He turned round and seeing me remarked with a smile, "This is my last effort (*ai amar sesh*)!" I thought he was tired and did not want any more stragglers to come up for another session of *anjali*. Maybe he did not know himself but the words were prophetic. This did indeed turn out to be his last Durga Puja.

My parents returned home. I came to Allahabad to spend the Deepavali holidays with them, which continued until 8th November

Bindu and I Take up Jobs

that year. At the time of my departure for Varanasi, my father said he would also come to the station to see me off. Bindu and my mother were already coming. My mother said, "In that case, we shall have to lock up the house." He said, "So, let us do it." My mother realised he had made up his mind so we all went to Rambagh Station. Bindu drove us in his new car. My father never went to see people off because he did not like to do so. I was a little taken aback at his accompanying us this time. Some of my friends from Prayag Mahila Vidyapeeth where I had taught for three years had also come to the station to meet me. I cannot say that I had any premonition but it so happened that I kept looking at my father to the exclusion of everyone else. As the train gathered speed I leant out of the window and saw my father standing tall and straight with his hands in the pockets of his checked woollen brown *sadri* (a sleeveless collared jacket), the walking cane hanging from the crook of his right elbow. It is still a clear image in my mind bringing unaccustomed tears to my eyes. I wish I had talked to him more, told him how much we appreciated his care and concern for us — pointless regrets. I could not have known that I would never see him again.

Some time during the evening of the 12th my friend Gyanvatiji came over and told me that there was a message from my mother that I should go to Allahabad immediately as my father was ill. I took the message lightly because I had seen him just three days back. However I just had time to catch the evening train, the famous, or rather infamous, Upper India Express of those days, the only broad-gauge train which connected Varanasi and Allahabad across the Ganges. From Varanasi we entered Allahabad in the dark over the bridge at Phaphamau. I must have been a little upset in spite of myself because I got off the train at Phaphamau. When the train started moving, I realised that I had not heard the typical sounds of crossing the bridge which prepared us for our own station, Prayag on the other side of the river. I just managed to board again one of the last compartments which was in motion and passing slowly in front of me.

At Prayag, I looked for Bindu as usual but found his friends Subodhda and Rajeeva Dave instead. To my question, they answered that my father was all right. When the car entered our road, I was surprised to see a line of other cars and the whole house ablaze with light. By this time, I did not know what to expect. I fleetingly thought that they must have called in a lot of doctors. I entered my father's bedroom and found him lying very normally in his usual posture of sleeping in his big four poster bed. A sheet was pulled up to his chest. His face was very serene. My mother was sitting at the foot of the bed. She looked calm and a little withdrawn. There were other people sitting around quietly or standing about outside the house. The realisation came to me that my father was no more. It was about 10.30 p.m. by now. I was surprised to see my sister-in-law who I knew was in Meerut with my brother. She obviously had been crying and was very upset. From her I heard and pieced together the events of the evening. This was the week of the *samyam saptah* of our ashram. This *saptah* was being celebrated in Calcutta. My mother like many others observed the regimen as far as they were able during the week. My father and she had eaten a light lunch; my father then had lain down as usual for an afternoon nap. My mother had sat in meditation from 3 p.m. to 4 p.m. in the next room. At four she had made tea and brought it to his room. She was surprised to find him still in bed and touched his shoulder to awaken him. Although he looked as if asleep she immediately knew he was no more. Thereafter all that my mother did, seemed incredible to us till she told us much later privately that as she touched my father she felt that her wrist had been grasped strongly by Sri Ma and that thereafter she was guided in her movements. It seems my mother first went outside, calling out to the gardener Jagdeo to fetch Madan, a friend of Bindu's who lived at the end of the road. She then rang up the family physician and friend, Dr. Chatterjee, who was out; she told his wife who took the call to send him over as soon as he returned. Before this day my mother had no occasion to use the telephone for calling anyone; she may have once or twice taken incoming calls. Not only did she make the local calls but she got through to Varanasi by trunk call. She was alone in the house; that she could locate the relevant numbers, that she could call the operator, was truly astonishing. Madan said later, that when

Bindu and I Take up Jobs

he arrived he saw her holding the receiver and speaking to Gyanvatiji. My mother finally relinquished the receiver to Madan and went back to my father's room where she sat at the foot of the bed for almost the whole of the next 24 hours. Our friends and relatives told us later that they had marvelled at her serene expression; and said they understood what it was like to be in the presence of *kripa* (grace).

Bindu was not at home. Madan got hold of his other friends and by dint of persistent enquiries located him at a party. They made the mistake of not preparing him in anyway for the bad news. He walked in to find my father lying as I saw him. He took it very hard but there were doctors in the house who took care of him. When I came he was sitting quietly in the drawing room looking drained and exhausted. He had cried for hours, his friends said.

My sister-in-law was expected to arrive from Meerut that evening. Her brothers were going into the army. She wanted to consult my father regarding the paperwork and other personal matters. Again, Bindu's friends received her at the station. She arrived, carrying carefully, the new rose Perfecta by Kordez sent for my father by my brother, who was a very keen rosarian. She placed this bloom in a vase on his bed-side table and also removed the cup of tea which was still sitting there.

Rajeeva Dave was all this time trying to contact my brother Manuda in Meerut, my sister Renu in Calcutta and Babu, who at this time was in his first place of posting, Jamshedpur.

Manuda could start for Allahabad very late and it was calculated that he would not reach home till late in the afternoon the next day. The story that my sister had to tell about this event was the strangest of the lot. The *samyam saptah* was in progress at Calcutta. Sri Ma was as usual sitting on the rostrum during the hour of meditation from 3 p.m. to 4 p.m. Some time before 4 o' clock she got up unexpectedly; with her hand she gestured that nobody should leave her seat, otherwise her entourage would have got up to follow her. She beckoned to my sister who was sitting in the first row of ashram girls. Holding Renudi's wrist she walked slowly to her little cottage where she lay down on her bed. Renudi sat near the entrance till Sri Ma again got up and walked back to the rostrum to participate in the on-going programme. Some time after the *maunam* which was at 9 p.m., the ashram received the news of my father's death. Nirvanananda went up to the rostrum to Sri Ma and gave her this news quietly. In the agitation of the moment he did not realise that there was a microphone just in front of Sri Ma. The entire congregation heard clearly that Sri Ma's devotee Niraj Nath had passed away in Allahabad a short while ago. The strange thing was that only Renudi did not hear this announcement. My cousin Sidudi sitting next to her realised that Renu had not heard anything and did not know how to deal with the situation.

On the conclusion of the evening session of the *satsang* Sri Ma sent for Renu and Sidu. People like Anil Ganguly and Gopal Dasgupta and other friends were in tears but a message came from Sri Ma that no one was to say anything to Renu. To Renu Sri Ma said that it was her *kheyala* that she was needed at home so she should return to Allahabad as soon as possible. Swami Paramananda, another person very close to my father, quietly carried out Sri Ma's *kheyala* and made arrangements for Renu and Sidu to catch the first flight to Allahabad next morning. While Renu slept, Sri Ma went on dispatching people on various errands. Our cousin Buba who was standing near said Sri Ma was up almost the whole night. She lay down for a little rest after Renu and Sidu had left for the Airport. They arrived earlier than Manuda from Meerut, who was obliged to come by car having missed all train connections.

Throughout the night and day, the people of Allahabad kept vigil with us. Many people came into my father's room just to see the utterly tranquil expression on his face and pay their last respects. I heard some whisperings regarding the advisability of fetching blocks of ice but ultimately nobody did anything about it as my father's body remained in perfect condition. People were evidently ready with loads of flowers; as soon as my brother arrived, a funeral procession was organised. Aloke Mitra, the young proprietor of Mitra Prakashan decorated the cortege. He used to come and talk with my father very often; there were other young people who had loved to chat with him. My father's contemporaries and friends filled the long approach

Bindu and I Take up Jobs

to the house. Somebody remarked that such a death was possible only in a yogi of considerable spiritual eminence, especially as the face and body showed no trace of deterioration even after 24 hours. This was my first encounter with death. Since then I have seen other beloved persons' bodies whence life had departed and been troubled by the memory; therefore, in retrospect I too marvel at this phenomenon. Father could not have struggled with a heart-attack, otherwise my mother would have heard him or his bed-clothes would have been in disarray. He seemed to have passed away in his sleep. Sri Ma took him away as easily as one gathers a flower from the garden.

The house slowly filled with our relations; Babu, poor fellow, came the next day. Within the first few days Sri Ma passed through Allahabad on her way to Delhi. We went to the station to pay our respects. She told us not to grieve but to make it an occasion of an on-going *satsanga*. So Bindu and all of us gathered in my father's bedroom every evening and he began by singing his favourite song: "*Ma jar anandamayi, se ki niranande thake* (it cannot be, that one whose mother is the Blissful One suffers unhappiness)" All visitors who came to mourn with us joined us for the *kirtana*. On the eleventh day the most elaborate funeral rites were performed by the three brothers. A chapter of our lives was over.

Sri Ma returned to Allahabad in December and stayed in Bindu's cottage for nearly 3 weeks.

She had no other programme in Allahabad. She gave audience to all who came. She chatted to Bindu throughout the day. I think this was the time during which Denise and Arnold Desjardins came to visit her. When the University closed for the winter vacation I had a strange reluctance to return to 31 George Town. I who had rushed home almost every weekend, now could not face the emptiness. Padmaji was going to Lucknow. Seeing my restlessness she took me with her to her home. After a couple of days, since Sri Ma was continuing in Allahabad I came home to find a festive atmosphere in the house.

Sri Ma and Bindu had a good laugh at my expense. On seeing me Sri Ma said to him, "Now she turns up! What does she care that I am here? She goes to visit a friend!" Bindu endorsed all these sentiments in high good humour. It was not possible to be sad in Sri Ma's radiant presence. We really enjoyed this visit very much. Sri Ma was relaxed, with no appointments restricting her movements.

One day a European young girl came to visit her. This girl was learning yoga in India. Sri Ma asked her to show her some of the postures. She demonstrated a few and then lay down in *shavasana*, the last relaxed posture. She said it is difficult to hold this posture correctly because in spite of oneself the muscles remain tensed. She demonstrated with the girls who were in the room. She would lift a hand or foot, or even a finger and say, "See, there is slight resistance. The body should become as if lifeless in this posture." Sri Ma said, "Alright, try with mine." She lay down on her chowki. Her whole body became as limp as a rag doll. The yogi tested her by lifting her head and one or two limbs. She was amazed. She had not seen such perfection even in her own guru. Sri Ma laughed and sat up. She said, "These postures are often used as exercises by people, so they only succeed to a certain degree. In the *sadhana* for spiritual emancipation, the postures happen naturally and therefore happen as they should."

I remember another occasion. We were all sitting in Sri Ma's room, when suddenly she got up from her chowki and folded her hands in a *namaskara* to someone standing at the door. We made way for him. My mother recognised him as the eldest brother of our family priest. A square of carpet was brought for him. When he was seated Sri Ma sat on the floor in an attitude of deference toward an important personality. In the course of conversation that ensued we came to know that this family of priests was related to the family priest of Bholanathji. Sri Ma and Bholanathji had visited Allahabad once in the late twenties. They had stopped for a single day in the temple of Kali at Muthygunje. Bholanath and Sri Ma had paid a call of courtesy on this family of priests. It was amazing that Sri Ma had recognised him at a glance after almost 30 years. Sri Taracharan Bhattacharya on his part recalled with wonder his first impression of Sri Ma.

Bindu and I Take up Jobs

After Sri Ma left our home we talked amongst ourselves. She had obviously stayed with us to help us out of our depression. We realised that she had kindly sustained us through our feelings of being suddenly plunged into deep sorrow. In retrospect we all think that Bindu suffered his first heart-attack then. He said quietly, "It was as if a stone weighing on my chest was removed by her." My mother was not demonstrative, so she continued in her usual calm and dignified way. I once heard her remark to a contemporary who had come on a visit of condolence, "How do you adjust to the sudden loss of a close companion of nearly 40 years?" But Sri Ma had helped her from the first day. We also saw as the years passed that Sri Ma's *kheyala* was constantly with her, and also with each one of us. We became busy in the world and forgot her sometimes, but she never did. Whenever anyone stretched out a hand it was held in a sustaining grip. I would rather say that from time to time we were turned away from such chosen courses of action as would have got us entangled in the meshes of the world by an ever-vigilant *kheyala*.

CHAPTER SEVENTEEN

Sri Ma's Birthday Celebration at our Home

Manuda was understandably very upset by the turn of events. He could not have stayed in Allahabad because he was in a transferable service. Bindu was at his first posting in Allahabad as promised by Bhaiya. He now offered to take charge of the house and try his hand at maintaining the establishment for at least one year. In case he felt inadequate, he would let us know, he said. Bindu, thereafter, rose to the occasion very successfully indeed. He stayed at 31 George Town for the next 5 or 6 years; during this time many important events took place. The mantle of the head of the house descended on him which he wore very gracefully and competently. My mother and sister stayed with him.

Sri Ma continued to visit Allahabad frequently. Once Prabhudattaji Maharaj received her at the railway station and insisted that she came with him to Jhunsi. Sri Ma in passing whispered to Bindu to try and fetch her back the same evening because she had the *kheyala* to proceed elsewhere next day.

Bindu went to Jhunsi in the evening and, meeting Prabhudattaji, prostrated himself at his feet. Brahmachariji was always kind toward Bindu for his gift of a melodious voice. He bent down, slapped him on the back and gave him his blessings; but Bindu continued in his posture of obeisance. Brahmachariji was non-plussed and everyone else started laughing. Then the Mahatma said Bindu only had to ask and he would get his wish! Bindu raised himself and said, he wanted permission to escort Sri Ma back to Allahabad for the night. Mahatmaji had a sense of humour and laughed with the others at being tricked into giving his consent to Bindu's prayer!

Sri Ma's Birthday Celebration at our Home

The village-style hut erected for Sri Ma at the side of her main cottage

The Janmotsava, or the Birthday celebrations of 1961, took place at 31 George Town. Swami Paramananda put this idea into Bindu's head. This year the celebrations would be for one day only. The duration of the celebrations depended upon the difference between the English Calendar date of May 2 to the Indian Calendar date of the 4th day of the dark fortnight. In 1961, the dates were just one day apart. It was a great occasion. Actually, Sri Ma and her entourage stayed with us for nearly 3 weeks. Innumerable functions were organised. The entire compound was one big ashram. The Delhi-party came to perform their *nama-yajna*. The mahatmas came and were suitably housed in nearby residences. Swamiji had supervised the putting up of the *pandal* (marquee) where a rostrum had been built for the holding of daily satsangs.

It was characteristic of Sri Ma that she achieved important tasks with the minimum of fuss. One of these days I was surprised to see Bindu and Babu dressed in the Indian garb of *dhoti* and *chaddar* (that is, unstiched clothes), sitting quietly in the small room adjoining Sri Ma's bedroom. They were awaiting my mother who had been sent for, and when she hurried in, Bindu said in exasperation, "Ma, where did you disappear, we have been waiting for you!"

Sri Ma at 31 George Town (1961).
Clockwise: Manu, Babu, Protima, Mimi, myself, Bindu, Renu, my mother.

Sri Ma's Birthday Celebration at our Home

I realised that Sri Ma had arranged for their initiation, as she had done for my sister and myself more than a dozen years ago. All of us came away leaving Sri Ma to direct and guide my mother in the proper procedures. Sri Ma said later to the small gathering in her room, "There is a special bond of uncritical attachment between these young men and their mother — this is why I have had this *kheyala* for them. See how fortunate for Bindu and Babu is today's ceremony. The Goddess has established herself right in front of them for this occasion!"

Sri Ma was referring to the Holy Icon of Tripurasundari which Raja Pratap Singhji had placed in the small room in the morning. This rare *yantra* was especially sacred to his royal house and went everywhere with him. Now, the Goddess had come to our abode to be in Sri Ma's cottage for the duration of the festivities.

It happens to be a fact that amongst all the families devoted to Sri Ma, ours is the only one where the brothers and sisters have been given the *tantrik diksha* by the mother. Sri Ma had not asked Manuda to join the others. Didi did suggest to him to take advantage of this opportunity. He laughed and said, "Nothing so simple is going to help me; for my cleansing Ma will have to apply caustic soda at least!" I think Sri Ma herself spoke to him later and gave him something to do.

One day we received a message that the Prime Minister, Pandit Jawaharlal Nehru who was visiting his ancestral home "Ananda Bhawan", wished to call on Sri Ma for her *darshan*. He, accompanied by Upadhyaji, his private secretary, and his daughter Mrs. Gandhi came in the evening in a limousine. There were no security outriders or any other car preceding or following his. Panditji, Indiraji and Upadhyayji were escorted to Sri Ma's cottage, where they sat for a while.

Soon it was time for Sri Ma to proceed to the public *pandal* for the satsang. As Panditji spoke no words of farewell, it was understood that he was not in a hurry to go away but would accompany her to the rostrum. Sri Ma sat with her guests on the rostrum. The people of Allahabad were very pleased to see the Prime Minister. They greeted him and some of them requested him to address them. Pandit Jawaharlal Nehru smiled and said that this day he had come to listen and not to speak. This statement pleased the audience; they also prepared to listen to Haribabaji's discourse. Sri Ma began the *satsang* by leading a *kirtana* for a few minutes. The Prime Minister seemed very relaxed; but he had another engagement at the Holland Hall of the University of Allahabad, so after some time he made his obeisance and went away.

After all the festivities were over we suffered a little from the reaction but also felt very happy that such an important function could be achieved so satisfactorily without any mishaps. Of course, Sri Ma's presence always precluded any untoward events, anywhere, or even if they did happen her way of dealing with unpleasantness made them seem not so.

Additions to our family

This Birthday Celebration seemed to put in train a series of happy events in our family. Babu got married in November 1961. Once again our family gathered at 31 George Town, on this occasion for almost a month's celebrations. The young couple, Babu and Meera, went all the way to Vrindaban to pay their respects to Sri Ma right after their marriage. Sri Ma was most gracious toward them. Meera developed a close tie with Sri Ma, independently and not only as a member of our family. They then went away to Jamshedpur.

At about this time the family arranged a marriage for Bindu. Bindu had declined to entertain any thoughts of marriage because he had been suffering from arthritis since his college days. The medical sciences were not quite clear at that time regarding the treatment of this disease. Instead of exercises for the affected area, the doctors had immobilized his lower spine in a plaster cast for six months. He himself had the wisdom to get rid of this cast but some damage had been done. All his life he suffered from this initial setback. At the time of Babu's marriage, he was well-established in his service, gaining prestige and status day by day. While he was driving Sri Ma from Varanasi to our house in Allahabad, she herself persuaded him to get married. Swami Paramananda, sitting in the back, broached the subject of his marriage. Sri Ma took it up, saying one should adopt a clear-cut aim in life. If one were religiously inclined then one could eschew worldly

Sri Ma's Birthday Celebration at our Home

entanglements, but just to enjoy life in the world without taking up any of its responsibilities was not right. Bindu mumbled some excuses, but Sri Ma overrode them saying he must choose between a life of complete dispassion or a life of a householder. She then laughed and said, "You must make your decision before you enter the gates of your house!" Bindu was heard to mutter his choice of a householder's life.

At first, poor Bindu was very unhappy. He was like the uncrowned king of Allahabad and enjoyed his own popularity immensely. He said, "If I get married, I shall become so ordinary."

He need not have worried. He remained what he was because his wife was so beautiful that a lot of glamour was added to his charm. Bindu's marriage was a very special occasion. As soon as news of this event spread in the town, the whole thing went out of our control. In our system of arranged marriages, the bridegroom's select entourage is entertained for one night at the bride's house. The bride's father prepares to receive ten, twenty or at the most thirty people or so. Now, we just could not tell how many would be accompanying the marriage party. Everyone wanted to come. The bride's father Professor Shambhu Charan Chatterjee of Varanasi rose to the occasion nobly, our rather apologetic estimate of at least a hundred people he took in his stride.

Ustad Ali Akbar Khan came to Allahabad for the occasion and he lead the procession of about 20 cars to Varanasi. The whole motorcade stopped in places where he himself let off rockets and other noisy devices. Poor Bindu was embarrassed, but he naturally could not say anything to his revered Ustad.

After the marriage ceremony we returned to Allahabad with the bride. In our turn, we made arrangements for a large number of people who could come to the marriage reception. The invitees included High Court Judges and other elite of the town and also Bindu's master tailor and other shopkeepers who served him on a regular basis. The whole of the shopping area of Civil Lines was closed down that evening because all of them came to attend the reception.

We were happy to receive Shyamali as another bride at 31 George Town. Babu's marriage had been very well organized as a successful function by Bindu and all of us, but Bindu's marriage was quite like a *mela* or a jamboree which has come to town.

Shyamali learnt how to arrange matters when Sri Ma came to our house and also to take care of the dozens of people who automatically became our guests for the duration of her stay. There was no end to Bindu's daring. He asked Sri Ma to come to us on the occasion of the Saraswati Puja in February 1964. We prepared for the occasion with great enthusiasm. Sri Ma most graciously occupied the cottage for a week or so. The presence of Sri Ma always enhanced the beauty and grandeur of these festivals. These were happy times; especially when Babu was transferred to Allahabad by his Bank. He was asked to open a new branch in his home town. He now had two daughters Neelanjana (Nilu) and Indrani (Tulu). The house was now full. My sister had stayed on with my mother since my father's death. Manuda and I came whenever we were free to do so. Sri Ma continued to use her cottage off and on, much to our delight.

Mimi's marriage to Professor Sheelbhadra Banerjee of Bombay took place in November 1966. Again we had a happy gathering at 31 George Town. This marriage seemed to round off the cycle of family festivities because the other two girls in the family were mere children at this time.

Sri Ma with new members of the family at 31 George Town. Shyamoli, the two girls Tulu and Neela, and Meera (hidden behind Neela and Renu (1976).

Sri Ma's Birthday Celebration at our Home

CHAPTER EIGHTEEN

Random Memories

After I joined the B.H.U., I was not able to follow Sri Ma around on her travels. I just kept up the routine of attending the Birthday celebrations. I attended the *samyam saptah* at Sukhtal because Sri Ma had sent for me. I also went to Vrindavan for another *samyam saptah* because the girls told me that Sri Ma had remarked on my continued absence. I had not seen Sri Ma for a long time. When I arrived at the ashram I found *satsang* was in progress in the hall. I stood at the door to have *darshan*. Sri Ma looked at me from her distant seat on the rostrum and then very deliberately turned her face away. I was actually amused at this so human reaction. While bowing down in *pranam* I said to myself, "Turning your face away will do you no good — you cannot desert us and we have no other refuge to turn to". When I raised my head and stood up I found her gaze on me and with a most beautiful expression as if she was endorsing the sentiments. I somehow remember this incident very clearly.

Other random memories go back to earlier years. The *maunam* (silence) of 15 minutes from 8.45 p.m. to 9.00 p.m., which is observed in all our ashrams, was begun some time during the year I was in the Kanyapeeth, 1948-49. This short period of *maunam* always used to be observed near Sri Ma, that is to say, wherever she happened to be in the ashram. One evening Sri Ma was lying on her *chowki* (cot) in the red verandah of the Kanyapeeth building. Didi and one or two of us were sitting around chatting desultorily. Sri Ma spoke about the period of *maunam*. I understood her to say that the entire ashram should become silent and still during this time. "How nice it would be", she said, "if at the stroke of the hour a quiet should descend to envelop the entire building, but it is too sprawling and there are too many people busy with various activities". I asked if I should try to organise the *maunam*. Sri Ma said, "Can you? Try and see".

I thought for a while, then went to Atulda in the Annapurna Mandir. I explained to him the details of the project and asked him if he would blow upon the conch-shell loudly from the parapet thrice at exactly 8.45 p.m. He being a very helpful person agreed to do so. Then I went to each department, up and down the staircases and through corridors. The general kitchens were right down near the Ganges. Our own kitchens were behind the main building. The kitchen staff everywhere were either amused or disgruntled at the idea that they would be required to stop work for a while at the sound of a conch-shell. Some wanted to know if everyone was to come to wherever Sri Ma would be sitting. It took me some time (and it took a few days for all this to become a habit) to explain that the idea was for everyone to keep *maunam* while doing whatever they were engaged in during those 15 minutes. Utter silence should prevail in the entire ashram.

Years passed, nobody remembered that I had first organised the ashrams for this period of silence. I myself was amazed when, after almost 30 years or so, Sri Ma once mentioned this fact in my hearing. She let me know that she remembered it on an occasion when she was asking me to arrange some function at a particular time. She said, "Do it the way you organised the time of the *maunam*".

Many awkward situations developed when mahatmas became frequent visitors to our ashrams. Sri Ma postponed all her appointments in order to keep herself free for the ensuing *satsang*. The young girls surrounding Sri Ma at all times had cause for resentment because they had to keep their distance while the *sadhus* were in *satsang* with her. Life became extremely difficult when Sri Krishnananda Avadhutji became an ardent devotee of Sri Ma. He was a great renunciate of exemplary reputation, but he seemed positively to dislike the sight of the girls forever surrounding Sri Ma. So whenever he came to see Sri Ma, she made it clear that we were to leave the room and wait outside. One rather amusing incident happened because of this situation. We were in Puri at this time. It was during a vacation, because a lot of us were there. From the open window in Sri Ma's room Avadhutji was seen to be coming along the seashore. We hastily removed ourselves to the next room and to the open verandah outside Sri Ma's room. Only young men like Abhayda, Bibhuda and Bindu remained. When Avadhutji was seated in Sri Ma's room she asked Bindu to sing a *bhajan* because the Swamiji was very fond of devotional music. Bindu began with the well-known song "*man ko range jogi sache rang me* (O ascetic, soak your garments in the true colours of detachment. Saffron clothes alone are not enough)".

While Bindu sang in his melodious voice, we watched Sri Ma fidgeting on her *chowki*. She would glance at us and then quickly avert her eyes and stare out at the ocean. Avadhutji sat still and seemed to like the song. He then did his *pranam* to Sri Ma and went away. With a sigh of relief, we trooped in to find Sri Ma almost helpless with laughter. She was half scolding Bindu for his choice of song. She was saying to him, while wiping tears of laughter from her cheeks, "Bindu, Bindu, how could you! To sit under the nose of the *sadhu* and sing this song! I did not know how I kept my countenance. Thank goodness the girls were not here, otherwise if they had broken into

Sri Ma at Puri

even the ghost of a smile, I certainly would have lost control. You will see, the *sadhu* will not come again!" Poor Bindu scratched his head and said he had not chosen the song with anything particular in his mind, which of course Sri Ma already knew. Needless to say, the revered Swamiji had not taken it personally either.

How endearing was Sri Ma's behaviour with her retinue of young people, how circumspect with the ascetics, and all this done so gently and so joyously. Joyousness was the keynote of our experience of those days we spent with Sri Ma.

The person most annoyed by this intrusion of the *sadhus* in our lives was Bunidi. Bunidi never attended *satsang*; she would await Sri Ma in her own room and be ready for her with a glass of water or some small pieces of fruit. Very often Sri Ma had no time even to take these refreshments, but Bunidi was always ready with them in case she did. Renu once told us a story about Bunidi and the *sadhus*. In Almora the buildings where the *brahmacharis* (young ascetics) stayed was at a distance from the living quarters of the young girls with Sri Ma. The girls were not supposed to trail after Sri Ma when she went to visit the *sadhus*. Sometimes she, accompanied by Didi, spent the night in her room within the sadhu-building. This was too much for Bunidi. She prevailed upon Renudi and Ksamadi (and perhaps Billoji) to set up an *akhanda kirtana* for Sri Ma begging her to come back to their part of the ashram. She improvised by singing. "Please, to us come back, we suffer from your lack" and many more nonsensical lines to rhyme with the *kirtana*. She said they would keep on singing till Sri Ma came back. Late at night somebody suddenly realised that Abhayda was sitting in their midst. Bunidi at once embraced the lady sitting next to him and discovered Sri Ma. Sri Ma had quietly left her *chowki* and had unobtrusively entered the girls' room and had sat quietly in their midst for quite some time. With her head and face covered, she had looked like any other white-clad ashramite. Abhayda, discovering that her *chowki* was unoccupied, guessed her whereabouts and disobeying the rules of entry came over to the girls' quarters. The girls were joyful but Bunidi berated Abhayda since Sri Ma went back to their part of the ashram because he would not leave without her.

Once Didu (Chhabi Chowdhary), Bunidi and I were with Sri Ma, on her visit to Bishtupur. We were told that it was Sri Ma's *kheyala* to proceed further without her entourage of girls, accompanied only by Swamiji (Paramanandaji) and Didi. The three of us were told to go back to Calcutta and await her return. Didu and I were not given to protest and we sadly began to pack our things. Bunidi was not reconciled to this parting at all. She cried and cried and made everybody miserable. At Kharagpur Junction, we boarded our train while Sri Ma and her one or two companions stood on the platform to see us off. Didu and I looked out of the window but Bunidi was slumped in a corner still wiping away her tears. As the train started, Sri Ma took a corner of her *chaddar* (shawl) in her hand and started waving it in the manner of a handkerchief. She then proceeded to move along with the train almost running, just as we always did when she was travelling and we were left on the platform. I cried out, "Bunidi, Bunidi, look at Ma!" Bunidi then sprang to the window and leant out (there were no bars to the windows in those days) and laughed to see Sri Ma waving farewell to us while running with the train. So Sri Ma saw Bunidi's laughing face before we left. Bunidi sat back saying, "She did it just to make me laugh, but I am very annoyed all the same". But her mood had changed.

Sri Ma never countenanced emotional displays in any of the young people who surrounded her. Tears, sulks, or hurt feelings she ignored or dealt with in a hundred different ways. However, Bunidi's case was exceptional. We all admired her commitment to the service of Sri Ma. Among the girls, she came closest to gauging Sri Ma's *kheyala* and acted accordingly. She used to suffer from asthma very badly, but she would always be neat and trim and so would she keep Sri Ma's miscellaneous effects. Memories crowd in — Bunidi was a person who felt happy when Sri Ma was joyous and radiant. If Sri Ma were grave or serious, Bunidi would try to divert her *kheyala* toward something light and funny, so that Sri Ma would smile or laugh. Sri Ma, however, seemed quite often to prefer disorder and impromptu arrangements. Once when she left on a short visit to Etawah from Dehradun, she only took Renu with her, leaving Bunidi at the ashram.

Bunidi was so upset and so given over to crying that she forgot to pack Sri Ma's clothes for the journey. Arriving at their destination, Renu was appalled to see that there were no blouses or petticoats for a change of clothes. At night when all visitors had gone away, Sri Ma asked Renu to fetch one of her *dhotis*. Under Sri Ma guidance, Renudi sewed a blouse and petticoat from this cloth. Sri Ma managed with these few garments — nobody came to know that she had so few clothes to wear and change into; actually people noticed only the spotless white *chaddar* (wrapper) that Sri Ma used in all seasons.

Bunidi, in spite of her occasional lapses, was irreplaceable as a custodian of Sri Ma's effects. Sri Ma lived in a perpetual state of disarray after Bunidi's regime was over. The other girls who came after her were never so competent. I take this opportunity to pay my tribute to Bunidi who was totally devoted to Sri Ma and was like an older sister to the younger cadre of girls like myself, Gini, Tara, Buba and many more. In retrospect I realise that not the least rewarding experience of our life with Sri Ma was this richness of many friendships with contemporaries.

Letter writing sessions with Sri Ma were always very rewarding. The ever-increasing bag of letters which Didi carried with her with such care was a regular item of her baggage. Every so often she would request Sri Ma to give some time to the letters. Important or urgent letters were read and answered as occasion demanded, but the bulk of them consisted of homely news from devotees who just wanted to keep in touch with Sri Ma. Sri Ma herself developed a pattern for disposing of her letters in one session. Five or six of us would take out all the letters from the bag and distribute them amongst ourselves, generally according to language, such as Bengali, Hindi, Gujarati or English. We would read them carefully, mark the important sections or just make a precis. Sri Ma sat on her *chowki* while we sat in a semicircle in front of her. Turn by turn we would "read" out the letters and take down her answers. She was very swift. She gave her full attention to each correspondent and dealt with each seriously. There were a few correspondents who wrote prolifically. There would be five or six letters from the same person in the bag. We were not supposed to ignore any of them. She listened to each one after which we had arranged them date-wise. Sometimes certain letters amused us but they evoked no answering smile from her. She gave all of them her serious attention. But she would clap her hands if we could empty the bag in one session and say, "Now Didi will be happy".

Sri Ma's answers are preserved verbatim in Didi's priceless collection of *vani*. I reproduce a few here to give samples of Sri Ma's care and concern for each of her correspondents.

To a woman who wrote in anguished terms about her affairs, saying she was angry with Ma for her unconcern:

"This body has caused you sorrow, think nothing of this body, disregard it if you can. All of you should engage only in the pursuit of that Ultimate One. He is compassionate, merciful. He is ever beckoning you to him. My mother (the correspondent) feels hurt — but that has also a beautiful side to it."

"You have been given this valuable human life — Do not waste time in useless thoughts. Render service to everyone in the household in the conviction that all forms are different aspects of God. Make friends with 'the personification of anger'. Think that you are rendering service to Him, to Him, to Him alone. If you can maintain the spirit of service, you will see you are being enriched with love, devotion and reverence toward Him. Time is short. Is it intelligent to waste time over thoughts which cause obstacles? You must not say, 'I cannot'. All relationships are temporary after all. You do not know what the morrow will bring — everyone must pack his own belongings for that journey.

> *Get ready for that journey on your own*
> *That is one path that you will travel alone.*

"You feel like scolding this body? Why not? Whatever you feel is welcome here. It is my *kheyala* that since this body cannot do anything for anybody, in becoming the object of your scolding it is rendering some little *seva* (service) after all."

Another devotee who was a renunciate wrote to her about the administrative problems in his ashram. She answered:

"Pitaji knows that this body does not have anything to say regarding these controversies. Had it been otherwise this body would surely have obeyed (given directions). But I ask, what is the use of engaging yourself in these matters? You have donned saffron robes, the colourful uniform of the navigator of the boat for crossing the river of life; your own *sadhana* is the wherewithal for the propelling of the boat. Whatever you have written about pertains to the world; these thoughts are not conducive toward crossing the river. No help whatsoever. Whoever or whatever is creating these hazards which must lead to drowning midway — beg of them with folded hands to allow you to proceed unhindered. Whatever is clouding your mind now are obstacles, obstacles, and obstacles. Engage your mind in the thoughts of the *atma* only."

Sri Ma had a quick way of answering questions put to her in passing. Once a woman said, "Ma, how do you keep your equanimity in spite of being constantly troubled by so many of us without respite for days?" Sri Ma said, "How do you keep your sari in orderly folds in the face of constant changing conditions? You do it automatically, not even becoming aware of the movements of your hands, don't you?"

The woman was very much struck by this answer. She exclaimed, "Now I understand what the Geeta describes as *abhyasa-yoga* (yoga by practice). The effort which becomes a normal way of life". I do not think Sri Ma meant quite what the lady understood her to mean but such exchanges happened very often.

Another woman said to her, "Ma, you have to deal with crowds of strangers all the time, nowadays. Don't you ever feel tired of this constant influx of outsiders?" Sri Ma smiled and answered, "Don't you get relatives as guests staying in your house? When kith and kin come, don't you treat them as family? You don't even notice the extra work. Isn't that so? Nobody is an outsider here".

Once she happened to come across a group of elders who were indulging in jokes not to be spoken in public. Sri Ma overhearing their talk added a jocular statement of her own which made them burst out laughing. One of them, a judge (Benoy Bhuson), said in wonderment, "Ma, you have no experience of the matters we were discussing; how do you understand this nonsense and moreover comment so wittily on it?"

Sri Ma said, "Baba, you are required to listen to tales of crime. Do you have to experience them before you pronounce judgement?"

The quick rejoinder was appreciated by Benoy Babu and his friends.

Shastra-vachana (scriptural authority)

Sri Ma was residing in Varanasi. Every evening after College, I went to the ashram and returned to the University late at night. One evening I entered Sri Ma's room to hear a lively discussion about the four *ashrams* of life. The first is that of the student who lives in his Guru's ashram for twelve years learning arts and crafts and the scriptures. After this period of *brahmacharya* (strict celibacy) at the age of 25 or 30 he returns home to get married and assume the duties of a householder. It is expected of him that he will uphold religion, family, social customs and moral traditions and be kind to animals under his charge. This is the second ashram known as the *grhasthasrama*.

After 25 or 30 years of this life of exemplary righteousness he and his wife together would go back to forest hermitages of their choice to practice *sadhana* leaving their sons to carry on their traditions. This third stage is called *vanaprastha*. The couple together strive for dispassion (*vairagya*) and devote themselves increasingly to a life of spiritual endeavour. There are some obligations. They are to visit villages and undertake such social services as are conducive to *sadhana* — men could teach scriptures, women also if they are qualified, or they may do some work more suited to their abilities.

After this comes *sanyasa*, the final stage of renunciation. The renunciate is free to devote himself totally, one pointedly and relentlessly to the quest for Truth. He has no more obligations to family, friends or society because his dedication and success is of paramount interest to the whole of mankind. To realise the meaning of being born a mortal in this world is to discharge a debt to humanity, forge a link in the chain of such teachers who have achieved ultimate bliss and can promise the same to other seekers.

Someone had raised a question in Swami Paramanandaji's presence that all the young women surrounding Sri Ma had no spiritual future because they belonged to none of the regular *ashrams*. Swamiji had posed this question to Sri Ma. When I came in Padmaji, Buaji (Miss Lalita Pathak) and my contemporaries were gathered in Sri Ma's room. Each was answering this question according to her own perception of her own way of life. Padmaji looked amused, Buaji impatient of such irrelevancies. Swamiji said that according to the scriptures one may proceed from *brahmacharya* to *sanyasa* eschewing the intervening stages, or proceed systematically; but we were beyond the age of the first stage (from 12 to 25 or so), but had not entered the married state, so were neither this nor the other; instead we were all *pandashramis*. The term *pandashrama* is pejorative, implying a state ending in futility. It is also a word parodying the Sanskrit terms.

As soon as I happened on the scene Sri Ma asked me, "What do you say? Paramananda says unless all of you get married you will remain in a *pandashrama* and will not qualify for spiritual emancipation". The discussion was being carried on in a light-hearted manner. Swamiji evidently was teasing Buaji, Padmaji and other senior persons present. I said, "Do we live by scriptural injunctions alone? I do not think we need to follow this particular tradition (of getting married in order to belong to the *grhasthasrama*)". I had not given any serious thought to this problem and had spoken the first words which came to my mind. Sri Ma's laughing expression changed. She became grave. She said to me very seriously, "I did not expect to hear such sentiments from you. That you should say such words (about not paying heed to the scriptures)."

I was a little taken aback. The discussion went on for some time but thereafter I took no further part in it. Sri Ma's words had made a deep impact on me. I do not recall that any conclusions were arrived at on that day. Thereafter, I began to study the meaning of the role of scriptures in our tradition. As a student of philosophy I was already familiar with the question of a difference between reason and faith, the rules of exegesis in interpreting scriptures and other such related matters, but had not interiorised or thought about them from a personal point of view. This self-education became an ongoing process. I listened carefully to the talks of Swami Akhandananda Saraswati, a most erudite scholar of our times. I read the very illuminating writings of Karpatriji, another renowned scholar. All this however, remained as if gathering dust, till I had the opportunity of going abroad and coming into contact with spokesmen of other traditions. I had much to learn before I understood Sri Ma's disapproval of my answer.

The Opening Ceremony of Sri Ma Anandamayi Seva Hospital

We have some very pleasant memories of this function in the ashram at Varanasi playing hide and seek with rather grim ones as well. Bindu had his second brush with death, but this time he was miraculously kept safe for us by Sri Ma's protective care.

The well known doctor Gopal Dasgupta of Varanasi had become a devotee of Sri Ma. He had started a milk-distributing centre for all such children whose parents could not afford this necessity for them. It was named Anandamayi Karuna. Over the years, this institution had grown into a medical-centre; finally a fully equipped hospital had been built near the ashram as a Charitable Institution. The then Prime Minister, Smt. Indira Gandhi had been invited to perform the opening ceremony.

Since Sri Ma was making a longish stay at Varanasi, Bindu brought my mother, sister and his wife Shyamoli to stay with me at B.H.U. from where they could go to the ashram every day. By this time, he had so expanded his jurisdiction, that he himself was kept busy at the regional office and with tours to nearby places. Sri Ma had let him know that she would like him to be in the ashram when the Prime Minister came because she had a *kheyala* that he should sing a devotional song on the occasion. On the eve of the opening day, Bindu did his *pranam* to Sri Ma, telling her that next morning he would be going on a tour but he would be back in plenty of time for the visit of Indiraji, the Prime Minister.

Random Memories

Sri Ma said, "Can't you postpone your tour?"

Bindu answered, "No, Ma, because many people will be waiting for me at various places. I shall start very early in the morning so I can return in time."

"Very well, then come to see me before you start on the journey (*dakha kore jeo*)". "Ma, who will let me disturb you at 5 o' clock in the morning? Udasji will certainly not open the door to me."

"Never mind. You come to the door and shout for me (*Ma bole jore dak dio*). I shall open the door to you."

Udasiji and others naturally smiled at this and so Bindu got a rare *darshan* and the *prasada* of a garland before his ill-fated journey to Faizabad. Within five miles of Varanasi, the car skidded on an oil patch on the macadam road and overturned into the ditch. The car actually made a complete somersault and landed again on its wheels. At first glance, nobody seemed to have been hurt, a miracle in itself. Bindu was accompanied by his junior officer Mr. G.K. Kapoor and his driver Tripathi. Tripathi scrambled up on to the road and stopped a truck going toward Varanasi. This truck helpfully towed the car out of the ditch on to the road and back to the town to Kapoor's house, where they changed over to another car and so drove to my quarters in B.H.U. Bindu was seen to be in much pain. He could not enter the house because all of us were at the ashram for the function.

The ashram that day had been taken over by the department in charge of security for the Prime Minister. All approaches to the ashram were sealed off. Indiraji would come by launch along the river. Entrance to the *pandal* (marquee) was by invitation and passes only. The magistrate had probably seen Sri Ma's entourage of more than a dozen young women on his previous visits to the ashram. He told Panuda that when Sri Ma came to the *pandal* she should be accompanied by two people only. This created a consternation. The girls looked askance at each other, not knowing which two would be the lucky ones. When Panuda posed this problem to Sri Ma, she in her usual calm fashion said, "Padma and Bithu will come with me", naming the two outsiders, thereby forestalling all controversies or heart-burnings.

Padmaji and I went to the ashram quite early as asked by the management. We accompanied Sri Ma at the proper time to the *pandal* and on to the very spacious rostrum. Sri Ma's *asana* (square of carpet) was placed at one side, we sat behind her. An *asana* was placed in the centre for Indiraji.

The Prime Minister was punctual to the minute. She was accompanied by Dr. Sushila Nayyar, the Health Minister, and other local officials. She came swiftly up the stairs to the rostrum and kneeling in front of Sri Ma, made her *pranam*. Sri Ma greeted her with a smile and a few words of welcome. While getting up Indiraji looked smilingly at Padmaji and myself and then realised that we were strangers and not Chitra, Udasji, Pushpa, Shanta or any of the others she was in the habit of seeing with Sri Ma. I also saw her from such close quarters for the first time. I had been under the impression that she was taller, but she seemed petite and of course very smart. She spoke to the audience and performed her part gracefully and competently.

After the public function, Sri Ma returned to her room in the Gopal Mandir of the ashram. She had been as much a V.I.P. guest at the function as any of the other invited notables. On behalf of the ashram, H.H. Maharaja Manavendra Shah of Tehri Garwal and H.H. Maharaja Kashi Nareshji had received Sri Ma at the rostrum steps. There must have been a host of notables but the police cordons were so rigid that we remained very isolated throughout the function.

After the function, Sri Ma received Indiraji in her own room and talked with her privately for some time. I was now free to leave the precincts. Not seeing any of my family in the crowd I walked to the entrance of the lane to our ashram and was surprised to see Tripathi, Bindu's driver, beyond the police cordon. He said, "Sahib wants you to come home as soon as possible. I have a car here." So I went home to find Bindu and Kapoor standing outside the house while Pickie, Bindu's small dog who was locked in inside was yapping fit to deafen anyone and was ready to break down windows or doors. I first released Pickie who scrambled all over Bindu for a few minutes much to his discomfort. I was concerned to hear about the accident. I took Bindu to the University Hospital immediately. We were lucky to find

Professor S.M. Tuli the Orthopaedic Surgeon still on his rounds. Bindu was examined and X-rays were taken. Dr. Tuli advised complete rest and prescribed the necessary medicines. Later, he told us that there were hairline cracks in the lower section of the spine which must have received a tremendous jolt when the car turned over. A miracle that Bindu had not broken his bones, since due to arthritis his body had already lost much of the litheness natural to ordinary people.

Sm. Indira Gandhi with Mataji and myself at the Varanasi Ashram

By the time we returned from the hospital, my mother and sister were back and Tripathi was sent to fetch Shyamoli from her parents' home. The front sitting room was quickly converted into a bedroom and Bindu could lie down at last. He did not seem to derive any greater comfort from this position and was evidently in great pain. We were kept busy with the various arrangements for his care, the visits of doctors and concerned friends who came to enquire about him.

Late in the evening we took it in turns to visit Sri Ma. She was told about Bindu's accident. It seemed she was expecting to hear some such news. My mother stayed at Bindu's bedside. It was not her way to pray for the recovery of any of her children when they were ill. She just depended on Sri Ma to do whatever was best according to her own *kheyala*. Bindu remained bed-ridden the next day also. He has in excruciating pain. Bindu had been ill many times but we experienced terrible anxiety this time because we had never before heard him groan, as if in spite of himself. The pain was so bad that he could hardly breathe properly. On the third day Miss Pathak, or Buaji (auntie) as we called her, came to see Bindu. She was very affected to see his suffering. She went back to Sri Ma and said to her, "Bindu is in a very bad way. I have never before seen tears in his mother's eyes. Truly he is in great pain". Sri Ma said nothing.

In the afternoon, when the ashram experiences a period of lull after the midday meal and before the evening *satsang*, Sri Ma quietly left her room and came out. Vimaladi (Dayanandaji) was in the lobby and was surprised to see her standing in front of her without her sandals or *chaddar* (wrapper). Sri Ma, without giving her time for any questions, asked her to prepare a medicinal dose of some edible ingredients she named. When this little pellet was ready Sri Ma held Vimaladi's arm and started to descend the staircase. Vimaladi realised that Sri Ma was going out. Disengaging herself for a minute she ran to fetch Sri Ma's sandals and shawl. Sri Ma accompanied by the wondering Vimaladi walked along the lane to the main road. Strangely, not one of the devotees who teemed round the ashram when she is in residence saw her.

Arriving at the main road, they saw Patalda about to enter the lane. He naturally was amazed to see Sri Ma. She asked him "Do you know Bithu's quarter in the B.H.U. Can you take me there?" Before he could even answer in the affirmative, a friend of his driving a car stopped near them. He was coming to the ashram. He hurriedly got out of the car, carrying two garlands in his hand as offerings. Sri Ma took them in her hand saying, "All concatenation of events (yoga) augurs well." (Later she enumerated them, as for example, she could walk out without a lot of people asking her all sorts of questions or wishing to stop her so as to make proper arrangements for her, that she met Patalda at the right moment, one of the few people who knew my house in B.H.U., that a vehicle with a willing driver arrived on time and lastly that he presented her with a couple of garlands instead of the usual one).

We in the University were amazed at the sight of Sri Ma quietly entering by the garden gate. She hesitated a little before the steps to the house. Pataldi said very robustly, "Ma, these houses belong to the University. Members of the staff come and go; they are not permanent homes but rather like a *dharamshala*."

In any case Sri Ma had the *kheyala* to enter. She came into the house and stood near Bindu's bed. She started to find fault with all my arrangements, "Look at this bed, how can he be comfortable in such a narrow one; bring another *chowki* and make it broader". While we rushed around, doing her bidding she made Vimaladi, unseen by us, put the medicine in Bindu's mouth and gestured to him to swallow it. She spoke to him about his accident. She then lightly put both her hands on his chest and made rubbing downward movements a few times, probably thrice. She gave the garlands to Shyamoli and Bindu, referring to the coincidence of there being a pair for them.

Shyamoli, finding Sri Ma so close and approachable ventured to speak about Bindu's current situation. She said, "Ma, he will not allow us to stop an unending stream of people from coming to see him. Dozens of his office staff have already visited him and more will come as news gets about to neighbouring towns. The doctor told him to rest but he is constantly being disturbed."

If Shyamoli had expected to meet with sympathy, she was disappointed. Sri Ma smiled at her and said, "You see, he is so charming in his ways that all kinds of people feel concern for him."

After a few more minutes, Sri Ma went away, leaving us to wonder and marvel at her *kripa* and graciousness. Very soon my mother noticed that Bindu's shallow breathing had become normal and he seemed not to be suffering from the pain which had held him almost as if in a strait jacket. He was lying very much relaxed and at ease. He improved rapidly, so much so that next day he persuaded Kapoor to drive him to the ashram. He mounted the staircase to Sri Ma's audience chamber without help. Everyone was astonished to see him and exclaimed joyfully at his recovery. Sri Ma laughed and held out a garland for him. He came up to her and bowed in *pranam*. When he raised his head his face was a little flushed. Sri Ma said, "Why do you go in for this extra exertion now". She put her hands on his head and shoulders in a gesture of blessing. She asked the girls to get a harmonium. When it was brought to him, Bindu sang a couple of songs for Sri Ma. Her *kheyala* of hearing him sing had brought him safe out of his accident which everyone said could have been fatal.

Sri Ma and Bindu

Another interesting incident comes to mind concerning Sri Ma and Bindu. Once in Vindhyachala, Buni became very ill at night with one of her periodic attacks of asthma. Sri Ma asked Renudi to prepare a paste of ginger and honey and give infinitesimal drops of this medicine to the patient at regular intervals. Renudi stayed awake with Bunidi the whole night. In the morning Sri Ma stood on her first floor balcony looking out toward the road as if waiting for somebody. A car was seen to begin the slow climb on the very steep road to the ashram. Sri Ma took a corner of her shawl and waved it like a handkerchief saying, "Come, Bindu, come". Bindu's car was an ordinary coloured Fiat. At that distance nobody else could have made out that he was the driver. By the time the car approached the gate, Sri Ma had gone round to the north-side balcony. As soon as Bindu stepped out she said, "Do not come up now. Go and fetch a doctor from Mirzapur, Buni is very ill."

When the doctor came, the patient had recovered a little. He approved of Sri Ma's interim relief-giving medicine, saying it was just the right thing for an asthmatic patient.

The fates tried to take away Bindu from our midst once again in the summer of 1981. At this time, he was in New Delhi. Sri Ma was in Haradwar. Bindu had gone on a tour of Rajasthan. On his return, Shyamoli insisted that he go to the hospital for a check-up because he looked so ill. The doctor detained him and transferred him immediately to the Intensive Care Unit as he had suffered a massive heart attack. Shyamoli came home without him to give this devastating news to my mother and sister who were at his flat at that time. Renudi rang up the ashram at Haradwar to give the information to Sri Ma. Sri Ma, it seems, looked grave and said, "I do not see any good future".

All the girls standing around exclaimed, "No, no, Ma, Binduda must get well."

Before she could repeat her statement they reiterated their faith in his recovery twice more, asking for her *kheyala* for it. Thereupon Sri Ma said, "Well then, let us see". She used to send someone with a flower, or garland or a fruit every day to the hospital for Bindu. By her grace he survived his serious illness and resumed his normal way of life. He was able to visit her as usual and also to sing for her on occasion. Sri Ma had once said that his voice had a touch of dispassion in it. Perhaps it was especially appealing because of it. Lately he was very much out of practice and used not to recall the songs in their entirety. Once while singing he forgot the lines. He was very embarrassed and apologised to Sri Ma. Sri Ma presented a garland to him and said with a smile, "The song was beautiful, the forgetting also was sweet (*Gan sundar hoyechhe, bhule jawao misti hoyechhe*)."

Bindu was very conscious of his lack of practice in singing, especially because in his leisure hours he preferred to play the sarod. He never put himself forward when experts were performing in Sri Ma's presence, but somebody or other would push the harmonium in front of him because everyone knew that Sri Ma would like to hear him sing. Once Bindu arrived a little late for the evening *kirtana*-session in Varanasi Ashram. Sri Ma had retired to her room which opened on to the first floor balcony near the temple of Annapurna.

The musical instruments were still to be taken away from in front of the temple which was now quite empty of crowds. Bindu sat down with the harmonium and began to sing one song after another. A small knot of people gathered round him in no time. Dasu came to play the *khole*. Not many people know that Dasu and Bindu were given the sacred thread in Sri Ma's presence in Varanasi in 1941, so they were friends of long standing.

Sri Ma in her room stopped conversing with the few people sitting around her chowki. She said, "Keep quiet, I shall listen to Bindu's singing." She lay down on her chowki and in the ensuing silence, Bindu's quite remarkable voice came floating in clearly to Sri Ma's room.

I would like to end this chapter with a quote from Richard Lannoy's letter dated May 23, 1997. I had asked him if he had met Bindu on his visits to Varanasi. He wrote:

"My memories of your brother are very sparse, alas. I met him only once when he visited Varanasi Ashram, probably in 1954, but just possibly 1957 or 1958-9. I remember him telling me he was called Bindu when a little boy because he was so small. And that he would crawl under Ma's bed. But the Bindu I met was a fine upstanding and handsome man with a magnificent voice. During Satsang that day he sang a Raga with exquisite musicality and spiritual devotion while Ma and everybody listened in rapturous silence — Bindu's voice rang out from the Satsang hall and could have been carried in delicate sound-waves across the placid surface of the Ganga to worshippers on the ghats, as in the accounts of legendary singers in olden days. But if these memories be called 'sparse' the simplicity and the clarity of them has remained undimmed for close on half-century. He was a big-hearted man of great charisma."

CHAPTER NINETEEN

An Invitation from Abroad

At the beginning of the Seventies, my college underwent a change of management; working conditions deteriorated. I had been teaching undergraduate classes since 1954 (initially in Allahabad) and wanted a break from routine. Coincidentally a change came my way at this time. Our Head of Department, the distinguished scholar Dr. T.R.V. Murti, was kindness itself to his younger colleagues. When two of his senior colleagues, Dr. Mehta and Dr. Sivaraman, went abroad for the academic year as visiting professors, he immediately invited those of us who were teaching in the Women's college to come to the department and take some post-graduate classes. This was a great relief. We now came in closer touch with our department and could deal with subjects more in keeping with our specialization.

It was around this time that I met several professors from Canadian universities who were on sabbaticals and had come to B.H.U. to be in touch with Dr. T.R.V. Murti and other scholars of the town. Professor G.M.C. Sprung from St. Catherine's was very interested in every aspect of Indian life. Several of us gathered in his room for general discussions. I met also his wife, Ilse, when she joined him for a while. She happened to be in B.H.U. when the Prime Minister of Canada, Pierre Trudeau visited Sri Ma at the ashram. Ilse came to the ashram with me to see how Sri Ma would receive the Prime Minister of her country. She waited in the hall with the public while the Prime Minister had his private interview with Sri Ma. Sri Ma had chosen me to interpret for Mr. Trudeau. Since his questions were not of a private nature although personal, they may be published now because they reveal Sri Ma's easy way of communicating with a man belonging to another religion, another country and a different tradition altogether.

After he had greeted Sri Ma, she said to him, "You are coming from a far away country, did you have a comfortable journey? Is everything congenial and comfortable now?"

After the visitor had replied suitably, a few more questions and answers of like nature followed. Then she said, "There is One Supreme Reality in and beyond the universe. That alone (The Reality) in this form (of yourself) has come to meet with this body, to whom nobody is a stranger or a newcomer. There is but one Reality — one Atma — It is that which has always been, is, will be. It is eternally abiding and yet ever new". The visitor quietly contemplated this statement then asked, "Is progress possible?"

Answer : Yes, always. With effort you may achieve an experiential truth which is direct, palpable and real. Just as a student may achieve a state of knowledge which to begin with was not within his grasp, so a human being may attain to a level of awareness which is permissible to his state of creature-hood.

Question : This attainment, does it happen all at once or after long efforts?

Answer : Both. You keep on striking a match — the flare is always sudden, it may happen after much effort or at the first stroke. In God's creation everything is possible.

Question : How can a man know that what he is doing is the right thing to do? Whether he is being true to himself or not?

Sri Ma : Is this question about things in this world or the other?

Question : To me, the two are not separate. I can understand the other only in relation to this world.

Sri Ma: There are stages, or levels, of understanding. The student of the lower grade has potentiality but he cannot be expected to grasp the lessons of the higher grades. The veil of unknowing or ignorance is pushed back from time to time. Man can act according to his best knowledge of a situation; but his efforts are relative and not absolute. For this reason, you see, you make an all-out effort but the result is not to your satisfaction. It is not possible for human beings

An Invitation from Abroad

to know what is best. What you said about not differentiating between two worlds is very just. This world is dominated by the mind and so is divisive. The mind operates in the realm of creativity, fruitfulness, the better way of life etc. The mind measures. We are determined by our sense of values. The mind sets out norms. The Immeasurable is perfect as it is. This realization dawns with the liquidation of the mind. The realization that whatever is, is That only. It is just as it should be and not otherwise. It is true, however, that unless one obtains that comprehensive vision of totality one may not give up his best efforts to do what he thinks is the right thing to do.

There was a little more conversation joined in by the Ambassador who was already well-known to Sri ma. Mr. Trudeau and Sri Ma walked out on to the terrace for a while. Mr. Trudeau seemed quite happy and relaxed and gave as much time as possible to the Press. He insisted on carrying the very special *asana* given him by Sri Ma instead of allowing his aides to take it from him.

Sri Ma on the terrace with Pierre Trudeau

My Days with Sri Ma Anandamayi

At this time there was a resurgence in the use of Hindi at B.H.U. Many of our non-Hindi speaking professors became unhappy with working conditions in our department. Professors from South India or other provinces had no students who could audit their lectures in English. One of our professors, Dr. K. Sivaraman, like many others thought seriously about emigrating abroad or transferring to another university.

Dr. K. Sivaraman was a scholar with many interests. His grasp of Western as well as Eastern systems of philosophy was truly phenomenal. His real talent lay in being able to use lucid language to explain the most abstruse problems of philosophy. His genial and outgoing personality attracted a whole group of young scholars and students for informal sessions of inter-religious discussion. In time, I came to know many in this group because I had taken a sabbatical from my college and had joined the Department of Philosophy to work on my project: "The systematic exclusion of tragedy from our indigenous way of looking at the world around us". This topic had intrigued me for a long time and I wished to make an in-depth study of it. During this period, I also went to the Calcutta National Library for a month and worked hard at amassing a mountain of notes on the subject.

The Department of Philosophy at this time was visited by other professors from Canada. Prof. and Mrs. Sprung introduced me to Dr. and Mrs. Paul Younger of McMaster University in Hamilton. One day I met Kapil Deva Tiwari, a research scholar from McMaster. Kapil Deva was junior to me in Allahabad University while we were doing our postgraduate studies. He had retained very flattering memories of my university career and was very glad to see me at B.H.U. He was working under the guidance of Prof. J.G. Arapura of McMaster University. Professor Arapura was spending his sabbatical year in India. McMaster had allowed Kapila Deva to accompany his guide so that he could continue with his work. Kapila Deva urged me to apply for a fellowship at McMaster University in case I really wanted to take time off from teaching and go in for research and study. He introduced me to Professor Arapura and broached the subject on my behalf. The Professor was neutral in his attitude, which was right. He

An Invitation from Abroad

said if I so wished I could apply with two letters of recommendation. Professor Arapura must have endorsed my application because I did get a post-graduate fellowship for the term 1972-74. But due to many unexpected events I could not go to Canada before 1973.

Many people are interested in knowing how Sri Ma affected the lives of the most unlikely people, to say the least. At this point in time, I think I can disclose this story about Dr. Sivaraman's emigration to Canada. Dr. Sivaraman's wife Smt. Parvathy is a good friend of mine and I am sure she would give me permission if I were to ask for it because it is a very touching and heart-warming incident.

During the occasion of Mahasivaratri of 1972, Sri Ma happened to be in Varanasi. Dr. Sivaraman was newly interested in Sri Ma, after hearing me talk about her. He asked me about the *puja*-festival which was to be held in the ashram. I was surprised because the previous year when I had spoken about Sivaratri at the ashram he had said rather disparagingly, "What do Bengalis know about Siva! In the scriptures Bengal used to be considered a *mleccha* (outcaste) country outside the pale of Aryan culture!" I was annoyed and sought to convince him that we have a history of Siva *puja* and many ancient temples to prove it. He remained sceptical saying "So what? They have temples and worship Siva in America nowadays. Read the *Dvadasjyotirlinga stotram* [1]. You will not find Bengal mentioned in it." I read the hymn with reawakened interest and to my chagrin found he was right! But the commentators wrote that the exact location of two of the *lingams* were not known but conjectural only. When I related this to Padmaji, she said promptly, "Take one for Bengal and give the other to the Americans!" I laughed and my gloom was effectively dispelled.

In Varanasi I had come to know many things about our own country. The disparities between North and South India were astounding. It is as legitimate to use the word 'European' when referring to a Spaniard, Italian or Norwegian as it is to say 'South Indian'

---

[1] The classical hymn to the twelve luminous lingams, extolling their self-revelatory authenticity and describing their hallowed sites for devout pilgrims.

when referring to a Tamilian, Andhrayan or Malayali. The strong tradition of Saiva Siddhanta is a living force in the South; it has a lively history of opposition to the equally prevalent Vaishnava traditions. In the North, we were no doubt aware of such distinctive religious orientation, but for all practical purposes it has a more fluid spiritual outlook. Everyone observes all the religious festivals dedicated to the worship of Krishna, Rama, Ganesha or the many aspects of the Goddess. I came to appreciate the missionary zeal of the Saivaite South when I realised that a special chair had been created in the Department of Philosophy at B.H.U and Dr. K. Sivaraman appointed to it to teach this system of thought. All religious sects have a yen for spreading the good news of their faith, whereas Sri Ma's devotees were not concerned with this kind of proselytising, partly because they wanted, most of all, just to remain close to her. I, for example, never talked about Sri Ma unless specifically asked; if a colleague asked me to take her along with me to the ashram I did so, but I did not seek to influence her in any way.

Sri Ma's divine aura was so palpable that actually there was nothing one could say which would describe it adequately. I get tired of using the word 'divine' with reference to Sri Ma. It can add nothing to describe her vibrant and luminous presence, the sheer majesty of which made her incomparable.

At his request, I had taken Dr and Mrs. Sivaraman to the ashram for *darshan*. Thereafter, he went on his own many times. He told me one or two of his remarkable experiences. Once, he wanted to purchase a garland of red roses for Sri Ma, but coincidentally on that day they had all been sold out and there were only marigold garlands left in the basket of the flower-vendor. So, he took a yellow garland and joined the queue in front of Sri Ma. Generally, Sri Ma used to take the offered garland in her own hand and with the other pick up the topmost from the heap next to her and put it on the neck of the person bowing in front of her. She was very deft with this process of exchanging garlands and the queue moved quite quickly. When it was Dr. Sirvaraman's turn to bow before her, she kept his garland in her lap and sifted the heap near her. The queue halted. She extracted a red rose-garland from under the heap and put it round his neck. She gave him what he had wanted to offer to her!

The other story was very private and close to his heart. He told me that he had a desire to be initiated by her in the very sacred *panchaksara mantra* of the Saivas, but together with this, he had a strong inhibition against the female form of the Guru. South Indians have a very robust male-oriented culture. I told him, "If you wish you can state your problem to Sri Ma quite openly and candidly". So Dr. K. Sivaraman asked for and was given a private audience on one of the days that he visited the ashram. I went every day while Sri Ma was in residence.

On that day I, along with other visitors and the ashram girls as usual stood around in the lobby while the people who had appointments went into Sri Ma's room one by one. We saw Dr. Sivaraman go in for his interview and come out after some time, while the next person was asked to step in. I went up to him to ask about his talk with Sri Ma but I was deterred from saying anything. I saw that he was looking a little overcome; his face was flushed and his eyes were bright with unshed tears. Obviously, he was not in a mood to talk. After a while, Sri Ma came out for her public *darshan*. There was a crowd in the lobby which sat quietly all around her for some time. I did not see Dr. Sivaraman again that day.

At our next meeting he told me in confidence his experience of the initiation. He had said to Sri Ma that he had a great desire for a formal initiation, without which no progress can be made in one's spiritual quest, but he could not accept anyone he knew as his Guru. Sri Ma said, "Look inside you, the Guru resides in your heart; then listen to what comes out of yourself". While she gazed steadily at him, Dr. Sivaraman felt the sacred mantra welling forth from an inner source and as compulsively he pronounced it aloud in her presence. Sri Ma did not need to say anything at all. It all happened automatically! Having understood his problem at a glance she granted his desire in a way which was itself fulfilment for him. At that moment he knew her to be what she was. I regret that I did not write down immediately the exegesis propounded by him on this initiation. His language was profound but lucid. I was impressed but I do not think I can reproduce it. He had a gift for languages.

It was after this experience that he had asked me if he could participate in the *puja* on Mahasivaratri night at the ashram. Sri Ma had introduced a novel way of performing this *puja* by general participation. In the big hall of the temple she helped to arrange a dozen or more huge flat receptacles in each of which a *sivalingam* decorated with flowers and garlands was placed. A ring of worshippers would sit around each *lingam*. In this way almost a hundred people could be accommodated in the hall. There were more such places for women on the balcony over the hall. In the main ashram, the girls of the Kanyapeeth and their teachers found places in the Chandimandapa. The devotees provided their own asanas. Other items were provided by the ashram: flowers, mountains of sweets, incense, garlands, *bilvapatra, arati* and the *panchapatras*. In front of every asana all these items were arranged artistically for each individual. Small earthen containers were provided filled with milk, curd, ghee and honey for each worshipper. These are required for the *puja* of the four *praharas* that is, from 6 to 9 p.m., from 9 to 12 midnight, from 12 to 3 a.m. and 3 a.m. to 6 a.m. There were a hundred and one other details, all carefully supervised by Sri Ma who worked around all the groups, pointing out deficiencies and adding to the festive decorations. The *sivalingams* were adorned with sandal-paste and garlands. Oil-wick lamps on decorative stands stood inside every circle. All the participants (nearly 200 in all) were expected to take a bath in the Ganges around 6 p.m., then they came into the hall in clean and unstitched clothes and occupied their own particular asana reserved for them. Bibhuda lead a *kirtana* party which had already begun the evening *kirtana*. They would sing the whole night, stopping only for the duration of the *puja*. Kusum Brahmachari (Swami Nirvanananda) was chosen by Sri Ma to lead the *puja*. There would be four *pujas* of about 45 minutes each during the four *praharas*. The magnificence and the quietude of this unique version of the festival is inimitable except as presided over by Sri Ma.

An Invitation from Abroad

Sri Ma herself made her rounds throughout the night to all the places where *puja* had been set up, making this experience — sitting for many hours in one place — a thing of beauty and unalloyed joy. Nobody felt fatigue or bored, and where else could one listen to such splendid hymns to Siva sung in so memorable a way by Bibhuda. The night flashed past as a single moment of purest delight.

Dr. Sivaraman told me later that while sitting in front of the Sivalingam, in Sri Ma's presence he had prayed for a secure future in some foreign university where he would be able to teach properly in the language he was used to, that is, English. When he lifted his eyes he saw Sri Ma in front of him and he had a strong impression that his prayer had been answered.

So he was not too surprised to receive an invitation from McMaster University in Canada. After he had accepted this invitation from McMaster, he received another invitation from the World Council of Churches in Geneva to participate in a programme of dialogue for the Graduate school at Chateau de Bossey under the sponsorship of the University of Geneva. He was on the point of declining this invitation when his wife said to him that he should suggest my name to them as a substitute. It would be easy for me to go because I was already on leave from my college.

I came to know about this when I received an invitation from Dr. S. Samartha in Geneva and Dr. N. Nissiotis, the Director of the Graduate school. Parvathyji (Mrs. Sivaraman) was very pleased that her idea of promoting my name had borne fruit. I asked Dr. Sivaraman what he had written about me which might have persuaded them to accept the replacement. I was not known at all in the academic world of foreign universities, whereas his was a well-known name even at that time. He said he had written to say that I was as able and competent as he was (which was very generous of him), only that I lacked the experience of teaching abroad which he had already. He then told me a little about the World Council of Churches and their programme. It sounded very odd and unrealistic to me. I asked him how I should deal with their problems about dialogue with other religions and he answered lightly, "Just be yourself."

Now, I had a problem; I knew that Sri Ma did not approve of people going abroad. I had heard her say so to many young people, and that it was better to remain in their own country even in reduced circumstances rather than live abroad in affluence. To be quite fair she gave the same advice to foreigners who asked if they should settle in India. She seemed to consider everyone's cultural background as crucially formative. It is easier to swim with the current than against it, as it were. My problem was that knowing all this, how should I ask Sri Ma for her permission to go abroad at my age?

In the end, after much thought, when I sat in front of her, for my private interview, I explained about the invitation from Geneva. I then said, "Ma, I am tired of the working conditions in my college. This is a rare opportunity for me to go abroad and learn more about the academic world. I would very much like to accept this invitation. Now tell me your *kheyala*, should I go or not?"

Sri Ma was observing silence at the time. I had gone to the Kalkaji Ashram in Delhi to seek her permission. She was half-reclining on her *chowki*. She looked at me for a few moments and then asked me a number of questions regarding the assignment. She spoke in a soft voice just audible to me. It gives me a thrill now as I write this, remembering her incomparable leniency toward the self-indulgent request I made. At that time, I did not even appreciate the fact that she was breaking her silence and would speak to me at length. I eagerly answered her questions — explaining about this Christian dialogue with other religions at Bossey. It did not surprise me that she instantly understood the whole background and its problems. She spoke of the situation as it would develop for me later on. I made hasty notes in a small notebook. There was little light where we were and I wrote by feel rather than looking at what I was writing, because I was also looking at Sri Ma's face and at the slight gestures of her beautiful hands, which always gave her words such expressive emphasis.

I put forward my own understanding of Christianity to Sri Ma, saying I would be expected to enter into dialogue with its spokesmen.

An Invitation from Abroad

I asked her: "Ma, how can one explain the personification of the Supreme Being as God?"

Sri Ma: (Whether you say) Personal, Impersonal — The Lord is Himself as He is. He is ultimate reality, pervading the universe as well as indwelling the innermost being (*antaryamin*). He is beyond all comprehension as well as being the innermost self in each, would you not say? He alone is, whether you say unknown, or knowable, the one who is nameless, formless, yet all Names are His, He is all-pervasive and universally manifest. Where is He not? When you touch the hand of a person, he says, "It is I", when you touch his head or foot, he says "It is I". Even his clothes indicate his presence.

All religions recognise His presence — they originate from Him. How to grasp this vastness? Take the example of a single person and the eddying relationships (radiating from him) — he is father, son, husband, brother etc. So it is with all religions. All are intimate relationships and each unique in itself.

Question: Christians believe that Christ is an Incarnation, the only Incarnation sent to save mankind. He is the sole mediator between God and man.

Sri Ma: Well, certainly it is right for the Christian to believe so, why not? Faith loses in spiritual vigour if it is universalised. It is unnecessary to do so. The boundless mercy of God is all-pervasive; He alone knows what is good for everyone. If every individual looks to his own spiritual journey then he renders the best help to his fellow travellers.

Any dispensation of Truth is a unique event. Not one may be compared with another. In celebration of this Truth, brotherhoods (*sampradaya*) are formed or come into being. Brotherhoods are also necessary. They provide cohesion, general unity of purpose, and provide courage to flagging spirits too; it is a good idea to belong to a brotherhood and follow its guidance for enlightenment. It is not necessary to distrust the faith of fellow seekers of Truth.

Question: Christians hold fast to the unique historical event of Christ's Incarnation. They are committed to their mission.

Sri Ma : Why should one put limits on the infinite or restrictions of time on the timeless, the eternal? The infinite has infinite ways of revealing itself. No one is entitled to say 'It is only thus and not different' — although strictly speaking such a creed is also allowable because every perspective is true. Where, after all, is the scope for rejection within the entirety of Truth? To claim exclusivity is a way of strengthening one's own faith and devotion, but to decry the loyalties of others is uncalled for. The true pilgrim should appreciate the efforts of fellow wayfarers.

Question : If one believes in a one-only Incarnation, how can one understand the truth of other manifestations?

Sri Ma : Incarnation is truly one only, a descent, a coming, an advent, each unique in its way. As I said, there is nothing or no one apart from God. The real crux of the matter is, keep walking! To advance in one direction, a supreme effort, single-minded and undeviating is required. To distract oneself by comparisons and contrasts is to slow down; unless they are used for a strengthening of purpose in a spirit of togetherness. The One encompasses all paths to the realisation of its truth.

Question : Ma, they do not, cannot believe in the One only — the creature is forever separate from God.

Sri Ma : Yes, indeed. Because God cannot be grasped by the mind, He is forever separate. To be human is to dwell in the world of mental images. The mind circumscribes the understanding. God is separate from the creature because he remains beyond mental idealisations. The supreme is, therefore, ever beyond, so it is right to say God and his creature. *The understanding of the separation is itself the divide* (emphasis added). He is one's innermost self, the inner witness, most intimately you yourself.

Question : Is a mediator necessary for knowing God?

Sri Ma : Yes, but God himself reveals himself as the Guru (Mediator). The Guru is God himself. He alone knows the requirements of the true disciple. To invoke the presence of the Guru one must become a true disciple.

Question : Are all paths of equal value?

An Invitation from Abroad

Sri Ma : In as much as a path is followed one-pointedly, sincerely and persistently. However, there are highways and by-ways which turn out to be deviations. You see, one is born with certain predilections which shape attitudes — your way of life is an amalgam of actions, beliefs and knowledge (*karma, bhakti, jnana*). The way you organise your life will determine the path you would like to follow. In the sphere of God-seeking, help is inevitable — even if one is ignorant and not given to evaluations, our path is straightened out by the Guru who appears invariably in order to render help and give guidance. It is your own effort and sincerity which are to be evaluated, not faiths.

Question : How should one know if one is not wandering around aimlessly?

Sri Ma : Whoever is on the path of the quest for That is touched by the peace of Truth. In this realm of seeking and finding, there is no possibility of any true effort going to waste, or non-sincerity producing results. Effort is required because man uses his will toward the achieving of worldly goals. So the will can also be harnessed toward carrying man beyond its limitations. Actually God's mercy prevails. You walk one step toward Him, He will come forward ten steps. He, in fact, is ever with you. The seeking itself, therefore, is a finding.

In all my dialogue with other religions these words of Sri Ma worked as a sheet anchor. As I studied and researched in later years they acquired greater meaning for me. In juxtaposition with Western streams of thought I learnt to see great wealth of significance in the Eastern heritage. This enabled me to hold meaningful conversations with Professor George B. Grant, the well-known philosopher of Canada at that time. Incidentally, I may say that although Sri Ma did not say, "Yes, you may go!" she must have had a *kheyala* toward it because I received invitations to go to conferences in later years also — till a time came when I was myself obliged to decline two or three of them as not convenient. The fact remains my wish to go abroad expressed in Sri Ma's presence flooded me with opportunities for this kind of fulfilment.

With great excitement, I started on my preparations for going abroad. Friends advised me on suitable clothes. Bindu helped me with the paper work. In Varanasi, he arranged for a friend who was a magistrate to sign on my photographs for my passport. He drove me to the *kachahri* (civil courts) a distance of nearly 20 miles from B.H.U. so that the seal would be available. When we arrived to this friend's chambers, I found on rummaging in my purse that I had forgotten to bring the photographs! Bindu looked at me sadly, but to my eternal gratitude, he did not say a word in exasperation. The next day was Sunday so the courts would be closed. The magistrate smiled and said, "It is all right, I have now seen you, so I shall recognize the photographs. Send them by a messenger tomorrow. I shall take the seal home with me today". Bindu's equanimity under stressful conditions was always admirable.

Bindu and Shyamali were in Bombay when the time came for me to go abroad so I chose Bombay as my port of departure. My erstwhile colleague Priyamvada Shah was in London at this time. She came to meet me at the airport.

We came to Crosby Hall which was a very large and commodious hostel for university women from all over the world. Priyamvada was staying here and she had booked a room for me on the same floor. The locality was beautiful and in those days calm and quiet prevailed. I was told of the historic importance of Crosby Hall. The dining hall (mentioned in guide books) was hung with antique tapestries. Breakfast and dinner were provided. Inmates were generally out the whole day, so there

Crosby Hall, Chelsea (Dining Hall)

An Invitation from Abroad

were no arrangements for lunch or tea. On every floor, there was a kitchenette where we could make tea or coffee. There was a gas fire in every room. In 1972, we were still required to use shillings to feed the meter and light the gas with a match. On a later visit, the charlady seemed amused at my attempts with the matchbox. She flicked the automatic switch and said with a smile, "You must be coming after a couple of years. It is all automatic now!"

Priyamvada explained to me the scene obtaining in the dining hall. All members were expected to occupy seats at tables already in use. None was supposed to sit alone by herself. Moreover, everybody would talk to her neighbours on either side during meals but certain subjects were taboo, such as all controversial political situations, any personal questions, any gossip about inmates etc. I saw that the English had developed dinner-table-talk to a fine art. I stayed at Crosby Hall off and on throughout the years I travelled abroad. Once I was accompanied by Gertraud Kiem, an Italian girl I had met in Varanasi. I explained to Gertie, as we called her, all the unwritten laws obtaining in Crosby Hall. On the first night, after dinner, I said I would take my mug of coffee and go up to my room (I had done this on previous occasions too). Other members used to congregate in a common room to watch their favourite T.V. programmes and for after-dinner coffee. Gertie told me helpfully to go up and that she would bring my coffee to my room. She arrived with two steaming mugs of coffee after quite a long time, remarking smugly that she had been talking to the lady sitting next to her. The lady was telling her all about her difficult family affairs. I was appalled and said, "Gertie, you did not ask her about her family, did you?" Gertie was unrepentant, she said, "Why should I not? She asked me first!" So, English good deportment was set at naught by Italian friendliness!

It was at the end of August 1972. I had a pleasant time with Priyamvada. My first impression was that there were very few people on London streets. Priyamvada took me to the tube stations at rush hour but I remained unimpressed. The crowds were very civilised and it all cleared up within half an hour. It was very restful to be in a big city which seemed to work at the reasonable pace of a small town in my own country. But alas! London also changed as the years went by. Margaret and Peter Fletcher's lovely home in South Kensington, which for me remained a favourite place for later sojourns in England, became more and more inaccessible due to traffic congestion. The once wide street became almost a narrow lane due to four rows of parked cars!

Chapter Twenty

At the Chateau de Bossey

I arrived in Geneva on October 3, I think. It was a very short flight from London. We came via Paris because the airline was Air France. The gentleman sitting next to me asked me about my destination and offered to give me a lift if it so happened that there was nobody to meet me. Everything was simple in those days. He helped me to collect my baggage from the carousel and we went through the customs counter without any hitch. I looked round to see if anybody had been sent to fetch me. Professor and Mrs. Nissiotis had come themselves and Marina spotted me in my sari immediately. I turned to the gentleman, standing patiently by my side thanking him for his offered escort and that I would not need it any more. He smiled, shook hands and went away. As soon as we had settled in the car Marina wanted to know who the man was whom I had spoken to. When I told her, she immediately took me to task for getting into conversation with strangers and agreeing to ride in their cars. I was amused and at once felt at home in a strange new country. Marina could easily have been an elder sister fussing because I did not know the dangers of accepting help from unknown people!

Switzerland was beautiful. The drive from Geneva to Celigny (17 miles) which I subsequently travelled many times was through gorgeous belts of woodland which were taking on the colours of fall. I was quite enchanted when we drew up at the Chateau de Bossey, the building where our residential school was housed. The hostess, a smart young lady named Eva Maria Schneck came out and welcomed me. I liked her very much and we became great friends as the days went by.

I was shown to my suite of rooms with a private bathroom. The small hall opened on to another suite occupied by Barbel, our translator. She and I also became good friends. In fact, as I realised by the end of the term, I was given a place in the hearts of the entire body of staff and students. I also was very happy to come to know so many congenial people and never felt like an alien even for one day.

A rather interesting incident occurred right at the beginning of the session. When the whole school had assembled, a picnic was organised so that we would come to know each other in pleasant surroundings. Buses were lined up to take everyone to the picnic-site. Barbel told me to wait in the front lounge as she would take me in her little Volkswagen. After everyone had left I saw Eva-Maria rushing about, evidently, very upset about something. To my inquiring look, she said that one of the students from Fiji Island had gone into shock and was refusing to talk or communicate with the staff. They had sent for the doctor. She was very distressed. She said almost every year an incident like this marred the session. Some of the coloured students who had not seen even one white-skinned face in all their lives, when suddenly brought into a European city were frightened and could not handle the situation at all. She said that the churches, which sponsored their visits, should allow them a little experience in places or towns where they would meet some Europeans.

The Chateau de Bossey

Before going abroad, I had been so tired of involvement in my own university situation, that I had vowed to myself to stay aloof while I was in Bossey. All such vows were forgotten in the face of Eva-Maria's distress. I said, "Can I be of any help?" She was very relieved, and said "Would you? Come with me then."

With Prof. and Mrs. Nissiotis (second from right) at the Chateau de Bossey

I went with her to this student's room. He was lying on his bed with his face turned toward the wall. While she stood at the door, I approached him and put my hand on his shoulder. I said, "Are you feeling alright? We are all here to help you. The doctor will be coming soon." Hearing my non-European voice, he opened his eyes and turned round. He joined his palms together in the manner of uttering a prayer and said clearly. "Please tell them to send me home!"

Eva-Maria on hearing his voice came in eagerly and spoke to him. Unfortunately, as soon as he saw her, he again turned to the wall and would speak no more. The doctor came to examine him at about this time, so I went down to the lounge once more and from there to the picnic with Barbel.

As the school began to take shape we nevertheless remained concerned about the young man. Once a week the staff met with the Director for an exchange of views and instructions. Professor Nissiotis always invited the seminar-leaders to attend this staff meeting, so we became very close friends also. The first meeting was mainly taken up with the problem of the student who wanted to go home. Eva-Maria made out a strong case for giving him time to adjust. Her concern was that he would be put to shame for failing when he went back home. It would affect the credibility of his church when they sought to sponsor other students in future. She was very committed to the care of the students and took this case of rejection very much to heart. Professor Nissiotis must have been informed about my visit to the student. He now asked my opinion about him. Although a bit surprised, I said that as far as my experience of working with young students went I did not think that he could come out of his inner retreat to be able to co-operate with the staff in the near future. Professor Nissiotis said "I agree with you, but since Eva-Maria is so hopeful we will abide by her decision. It will be for her to say if he should be allowed to continue or not". Within a couple of days, however, Eva-Maria acknowledged that the student should be allowed to go home.

I had a very illuminating time at the Chateau de Bossey. My knowledge of Christianity at the time was rather elementary; we knew the broad outlines of Judaism, the history of the rise and spread of Christianity and its subsequent split into Roman Catholicism and the various Protestant movements. We in India are familiar with this scene of diversification and proliferation of religious commitments. At the time I did not have the experience to appreciate the superficial nature of this resemblance.

I had been invited to lead a seminar on "Dialogue on Salvation from the Hindu point of view". I remember I went prepared to discuss the topic from a metaphysical point of view, taking for granted that the soteriological positions of all religions were widely divergent and mutually exclusive. After all the question of *moksha* (salvation) had been debated in our country for centuries.

It took me a couple of weeks to orient myself to the atmosphere of the World Council of Churches. The school session of 1972-73 consisted of approximately 50 Christian students of theology belonging to 13 denominations including one Jesuit and one Greek Orthodox. They came from 26 different countries of the world, representing a vast panorama of cultural heritages. They were not students of philosophy working for academic degrees but committed men and women, who were either priests already or shortly to be ordained after completing their courses. These young people were well versed in theology but singularly ignorant of other religious affiliations. All that they knew of Hinduism, for example, was that we worshipped the cow, many idols and had a fierce caste-system. Truly a sobering thought as far as I was concerned but I was aghast at their lack of knowledge of other cultures. Some students asked me if we had a script; one or two asked if we still had tree-top houses; obviously as far as most of them were concerned, all dark-skinned people had just emerged out of their bush-culture. To their greater confusion, I told them that we were still at home in our "primitive culture" and had no wish to discard it as inoperative.

In contrast, the staff and personnel of the school were well-educated and very cosmopolitan in their outlook. The senior-most secretary Miss Simone Mathil was an admirer of Tagore. She and I had many a discussion about the tragic muse in poetry. I learnt a lot from her. Mr. De Graaf, the Chief Accountant, was very knowledgeable about India.

For the first week of the school Dr. Nissiotis requested the six Seminar leaders to give one introductory lecture each. I scrapped my carefully prepared lecture-notes on *moksha* and started afresh. I began with the level of understanding which envisaged a whole nation kowtowing to the homely cow. I told them that not only the cow, but many other creatures, rivers, trees, shrubs, rocks and stones were sacred to the Hindu. Children also were worshipped (on special occasions) as mirroring the divine spark in their as yet unsullied and pure persons. The transcendent was also immanent in every being, hence this celebration of pervasive divinity. The Hindu is normally a devout person; he believes that Divine presence can be evoked by heart-felt prayers anywhere and at any time because God is ever present with us. The myriad ties which bind God and his creatures together are celebrated in joyous festivals. The 'idols' in various temples are not so many gods but Images of the same Person who, being nameless and formless, assumes many to delight the hearts of his worshippers.

The introductory lecture went very well. The large hall with entire walls made of glass looked out on pleasant gardens and big trees. At the back of the hall were two booths for simultaneous translations into French or German (or English). The atmosphere was informal. If the speaker went too fast the translators could flash a small red light on the booth but all in all they were very skilful. I was amazed at the speed of their translation. They would finish a sentence actually simultaneously with the speaker. Even the emotional overtones came through. I asked Barbel about this "How do you know what the speaker is going to end up with?" She said "I do not know, it just happens that I somehow enter into the mind of the speaker, as it were!" Their concentration was terrific. I noticed that there were beads of sweat on Barbel's brow if the speaker went on for more than one hour. Fifty minutes were comfortable for them, one hour was difficult and over an hour was exhausting.

On the occasion of my first lecture I sensed that many of the students from Africa (erstwhile French and English Colonies) understood me better than the Europeans. One student from Dahomy who was fluent in French became so excited that he spoke to me directly in English. He apparently wanted to know if Hinduism would accept a marriage between two people belonging to different religions. What he came out with was, "Now if I wanted to marry you, can you accept?" I smiled at him and said, "Is that a proposal? Thank you very much!"

This brought the house down. The students were delighted. I think it was from this moment that they accepted me as a sympathetic companion rather than a spokesperson from an alien culture.

We very soon settled down to a routine at Bossey. After breakfast we walked over to the Lecture Hall to listen to the speaker of the day. One or other of the dignitaries of the World Council of Churches which sponsored the graduate school came to speak to the students. I had the opportunity of meeting many eminent theologians. I as an outsider had a very educational insight into the whole question of the mission of Christianity. There was an obvious gap of understanding between the older generation of theologians and the new generation who could raise very pertinent and uncomfortable questions. One or two of them gained recognition in this matter. Nicholas Bradbury (Oxford) who was the youngest of the group raised his voice very often to the exasperation of the speakers.

It took me a while to assess the 'dialogue' situation. Its obvious intentionality to persuade with a view to conversion came as an unpleasant surprise. Perhaps surprise is not the right word. The 'dialogue' was in fact a monologue because the Christians made no real effort to understand their partners' points of view. It was developed as far as I could see as a strategy of "know your enemy better!" I was also taken aback by the use of such words as 'threat', 'encounter', 'confrontation' etc. within the framework of the dialogue. As far as the Christian groups themselves were concerned, I saw that they preferred to preserve their identities. The ecumenical movement had a very limited success in this field. I also experienced the unhappiness of the students from Africa who keenly felt their anomalous position in the modern world. I remember the same student from Dahomy who had questioned me, speaking sharply to the eminent scholar Roger Garaudy. He said, "You now talk of roots after destroying all the roots we had!" There was considerable resentment against the missionaries who had alienated them from their culture. Olivia, a slim girl from Rhodesia used to admire my saris saying, "If the Christians had not taken us out of the jungle dressed in stupid Mother Hubbard skirts, perhaps we would have developed national dresses of our own and not be obliged to wear European clothes which look so incongruous on us."

The students from the Western world had their own problems. Their main focus was not the 'other' but sheer indifference on the part of their congregations. They wanted to know how to contain the forces of secularism. As far as I could see none of the eminent theologians addressed himself to this question. For all of them the emphasis was on mission and dialogue.

After a month or so, I was ready to give up my assignment and return home, not having the heart to be constantly in the position of the 'other' or a 'threat'. The question of identity and communication is a problem which does not arise out of our understanding of the religious way of life. I had to shift my perspective almost totally to appreciate the magnitude of it for the West.

My students, however, would not hear of my withdrawal from the school. They insisted that they themselves were in a conflict situation on many counts and that I should participate by suffering along with them in the cause of creating even a minimal level of understanding.

After six months (1972-1973) of lectures, dialogues, seminars, discussions and participation in each other's ritualistic ways of worship we remained where we were. The world religions made no headway toward a rapprochement, neither did the strongly entrenched denominations within Christianity coalesce into a harmonious company. Sometimes I used to feel nostalgic for a *satsang* at home. In India it is possible to invite an erudite advaitic (monistic) scholar to give a discourse on the *lila* of the Child Krishna. The audience may consist of Saivaites or other sects who do not worship the image of Krishna. The identity of the Advaitin is not diminished in extolling the glory of a particular Image nor are the devotees of Siva, Rama and so on, alienated amongst themselves or from the monastic speaker. To talk of God and to listen to God-talk is a joyous occasion for all participants. A happy extolling of the many magnificent qualities (*aishwarya*) of God and His ever-present compassion for his creatures was not the theme of these meetings. I used to get an uncomfortable feeling that these men operated as if they knew better than God as regards His creation. The Graduate School at Bossey was not a harmonious group of devout people. The one quality which is indispensable to devotion is humility, but this quality does not sit easily with the burden of exclusivity.

Although the Graduate School failed in its primary objective, it achieved a tremendous sense of cohesion between people of different cultures, traditions and countries. Strong ties of friendship were forged between unlikely people which have endured to this day. We achieved a level of sympathetic reciprocity, not due to dialogues but in spite of them.

At the Château de Bossey

It was not all hard work and confrontations at Bossey. I was invited out for the weekends by one or other of the secretaries. I went to Montreux with Eva-Maria Schneck and was thrilled to see the castle of Chillon. The poem "The Prisoner of Chillon" was prescribed reading for us at college. I now saw the dungeons I had read about and the pillar with chains where Lord Byron had signed his name. Eva-Maria was truly a good friend who from the first day had accepted me as one of themselves. I spent other weekends with Idelette and her daughter Veronique in their beautiful chalet and also Margaret Koch, the librarian, a very well qualified and studious person.

The most exhausting weekend that I spent while at Bossey was with Nicholas. In a spirit of adventure, he took me to Zermat in order to get a clear view of the Mont Blanc. The time was close to Christmas and the snow was knee-deep everywhere. He made me walk through wide snowfields in my unsuitable dress: when I was thoroughly upset with this marathon race he fetched up at a bookshop where he very engagingly bought me an Agatha Christie book as a peace-offering. When I saw it was in French, I felt like throwing it at his head. We however had a hot cup of coffee at a restaurant where at his request the band played some of our favorite tunes for us. (I was learning how to appreciate Western music from Nicholas). Incidentally, we did not see the Mont Blanc, which remained hidden by clouds.

Christmas night was celebrated in Bossey with an elaborate ecumenical service. I attended the midnight Mass. By this time I was quite familiar with the ritual and was content to attend it, probably with more devotion than many Christians.

Peter Neary (Jesuit), another member of my seminar, and I had been invited by Nicholas to spend a few days with his family at Ilkley in Yorkshire. So after Christmas we went over to England for a few days. The English countryside is beautiful. Nicholas' parents were gracious and very welcoming. Everywhere down the village street and in the local pub, I was introduced as 'Nick's teacher from India'.

There are so many different memories of these days. One day, we were all shocked to hear that one of the secretaries had heard about the sudden loss of her mother in far away America. I went up to her office and saw that she was quietly sitting in front of her typewriter, looking quite blank. When I stood near her, she suddenly turned and putting her arms round me, broke into tears. She was a strong-minded American girl, well able to take care of herself, so I was very touched as well as surprised. I said all the things I remembered to have heard Sri Ma say on the occasion of such bereavements.

I said, "We shall pray together". She looked at me with bewildered eyes and said, "I do not know how to pray". I stayed with her until it was time for her to board the flight to her home-town in America. She was such a good girl but untouched by the quality of devotion. There were others like her but this type of modernity was not uncongenial to me. If modern people could be happy and self-sufficient, so be it. God is too precious to be commandeered in anybody's life.

At the end of the session, Prof. Nissiotis asked me if I would speak to them about my impressions of the school and its objectives. He said they would all like to hear what I had to say about their programme. This was an unexpected assignment but my seminar people insisted that I accept it. A student from Africa, Michael Jackson, came to me and said that I should take full advantage of the opportunity and be as tough on the Christians as they were on other religions. He said if I was not tough enough he would get up and leave the hall. He was one of the committed Christians and yet very nostalgic about his cultural background which he had left behind.

I collected my thoughts together. We had come a long way from the introductory lectures, I had acquired some knowledge about the ecumenical movement and the problems endemic to it. This lecture was one of the most difficult for me, before or since. The audience consisted of personal friends. Many of the secretaries came to listen to the talk. I did not wish to give offence to their susceptibilities as Christians and I myself had nothing but high regard for their religious commitment. I spoke for just under fifty minutes remembering Barbel's stricture regarding the time limit. I kept looking at Michael Jackson's attentive and serious face and knew that he was not disappointed in me.

I summarised for them what I had understood Sri Ma to have said regarding human destiny and the possibility of dialogue between different world religions in roughly the following words:

"Truth is timeless. It is all-pervasive and brooks no relational categorization. Man, in search of this Truth is a pilgrim who is desirous of unraveling the mystery of his presence on earth. We are born to a tradition, a cultural background, a geographical situation, a religious faith. The starting point is therefore given to us. Religions are necessarily time-oriented and space-bound. To seek to universalize a particular mode of revelation is neither necessary nor very realistic. They are facets of the same Truth and so bear witness to its omnipresence.

"The Church however, takes its mission very seriously. The symbol of the cross can be understood very easily in the East as the tangential descent of transcendence to become immanent. A coming together of heaven and earth, so that man may look up and be filled with the joy of the message. But the men and women who took up the role of savior for the whole world were not enlightened in themselves. They interpreted the will of God, which is a very dangerous procedure. Instead of marveling at the many-splendored 'creation of God' they hastened to divide people into 'civilised', 'primitive tribes', 'pagans' and so forth.

"To the Christian, the world looks like a confused jumble and beyond the provenance of God's jurisdiction! Otherwise why should a Christian be called upon to improve upon the creation of God? In this context it is worth considering the famous sermon at Athens by Paul, which serves as a model for evangelists at all times.

"For as I passed by, and beheld your devotions I found an altar with this inscription, TO THE UNKNOWN GOD. Whom therefore, ye ignorantly worship, him declare I unto you."

Acts VIII, 23.

"The question arises as to whether the Athenians might have replied to Paul,

'Him that you have found now, we already render homage to, because he is truly unknown but not unknowable'. We might imagine that Paul would then have identified the philosophy of the Athenians as the heresy of gnosticism.

"It is true that the Second Vatican Council has given some sort of recognition to other religions. This could have been a welcome move on the part of the Church, had it not been accompanied by a suggestion that the non-Christian multitudes should listen to the Gospels and thus acquire the necessary prerequisite qualification for acceptance into the Church.

"This is doing needless violence to the feelings of other fellow pilgrims. Many of you are no longer in sympathy with those who consider all other religions to be threats or challenges. The readiness to *listen* may gradually overcome the tendency to preach. If the 'other' could be seen also as a pilgrim, a wayfarer, a friend engaged in the same quest for God's grace, only then could dialogue become the basis for a togetherness, a greater understanding of the magnitude of the task ahead, a supportive rather than a disruptive attitude toward the religious life. Dialogue, after all, can only be carried on in commensurable language. If participants use terms which vary in meaning, there can be no significant communication.

"Dialogue is an ambivalent term. The Hindu tradition itself is structured on the dialogue. From the Upanishads to the Dharma Sastras (law books) the format is uniformly that of a conversation between the seeker of Truth and a Teacher (*Rishi*) who has realized It. The whole of the Sanskritic tradition may be summarised in the oft-repeated verse:

Awake, arise; approach the great (sages) and learn:
As sharp as the edge of a razor
Is the road (to Him) difficult to traverse;
So say the wise.

(Kathopanishad II. 14)

"All scriptural texts pivot on this call to look beyond the given condition of man in this world. The search for Truth is sometimes spoken of as the quest for self-realization by the *advaitin* (monist) or God-realization by the devotee (monotheist). The Self is the *antaryamin* (the inner witness) who appears as the *Ista Devata* (the adored Image within the heart) to the devotee. The search therefore must begin with an attempt to focus on the inner being.

"As I said, why should one feel called upon to go on a mission to preach? This could be based only on the belief that God has withdrawn from His creation and is no longer concerned. Compare the Enlightened Teacher. He is sufficient unto himself and is joyousness personified, because he regards the world as the perfect expression of a perfect being. He has no calling to preach, makes no demands nor commands allegiance. He responds graciously to the sincere seeker, dispels doubts and strengthens resolve. By his very presence, he establishes the viability of the spiritual quest [1]. Dispensation of Truth must hold together time and timelessness. God is not in the past only but also in the present and for evermore.

"One of the earliest dialogues recorded in the Sanskritic tradition is the Gita. It is the first text in which the words 'the Lord said' (*Sri Bhagavan uvacha*) are used. Even so, the dialogue does not change into a discourse till the disciple (Arjuna) acknowledges himself as such and specifically asks for guidance (Gita II. 7). What is remarkable here is the Teacher's concluding remarks:

> *This wisdom, more secret thān all that is secret,*
> *has been declared to thee by Me:*
> *reflect then over it all and do as thou pleasest.*
> (Gita XVII. 63)

"The freedom to be oneself even in the presence of God is neither denied nor trivialised. Unless man is seized with the yearning to know God, a hunger for freedom to be himself, the desire for unqualified bliss promised to him by the scriptures (*shastras*), he is not metamorphosed into a seeker (*jijnasu*). To become a true seeker is the aim of religious life.

"The language of seeking and finding is based upon a dualistic concept: God and his creation. The whole idea of duality is meaningful only as a bondage of love. This is why the Hindu celebrates as

---

[1] The Upanishads are a treasure-house of such meaningful dialogues.

many ties of love with God as are experienced by man on earth. God may be known as Father, Mother, Beloved, Friend, Master or Child. A fear of hell, redemption from sin, even hope of salvation as parameters of the life of devotion do not add to the majesty and compassion of God. How can any religion justify its ministry unless it can present God as the only worthwhile quest for human endeavor!

"Religious brotherhoods are very important. The individual gains strength from his *sampradaya* or brotherhood; it lends cohesion to desultory effort. A sense of solidarity, commonness of purpose, the togetherness required for celebrations and rituals, are conducive to a life of spiritual endeavor, or *sadhana*. If a commonwealth of nations could be a politically viable concept, then we should be able to look forward to a future of a commonwealth of religions. It would be a celebration of the infinite ways of God's advent amongst his people. The religious way of life could be a matter of rejoicing, a joyful participation in each other's modes of worship. Let the dialogue, therefore be an instrument of celebration of the many faiths which enrich civilization."

I was exhausted at the conclusion of the talk. Nicholas said later that he had lost a pint of sweated blood on my behalf. There was just a little clapping but a sustained standing ovation. They were moved and showed it clearly. Professor Nissiotis got up from his seat, fetched me a glass of water and spoke words of appreciation unreservedly as did many others. He said, "In your presence I felt the futility of this entire programme. Your smiling acceptance of it seems to nullify it". Could there be a greater vindication of Sri Ma's message to the Graduate School of the year 1972-73?

CHAPTER TWENTY ONE

On the Way to Canada

The Graduate School came to an end with a big valedictory function held in the beautiful lecture hall. The time of parting was truly sad because we had become more than family in many cases. Professor Carl Van Peursen of the Free University at Amsterdam invited me to come to Holland before I left Bossey. Other students asked me to visit them if I happened to travel in Europe. In a flurry of invitations, exchanges of addresses and promises of correspondence, the Chateau emptied of its inhabitants in a couple of days.

The Chief Accountant, Herr Herman de Graaf, provided me with tickets to Amsterdam on the Rhine Express. So I had this marvellous experience of travelling along the river Rhine on this train. Professor Van Peursen met me in Leiden. He had scheduled two lectures for me, one at Leiden and the other at Amsterdam. I so wished that I could have spoken the language and so deepen the feeling of belonging to these ancient seats of learning. The Professor, seeing my interest, took me to visit Spinoza's house near the sea coast. Leiden, I was told, was the oldest University of Europe, made notable by Descartes, whose favourite path is known as the 'philosopher's walk'.

From Leiden we came to Amsterdam. This was a new and modern university. I tried to speak in the language of philosophy since the venue was the Department of Philosophy, but again I had to mould my talk to the everyday language of basics. The audience was not interested in Hindu Philosophy but only in yoga, transcendental meditation and such topics. I, not being interested in these, was disappointed by the questions from the audience. It was as if, when I was ready to serve delectable dishes, all that the clients wanted was boiled potatoes. Gradually, I came to realise that there was a noticeable apathy concerning religion. Hindu philosophy, consisting in interpretation of the Upanishads, was considered religion. The unity of religion and philosophy sounded alien to most of them.

Professor Van Peursen took me to his home for dinner where I met his family. The next day the Professor's daughter Albertina took me in a barge down the river to the sea, pointing out the gabled houses on either side of the canal. We had hot chestnuts from a roadside vendor who was roasting them on an open fire. Just like buying hot monkey nuts from such vendors at home. I had acquired another lifelong friend. For more than 25 years my Christmas began with Professor Van Peursen's greetings card. I had the privilege of writing an essay for the commemorative volume published on his retirement by his university.

On my way back I visited two of our erstwhile students, Harry Menting at Utrecht and Gerhard Dietrich near Koln. I had the opportunity to see the famous paintings of Van Gogh and also a whole waxworks tableau of Rembrandt painting "The Night Watch". I was a little amused to see the figure of Mata Hari by the side of Mahatma Gandhi in the museum. After all why not!

Before coming to Bossey I had taken permission from McMaster to join very late in the academic year. I applied for a visa to Canada from Bossey. Now I saw I had a problem. The Canadian Embassy wanted a full medical examination, spread over 9 weeks or so. Although Professor Nissiotis extended an invitation for me to stay on in Bossey I did not like to do this. As a matter of fact I was ready to go home after spending 9 months in Europe. My desire for a break in the routine of teaching and a change of scene had been fulfilled. I wrote to Paul Younger at McMaster, apprising him of my medical problems and that I would not be able to join before June, if at all. Paul wrote back to say that my fellowship would be kept open for me and I could come whenever the formalities were completed.

In the face of this supportive gesture, I felt I had no choice but to do my best and complete my visa formalities for Canada. I agreed to

On the Way to Canada

the medical tests. The clinic said they would let me know the results of the tests in due course. After my visits to Amsterdam and Mainz (with Peter) I left for England and stayed at Crosby Hall.

Melita Maschmann was visiting her home this year. She invited me to come to Darmstadt for a few days and I had a very good time with her. She and I celebrated Sri Ma's *Janmotsava* together. It was nice to sit in meditation about the time the ashrams in India would also be observing it.

At last the message came from Koln to come for an interview. When I met the officer, it was apparent to me that he was on the point of refusal but changed his mind after talking with me for some time. He said, "You know, we never, never allow anyone with your medical history to enter Canada. However, I am making an exception in your case at my own risk. There is one stipulation. Immediately on arrival you must put yourself under a doctor who will examine you from time to time. If you promise to do that, I shall sign the papers". I had no difficulty in agreeing to this stipulation since I knew myself to be free of the disease they were so afraid of.

I took a plane to Canada from Frankfurt. Peter drove me down from Mainz and saw me off on my first flight across the Atlantic. The plane was 4 hours late at Montreal. When I arrived in Toronto, I was so happy to be received by Mervyn and Ilse Sprung who had been waiting for me almost the whole day. He drove us back to St Catherine's where I spent the night in their beautiful house. This house and later another one in the woods became a home for me away from home for the 4 years I stayed in Canada. Mervyn took me to Hamilton the next day and to the Department of Philosophy, a beautiful old-world building. I was so pleased to see that the rack of letter boxes contained one with my name on it. This immediately gave me a feeling of belonging to the university.

At McMaster University

Professor Paul Younger welcomed me and found me a flat to stay in. This was at 89 Dalewood where I stayed happily for the next three years. The owners, Louis and Martha Frohlinger, from almost the first day accepted me as a member of their family. Martha helped me to familiarise myself with Hamilton. Being summer, the University was quiet. The campus was very beautiful. I called on the family of Dr. Sivaraman who was away in India for the summer vacation. His wife Parvathyji looked rather unsettled but the two children, Kartik and Gauri, seemed happy and full of plans.

In order to keep my promise to the office in Koln, I asked Martha to introduce me to a doctor. She took me to her own physician, Dr. Jacqueline Grant who entered me in her books. This stipulation proved to be very ironic. I did not suffer from a recurrence of tuberculosis but, it seemed, I might have cancer. Dr. Grant referred me immediately to the Department of Cancer Research at the hospital in McMaster University, a landmark in this part of the world. They promptly decided on an operation. I was completely flabbergasted. I had no feeling of discomfort or any sense of illness. The nodule they suspected to be malignant had been there for more than a year at least and was not any different from what I could remember, and caused me no discomfort. In those days, cancer was as dreadful a disease as tuberculosis was twenty years earlier. New forms of treatment were just beginning to be adopted and much still remained at the conjectural stage. When I came home with this news, poor Martha dissolved into tears. I was disgusted with myself. When people go abroad, they wish to be a credit to their families and friends. Here was I, who not only had put her family through one traumatic experience but was now going to put them through a worse one. I suggested to the doctors that since I was not even aware of the nodule, it could be allowed to remain undisturbed till I felt some discomfort but this suggestion was rejected out of hand. Martha sat me down and explained the pros and cons of the operation and showed me the overwhelming weight on the side of the pros. She came to the hospital with me and asked the surgeon to postpone the operation for ten days because she was obliged to go away from Hamilton for that time. The doctor said, "Do not worry, we shall take very good care of her. She will be ready to go home with you on your return."

On the Way to Canada

So, I admitted myself to the hospital on a Monday, two days ahead of the operation as required by the doctors. They were very thorough with pre-operation tests and examinations. I told myself a little bracingly that if one had to be ill one may as well enjoy the comforts of one of the best equipped and staffed hospitals in the world. I remember wondering if all the psychedelic colours and beautifications did make a difference to the patients. Perhaps they did. It is more agreeable to be ill in gracious surroundings than in severely practical ones. I also liked the complete anonymity. I told the staff of the hospital that I would not have any visitors. Martha, however, said she could not go away without leaving somebody to take her place at my bedside. She said, "I shall ask Mary West to visit you. You will like her. Although she is English, she is a very good friend". I already knew about the prejudice against the WASP in Canada and was amused at Martha's choice of language. Thus, I acquired yet another life-long friend in Canada. If I write about Mary's and Martha's care and concern for me, it would be an impertinence. I was so surrounded by their love and friendship that I remember only the good times that I had in Hamilton and those I had in profusion.

I was not afraid of the operation because although a major one, it was not likely to go wrong or to cause complications. I was, however, surprised by the reactions I evoked in the hospital staff. I was kept in the post-operative recovery room almost the whole day. Whenever I opened my eyes I found a nurse sitting beside me. She would smile and say, "How are you feeling?" I would try to smile back and incline my head or say "Fine". Once or twice she said, "Do you know what has happened to you?" To which I said, "Yes". Again she asked "Are you all right?" To which again I answered, "Yes".

I was brought back to my room in the evening. I have seen many patients come out of sedation in a most uncomfortable way, but I suffered no ill effects; I just slept if off. Maybe this was due to their superior technique. One nurse, who was detailed to my care especially was constantly with me. After a couple of days, I asked her "Why do you ask so often if I know what has happened to me?" She said, "You see, we have never seen a patient like you. You are so calm and reserved that the doctors and all of us are doubtful if you realise the consequences of this operation."

I do not know what they expected me to do. It was a very personal experience which I would not think of sharing with anyone else. Besides, I truly was not very upset. How would they know about the inner quietude, which envelops one due to the constant remembrance of one's *ista mantra* and the abiding presence of the personification of the mantra. In a way, I was amused at the bafflement of the social worker who came to chat with me one day. I think the doctors sent a psychiatrist also but I was able to convince everyone that I was all right and also very grateful for their thoughtfulness.

Mary came every day and took care of small necessities as they arose. Martha was in communication with her and got daily bulletins regarding my recovery. As soon as Martha returned from Montreal the surgeon discharged me from the hospital. Martha fetched me home in her red Toyota and fussed round me for a few days till she also realised that I was as sanguine as my normal self.

I would have avoided mention of this bit of medical history if it had not led to a very endearing *matri-lila* back home in India next year. I had taken pains to keep it under wraps because in Hamilton there were many Indians from our part of the world. If any version, garbled or otherwise, had reached my family they would have suffered terrible anxiety. From a distance a medical disaster always sounds worse than reality. I kept on writing cheerful letters so that even if they heard rumours they would be able to discount them as such.

The university opened for the session of 1973-74. After quite a long time, I sat happily on the other side of the table and took up the work of research and study of the courses I was interested in. The library also was very fine, well-equipped and student-oriented. I was impressed by their ability to get me any paper or book from any corner of the world within three weeks of requisitioning it. Beautiful surroundings and nothing to do but read and write and drink innumerable cups of coffee — what more could anyone ask for!

On the Way to Canada

When we closed for the summer term, I planned to go home for two months; I needed a break more than anything. Moreover, I wanted to break the news of my illness myself so that the family could see for themselves that I was all right.

I returned to India to be received in Bombay by Bindu and Shyamoli. My mother and sister had come to Bombay to meet me on arrival. From them I came to know that Sri Ma was in Pune at the time. This was very convenient for all of us as Bindu drove us down to Pune to have *darshan* of Sri Ma.

Everyone was pleased to see me and asked me lots of questions regarding my travels. At the end of the day visitors to the ashram departed and inmates only remained. I asked for a private talk with Sri Ma. Didi and the other girls removed themselves to their own rooms. Sri Ma was lying on her *chowki* on the verandah. I sat on the floor near it. I said, "Ma, I have some bad news to give you". After that, I told her about the unexpected diagnosis of cancer and the consequent operation I had undergone. Sri Ma sat up on her *chowki*. She asked very penetrating questions; as usual she quickly assessed the entire scenario, the logistics of post-operative treatment which would be long drawn-out over a period of 3 years at least. I said to her, "Ma, I cannot bring myself to tell my mother about this latest disaster. As you know, she nursed me through the previous serious ailment so bravely and competently. How am I to tell her that by all reckonings, I am suffering from a worse disease? Please do this for me."

Sri Ma agreed, thereby lifting a burden off my shoulders. I went to bed that night feeling light and easy. The next afternoon it so happened that all my family were sitting in Sri Ma's room. There were no outsiders but only some people residing in the ashram. Sri Ma spoke in a brisk tone to my mother, "Come here mother, have you had your lunch?" My mother nodded her assent. Sri Ma said, "Shall I tell you about your daughter's courage and fortitude? She is a girl in a thousand. You can be proud of her". Sri Ma went on in this strain, somehow working in the operation so deftly and lightly that my mother was completely distracted from the main theme. I stole a glance at

Bindu, saw his flushed face and knew he had not missed the message. Shyamoli and my sister were frankly in tears, but my mother, due to the unbounded compassion, the all-encompassing *kripa*, had been saved the shock of realisation or its traumatic aftermath. My mother was not stupid at all; she was quite capable of assessing the repercussions of this operation. The words of Sri Ma just took away the fear and the dread pertaining to the situation. I saw this happen before my eyes and knew my prayer had been answered. My mother went on listening to Sri Ma. She even had a look of gratification on her face. Sri Ma referred to a recent case of a cancer operation in the ashram. The patient was an eminent person, a scholar, but he had been so afraid that he had asked her to come to Bombay with him and be in town while he was hospitalised. Sri Ma said, "And look at this girl, all alone in a foreign country", etc., etc. I was embarrassed at the unmerited praises she was showering on me. Unmerited because I had never been afraid or unequal to the situation I had faced.

It all ended well. Didi Gurupriya also spoke words of concern, her eyes filling with tears, but at last I was relaxed and happy. Sri Ma asked me if she could tell about my illness and operation to others if she felt called upon to do so. "Yes", I answered. "Now that my family has been told, I have no objection to other people being informed about it". I had seen in Canada that people were afraid to give this disease its name; in general they camouflaged it by using technical terms but I saw no reason to adopt such measures. I am sure anyone suffering from what could be a fatal disease would like to know about it in order to deal with it in a proper frame of mind.

After a very pleasant interlude in Pune, we returned to Bombay. From there, my mother, sister and I travelled to Lucknow to be with my other two brothers who were both posted in this city. We stayed with Babu and Meera for a few days and then came home to 31 George Town, Allahabad. From Allahabad, I went to Varanasi because Sri Ma had gone there. I had another chance to visit her. I also went to the university and met such friends who were on campus during the summer vacation. Then it was time for me to return to Canada to get on with my research project.

On the Way to Canada

I got a welcome from Martha. She produced for me a bag of frozen cherries. She knew that the season for fresh cherries would be over by the time I returned from India, so she had put bags of them in the deep freeze.

Martha and myself

Chapter Twenty Two

My Research Project

In Bossey I had come up against the tension between reason and faith from the point of view of religion. At McMaster, I came closer to its philosophic dimension. Here was a civilisation which had completely divested itself of its heritage of mythology and chosen to embark on the path of reason. History was important as a way of understanding their own past, present and future. I seemed to have been brought up against a brick wall. I was used to a culture which did not distinguish between mythology and history, or rather drew no line of demarcation between the ages of mythos and logos, to use the language of philosophy. Mythology was also a dimension of truth for us. No longer was it so in the West. We in India do not see the real significance of the movement of thought which broke away from Plato and demystified nature. Nature no longer was a mystery, a refuge to be sought for constant renewal. Nature could be questioned and made to give answers, which enhanced human knowledge and power. This was the beginning of science.

Parallel with this expanding horizon of mental powers, man in the West found himself emerging from what he regarded as the dark ages of religious dogma. Moral behaviour assumed importance independently of religion. Religious behaviour so often was neither good nor ethical. This problem is endemic to all religions. It is generally acknowledged in Western philosophy that the definitive separation of morality from religious belief was brought about by the German philosopher Immanuel Kant. The gigantic shadow of this gentle teacher of philosophy of Konigsburgh lies over the entirety of Western civilisation. I had read in one of his biographies that the poet Heine had said, "If people knew the significance of what this little man was writing so quietly in his study, they would have trembled in fear as if in the presence of an executioner!"

Kant refuted the traditional proofs of the existence of God and established the supremacy of the moral law as the only object of reverence. Kant himself was a man of moral uprightness. His gentle dignity and piquant humour were admired by his friends and neighbours. He had said that man need not look beyond himself for knowing what is morally good and what is not. The will to goodness is inherent, it needs to be appreciated and acted upon. If man were to abide by the rule of his own will toward his duty, his obligations, he would not commit wrongs. To the question that man is often bewildered by the pull of diverse obligations, he laid down criteria by which one may know the only one duty to be followed on a given occasion. The moral law, it is true, commands without promise of reward, but it is unthinkable, indeed irrational, to suppose that virtue will not bring about a state of happiness.

Kant brought the age of innocence to a close. Man was now supposedly fully adult, responsible for his own action; since his destiny was to be virtuous, faith in God is posited as guaranteeing the fulfilment of the Good, that is, a state of perfection.

Needless to say that I have oversimplified two great works of philosophy here for the purposes of this chapter.[1]

The exhilarating experience of freedom gave a new dignity to man, who now occupied the centre of the stage and felt powerful enough to command destinies. The repercussions of this philosophy were far reaching. In time, the moral will was metamorphosed into the will to power and lead to the phenomenon of Hitler; freedom, utter and all-encompassing, brought about a loneliness of the spirit, and anguish which overwhelmed the heart, giving rise to Existentialism and its subsequent schools of thought. Philosophers have traced back the sources of modern liberalism also to the philosophy of Kant.

---

[1] The *Critique of Pure Reason* and the *Critique of Practical Reason*. I hope to be forgiven by all Kant scholars.

One of the most poignant epitaphs to be written about the "Freedom of the Will", perhaps is:

"The same act which appropriates the God-given moral law reduces its God-givenness to irrelevance." [2]

Moral autonomy was bought at a great price. The dichotomy between religion and ethics remained unbridged.

In Indian colleges, Kant and Hegel were taught differently. My own teacher, Professor A.C. Mukerji, taught them as metaphysicians who could be compared with Samkaracarya. It was his life-long grief that Indian philosophy was not accepted as "Philosophy" in foreign universities, but delegated to departments of religious studies. He used to tell generations of his students that if they wanted to render some service to their country then they should strive to put Vedantic thought on the philosophic map of the world.

I was lucky to arrive at McMaster during the last years of Professor George B. Grant's tenure as one of the founder-members of its Department of Religious Studies. He was the most well-known thinker of his time in Canada. I was happy when he agreed to become one of my examiners because this gave me many opportunities of exchanging ideas with him.

It was George Grant who made me see the futility of comparative studies, which was almost a full-time occupation of research scholars in India. I also learnt to see Western thinkers within the framework of a historical background and not out of context as we did at home. As for example, Kant in the West was more important as the father of modern liberalism, rather than as a metaphysician. In Bossey I had found that there was no commensurable language for "dialogues". According to George Grant there could be none for metaphysics or ontology either, until the different orientations were recognised and appreciated. He said to me once, "People do not understand the implications of living in a society guided and controlled by technology. The will to create is rampant; the checks and curbs are not *from without but from within the same order of functionality*. To say

---

[2] Fachenheim, E. *Quest for Past and Future*, Indiana University Press, 1968, p. 215.

My Research Project

that technology will be used for welfare only is silly because it preempts the renewing processes of nature and so advances along irretrievable paths... 'the wasteland grows' ...if we choose to recall Nietzsche's prophetic words. We in the West have achieved our future; there is nothing for us to look forward to anymore [3]. With these thoughts in my mind I founded the Department of Religious Studies where other traditions would be taught by spokesmen from the East. I wished to find out if radically different traditions would teach us something which we once had but have now lost". He added a little ruefully, "But all scholars who come from India seem to have a 'me too' syndrome. If Vedanta is like Kant, or Visistadvaita like Pringle-Pattison then we do not need to study Samkaracarya or Ramanujacarya. We could be interested in originality only, but alas, the East needs must ape the West. It is a pity!"

George Grant said this all very lightly but there was a tinge of sadness in his voice. This truly, for me, was an encounter session between A.C. Mukerji and George Grant! I had been impressed by Professor Mukerji's sense of commitment and now I began to understand George Grant's anguish regarding the overcoming of moral and religious values in the name of liberation and progress. I was coming from an atmosphere of a resurgence of Vedantic thought in Indian universities, but it is a curious fact that I learnt much about our philosophy in Canada — Professor J.G. Arapura was a pioneer in this field, now ably supported by K. Sivaraman. Under their able guidance I decided to research the so-called "renaissance" of Vedanta as the neo-Vedanta of our times.

The influence of Western education in India had been profound. The nineteenth century saw an ancient civilisation smarting under the onslaught of disparaging criticisms of its cherished ideals. The British educators [4] thought they could sweep away the cobwebs of the

---

[3] What he meant was that due to present-day technological knowhow all problems, in theory, were amenable to solutions; moreover moral questions also were getting diffused into expediency situations and could not be resolved by a 'yes' or 'no'.

[4] This was the era of the tremendous popularity of one Balyogi (Boy-yogi) in the West. One evening we happened to see a T.V. programme of a reception given to

wisdom of the East. Indologists condemned the concept of *maya* as negative and life-denying. The scaffolding of philosophy on religious texts (the Upanishads) was found to be dogmatic and unrealistic.

This disparagement produced a sharp reaction (not in kind, because it is not in our culture to decry the faith of others) from the academic world of newly created universities. Eminent scholars sought to prove that Vedanta was also a rational system of thought, which believed in the practical reality of the world and its demand upon man as a moral agent. A galaxy of erudite professors wrote in the modern terminology of Western thought, but the profoundest exposition could not be called anything but apologetics. It is true that Dr. S. Radhakrishnan's brilliant lectures created a stir, but his own philosophy was looked at a little doubtfully as a form of universalism.

My research project took shape from these studies. The Sanskritic tradition poured into the mould of Western thought had not gained in fruitfulness. Cogitating on George Grant's question, together with this phenomenon I drew the conclusion that there was a crucial difference between the two traditions. This difference lay in hermeneutics, that is, the methodology by which we understand our heritages. Time and events (history) create barriers toward identifying oneself with the mental horizons of ancient peoples. If the tradition is radicalised from time to time then the task becomes almost impossible. On the other hand if a tradition undertakes to preserve itself as given originally, without adjustments from time to time, then it seems monolithic and unrealistic. All other faiths become 'other' to it, leading to enmity and alienation undermining the unity of global concerns.

Studying the methodology of preserving the *sastras* (scriptures) in the Sanskritic tradition, I saw that there were no occasions calling for total transformations. The scriptural aphorisms were the material on which exegeses, commentaries etc. were written; everyone was free to interpret the *sastras* according to his own understanding of them,

---

this rather plump little boy in America. Hundreds of his American devotees were bowing in adoration in front of him. Next day George Grant referred to this programme in his seminar. He looked at me and said with a laugh, "He is Lord Macaulay's Nemesis!" Lord Macaulay was the architect of modern Indian education.

staying within the parameters of exegetical rules. There was no clash between reason and faith because the ideology was presented as a reasonable thesis which could be questioned. The Enlightened Teacher was always ready to expound and carried conviction by his own palpable state of enlightenment. A very delicate balance between the appropriation of that which is given and an updating according to the demands of the times was achieved in India.

Many things fell into place for me. I was thrilled to gain a new perspective on the teachings of Sri Ma's that I had imbibed from childhood. I saw the simplicity of her words arising out of the most profound understanding of every dimension of the human quest for transcendence. The Enlightened Teacher (*rishi*) alone may harmonise the immanent and the transcendent. In India, therefore, we come across the phenomenon of great teachers who have accomplished this task from age to age, from century to century. I believed that an entire volume could be devoted to the continuing teaching of the Advaita from the *rishi* Yajnavalkya to the Adi Samkaracarya, Sri Ramakrishna, Bhagavan Sri Ramana Maharshi and for the modern age Sri Ma Anandamayi. Sri Ma had understood the pervasive power of the demanding world in our time. She had neither endorsed it nor denied it; she was showing a way of dealing with it easily and successfully, and yet also how to seize upon the question of ultimate freedom and thus attain supreme bliss. No wonder the *mahatmas* had seen and recognised in her the very personification of ancient wisdom. It truly needed a personality like her to reaffirm the timeless truths of the *mahavakyas* of the Vedas. In an increasingly westernised social atmosphere, she, by her commanding and radiant presence as a living exemplar of forgotten truths and half-remembered aims of life, placed a new accent on the viability of the quest for self-enlightenment in the present age. People, it seems, had lost faith in these ancient modalities, but here was a person living in our midst through all the convulsions attendant upon the establishment of a modern Indian state, who embodied what we thought were ideals long since dead and gone, with stunning vibrancy. By the precept of living in the world in the ordinary way, but with extraordinary intensity, she opened up a new dimension in the concept of renunciation. She demonstrated that no one needs to forsake his duties or obligations in the world. Anyone, just anyone, man, woman, or child, may live as ordained by God and yet engage in the most rewarding quest of all which it lies within his power to undertake. She made no distinction of religion, race, caste, status, sex or age. She brought God and man together in bonds of love, faith and hope of mercy which flows in an inundating stream for ever and ever. I had now an answer for George Grant. I drew a line of demarcation between a radicalized tradition and an abiding tradition. I received much valued support for my view from the well-known German Professor Hans Gadamer (visiting Canada at the time) when he said that the West needed a Plato again to recover their own vision of unity.

Farewell to McMaster

By the end of 1977 I was ready to take a break. The doctors had released me from the routine procedure of periodic check-ups. I met the Dean and asked if I could go home and submit my thesis from India. I knew I would have to come for the viva-voce. The Dean very thoughtfully made allowances, saying, "If you finish and submit your work, there will be no problem about your return visit to McMaster."

Nicholas, who was in New York, now came to my flat in the Hess Village to help me to round up my affairs in Canada. I had had to change my residence earlier because Martha and Louis had gone away to Winnipeg to be near their son Tom. Martha and Mary found me a very agreeable flat in a very old building right on the corner of Hess and Main Street.

I wished to give a party to all my friends in Canada before I left. This became a big and lavish affair thanks to Nicholas. Parvathyji came and prepared a lot of food; other friends gathered round and added a mood of festivity to the occasion. Mervyn and Ilse came from St. Catherine's.

A few days earlier, I had invited Dr. and Mrs Grant and Professor Sivaraman and his wife to dinner and a show afterwards. I introduced George Grant to the after-dinner mouth cleanser (*mukheshuddhi*) — the betel leaf. He and Sheila were fascinated by the silvery covering and could hardly believe that it was truly silver beaten to feathery lightness. I had of course left out the lime and other ingredients which only veterans can enjoy. After dinner we walked over to the theatre close by. I had already bought the tickets and our seats were near the stage, which was almost a part of the auditorium. The play was "The Mousetrap" enacted by a visiting company from England. It was very thrilling. The actors used the auditorium itself for some of their entrances and exits. A modern technique I had been introduced to by Guy Sprung (Mervyn's son) in London. [5]

Dr. and Ms. Grant at my flat in Hess Village

We had a very nice relaxing evening. I did not see George and Sheila again because when I returned to Canada in 1981 they had left Hamilton for Nova Scotia.

Partings are always sad. Mary came to see me off at the Airport Terminal. She and Derek were about to leave for their home in Yorkshire so I did not see them again either. There is a couplet in the Yogavasistha on human relationships. Rama says, "Just as two pieces of wood floating on the tides of the ocean come together for a little while and then are separated by the movements of the current, so are all relationships in the world."

---

[5] A delightful memory. Following instructions given by Guy I arrived from Crosby Hall by Tube but got a bit confused when I reached street level. I thought I would take a taxi to be quick and sure. The cabby, listening to the address, got out of his taxi, took me by the elbow and said, "you don't need a taxi, love, its just round this corner"!

I stopped in New York for a few days with Peter Neary and Nicholas. By this time, I had a working knowledge of some of the denominations of Christianity. I saw a little of the functioning style of the Jesuit order at Fordham from close quarters because this is where I stayed.

I returned in India just before the Janmotsava of 1977 at Ramtirtha Ashram in Dehra Dun. We first went over to Kankhal, Hardwar, to have Sri Ma's *darsana*. Everyone was pleased to hear that I was back home for good. We went up to Dehra Dun in Sri Ma entourage. The mahatmas had made admirable arrangements for a mammoth crowd. They spoke in glowing terms of Sri Ma's message of detachment. One swamiji said, "What had once been exclusive, esoteric, known and practised by a few renunciates in the seclusion of Himalayan caves has been distributed kindly and freely by Sri Ma to all and sundry. A veritable descent of Grace for the benefit of mankind!"

After the Janmotsava we returned to Allahabad and I went back to B.H.U. to resume my post at the beginning of the session 1977-78. It felt to me sadly depleted of my particular friends. Padmaji had retired but was still on the campus in order to finish her work with her research students. Shakuntala, Hiran Malani and Shail Dubey were still at work like me. Only Priyamvada Shah was away in London. At my invitation the three friends who had retired came back for a short visit so we had a grand get together again and enjoyed ourselves very much.

Sri Ma's birthday celebrations were held in Bangalore in 1978. So I planned to take my mother and sister on a pilgrimage to the temples in the South after attending the Janmotsava. Govinda Narain was Governor of Karnataka. The Maharaja and his family were devotees of Sri Ma. The entire function was arranged in a manner appropriate for hosts of such exalted position. The huge rostrum was beautifully decorated. Every eminent monastic order was represented by either its head or his representative. Amidst a galaxy of ochre robes, Sri Ma's resplendent white dress looked delicate and angelic. We never paused to think about this remarkable phenomenon, the spontaneous obeisance accorded to her by so many of our *sadhus* and mahatmas. The unanimity with which the ascetic orders affirmed her presence was unique. After all what was Sri Ma? She was not a scholar, she had never renounced the world (or engaged in *sadhana* in a retreat). Her whole life was spent among her people in the full glare of the public gaze. But when she spoke she did so with the authority of knowledge acquired not in this life nor an outpouring from a source beyond her. She was sufficient unto herself. Therefore, she did not *need* to speak but when she did it was the articulation of a self-authenticating perfection, completely satisfying to her auditors. For this reason the mammoth congregation sat for hours waiting anxiously for the last item of each session, Matri-satsang — that is, a conversation with Ma.

The *sadhu* who was acting as the master-of-ceremonies on the rostrum was very stylish in his presentation of all the questions which were handed up to him from the auditorium. One evening he began with almost an anguished cry from the heart, "Ma, I am subject to fits of anger which I cannot control. I lose all sense of proportion when I am angry. How can I control my fits of diabolical anger?" In the ensuing silence Sri Ma's light words fell as a benediction. "Drink a cold glass of water!" When the burst of spontaneous laughter from the audience subsided, Sri Ma addressed the question seriously. "All of you have been listening to very grave topics the whole evening and were in a sombre mood. This is why I made you laugh to ease the tension. From your question, it is obvious that you yourself do not think anger is justified under the conditions which provoke it. Start from there. The reason then must lie within you. Analyse your own reaction to a situation carefully. Take time to think if the provocation is great enough for you to react in anger. Fill your mind and thoughts with *nama-japa* to counteract resentments. If you get into the habit of living with the name of God then other things will evaporate because the name which is God himself is of the nature of peace; as this peace pervades your mind and heart, your anger will dissolve."

Sri Ma's answers always contained practical teachings; her words were like beams of light which illuminated the mind so that one felt capable of engaging in *sadhana* immediately, no matter what one's circumstances were. Her oft repeated *vani* "God-remembrance alone is the only desideratum for human beings", came alive in her voice, accompanied by the bright encouraging glance of total understanding. Any auditor would, for the moment at least, be convinced that he was capable of treading the razor's edge path, especially as Sri Ma never sought to pluck anyone out of his given conditions. So many times we have heard her say, "Make a beginning, any beginning. The rest will follow. If you cannot believe in God, then at least open up your mind and pray to him to enlighten your heart with his presence. I tell you to make a beginning because it is your nature to strive in the world, so your effort is necessary in this dimension also. It is true nothing happens unless God wills it so, but you do not know this of your own knowledge. You are used to taking decisions and acting on them. So it behoves you to make a beginning in this dimension also. Believe me, if you take one step God will come forward ten steps. This is language only. The truth is that he is ever with you. That you do not feel him in your inner being is the distance artificially created which needs to be dispelled."

The written word cannot recreate the glowing atmosphere of *matri-satsang*. When we heard her speak of *sadhana* in its simplest forms, it seemed so easy of accomplishment and the realisation of God within easy grasp.

All the mahatmas occupying the stage paid fulsome tributes to Sri Ma. She was the most important person for all of them. I remember Swami Chinmayanandaji said, "What is there to say about Ma? When the sun rises in the east, is it necessary to point it out to anyone? It is self-authenticating". Swami Chidanandaji took up the difficult task of translating for her, although Hindi was understood more widely now than on her earlier visits to the south.

We parted from the entourage at the conclusion of the celebrations and went to Madras to begin our pilgrimage. We had been invited by Professor Sivaraman and his wife to make the round with them. They were in India for one year on leave from McMaster. Padmaji came with us on this trip saying she would like to visit the temples in the company of a Saivaite. So we were a group of six. The professor and his wife, Padmaji, my mother, sister and myself. We had a very rewarding trip. Professor Sivaraman was greeted with respect at Chidambaram where his father was gratefully remembered as a noted Saivaite scholar and devotee.

We saw the famous panel of Dakshinamurti and many other precious icons which we would have missed had we not been guided by Parvathyji and Sivaramanji. We experienced the very interesting line of divide between Vaishnavite pilgrims and their Saivaite counterparts. Every famous temple housed both images of God, namely Narayana and Siva. At the temple of Chidambaram we sat for a while inside the precincts waiting for the *prasad* (food) which Sivaramanji had arranged for us. I noticed that many people who came in for a *darshan* of Siva Nataraja were holding up a palm leaf fan against the left side of their face as they approached the inner sanctum. On their way back they entered another sanctum which was now on their right and was dedicated to Lord Narayana or Govindaraja. I asked Parvathyji about this oddity. She said the Saivaites while coming in would not "see" Govindaraja before paying their respects to Nataraja (Siva). After making their obeisance to Siva, on their way out they would also pay their respects to Govindaraja. The Vaishnavites would follow the opposite procedure. The same routine obtained in temples which housed Govindaraja as the main deity. All temples as a matter of course housed many images of God. Each was named after the main image in the inner sanctum.

This pattern of behaviour could only obtain where the belief in unity was as strong as the preference for and loyalty to one's own *ista devata*. Now I understood why Parvathyji had hurried us all away from the temple of Srirangam to visit another temple to Siva before all doors were closed to pilgrims. She said, "My father-in-law taught me that one must begin and end with a *darshan* of Siva when on the pilgrimage". So, being with Saivaites we also behaved like Saivaites.

After this rather strenuous journey we went our different ways. Padmaji went home to Dehradun, Sivaramanji and his wife returned to Canada. We came back to Allahabad via Calcutta. I rejoined my university in July 1978. I devoted myself to the writing of my thesis for McMaster in all my leisure time.

When I felt I was ready with it I wrote to the Dean, who immediately sent me a letter of invitation with some provision for work and an honorarium in order to cover all expenses. The summer vacation of 1981 seemed a good time for my visit. Before leaving I had to seek Sri Ma's permission for this project. I waited for a chance to do this as early as possible.

CHAPTER TWENTY THREE

The Ati-Rudra *Yajna* at Haradwar

Sri Ma came to Varanasi at the beginning of 1981. Most of her entourage was with her. Padmaji and I went to the ashram to find all the younger people full of some exciting news. Shanta Pathak, Parul, Nirmala Handoo and Aruna Pandya told us that they were thinking of arranging an *ati-rudra yajna*. While watching such a *yajna*, they had simultaneously felt that it would be nice if they could perform such a ritual in Sri Ma's vicinity themselves. But such Vedic rituals had been the prerogative of men for thousands of years. How would they know how to set about it? When one of them voiced these thoughts in Sri Ma's presence, she responded by saying, "Why don't you?" very quietly as if it were not at all an overwhelming idea to begin with. The girls looked at each other, thinking, "Can we? Should we go in for this?", "Everyone will say we are too ambitious" and such other doubtful thoughts. In this mood they had come to Varanasi.

Padmaji listened to their hopes and fears and said that one of her young colleagues, Pandit Vamadeva Mishra, was very well-qualified in Vedic ritual. If he were to agree, they could work out the entire logistics of the *yajna* from constructing the building to the last ceremony of the final oblation (*purnahuti*). Sri Ma said, "Why don't you ask him?" We took this to mean a favourable *kheyala*. Padmaji then entrusted Vyas Mishra, her research student, with the errand of getting in touch with Vamadevaji and inviting him to the ashram. Vyasji returned to say that Vamadevaji had gone to Allahabad for a few days. Sri Ma said, "Why don't you all go to Allahabad to see him?"

In surprise, somebody said, "All of us?"

"Why not? What is the difficulty?"

We felt that the scheme was taking hold of us and directing us. In some confusion the seven of us travelled to Allahabad almost at a minute's notice. Padmaji, Shanta, Aruna, Parul, myself and Vyas in a taxi and Nirmala accompanied by Hrday Narain, another student of Padmaji, by bus. We descended on 31 George Town late in the evening much to the astonishment of my mother and sister. Leaving them to prepare a hurried meal for eight people we proceeded to Sheokoti where Vamadevaji was reported to be staying. We were disappointed to learn from his hosts that he had gone back to Varanasi but felt we simply could not go back to Sri Ma without some positive news from Vamadevaji, and so decided to try and get in touch with him as quickly as possible.

We had a sumptuous dinner at 31 George Town, and drove back to Varanasi through the rest of the night. At break of dawn we were at Vamadevaji's home. He opened his door to us and was taken aback at the sight of Padmaji and her retinue.

After offering our apologies for disturbing him so early, Padmaji related our plans and problems in detail. He professed himself honoured and agreed to take charge of the proceedings. We breathed sighs of relief and invited him to come to the ashram to have *darsana* of Sri Ma. He said he would come after his classes.

In the evening Sri Ma sat awaiting him in her downstairs room which opens on to the red verandah. As usual we propped up the walls of her room. I remember that Narayana Swamiji was reading aloud an article he had written on Didi Gurupriya, who had recently passed away. He had brought it to her room saying, "Ma, will you listen to what I have written about Didi?" Sri Ma said he could read till the arrival of the person all of us were waiting for. Narayana Swamiji's article was well-written and full of praise for Didi in very poetic language. I admired his style and presentation. It was a lengthy essay; after he had read about half of it there were sounds of arrival at the doors of the red-verandah. Swamiji stopped immediately and asked if his account had been approved of by Sri Ma. She replied, "Oh! you did not say anything about judging your account. There are many errors in it and many things were not as you have represented them, but since you had asked me to listen to it, I listened and did not point out the mistakes."

Narayana Swamiji looked a little taken aback, but not as much as I was. Truly the expanse and profundity of an acquiescence to the temporal order could not be gauged by us. It was so natural for us to react that we constantly forgot that here was an enigmatic personality which was somehow not ruled by ordinary criteria of behaviour. There was however, no time for such reflections. Vamadevaji came in and made his obeisance to Sri Ma. This was his first *darshan*. Sri Ma picked up a garland from her *chowki* and held it out to me, so I knew that she meant it for Vamadevaji. I put the garland round his neck. Sri Ma said "So, the *acarya* (priest-in-chief) has been chosen". Vamadevaji expressed his willingness to conduct the performance of the *yajna* which is one of the greatest rituals in our tradition.

The questions of venue and time came up. The best time for such a *yajna* is April. Shanta and the others were happy with this time because it would be just before the Birthday celebrations. The venue of this most important function was not yet fixed. Some devotees were keen to arrange for it somewhere in Madhya Pradesh. Swami Paramanandji had half-promised these people that their wishes would be fulfilled. Sri Ma, in general, never made any decision on such matters. She abided by the convenience of everybody and those who arranged for such big functions. She never promised to attend them either, saying "*Ja hoye jai*" (whatever comes to pass will happen). The managers counted on her presence because they made sure of the attendance of eminent mahatmas. Now, if the Birthday celebrations were to be held in South India, it would be very hard to arrange for the *Yajna* at Haradwar. She said, "Ask Paramananda". I went to Swamiji's room and related to him all that had transpired in Sri Ma's presence. He at once understood that Sri Ma had a *kheyala* for the *Yajna* and also that it should take place in Haradwar. Haradwar is one of our sacred cities, situated in the foothills of the Himalayas and has for centuries been dedicated to the worship of Siva. The entire city is devoted to the service of the ascetics who congregate there. The sacred river Ganga enters the plains at Haradwar; there is a special place where every evening the river is acknowledged in gratitude and worshipped with flowers and lighted lamps.

Paramanandaji came over to Sri Ma's room. He agreed to the venue and the time. Since the time was close to the dates of the Birthday celebrations, these would also be held at Haradwar. Now everything moved very fast. Shanta, Nirmala and Aruna began on the stupendous task of shopping for the event. Vamadevaji made out a list for the grains, herbs and other items required for the oblations of one lakh mantrass into eleven fires which would be kindled in eleven newly constructed receptacles. The *yajna* would be of eleven days duration. Vamadevaji had hours of discussions with the girls. He made out plans for them of the building, its height, length and breadth and other specifications. The floor and pillars would be of brick and cement. The roof would be a scaffolding of wooden slats overlaid with straw. The meticulous details of these specifications had to be carefully written out for the engineer who would be entrusted with the job in Haradwar. I remember one interesting detail. The *yajna mandapa* would have four entrances, and the elaborately decorated gates would be constructed from the wood of four different types of trees.

Vamadevaji said he would require personnel numbering about 35 pandits to help him with the oblations and a few others for helping around the *mandapa*. So food and lodging for about 50 people would have to be arranged. There was no end to the extent of the jobs which lay ahead for us. It was mind-boggling if one had time to sit and think about it all, but luckily there was no such time. I suggested to the girls that they should ask Padmaji to take charge of finances. I knew from my long association with her that she had a very sharp eye for mathematical details and a memory to go with it. Padmaji was more than equal to this thankless task of keeping track of the money and acted as a steady bulwark to the committee of four people who registered themselves as such for the duration and purpose of the *yajna*.

The Ati-Rudra Yajna at Haradwar

The committee asked me to write out a *samkalpa* (intention, purpose) for the *yajna*. They had already proposed one in words which expressed their inner feeling, namely, "In order to please Sri Ma and seek her grace in our lives". When read out to Sri Ma she said that, in which case, she would have nothing further to say on the matter and they could proceed on their own. They should have known better. Sri Ma never shows acceptance or appreciation of such homage. I gave it some thought and changed it to: "For the propitiation of the Supreme Being who is the *Ista* of the whole of mankind". Sri Ma raised no objection to this so it was used at the proper time.

The work got underway and gathered momentum, while the girls were almost carried away on a tide of demands on their capability and resources. They could meet these competently at every turn because they felt themselves to be part of a miraculous concurrence of events.

On the eve of Sri Ma's departure for Haradwar, I found myself alone in her room for some time. She asked me, "What were you telling me about your trip to Canada?" I was very surprised. It had so happened that when Sri Ma was travelling down to Varanasi from Bombay bringing the seriously ailing Didi Gurupriya with her, we had gone to the station at Allahabad with refreshments for them. Bhaiya had made elaborate arrangements for Didi's comfort. There was a very competent nurse to tend her along with her other usual companions. Didi was in the next compartment to Sri Ma and seemed to be sleeping. We did not disturb her. I wanted to take Sri Ma's permission for going abroad and broached the subject while she was talking in a desultory way with us about Didi's illness. Just as the words were out of my mouth, I realised how thoughtless I had been to choose this moment for talking of something completely out of context. Sri Ma's look of indifference stopped me almost in mid-sentence. I felt ashamed that I could put myself forward when Sri Ma was fully preoccupied with Didi's critical condition. Truth to tell, we did not know that Didi had only a few more days to live. We were always confident that she would make a recovery. However, I said nothing more at the time. Sri Ma took Didi to Varanasi and returned to Vrindaban. As is well-known, she spent five consecutive nights in trains travelling back and forth at this time. Then we finally received the sad news of Didi's passing away. When Sri Ma returned to Vrindaban Bindu and I went there on a visit of condolence. Sri Ma did not talk of Didi, which was a little unusual because she generally spoke at length about the people who had just passed away, describing the events leading up to the event and in a way "eulogising" them. We had heard her talking about Didima for days, also about Haribaba and others who had been close to her. But now she was very quiet.

I met Sri Ma again when she came to Varanasi. In the meantime, I had no occasion to talk to her about going abroad. I, therefore, was surprised at Sri Ma's question. I did not even know that my words at the railway station had registered with her. I now explained that unless I went to McMaster to submit and defend my thesis, the work would remain incomplete. I had accepted a fellowship for three years. I felt I was morally obliged to finish this research project especially since the Dean had been so very helpful regarding facilities to be given to me if I completed the work and came to defend it.

Sri Ma listened very carefully. She agreed that the work should not be left unfinished but asked, "Can't you go a little later, after the completion of the *Rudra-yajna*? If you go away who will guide them with sound advice? (*Ke buddhi debe?*)" I knew that my presence was quite dispensable since Sri Ma herself was there to guide and to plug loopholes but I was very happy to be asked by her to stay and participate in this function. I postponed my visit to Canada till after the *Yajna* and the Birthday celebrations.

Haradwar became the centre of feverish activities when Sri Ma arrived back in town. The site of the *Yajna mandapa* was chosen. An eminent engineer came forward to take charge of constructing the building. The committee of girls started amassing stores for the *yajna* as well as cereals etc. for the expected pandits from Varanasi. I, with my mother, sister, a young colleague Krishna and my friend Premlata took up residence in a small house nearby. Padmaji, Nirmala, Shanta, Indira and a few other girls from the ashram came to this haven for their meals which, during the ensuing hectic days, were often missed.

Miss Sen and Miss Navlekar from Allahabad joined us here. I include these names here in fond memory of our erstwhile teachers who were devoted to Sri Ma. They rendered help where needed and a sense of solidarity to the council of workers who mainly came from Allahabad.

The only drawback to this memorable function was the indifference shown toward it by the male members of the ashram. All the brahmacharis (ascetics) kept aloof, giving us to understand that it was solely our own affair. This was quite uncalled for and not at all in accordance with Sri Ma's ways of doing things. She attempted to bridge the gap but the groups remained estranged. The *yajna* committee accepted the challenge and tried to do without help from the ashramites. Only Swarupanandaji remained neutral, and was most open to Sri Ma's *kheyala*. He accepted the responsibility of arranging for food for the heavy influx of visitors during the coming festivities. His arrangements as usual were impeccable.

Sri Ma was very frail. A wheel-chair was always at hand. One day she said a few words about the building under construction. I was standing near and requested her to visit the site. Slowly she walked to the Mandip and entered it. Swami Paramanandaji scolded me for asking Sri Ma to come to the Mandip as the floor was newly cemented and was damp and cold. But Sri Ma made a tour of the entire hall looking at the eleven receptacles being constructed for the installation of *yajna* fires. I was right to have thought that she had a *kheyala* for this inspection because she made many practical suggestions for improvements regarding the seating arrangements, and indicated how greater facility could be achieved for moving around in the confined space. She suggested that a 3 feet wide path should be marked all round the hall. Subsequently this path became a very important feature of the *yajna*.

The priests headed by Vamadevaji arrived. Sri Ma was sitting out in the courtyard to receive them. They assembled round her in distinct groups. We had read about the four Vedas and that each had a distinct rhythmic chant. Now we were thrilled to hear the priests pronounce *mangalacharans* (benedictions) in the tones of Sama, Yajur, Rik, and Atharva Veda one by one. Sanskrit is a beautiful language.

The sound of mantras pronounced in unison in rhythmic beats is quite distinct from any other musical experience.

The priests evoked an atmosphere of ashram life in Vedic times. They were then escorted to their living quarters. The Mahantji of Udasina Akhara (monastery) had agreed to provide his spacious guest house for this purpose. Renu, with a staff of four servants headed by Bechan from Varanasi, was in charge of their meals and general welfare.

Vamadevaji supervised all arrangements. However, he did nothing without consulting Sri Ma first. Although he had just met her he knew that her understanding of Vedic ritual was more exact and profound than that of any scholar supposedly well-versed in it. One day she asked him if the people at large could participate in a *yajna* in any way whatsoever. The priests had exclusive rights of entry into the hall. No one else would be allowed even to touch the outer walls of the hall once the completed building was consecrated for the *yajna*. Vamadevaji quoted a couplet in Sanskrit. Smilingly he explained, "The priests who perform rituals are akin to beasts of burden who carry a priceless load of books on their backs. The *yajmans* (those who organise and initiate *yajnas*) are like the owners of enterprises which derive profit from transactions. The real beneficiary is the auditor who can listen wholeheartedly to the text and give his full attention to it". He then explained that the public can participate by *parikrama*, namely circumambulation around the *yajna* hall, listening to the sound of the mantras, and looking at the rising flames. Sri Ma had anticipated this integral aspect of the ritual by providing for the path around the hall.

The day of commencement drew near; the *yajnashala* (hall) looked festive with red and gold adornments at the four entrance gates; flower garlands were festooned around the pillars inside. Decorative cloth was laid over the platforms and ritual articles which would be dedicated to Lord Siva and the Devi and also to all other gods of the Vedic pantheon. Renu had painted a big picture of Siva and Parvati. This was presented to Sri Ma. She balanced it on her lap and looked at it for some time. Then it was given to the priests who installed it on the main platform or *vedi*. Bindu was standing at Sri Ma's back.

He said that while Sri Ma looked at the painting it assumed the character of a portrait.

I learnt many things about our Vedic heritage. Temples, idols, the many forms of *puja* with flowers, incense, sweets clothes etc. did develop during *puranic* times but I saw no need to draw a sharp line of distinction between the two eras. The same gods were installed, invoked and worshipped during the Rudra Yajna but by mantras instead of the physical accessories. The mantra alone seemed to conduct the body, mind and intellect toward an appropriation of supramundane powers which could raise man to a level of awareness where he could commune with divinity. Fire, kindled for the purpose and rising high in flames of variegated colours, symbolised the coming-together of an earthly being and the powers which help him to advance on the quest for Truth. Fire is looked upon as the visible link, a liaison between earth and heaven, man and gods. It cannot be defiled and forever remains a symbol of the quality of *sat* connoting energy, light and buoyancy.

In a suitably impressive function all the priests were formally consecrated to the performance of the *yajna*. They were made welcome one by one, their feet were washed and they were asked to sit on squares of carpet. Presents were offered — yellow coloured silken clothes, garlands and sweets. After this ceremony of initiation, they would live in a sequestered manner of a "retreat", conducting themselves as renunciates for the fortnight of the *yajna* celebrations. A few local priests who had been included in the team by Vamadevaji also came away from their homes for this period.

The holy *yajna* fire was kindled by Vamadevaji using the ancient method of friction with fire sticks. The ceremony was watched by a galaxy of important people, namely the heads of all the ascetic orders who were invited to sit inside the hall. The hall was surrounded on all sides by crowds of devotees who felt they were extremely lucky to watch a Vedic ritual performed in all its meticulous detail. The kindling of the fire is an art. We watched Vamadevaji, who in turn would glance repeatedly at Sri Ma sitting nearby. At one point, we saw Sri Ma raise her hand very slightly; Vamadevaji stopped the rubbing motion and a flicker of light was seen. The accompanying recitation of mantras had a beautiful rhythmic cadence, a haunting sound, almost a crooning.

The fire was multiplied into eleven individual flames and placed in the eleven receptacles constructed for the purpose. Other rituals were set in train. I had other duties elsewhere so could not watch the activities all the time. However, very soon everyone concerned was impelled to rush back to the *mandap* (*yajna* hall). Black storm-clouds filled the sky, darkening the day into sudden night. The electricity connection snapped. A gale arose, bending trees, rain poured down, disrupting all the arrangements which had just begun to be set in train. We looked fearfully at the thatched roof of the *mandap*, scared that it would be blown off. The banners and flags had to be lashed down to their supports but now that the ceremony had begun following consecration of the building, no workmen could be sent up to do this. Some of the young brahmacharis who had been initiated for work inside, now very smartly climbed up the precarious holds of the roof. Although clad in unsuitable silken garments they managed very well. I remember I wished I had a camera to take a video of one lithe figure in yellow robes silhouetted against the black skies right on top of the roof struggling to lash down the main flag which was heavy and wet and threatening to get out of control any minute. I began to pray for his and his friends' safety who were doing similar jobs on the four slopes of the roof.

Vamadevaji told me later, that for a few minutes he had felt anxious that the priests would panic and there would be a stampede toward the doors. But no one moved from his seat. It was totally dark for quite some time. Against the chaos raging outside, the inner sanctum presented a beautiful and serene sight. It was lit up by eleven centres of orange flame rising upwards to the accompaniment of mantras pronounced in unison with perfect enunciation. Sri Ma, in her shining white silk sari, sat utterly still surrounded by ochre-robed ascetics. Gradually, the sound of the sonorous chanting rose above the howling wind. The dark clouds passed over, the sun re-appeared to restore order and normality. The fury of the storm could have laid to waste everything but we believed we had escaped miraculously and were most grateful to have done so.

The *yajna* proceeded on its well-defined and imperturbable course. The committee of girls made strenuous efforts to make it worthy of Sri Ma's gracious presence. No detail of ritual observance was omitted. The mahatmas were profuse in their praise for such a spectacular yet sombre event.

According to puranic history, a *yajna* of legendary fame was interrupted by the retinue of Siva because the performer, king Daksha, had insulted the great god. The site of that *yajna* had been Kankhal. The temple of Daksheshwar Mahadev situated nearby suggested the possibility that this had been the very site where now the new *yajna* was taking place. Many mahatmas were of the opinion that it was particularly appropriate that Sri Ma should complete the unfinished *yajna* of yore. Who else could wield the *shakti* (power) required for this impressive act of rejuvenation and fulfilment.

Much more could be written on the various aspects of this *yajna* but I leave it here to continue with my own story of travels and events. The Birthday celebrations of this year were also observed in Kankhal. After the *yajna*, Sri Ma seemed to withdraw into herself. The public again could only catch glimpses of her at scheduled times.

After the function we returned to Bindu's house in Delhi. I made preparations for travelling to Canada. I went first to England to stay with Nicholas for a few days. Nicholas was very busy but he took me along to his various appointments, so that we could talk in the car. I had been very tired when I came to London after all the functions in Haradwar. Although my programme in England was hectic thanks to Nicholas, I felt very rested and relaxed. Nicholas was now Vicar and the Vicarage at Tottenham Court Road was spacious and comfortable. The other friend who was equally restful was Margaret Fletcher. She saw me off at the airport. I arrived in Hamilton, full of determination to finish as quickly as I could. Everyone helped. I stayed with Dr. Sivaraman's family. I worked hard from morning till night revising and editing my work. Parvathyji kept up a supply of coffee. Grace Gordon very kindly typed the thesis, which I submitted within a fortnight of my arrival in Canada.

The Dean, Chauncy Wood, promised to expedite the collection of reports from examiners. I was now free for at least three weeks. I went to Winnipeg to stay for a couple of weeks with my friend Martha Frohlinger. We were delighted to be together again. She had a beautiful house. Louis was away but I met her son Tom and his wife Heather. I also spent some time with Mervyn and Ilse in their big elegant house in the woods near St. Catherines. The memory of drinking tea out of a Burmese copper tea service in front of a log fire in the library is undimmed and precious.

I returned to Hamilton before the oral examination. Dr. Grant had dictated his report by telephone. I received considerable help from my other examiner Dr J.G. Arapura also. The *viva voce* lasted for almost three hours but I was through. It was very exhausting but I was happy that it was all over. Parvathyji gave a party to all concerned after the *viva voce* examination. I was grateful to her and thankful that it had all ended well.

Nicholas had asked me to stop over on my return journey to India. At Charles de Gaulle I remember the lady operating the computer asking if she should route me to London or Delhi. I decided to go home. In Delhi, I found everyone suffering from the shock of Bindu's sudden massive heart-attack. I heard about Sri Ma's *kheyala* for him. As it turned out, she would spare him to us for another six years. When I came, he was on the road to recovery and looking fit. After a few days my mother, sister and I returned to Allahabad. I went to Varanasi to join my university.

We continued to hear rather depressing news about Sri Ma's health. We could not understand why she did not have the *kheyala* to shake off the bodily ailments as she had done so many times before. Moreover, she continued to travel and attend various functions in different parts of the country. This was also rather puzzling. Perhaps, the management knew best how to interpret her *kheyala*.

CHAPTER TWENTY FOUR

"I Am Ever With You"

1982 was the year of *ardha kumbha* at Allahabad. We knew that Sri Ma would come to the riverside camp for at least a few days. With the help of our servants, Renu and other assistants took on the job of preparing Sri Ma's cottage in our compound for occupation. The entire enclosure was made spotlessly clean. I took leave to go to Allahabad and await Sri Ma's visit. As winter is short-lived in India we are not equipped with central heating or anything like that. Sri Ma's cottage would become like an ice-box in January. So we covered the roof with a huge tarpaulin. We hung double curtains along the verandah which could be drawn aside during daytime. We lined the ceiling of her room as well. We worked hard to make the cottage as cosy and comfortable as possible, not forgetting the fact it should look beautiful and not clumsy.

Sri Ma came from Vindhyachala by car on January 9, 1982. The young Raja of Hathwa drove her very carefully in his big limousine. He had so arranged the back seat that she could lie down comfortably in it. When we saw the motorcade pause at our gate we ran to it, not knowing if Sri Ma was coming in or not. Sri Ma spoke to us, "I have asked to be driven to the Satya Gopal Ashram first. I shall not get down from the car. I shall just greet them and come back as soon as possible. Is that alright?"

We immediately begged her to do as she liked; it was like her to observe these niceties of behaviour. Since she was expected to stay at our house, she took our "permission" to go to another house first.

Panuda had told us that Sri Ma was in very poor health. We should discourage any public audience; close devotees also should come only at a specific time for *darsana*. So when Sri Ma came to 31 George Town, there were very few people to greet her. We did not find her any different from her usual serene self. As Renu approached her she forestalled the *pranam* by catching hold of her hand and saying, "Never mind (the *pranam*). Go quickly to look after the Raja of Hathwa and his people. They have been careful and circumspect about this journey from Vindhyachala to Allahabad. They will need some refreshments."

My sister was ready with a very elaborate and sumptuous breakfast for our guests. They were invited inside the main house and made welcome by her and other willing helpers. Sri Ma's entourage had come from Varanasi ahead of her. In a few minutes the house was full and echoing to the voices of a happy crowd, quite like old times.

Sri Ma sat on the *chowki* prepared for her on the verandah of the cottage. She seemed ready for a crowd. She looked her normal radiant self, pleasantly smiling and talking to the handful of people standing about. I felt sorry that I had followed instructions so literally. The devotees of Allahabad missed a rare opportunity of *darsana* and *matri satsanga*.

Sri Ma spent a quiet evening. Some people from out of town came around 9 p.m.. Udasji told them unequivocally that Sri Ma could not be disturbed. They were almost in tears but they handed over the box of sweets and a garland they had brought for Sri Ma. Udasji asked me to take the box of sweets into Sri Ma's room, touch the *chowki* with it and bring it back to the visitors as *prasad*. I entered the darkened room very quietly, touched the *chowki* with the box of sweets and retreated as softly as I had come in. I was halted by Sri Ma's question "What is it?" I explained about the box of sweets. Sri Ma said, "Ask them to come in". So these lucky people had *darsana* and an agreeable conversation with Sri Ma. They were devotees of long standing and withdrew soon, not trying to take any advantage of the situation.

"I Am Ever With You"

Sri Ma on her last visit to 31 George Town, January 9-10, 1982

Next morning Sri Ma told me that some mahatmas would come to meet her from their river-side camps at the site of the Kumbha Mela. We made elaborate arrangements for them to sit in Sri Ma's room. Lots of garlands, fruits, sweets were assembled as offerings. Sri Ma indicated that my eldest brother Manu, who had now retired and was living at home, was to be at hand to greet the *sadhus* and put the garlands on them when they came. We never put ourselves forward when Sri Ma stayed with us, leaving it to Swami Paramanandaji or Didi or Panuda to do the honours. Sri Ma, however, was careful to involve my eldest brother if he happened to be at home. I recalled that when the then Prime Minister Jawaharlal Nehru and Mrs. Gandhi visited her at our house in 1961, she had summoned my mother from the back of the surrounding crowd and introduced her to the visitors as her hostess. Panditji and Indiraji could not take any special notice because people were milling around, but Sri Ma was always scrupulous in her social observances. Now my brother did his part when the *sadhus* came to our house. We knew that he had no great reverence for *sadhus* in ochre robes but in Sri Ma's presence, he behaved most correctly and with genuine respect as they were her guests.

The mahatmas requested her to come to the opening ceremony and join in the procession that evening. They said they would be careful and no inconvenience would be felt by her. Sri Ma smiled and said, "This body is never inconvenienced. If you wish to take it to the *mela*, then do so if you can."

Before Sri Ma left for the *mela*-grounds she spoke for some time about our family. She addressed the small crowd, bestowing high praise on my parents as well as all of us. I actually felt so embarrassed that I left the assembly pretending I had work to do elsewhere. This was very unusual behaviour on Sri Ma's part in our house. We were used to mild scoldings for omissions and commissions in the past. For example, once she had come to our house from that of Gopal Swaroop Pathak in the same town. Sri Ma had stayed with Shanta Pathak (Purnananda) and her family for a couple of days. Shanta's brother R.S. Pathak drove her to our house where we were awaiting her arrival. At night, Sri Ma said to my brother Babu who was posted in

"I Am Ever With You"

From left to right: Satyananda, Nirmalananda, Nirvanananda, Bhaskarananda, Shantivrata, Swami Paramananda and others.

Allahabad at the time, "Why didn't you come? It was not right that Bhape (R.S. Pathak) should have had to bring me over. If Bindu had been here, this would not have happened. He would have gone to fetch me to his house."

Babu was contrite. He apologised profusely and begged that she would have the *kheyala* in future to call upon him for any service at all. Luckily for him, Sri Ma did come to Allahabad unexpectedly some time later. She came to 31 George Town and asked Babu to drive her to Varanasi to a small one-roomed ashram at Sankat Mochan. She did not have the *kheyala* to go to the main ashram at Bhadaini. Her usual entourage did not know her whereabouts because she had left them at Kanpur to continue on to Varanasi by train instead. She had come by car to Allahabad accompanied by a new companion, who was almost a stranger. Arriving at Sankat Mochan (Varanasi) she told Babu that he could go to the university and inform me but that I should not tell anyone else.

We hurriedly returned to Sankat Mochan. We found Sri Ma quite comfortably installed and chatting with the bewildered inmates, who were overawed by her presence but also very happy. She told me that Babu had driven her very carefully and had been very circumspect. She loaded him with *prasad* and blessed him by touching his head and shoulders when he took his leave of her to go back to Allahabad. Sri Ma's "reprimands" were rare occurrences. All who received them considered themselves privileged. In general, the veil of aloofness remained impenetrable. I must also add that she was so kind and compassionate that one word of "scolding" would shortly be overlaid by layers of approving sentences. Paramanandaji was always telling her that she should be more strict. But evidently all our faults, sins and errors were not great enough not to be washed away by the falling gentle rain of compassion. I have no words to describe the experience of being forgiven for shortcomings.

It is difficult to stop when one is talking about Sri Ma's *lila*. One is tempted down the byways of memory. However, to go back to January 10, 1982. Sri Ma for a long time paid compliments to Bindu, his attitude of not finding fault, his spirit of service. We should have

"I Am Ever With You"

realised that she was making a valedictory farewell speech, instead of just feeling happy that Sri Ma was pleased with us.

Sri Ma went away to the campsite in the evening. I went back to Varanasi. Our ashram always puts up a camp in Sri Ma's name in the Kumbha Mela. This year there was heavy rain, disrupting arrangements and demolishing many of the temporary structures. My sister related that nothing seemed to go right, a unique state of events where Sri Ma was concerned, because we knew from experience that nothing ever went wrong when she was near. But we never had any sense of premonition that the elements were presaging an ominous future for us. My sister said that once Sri Ma got up with some difficulty from her *chowki*, and holding Renu's arm walked to the window of the hut and looked out on the scene of disarray. This was one of her all-comprehensive glances, difficult to describe. It did not depend entirely on the movement of the head which was very slight or even on the movement of her eyes, but she seemed to take in the entirety of the vista all at once. Renu had a strange feeling that it was not a usual viewing of how things were but rather a gesture of farewell. She had been closely associated with the site of the confluence of the two holy rivers for a long time. [1]

Before leaving the camp Sri Ma entertained all the mahatmas assembled in the *mela* to a grand feast and also all the people known to her in the city. Not one single person was overlooked or forgotten. For nearly half a century she had paid regular visits to the site of the *kumbh-mela* at Prayag. This was her last visit.

Sri Ma continued to be ill and frail but we received news of her constant travels also. There was no respite from programmes in different parts of the country. We were surprised to hear that Sri Ma was going to distant Tripura in late March. When she returned from this long and strenuous journey, she indeed looked ill and weary. Tripura was the place of her birth. Did she have the *kheyala* to visit her *janmabhumi* (place of birth) before her withdrawal from the world?

---

[1] Later, we recalled Didi's accounts of similar gestures of farewell at Shahbagh and at other places which she would visit no more.

We thought of all this in retrospect, but at the time we merely blamed the management for not making better arrangements for a restful time.

Sri Ma's Birthday Celebrations were held again in Kankhal in 1982. Never had we witnessed such a scene of confusion before. Sri Ma was visible for short durations only. She lay on her *chowki* quietly. There was a queue in front of people who would go up to her one by one. Udasji would take the garland of flowers or box of sweets from their hands, place them on the *chowki* for a moment and then give them back as *prasad*. Others helped Udasji from time to time. I recall a lady who in a tear-choked voice said "Ma, do you remember me?" Sri Ma spoke softly to her asking about her children by name and about somebody's marriage in their family. The lady was overwhelmed with joy that Sri Ma was fully aware of all those who approached her although she was not going through the ritual of an exchange of garlands.

Our Kanyapeeth had a problem. We were suffering from a lack of sufficient funds, inflation had played havoc with our budget. We had been debating if we should ask for donations. The older girls, Jaya Guneeta, Kanti and others were trying to persuade me to publish an appeal for money in our quarterly magazine *Ananda Varta*. I was totally opposed to this, reminding the girls that Sri Ma always forbade us to ask for money. Brochures giving information about the institution were extant but nobody felt called upon to give monetary help to it, that is, apart from our regular donors. Giving in to the pressure of the girls I did write an article for the *Ananda Varta*. I spoke of Didi's dedicated work toward establishing the Kanyapeeth and its present important role in exemplifying Sri Ma's *vani*, "To talk of God alone is worthwhile, all else is pain and in vain". But I could not actually ask for contributions so nobody evidently took the hint which it was.

Now I wanted to present the problem to Sri Ma. We asked for a little time for a private interview. Padmaji, Premalata, Kanti, Jaya, Guneeta, Gita, Krishna and myself gathered near her *chowki* in the open courtyard while her entourage drew away to a distance. I was standing at the foot of the bed because I was elected spokesperson. I presented the monetary problem as clearly and as succinctly as I could. I added that we were thinking of ways and means of inviting contributions. One of the members of the Management Committee, the Rani Saheba of Gondal was keen that we should ask for contributions from those who are interested in this project.

Sri Ma went straight to the heart of the matter. She said, "How much more do you need, so that the monthly expenses can be met adequately?" Premlata answered quickly that we seemed to be short of about Rs 2,000 per month, that is, a fund of Rs. 2 lakhs deposited in investments would carry us through.

Sri Ma said, "The *yajna* has been very expensive. I am told that all available funds are bespoken, let us see how it goes."

I signalled to the others that we would not say anything more about money matters. From Sir Ma's response it was clear to me that we were not to ask for money. Jaya then said, "Ma, we can see that you are not at all well. Please come to Varanasi, to us at the Kanyapeeth. We shall ensure that you will have complete rest and we shall look after you in every way."

Sri Ma was looking at me since I was standing at the foot of the bed. With reference to Jaya's statement, she said, "She (Jaya) does not know what she is talking about. They do not understand the gravity of the circumstance."

I said what came spontaneously to my mind, "Ma, in this situation what should be our course of action?" Sri Ma continued to look at me for a few seconds. She did not answer. I still remember her look which I did not understand because it was a look of compassion. She seemed to commiserate with our state of bewilderment. She knew (as we did not at the time) that we could be given no shortcuts through our experience of shock and trauma in store for us". [2]

The management decided that they would not ask Sri Ma to come to the main hall of the ashram for the Birthday Celebrations. It would be held in her living quarters. A marquee was erected in front of the

---

[2] On their return to Varanasi the Kanyapeeth found a cheque for Rs 25,000 from a new devotee. Other contributions followed, thus solving the money problem.

house. Some professional decorators were constructing a chariot-like throne upon which would be placed Sri Ma's bed. When the chariot had taken shape, Udasji took great exception to it. She ordered the men to dismantle it forthwith saying, "Why a chariot? Do you want Ma to go away?" The chariot was dismantled and taken away. Rain poured down on the night of the *puja*; the canvas top was not proof against such a downpour. The assembled people had no place to go. Only a few could be accommodated in Sri Ma's room. The *kirtan* sung by a handful of girls was not audible outside. The usual atmosphere of solemnity could not be built up. The devout congregation wishful of sitting quietly and paying reverential homage to their *ista-devata* on this important night were obliged to disperse and seek shelter where they could. Never had we experienced such a Birthday night.

Next morning we were told that Sri Ma had said that the ashrams should not attempt to arrange *pujas* near her in future. Such *puja* could be offered to the portrait in the hall. We thought Sri Ma was referring to the discomfort suffered by everyone and was making sure that the management would make more proper arrangements. None understood this for the prophecy it was.

After the celebrations were over, we returned to our places of work. This was my last *darshan* of Sri Ma. As usual we made our *pranams*, received some token as *prasad* and came away, hoping we would see Sri Ma looking her radiant self on our next visit.

We continued to get news of her travels. At last, she returned to Dehradun and stayed in Kalyanvan from 5th July to 24th July. She seemed totally withdrawn. She did not respond to messages or letters. Bhaskarananda requested her to say something in reply to the hundreds of inquiries being received by them every day. Sri Ma said, "All of you should strive to live up to the grace of your Guru in your life". On July 24th, she came to Kishenpur Ashram. She had stopped taking food for about 3 months. She took a few sips of water now and then. This bit of news did not sound too serious to us. We had heard many times about Sri Ma's abstinence from food and also seen her take next to nothing and yet look her normal bright self. She had never suffered from lack of food before but this stint of fasting was definitely not in accordance with her usual *kheyala*. We had never seen her physical conditions, such as fastings, sprains and breakages of bone-joints or aches and pains disturb her serene countenance. So we all prayed to her to give up the *lila* of illness soon.

My sister Renu and my mother were in Delhi with Bindu and Shyamoli. My mother had undergone an eye-operation which had unfortunately not been beneficial. On August 27, Renu received a message from Nirmala and Shanta who had come to Delhi on some important errand. They said they were driving back to Dehradun and Renu should come with them if she wanted to see Sri Ma for the last time. These close companions had sensed that the end was near. So Renu was among the few who kept vigil in Sri Ma's room on the last day. Nobody could do anything to alleviate Sri Ma's suffering. Obviously, it was not a medical problem because even the doctors assembled round her bedside could find no fault which could be remedied. They also could do nothing but pray to her to bring her *kheyala* toward her recovery. Renu was told that instead of answering Dr. Surabhai Seth's prayer for her recovery she had said to him "Take care of Paramananda."

Sri Ma's "*anandamayi svarupa*" (persona of bliss) was totally in abeyance. She drew her last breaths in agony, watched with helpless despair by people who were close to her in devotion and allegiance. Our tradition does not teach us to associate suffering with divinity. Sri Ma somehow had got us accustomed to it. She who was joy personified had seemed sombre and sad in the last months. The enigma of her majestic and yet so kind personality was now eclipsed by the greater mystery of what looked like suffering to us. It needs to be pondered upon by all of us, all our lives.

For now, whenever I recall the evening of August 27, 1982, I am amazed at my insensitivity. In Varanasi I was not overcome by any sense of desolation around 8 p.m.

On the morning of 28th August, Premlata came and gave me the news which she had just then heard. A neighbour brought a newspaper announcing the headline news. Premlata had come prepared for a journey. I quickly packed a bag and accompanied her to Haradwar by the Doon Express. We met other people who had boarded the train at different stations. The railway service rose to this occasion most nobly. They allowed hundreds of people to board trains without reservations and sometimes even without tickets. I was told that such was the case all over India. The trains were held up at times to accommodate people running to board it.

When Premlata and I arrived at the ashram at Kankhal, Sri Ma's body had been installed in the main hall in front of the statue of Adi Samkaracarya. She was surrounded by her usual entourage. Everyone was quiet, each cocooned in a world of heart-breaking sorrow. They were all exhausted too. For the last three days nobody had prepared any food in the kitchens. They had been subsisting on liquids. Everyone was waiting for the time of the *samadhi* which was being organised by Mahant Sri Narayandas Puriji Maharaj in consultation with Panuda and others of the ashram.

I did not want to see Sri Ma's body. I sat in the enclosed verandah near the hall watching the queue of devotees who were approaching from the main gate. In a while Atmanandaji came and sat near me. She looked calm and quite undisturbed.

After some time she said "Why do you cry? She has not gone away. For almost the whole of the last two years she has not been available to thousands of people who wanted her *darshan*. Now she is free and will be available to everyone everywhere. She belongs to the world and not to a few devotees only". I saw that she spoke with great conviction and was comforted by these words. As days went by I found she had spoken truly. Sri Ma was ever with whosoever remembered her, thought about her or meditated on her message of hope for spiritual emancipation.

The ashram at Kankhal rapidly began to fill with crowds. I recognised many of the V.V.I.P.'s and some of the out-of-station devotees. The Prime Minister, Mrs. Indira Gandhi, came and was given a place among the girls surrounding Sri Ma. It was time for the *samadhi*. Shanta came and handed me a flower garland. She said, "Bithudi, why are you standing so far away". I said, "I do not wish to see Ma as she is now". Shanta said, "Come and put the garland on her. Remember, even this body will not be available to us within a very short time". She looked infinitely sad but composed. So I slowly went forward and offered the flowers as other girls were doing. I wish I had not been persuaded by Shanta. In place of the inimitably endearing smile which had always expunged the world from my mind for so many seconds there was this still and quiet face which I did not wish to remember or think about in any way.

The mahatmas came and took charge of the process of internment of the image which was Sri Ma Anandamayi. By a spontaneous consensus of opinion, the ceremony was to be performed with the highest honours prescribed in the Hindu tradition. Sri Ma alone commanded this unique homage from the upholders of our religion. No sectarian disputes arose. To all mahatmas Sri Ma was the personification of *brahmavidya* itself. All this was as it should be but I was not going to witness the scene of irrevocable farewell. I quietly went away to my room and waited on the time.

After days of constant attendance on Sri Ma the girls suddenly were at a loose end. Nobody had anything to do. We drew together in groups and talked about the preceding days. I heard about the visit of the Jagadguru Sri Samkaracharya of Sringeri Peetham on June 16. To him she had said, "Pitaji, this is not illness. It is a state of tension between the manifest and the recall of the Unmanifest."

Nirmala told me that when the Jagadguru was expected, Sri Ma had said, "Send a message to Bithu". I was astonished. I said, "But I did not receive any word from any of you?" Nirmala shrugged and said that they were so distracted and upset that they did not follow it up. Maybe each thought another would do it. So I had missed my chance of being with Sri Ma one more time. Perhaps she had some *kheyala* to say something. Profitless regrets. I sustained myself with the thought that she had a *kheyala* for me at the time.

Chandana told me that Sri Ma had been heard to repeat a few mantras from time to time. On the night of the 25th she had clearly pronounced the sacred *pancaksara* in its reversed form "Sivaya Namah". This gave me a jolt, because I had read in Saiva Siddhanta literature that this form of the mantra indicates a state of freedom from all bondage, especially the body. I marvelled that Sri Ma had all along in some way or other given expression to the fact that the end was near. She had withdrawn herself from crowds, she had suffered physically and had spoken words which, interpreted rightly, would have indicated her *kheyala* for making herself unmanifest very soon. Her last words spoken to her entourage were, *"Je jekhane acthho boshe padho."* The nearest translation, or rather meaning, could be "Wherever you are, commit yourself totally to *sadhana*, to the exclusion of everything else."

I have come to the end of the story of my days with Sri Ma Anandamayi. I wrote a farewell note for the special number of the *Ananda Varta*, October 1982. I reproduce it here as a conclusion to these reminiscences.

To Bid Farewell...................

We know only how to celebrate the coming of our beloved Sri Ma. We know how to spread the glad tidings that Ma is coming to town; we remember the joyous experience of preparing for her visit; we know how to put up festive arches, hang out colourful festoons and keep in readiness innumerable flower garlands for her. We remember the happy excitement of waiting for Sri Ma's car. We remember the thrill of hearing the first whispered message, "Ma is coming, Ma is coming!"

We also remember the unique experience of the first glimpse of that beauteous, majestic form; we remember the buoyancy of spirit, the uplifting of hearts in the vicinity of Sri Ma, but who, really, can describe the ineffable joy of the first vision of that inimitable radiant smile which forever removed all burdens weighing upon the heart, even as the suddenly shining sun puts to rout lowering rain clouds. We especially remember the bliss of fulfilment when we encountered the all-seeing compassionate glance which made naught of all earthly worries and set at rest all questioning of the spirit. We understood the meaning of the text:

> *All one's actions are nullified, the knot of the heart is penetrated and all doubts are resolved, on perceiving He who is Supreme.*
> Mundaka II.2.9

"I Am Ever With You"

We remember all this and more, but we are singularly unprepared for bidding farewell to that One person who had inter-penetrated the very texture of our being, Is it possible that we shall see no more that all-conquering smile which had captivated the hearts of all alike, the old and the young, the ascetic and the householder, the businessman and the artist, the sophisticate and the villager? Shall we no more thrill to the sound of that divine voice singing melodiously the Names of the Lord? Even when we did not see Ma for a few days, a few weeks or a few months, we knew she was with us in the same life's breath we drew, the earth we walked, the space which circumscribed us and the time which delimited us. How to convince ourselves now that this earth, this air, this time, these places and we shall know Her no more? Who can be more privileged than us and who more unfortunate?

We do not quite know how to relate to the festival of bidding farewell to the dearly beloved manifest form of Sri Ma, we tell each other that Sri Ma is still with us, that she has merely made Her visible form unmanifest; that she who belonged to one particular time and place, now belongs to the whole wide world and to the end of time and beyond. Yet the hearts which knew nothing beyond or apart from Her Image, today stand empty and bereft.

Let us then start out on the journey toward understanding the message of Sri Ma. Let us gather strength from each other and recall that grief is uncalled for in relation to that radiant Image which we have cherished for so long in our hearts. Let us unite in praying that we become deserving of that Grace which we know is forever being showered on all of us. We have so far lived in the joyous presence of Sri Ma, but now we must try to instil this joy in our hearts to fill out its emptiness. A new journey begins for us. We must carry the memory of Sri Ma's words with us as the only support and wherewithal for this journey, namely, that, "With pure, one-pointed and undeviating concentration one must seek Truth". Living in the presence of Sri Ma's manifest form, we understood the meaning of the Upanishadic Text. We must now begin the journey towards the realisation of the truth of the Text. For us who have known Sri Ma and for those who will come to know her it should be an easy and rewarding journey.

May Sri Ma's *kheyala* be fulfilled

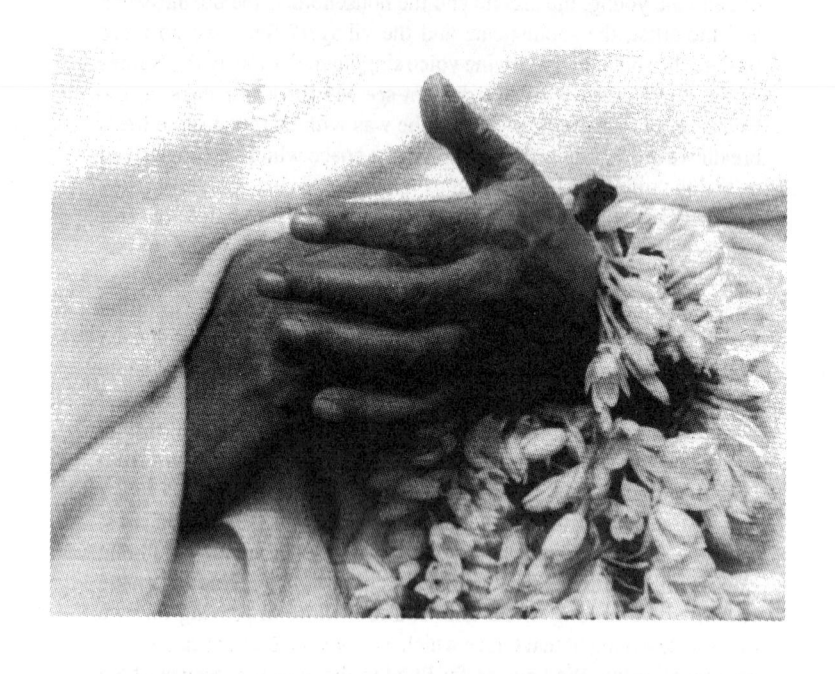

Photo by Richard Lannoy

Glossary of Sanskrit, Bengali and Hindi Words

Abhyāsa : practice
Ācārya : teacher
Ādya śakti : primordial energy or power
Agomoni (B) : song of welcome, invocatory song
Ahetuka kṛpā : spontaneous grace, contra grace merited by devotion
Akhanda : unbroken, continous
Akhanda kirtan : continuos singing of devotional music
Akhārā : monastery
Alkhallā : a loose garment worn by sadhus
Amaṅgala (B) : inauspicious, harm
Ānanda : bliss, ecstasy
Aṅgocchā (Hindi) : a light towelling cloth
Annaprāśana : the ceremony of giving the first morsel of solid food to a baby
Ārati : the ritual of offering lighted lamps, a part of *puja*
Āsana : a small square of carpet
Astra : weapon
Asura : demon
Ātma : the inner Self
Attahasa : loud laughter
Bachhī (H): small child
Bādhaka : hindrance
Bahirvāsa : an outer garment, a wrap-around
Bhajan : devotional song
Bhāva : a state of withdrawal of attention from the world and immersion in an atmosphere of quietude
Bhavanadī : the river of life in the world
Bhayaṅkara : terrible, horrifying
Bhoga : enjoyment; also the food offered to the deity during *puja*
Bhogirāj : man who enjoys himself fully
Bilva patra : the leaves which are sacred to Shiva

Brahmacarya : celibacy
Brahmateja : the buoyant energy accruing from asceticism
Brahmavidyā : the supreme knowledge synonymous with realization of Truth
Cakra : see *satcakra*
Calanta vigraha (B) : a movable Image. Many temples have such Images for taking out in processions.
Chaddar (H & B)): shawl
Chappal (H & B): sandals
Chowkī (H): a wooden bed
Chowkidār (H): a guard
Cit : intelligence
Dandee (dandī) (H): a sort of sedar chair used in hill-towns
Darśana : audience
Daśamī : the tenth day
Dāsī : servant woman
Dharmaśālā : inn for pilgrims
Dhotī (H & B): a white cotton piece of cloth worn by men in various styles
Dhyāna : meditation
Dikpāla : the deities who guard the ten directions
Dīkṣā : initiation
Donā : a receptacle made of leaves
Doṣa dṛṣṭi : fault finding
Durgāśaptaśati : a religious text, describing the advent of Devi (a part of Markandeya Purana)
Ekamevādvitīyam brahma : Brahman the one without a second
Ekkā (H & B): a horse carriage
Gāyatrī Japam : the repetition (in a ritually counted order) of the Gayatri mantra
Gopīs : the dairy maids of Vrindavan
Gufā (H): cave, underground room
Holī (H & B): the festival of colour
Iṣṭa-devatā : the adored Image of the devotee
Ja ta (B) : "whatever is, is"
Janmāṣṭamī : the Birthday of Sri Krishna
Janmotsava : the celebration on the occasion of Sri Ma's Birthday
Japa : repetitive way of pronouncing any of the Sacred names; it is done silently, sometimes with the help of a rosary
Jaṭā : matted locks of hair
Jayadhvanīs : loud acclamations in chorus
Jhoola (jhūlā) (H & B): swing

Glossary

Kaḍhāi : a frying pan
Kanyās : maidens
Karapātrīs : sadhus who accept only a little food which they can hold in their palm
Kharaū (H & B): wooden sandals
Kheyala : whimsical thought
Kīrtan : religious singing
Kṛpā : grace
Kṛṣṇa avatāra : the incarnation of Krishna
Kṛyās : rituals
Kṛpā-pātra : the worthy recipient of grace
Kulharas (H): earthen cups
Kulīna brāhmaṇa : a very special sect of brahmins
Kumārīs : maidens
Kumbha Melā : the yearly gathering at the river-side at Allahabad in the month of January-February
Kuṇḍa : a receptacle
Kurtā (H & B): a colourless loose garment worn by men
Kutiā (H): hut
Lakṣmī : the goddess of wealth
Līlā : play, enactment
Mahānāma mantra : a special mantra sacred to Vaisnavas, used widely for singing kirtana
Mahātmās : ascetics
Mahāyajña : a great yajña
Mahotsava : a great festival
Mandap : a place set up for a religious function
Matṛ-kathā : talking about or reminiscing about Sri Ma's words and deeds
Maunam : silence
Melā (H & B): a concourse of people, a gathering for a festival
Misrī (H & B): palm sugar
Mleccha : outcaste
Nagar-kīrtana : singing on the streets
Naivedya : sweets and fruits offered to a deity
Nāma : sacred name
Nāma yajñas : a festival of celebrating the names of God
Nāma-saṁkīrtana : the singing of the Sacred names, in a variety of tunes
Namaskāra : folding of hands in greeting
Neem (*nīm*): margosa tree

Pallava (H & B): the outer edge of the sari which hangs over the back
Pañcakṣara mantra : the special mantra sacred to Shiva
Pañcavatī : a grove of five special trees
Pañcapātras : a small brass receptacle for sacred water from the Ganga
Pandāl (H & B): marquee
Parāṭhas (H & B): special type of chapatis
Pisshu (H & B): an insect
Praharas : a time period of 3 hours approximately
Praṇām : bowing, obeissance
Prasād : a benediction, the partaking of food which has been offered to a deity
Prasanna : pleased
Preyas : that which is pleasing
Pūjā (H & B): the ceremonial worship of a deity with flowers, incense, sweets, camphor, etc.
Puṇya : religious merit
Purṇahuti : the final oblation into a sacrificial fire
Puśpañjali : offering of flowers
Rasamaṇḍala : the dance of Krishna and the milk-maids of Vrindavana. It is imagined that they have formed a ring round Krishna and Radha in the middle, but each maiden is partnered by Krishna who appears as many for this purpose.
Ṛṣis : enlightened seers
Śavāsana : one of the yogic asanas
Sādhanā : efforts made toward spiritual upliftment, e.g. japa, meditation...
Sādhus : ascetics
Sādhu-samāj : an assembly of ascetics
Sādhu-sammelan : the same as above
Sadri (H & B): a high-collared sleeveless jacket worn over a kurta
Sahaja : at ease, natural
Sākhīs : friends
Samiyana (H & B): a large marquee
Saṁskāras : predilections
Samyam saptāh, Samyam vrata : a week-long regiment of austerities to be undertaken by ordinary folk as fulfilment of a vow of dispassion taken for the duration
Sandhyā : evening, the evening prayers
Saṅgam : confluence
Saṅkalapa : resolution, objective
Saṅkīrtana : the same as kirtana
Saṁnyāsa : renuntiation

Glossary

Śāstra - vācana : scriptural authority
Sat : to exist
Satcakra : in the yoga system of thought, six centres that are recognised as important to the nervous system for spiritual exercises
Satcidānanda : a term denoting the Supreme Reality or Brahman. Sometimes it is used to denote the personalized form, that is, God.
Satsaṅga : an aseembly of devout people
Sevā : service
Sevābhāva : spirit of service
Śraddhā : respect, worshipful allegiance
Śreyas : the good
Stotra : hymn
Svarūpa : the nature, the inner being
Swāmījī : a title of respect for an ascetic
Tapasyā : austerity
Thālī (H & B): a metal plate
Tolis (H & B): groups
Tongā (H & B): a horse carriage
Tongāwālās (H & B): the coachmen of horse carriages
Tulasī : basil
Utsava : festival
Uttarakhaṇḍa : Northern regions, the foothills of the Himalayas
Uttariya (H & B): scarf
Vahana : mount
Vairāgya : dispassion
Vajra : thunderbolt
Vanaprastha : the third stage of life when husband and wife may be together in a forest hermitage
Vāṇī : utterance, spoken word
Vasanti Devī : an image of the goddess Durga
Vedī : platform
Veṇī : plait of hair
Vidyārambha : the beginning of schooling
Vidyāvaridhi : ocean of learning, a title
Vilāsa : indulgence
Viśvakalyāṇa : the good of humanity
Zamindārs (H & B): landlords